The Organization of Attachment Relationships

Quality of attachment has been a central variable in developmental research during the last two decades. However, even though attachment is relevant to all cultures and humans of all ages, the majority of research has focused on middle-class infants in Anglicized cultures. Further, the function of attachment to protect humans from danger has been over-looked, whereas a focus on the advantages of safety and security have been emphasized. This volume presents new theory on attachment that broadens its range to ages beyond infancy, to many cultures, and to endangered populations, including both psychopathological individuals and those living in threatening contexts. The intent is to provide new theory and methods to better understand human variation in interpersonal and cultural self-protective strategies. The expansion of the attachment classificatory system beyond its roots in infancy and to a broad range of cultures differentiates this volume from other work on attachment.

Patricia McKinsey Crittenden currently directs the Family Relations Institute in Miami, Florida.

Angelika Hartl Claussen is an Applied Developmental Psychologist at the University of Miami, working at the Linda Ray Intervention Center for children at risk.

The Organization of Attachment Relationships

Maturation, Culture, and Context

Edited by

Patricia McKinsey Crittenden
Family Relations Institute, Miami, Florida

Angelika Hartl Claussen
Linda Ray Intervention Center, University of Miami

CAMBRIDGE
UNIVERSITY PRESS

PUBLISHED BY THE PRESS SYNDICATE OF THE UNIVERSITY OF CAMBRIDGE
The Pitt Building, Trumpington Street, Cambridge, United Kingdom

CAMBRIDGE UNIVERSITY PRESS
The Edinburgh Building, Cambridge CB2 2RU, UK
40 West 20th Street, New York, NY 10011-4211, USA
10 Stamford Road, Oakleigh, Melbourne 3166, Australia
Ruiz de Alarcón 13, 28014 Madrid, Spain
Dock House, The Waterfront, Cape Town 8001, South Africa

http://www.cambridge.org

First published 2000
First paperback edition 2003

Printed in the United States of America

Typeface New Baskerville 10/12.5 pt.   *System* QuarkXPress™ [HT]

A catalog record for this book is available from the British Library

Library of Congress Cataloging in Publication data is available

ISBN 0 521 58002 1 hardback
ISBN 0 521 53346 5 paperback

To John Bowlby, who provided such a magnificent theory of human adaptation that researchers and clinicians from many disciplines, interests, and cultures are still extending its application, and to Mary Ainsworth, whose basic patterns of attachment opened the way to thinking about universal aspects of human self-protective strategies and who encouraged all of us to explore widely beyond the secure base that she provided.

Contents

Acknowledgments

Many people have assisted in the preparation of this volume, and we are appreciative of their efforts. The authors of many of the chapters have waited, sometimes a very long time, for the full set of contributions to be ready. Their patience has been outstanding. The organizers of many of my (PMC) international visits have been essential in introducing me to their various cultures and in enabling me to think about the effects of culture on patterns of attachment. Even when their culture is not specifically addressed, their contribution was essential to the overall understanding of culture that is offered here. Among these are Eleanor Ames, Juan Balbi, Lorenzo Cionini, Louise Ethier, Mateo Ferrer, Helen Gogarty, Helga Hanks, Hans-Peter Hartmann, Airi Hautamäki, Noel Howieson, Kari Killèn, Carl Lachrité, Michael Lenaghan, Aldo Matucci, Rigmor Grette Moe, Irma Moilanen, Louise Newman, Helgard Rauh, Joyce Scaife, P. O. Svanberg, Graziella Fava Vizziello, and Yiota Vorria. Several people have read and commented on various chapters included here; we are especially grateful for their efforts and for their guidance on the literature regarding their own cultures: Claudio Angelo, Gunilla Bohlin, Mirjam Kalland, Saara Katainen, Furio Lambruschi, Andrea Landini, Anna von der Lippe, Tanya Meischner, Irma Moilanen, P. O. Svanberg, and Simon Wilkinson. Finally, I want to thank the five "expert coders" who classified the "disagreement" tapes from the Ahnert sample. Their effort helps to clarify universal problems with classificatory procedures and highlight issues that need to be addressed in the future. We have made every attempt to deal with the issues of culture and adaptation with as little bias and judgment as possible. The people listed here are responsible for any success that we have had.

Contributors

LIESELOTTE AHNERT Interdisciplinary Center for Applied Research on Socialization, Berlin, Germany

VICTOR J. BERNSTEIN University of Chicago, Chicago, IL, USA

KATHERINE A. BLACK University of New Hampshire, Durham, NH, USA

GUNILLA BOHLIN Uppsala University, Uppsala, Sweden

KIM CHISHOLM Saint Francis Xavier University, Nova Scotia, Canada

ANGELIKA HARTL CLAUSSEN University of Miami, Miami, FL, USA

PATRICIA McKINSEY CRITTENDEN Miami, FL, USA

GRAZIELLA MARIA FAVA VIZZIELO University of Padua, Padua, Italy

CRISTINA FERRERO University of Padua, Padua, Italy

ELISABETH FREMMER-BOMBIK University of Regensburg, Regensburg, Germany

KARIN GROSSMANN University of Regensburg, Regensburg, Germany

KLAUS E. GROSSMANN University of Regensburg, Regensburg, Germany

BERIT HAGEKULL Uppsala University, Uppsala, Sweden

SYDNEY L. HANS University of Chicago, Chicago, IL, USA

ELIZABETH JAEGER Temple University, Philadelphia, PA, USA

ANNE KUNELIUS University of Oulu, Oulu, Finland

CLAUDIA LANG Emory University, Atlanta, GA, USA

ANNA VON DER LIPPE University of Oslo, Oslo, Norway

STANISLAWA LIS University of Warsaw, Warsaw, Poland

KATHLEEN McCARTNEY University of New Hampshire, Durham, NH, USA

TATJANA MEISCHNER Interdisciplinary Center for Applied Research on Socialization, Berlin, Germany

IRMA MOILANEN   University of Oulu, Oulu, Finland

BERND MÜLLER   Landesarbeitsstelle Frühförderung Brandenburg, Germany

MARINA MUSICCO   University of Padua, Padua, Italy

MARY F. PARTRIDGE   Syracuse University in Spain, Madrid, Spain

HELLGARD RAUH   University of Potsdam and Free University, Berlin, Germany

ALFRED SCHMIDT   Interdisciplinary Center for Applied Research on Socialization, Berlin, Germany

M. CAROLINA SILVA   University of Porto, Porto, Portugal

BELINDA E. SIMS   Johns Hopkins University, Baltimore, MD, USA

ISABEL SOARES   University of Minho, Minho, Portugal

DOUGLAS M. TETI   University of Maryland Baltimore County, Baltimore, MD, USA

TIINA TIRKKONEN   University of Oulu, Oulu, Finland

LEX WIJNROKS   University of Utrecht, Utrecht, The Netherlands

UTE ZIEGENHAIN   University of Potsdam and Free University, Berlin, Germany

CHAPTER ONE

Introduction

PATRICIA McKINSEY CRITTENDEN

Every theory faces occasional watershed periods. Attachment theory successfully negotiated one about 20 years ago after the publication of Ainsworth's *Patterns of Attachment in Infancy* (Ainsworth, Blehar, Waters, & Wall, 1978) and Bowlby's third and final volume of *Attachment and Loss* (1980). The central issue at that time was to establish attachment as an empirically and theoretically sound domain of study. Bretherton and Waters' monograph of the Society for Research on Child Development, *Growing Points in Attachment Theory and Research,* could be considered evidence of the successful resolution of that issue (Bretherton & Waters, 1985).

The outcome of the research that followed these volumes has been a consolidation of central principles and empirical findings. Specifically, the universality of Ainsworth's three patterns across a variety of cultures is well established, as is the relation of anxious attachment to risk conditions and developmental problems. Moreover, as Bowlby proposed, the effects of attachment are observed across the entire life span, and there is evidence of continuity of pattern across both individual lives and generations. There have, of course, been disputes about numerous topics, for example, the role of temperament, cultural variation, and the best way to describe the patterning of at-risk children. Nevertheless, there is now a large body of attachment research and theory on which a different sort of research program for the future can be built.

Today we may be in another watershed period. The very success of the work from the mid-1970s to the present and the broad acceptance of quality of attachment as a critical developmental variable mean that researchers are applying attachment theory and assessments to samples not seen in infancy, to clinically extreme samples, and to samples in an increasing variety of cultures. Successful negotiation of this expanded interest may require concurrent expansion of theory and methodology in ways that focus on differentiation rather than unity (van IJzendoorn, 1990). Such a change in perspectives is, in fact, quite common in science; see, for example, Lesch

(1996) and Mazumdar (1995) for discussions of the role of alternating patterns of unity/continuity and differentiation/discontinuity in scientific thought. Attachment now seems to hold great promise for a great variety of researchers and mental health practitioners. That promise may best be fulfilled if we venture away from our secure base of shared knowledge and explore different perspectives vigorously.

This volume attempts to effect that expansion by focusing on three issues: culture, maturation, and developmental context. These issues are quite similar to those proposed by Belsky (1995) with regard to the ecology of human development. That is, Bronfenbrenner's ecological model (Bronfenbrenner, 1979) addressed the issues of *how* developmental processes and context interact to shape both individual lives and, reciprocally, the contexts in which lives are lived. Belsky focused on the unstated central question of *why* these processes functioned as they did and proposed that evolutionary theory could illuminate the issue. Although both questions are important, the question of why we organize, mentally and behaviorally, as we do is central to the chapters in this volume that are devoted to theory. The answer that is offered is drawn from an extension of Bowlby's work. It is proposed that danger, including the need to prepare for and respond to danger, is the central organizing principle around which strategies for self-protection are organized.

The empirical chapters focus more directly on how this organization occurs. The selection of contributors expands the range of perspectives on attachment. The contributing authors have been selected from a wider range of countries and with fewer English-speaking investigators than usual, including, in particular, investigators from former Soviet bloc and Mediterranean countries. The intent is to expose attachment researchers to competing perspectives and to highlight a group of emerging attachment investigators. Doing so, however, creates tension between scientific methodologies and psychological/political theories. The theoretical chapters address both the common ground among these perspectives and the ways attachment theory itself might adapt to its broadening international environment. Another point of tension, tied to this broadening perspective, is the evaluative perspective implicit in attachment theory. Indeed, even the term *quality of attachment* carries implicitly the notion of good and bad qualities. Although this term will be used frequently in this volume, its preferred synonyms are pattern of attachment, attachment strategy, and (most preferably) self-protective strategy. It is proposed that attachment terminology should carry no implication of evaluation in either the moral or adaptive sense. Finally, the theoretical chapters integrate current thinking in other areas of science into the discussion of the meaning of individual differences in attachment among individuals and across the life span.

CULTURE

In recognition of the universality of the contribution of attachment to developmental processes, standardized assessments of pattern of attachment are being applied in an increasing array of contexts that are defined by culture (Marris, 1991). If, however, there is validity to Vygotsky's theory of the contribution of culture and history to development (Vygotsky, 1987) or to Bronfenbrenner's theory of the social ecology of development (Bronfenbrenner, 1979), we must account more fully for the effect of culture on the organization, function, and development of patterns of attachment. Indeed, Anglo-centrism could be an impediment to the growth of attachment theory (Takahashi, 1990). Culture, however, is hardly a neutral issue that can be resolved simply with the careful accretion of empirical data. Because of the thorniness of the problem, a brief discussion of cultural issues is relevant.

When this volume was first conceived, the clear plan was to look at attachment through the perspectives of culture, maturation, and context. Over the time it has taken to complete the volume, culture has come to stand out as the most challenging topic. In particular, the challenge seemed to be to describe each culture such that those for whom a given culture is home would nod at the description of themselves, as though to say, "Yes, that is us," while, at the same time, those outside the culture would think, "Yes, indeed, that's them!" Since then, I have traveled to all but one of the countries represented in this volume, spent time with all of the authors, and, with only two exceptions, viewed or actually coded some of the data reported here. I have packed and unpacked my bags, both concretely and metaphorically, until "home" has become paradoxically everywhere and nowhere. In the process, I have come to understand that what one sees is only partly a function of what one looks at. More intriguing is the impact of where one stands when one looks and what one has seen in the past (cf. Kelly, 1955). Time and place color observation such that it cannot be objective and be the same to everyone. Moreover, I have slowly come to wonder whether the empirical methodology that is intended to protect us from bias cannot also obscure our ability to see the bias. I fear this could be especially true in attachment research where the object of observation is a pattern of behavior rather than discrete behaviors and where it is so easy to impose both behavioral expectations and value judgments on the patterns.

For example, recently with a group of 18 Finnish, Russian, and Swedish colleagues, I played a Strange Situation videotape of an American girl whom I had offered as an exemplar of secure attachment, a B3. April was alone and facing the camera with her back to the door when her mother entered. Because of her position, we were able to see her face before she saw her mother; in other words, we saw her expectations before they were realized.

April's face changed expression as she heard the door open and I asked the 18 observers what they saw. No answers. We replayed the two to three seconds of videotape several times, and slowly the answers came: a smile, excitement, satisfaction. I played the tape yet again and narrated what I saw: stilling as she listened, closing of her mouth, pursing of her lips – in anger? – at her mother who had twice left without saying a word. No one else had seen that. After I narrated it, everyone saw it. Of course, April was also glad to see her mother, and, when she actually greeted her later, it was with joy and intimacy. So was there also a fleeting moment of anger? Can B's be angry? Was I right and did expectation bias what everyone else saw? Can we accept anger as a part of security when we have focused so intensively on the positive aspects of security?

Furthermore, when this group constructed a Swedish/Finnish reliability test, coders from each culture overidentified Type B in their own nationality and underidentified it in the foreign children. This effect has been repeated many times with different arrays of cultures. It appears that there is a confusion of normative with Type B.

These issues of what one sees and who can see it now pervade this volume. Sometimes, the issue appears to be methodologically resolvable. For example, chapter 19 presents a discussion of the widely discrepant classifications given to a single set of eight East German and Russian Strange Situation videotapes from the Ahnert et al. study by several "expert" coders. Which is the correct classification for each infant? What matters most in arriving at a classification: who trained the coder and how reliably they code, what version of the classificatory system the coder used, what culture the coder lives in or language they speak, whether the coder is "Eastern" or "Western," what the coder's personal attachment history is, and so on? We have not asked these questions, but they may matter. Possibly, as Klaus and Karin Grossmann suggested, we should hold an international seminar on classificatory procedures and resolve this issue (Personal Communication, December 1995). Or maybe new findings, new samples, and new researchers would necessarily undermine that agreement (presuming it could be reached at all). If that happened, would it be evidence that science was working or evidence of the failure of our methods?

This circumstance of disagreement among reputable coders and across boundaries of nation, culture, and training poses perplexing problems that must be faced directly if attachment theory is to represent human experience adequately. Although, in the natural sciences, standardizing units of measures has greatly improved international cooperation and empirical advance, it is also true that discrepancies have been highlighted. These then became the focus of future research and the basis for defining new measures. The difficulties of doing this in the social sciences and with observational measures are substantial, but the task needs to be undertaken with both an open mind to what will be observed and acceptance of the notion that change in understanding is the basic process underlying research.

Other issues are less amenable to objective resolution. The longer I travel and the more often I return to each country, the more I wrestle with describing cultural variation, understanding the effects of culture, and explaining to myself why cultures vary, that is, the function of culture. I'm a psychologist, not an anthropologist, and I feel ill prepared to do this. A quick look at the anthropological literature, however, confirms that the problems of observer and observed are universal (Devereux, 1968; Geertz, 1989, 1995; Lofland & Lofland, 1984; Marsella, 1998). These problems are also relentless; ignoring them creates greater bias and misunderstanding than confronting them (Gergen, Gulerce, Lock, & Misra, 1996; Marsella, 1998). I'm also an American and, of course, a specific American with my own developmental history. When am I viewing through human eyes? a woman's eyes? American eyes? uniquely my own eyes? Needless to say, I am the one person who cannot answer these questions, but because they apply equally to all of us, they are important.

One way in which the chapters in this volume addressed the issue of culture was by having each set of authors include, in their introduction, a section on aspects of their culture and national history related to attachment and, in their discussion, an interpretation of their results as they might reflect cultural themes or influences. These sections proved to be very difficult to write, and there were many queries about how to meet this request. I had naively assumed that each of us knew our own culture best and that, before I (the perpetual foreigner) was audacious enough to address the topic, members of each culture should have the opportunity to define themselves. It was not as I expected. Indeed, I have learned at least as much about being American by viewing America from other countries and through others' eyes as I have learned about the other countries. So, although I now think that few of us are prepared to describe our own culture, each of us attempts it in this volume.

Culture is the ground we walk on, but because it is always there and invariant, we rarely see it. Only when the ground is unfamiliar, and especially when one stumbles over it, does it suddenly become foreground. This has been my experience when viewing data gathered from different cultures. Often what seems odd to the outsider is so normal as to be invisible to investigators within the culture. I have been welcomed everywhere that I have traveled, and each of my hosts has offered me an opportunity to understand their culture's way of living. Sometimes I think I understood or at least made some progress toward understanding. Other times, I saw things so differently, particularly with regard to secure and anxious attachment, that the discrepancy became painful to me and a problem for us. A particular issue became the distribution of the patterns of attachment in different cultural/national groups. This issue appears throughout this volume and is the focus of the final chapter.

MATURATION

It is ironic that, although the great majority of attachment research has been carried out by developmental psychologists, the theory as practiced is substantially less developmental than most other developmental theories. That is, attachment researchers have paid more attention to the validation and temporal extension of the infant patterns of attachment than to the interactive effects of maturation and experience on the organization of attachment beyond infancy. It is not that the focus on infancy has not been fruitful; to the contrary, it has been very productive. Consider, for example, the important longitudinal research, generated from Sroufe and Egeland's Minnesota sample and the Grossmann's German samples. Furthermore, numerous other longitudinal studies of shorter duration also have increased our understanding of the long-term consequences of individual differences in pattern of attachment. The majority of such studies have in common, however, a focus on prediction from infant patterns of attachment to later outcomes. Where expansions have been made, for example, the controlling patterns (Cassidy & Marvin, 1991; Main & Cassidy, 1988), they tend to reflect observed behavior that is described rather than articulated in terms of developmental processes that are tied to neurological maturation and that have implications for continued elaboration at later ages.

It seems entirely possible, however, that the neurological limitations of the infant brain would constrain considerably the range of possible organizations of attachment in infancy. If substantially different or more complex organizations develop after infancy, longitudinal studies based on infant pattern of attachment may fail to capture these. Moreover, children live in more complex and varied environments than infants; this may lead to greater complexity, variation, and specificity of organization of attachment after infancy. Therefore, an important challenge facing attachment theory is to access other bodies of developmental theory, including, in particular, the cognitive neurosciences, to explore the possible elaboration of attachment strategies beyond infancy. Numerous other bodies of scientific thought ranging from biology to physics, astronomy, and geology are now fairly humming with ideas based on interactive processes and indeterminate outcomes. Especially as these notions affect the underlying genetics and neurology of human development, attachment can benefit from these nonlinear ways of conceptualizing temporally ordered processes.

Several of the chapters in this volume provide starting points for developmental theorizing. Rauh, Ziegenhain, Müller, and Wijnroks in chapter 14 consider the transition from infancy to the preschool years in a Berlin sample and demonstrate how the method of assessing pattern of attachment changes, sometimes dramatically, the nature of the findings concerning developmental change. In their study, depending on the method of classifying Strange Situations of 21-month-old children, the developmental transition is one of dramatically increased anxiety or substantially increased security. Grossmann and Grossmann in chapter 2, also observing German toddlers, point to the importance of different parental roles, even in relation to a single child. In chapter 6, Lippe and myself in a study of 5- to 8-year-old Egyptian children highlight the role of gender in interaction with development in some cultures. Hans, Bernstein, and Sims in chapter 15 follow the developmental pathways of two normally developing children whose context provides too little predictability and who, in middle childhood, begin to display relatively extreme patterns that, in adolescence, are contained and reintegrated within the normative range. Their chapter highlights both the variations within the Type C pattern and the interaction of maturation with development to create a changing array of adaptive possibilities. In chapter 16, Black, Jaeger, McCartney, and myself pick this theme up in a sample of 16-year-old adolescent girls and offer data that new organizations and processes are under way in midadolescence. Again, failure to account for maturational change in our methods would result in very different findings. Soares, Fremmer-Bombik, Grossmann, and Silva in chapter 17 carry the theme to the transition from adolescence to adulthood.

CONTEXT

Two decades of research demonstrate that children in high-risk circumstances are less often securely attached than children developing in more favorable circumstances. These contextual factors are of many types: dangerous families, poverty, parental psychopathology, institutionalization, and so on. In this volume, the focus is less on the lack of securely attached children and the identification of risk factors and more on the essential qualities of contexts that produce differential effects in children's mental and behavioral organization and on the self-protective strategies that children use in threatening situations. In particular, danger in its various forms is seen as the underlying experience associated with risk, and the need to predict and prepare for danger is viewed as central to human strategic organization. Thus, rather than comparing threatened (i.e., at risk) children with nonthreatened children and finding the former lacking in security, it may be more meaningful to ask how the threatened child's strategy reduces the danger. From this perspective, there is the possibility that without new conceptualizations of patterning and strategy, the study of attachment in the context of risk will prove to be a barren promise.

To date, the primary means of thinking about attachment and psychopathology have included type A/C organization (Crittenden, 1985a;

Radke-Yarrow, Cummings, Kuczynski, & Chapman, 1985), disorganization
(Main & Solomon, 1986, 1990), and, in the Adult Attachment Interview, the
"Unresolved" and "Cannot Classify" categories (Hesse, 1996; Main &
Goldwyn, under contract). Given the variety of human disorders and breadth
and detail of clinical classificatory systems (e.g., DSM-IV, ICD10), the current
interest of clinicians in attachment theory will fade if we do not adapt our
constructs to match, and exceed, the breadth and specificity of those already
in use. A particular contribution of attachment theory could be to emphasize
developmental pathways, mental processes, and psychological functions associated with psychopathology or risk for pathology (as opposed to the symptom clusters that typify more traditional diagnostic systems). These topics,
however, need considerable elaboration from their present state to be diag-
nostically and clinically useful above and beyond current clinical procedures.

Several chapters explore risk. In chapter 8, Moilanen, Kunelius,
Tirkonnen, and I explore in toddlers the dual contexts of twin status and living in Finland, a country with extreme seasonal changes in light and living
patterns. The startling finding that risk (being an unhealthy twin in the dark
months) yields higher proportions of Type B attachment forces reconsideration of the effects of context on maternal and child behavior. Lis's study of
institutionalized children in Poland (see chapter 9) is a reminder of both the
importance of detailed observation and the variation of effects, depending on
critical differences within the context. In this case, particular adaptations
within the institution moderated the expected negative effects of institutionalization on the children. Chisholm's two case studies of Romanian children
adopted by Canadian families expand this theme in chapter 10. Although the
Romanian institutions had few of the advantages of the Polish setting, differences in the receiving families were tied to differences in developmental pathway for the children. In chapter 11, Teti considers the context of maternal
depression and, like the other investigators, finds important differences in
the range of outcomes as well as evidence of patterning not seen in infancy.
Lange, Claussen, Partridge, and I (see chapter 12) consider directly the issue
of danger in a sample of abused and neglected children. We find both an
increasing array of patterning, as compared to the Ainsworth set of infant patterns, and evidence of dyssynchrony within a single individual's array of internal representations when these are tied to different memory systems. The
implications of this finding for behavior are considered. In the more normative context, three studies consider the effects of day care on children. The
Rauh et al. study (chapter 14) is particularly interesting because it suggests
that the process through which entry to day care is accomplished is significant
to the outcome; in this study, age at entry was not related to pattern of attachment. In chapter 3, Fava Vizziello, Ferrero, and Musicco explore day care with
somewhat older Italian preschool-aged children. They find that the parental
situation is predictive of children's adaptation, although, when the receiving

staff was attuned to children's needs, they moderated this influence. In chapter 5, Bohlin and Hagekull explore the issues of day care, attachment, and behavior problems in a Swedish sample of 4-year-olds. Their finding that entry to day care between 12 and 15 months of age was related to higher rates of Type C attachment is intriguing. Although these studies by no means close the issue of the effects of day care on young children, they do highlight the importance of maturation and cultural context on variation in effects. As Bohlin and Hagekull (this volume) and many others have noted, the effects of day care are tied to many differing factors. Sorting these out for children who differ in age, culture, risk status, and parental influence is necessary before this resource can be used consistently to benefit children.

CONCLUSIONS

Over the course of two decades, I have come to conceptualize attachment as a theory about protection from danger and the patterns of attachment as strategies for predicting and protecting oneself from danger. In this sense, I find all patterns adaptive – in the context in which they are learned. Do cultures differ in their dangerousness and in the types of danger to which individuals have been historically and are now exposed? I think so, and I address this issue in the final chapter. Here I want to point out that when we observe children with non-B patterns, we are observing children responding to the perception of danger. For the normative Al-2 and Cl-2 patterns, the danger is very slight and requires only a little cramping of one's possible self. For others, however, the danger is greater, and the self is more distorted in an effort to accommodate the threat and protect oneself. Sometimes, safety cannot be achieved with any strategy. Observing children in such situations is extremely uncomfortable and a challenge to our "scientific" distance.

Recently, I viewed Strange Situation videotapes with a group of researchers studying the effects of maternal drug addiction on children. In one tape, there was a 4-year-old boy who seemed extremely independent and distant from an intimidatingly withdrawn mother who exuded hostility. However, when he was left alone for three minutes, this seemingly competent, independent little boy fell apart. After a brief and silent search around the room, he sank to the floor in a corner, his body curled almost foetally and his wide-open mouth emitting intermittent and eerie wails into the vacuous space. Suddenly, his teeth started clacking together as he repeatedly whispered the words, "I want my mommy"; his lips did not move. When the stranger entered, he cried more loudly and fixed his gaze directly on her. Following the directions given to her, she tried to "jolly" him out of his crying: "Come on, you're a big boy," "You're not really crying – you don't even have tears!" When I asked my colleagues how the boy felt, they said he began with genuine distress but ended up pretending to cry; he was probably a Type C child feigning helplessness to coerce adults into taking care of him. Many questions later, I admitted to being astonished that no one felt his unspeakable agony as being beyond tears or thought that he needed, and deserved, to be held comfortingly, even if only by a stranger. I was even more surprised when everyone in the room, including especially the stranger, agreed and was openly relieved to discover that they were permitted to feel (for him and for all observed children). Where do scientists put their feelings when they work? Where should we put them?

Suffering deserves a voice, and attachment theory, by its very subject matter, is supremely suited to the task, whether it is for a child whose hope is dying, a mother whose hope died years ago, or a whole culture struggling with persistent threat. At the same time, we must acknowledge the uncertainty of knowing what we see. Each of us speaks with many voices and sees through many eyes. Failing to acknowledge this is fooling ourselves and deceiving our colleagues. Thus, there is a tension in this volume, one that I hope can be left as productive uncertainty that may lead to thoughtful reorganization of our theory and methods.

To understand anxious attachment, I think we must both understand a child's situation and feel for him or her. When assigned with informed compassion, an anxious pattern of attachment does not describe inadequacies, but rather acknowledges a child's attempts to cope with the challenges of his or her world. Knowing what children can do to protect themselves is at least as important as knowing how "securely" they would act if they experienced no threat. Indeed, so little effort is needed to survive safety that even the foolish, infirm, and stupid can manage the task. On the other hand, it may be that only the intelligent, capable, prudent, and wary can survive danger. The point is that I fear that we have taken a deficit approach to thinking about "anxious" attachment. No wonder no one wants their child, family, or culture to be associated with one of the anxious patterns. Recognizing the accomplishment and adaptation implied by the non-B patterns and placing them in the ecological context of family, culture, and history can help us understand human relationships better and change the negative value placed on the Type A and C patterns. From this perspective, I recommend John Bowlby's original advice to Mary Ainsworth that she name the infant patterns A, B, and C until she knew what they meant. Possibly, in spite of all our existing attachment research, we do not yet fully understand the meaning of the patterns, the full range of meaningfully different subpatterns, or the full implications of the interactions of history, maturation, context, and person that produce the patterns. By increasing the application of the attachment paradigm to more countries and cultural groups, we may reach a better understanding of the range and meaning of human variation and be given the opportunity to refine our theory and methods to reflect that variation more nearly.

PART ONE

MATERNAL SENSITIVITY

CHAPTER TWO

Parents and Toddlers at Play

Evidence for Separate Qualitative Functioning of the Play and
the Attachment System

KARIN GROSSMANN AND KLAUS E. GROSSMANN[1]

INTRODUCTION

Bowlby defined attachment as the "disposition of the child to seek proximity
to and contact with a specific figure and to do so in certain situations, notably
when he is frightened, tired or ill" (Bowlby, 1982, p. 371). He thus states that
the attachment system in the child, and the complementary caregiving and
protective system in the parent, is only one aspect of the parent–child relationship. Bowlby talks of various shared dyadic programs that make up the
whole of the parent–child relationship. He gives top priority to the attach-
ment-caregiving program with respect to the child's mental health.
Nevertheless, others such as the feeding–fed shared program, that of playmates, and that of learner–teacher are also important for the child's development as a full member of his society (Bowlby, 1982, pp. 376–378).

Maturational and Situational Influences on Parental Roles

The transition from infancy to early childhood is marked by a large increase
in the child's cognitive and language ability. In the familiar home environment, the attachment issue of protection becomes less prominent, and the
parental caregiving system is probably less frequently activated as compared
to their intentions to socialize the toddler. For the young child, issues such as
autonomy, self-control, sense of self, and power of language gain a larger
share of importance during daily parent–child interactions (Lütkenhaus,
Bullock, & Geppert, 1987). With their increasing ability to recall past experiences (Daehler & Greco, 1985) and to foresee regular occurring events, separation distress lessens and longer times in play with other children and at
other places can be handled.

---

[1] For further information on continuing research, contact the first author, Institute of
Psychology, University of Regensburg, D 93040 Regensburg, Germany

In infancy, the baby's compliance or willingness to respect the mother's guiding commands and prohibitions has been shown to be related to maternal sensitivity (Ainsworth, Bell, & Stayton, 1974). With the growing skills of the children and the demands of society on the family, the concept of parental sensitivity may have to be differentiated to allow for strictness in one area, such as aggression against peers, and leniency in other areas, such as timing of routines or wanting to be pampered. In this sense, the roles of the parents are expanding from being mainly a caregiver and an attachment figure to becoming a play partner, teacher, and socializing agent of society.

Crittenden (1988b, p. 139) specifies the three basic roles that parents have to fulfill relative to their child: They are expected to function as caregivers, as primary attachment figures, and as social interactants to their child, giving meaning to the child's behavior as well as guiding the child in his or her learning. In her paper on the role of parents in the socialization of children, Maccoby (1992) lists research findings on additional aspects of the parent–child relationship: parents as gender role models and as mediators of morality and altruism. Maccoby also points out that the resulting abilities of the children are not achieved by certain schedules of reinforcement and punishment or by mere identification of the child with either parent, but by less direct means such as observational learning in the context of group rules, self-definitions, and aspirations. Parents should be providing a loving and trusting relationship to facilitate attachment; achieve morality in the child by "other-oriented induction," that is, concern and empathy for others; enhance cognitive growth by scaffolding intellectual experiences; and motivate the child through their appreciation of his or her accomplishments.

Cultural Influences on Parenting

The tasks of parents in all cultures is to care for and enculturate their children. They can recruit help for their task, and as the child grows older, they are usually aided by others and institutions, but they have the ultimate responsibility for their child's health and behavior. Enculturation means to prepare the child for socially accepted physical, economic, and psychological situations that are characteristic of the culture in which they are to survive and thrive (LeVine, 1977).

Thus, parents are also supposed to grant their growing children enough autonomy so that they can explore their environment, establish peer relations, and profit from the knowledge of many other teachers besides their parents. Beyond infancy and after an attachment to at least one primary figure has been established, the parent–child relationship is no longer exclusive. The social world of the toddler widens as kin, neighbors, and possibly professional caretakers support the parents in their child-rearing task. Children establish a variety of relationships, with different people playing specialized roles in their lives. Rogoff, Mistry, Göncü, and Mosier (1991) view this development as a process of apprenticeship in which the child learns different things from different people.

Cultures differ in the role demands they make of mothers. Rogoff et al. (1991) report that U.S. and Turkish middle-class mothers considered it part of their role to play with their children, whereas "some of the Guatemalan Mayan mothers in our sample laughed with embarrassment at the idea of playing with their children, as this is the role of other children and occasionally grandparents" (Rogoff et al., 1991, p. 177).

Role Definitions of German Parents

In Germany, mothers consider it as part of their role to play with their child even well into the school years, until the child prefers age-mates exclusively. German society, and especially the toy industry, emphasize the role of parents as teachers, demanding that they inform themselves about and buy "Lern-Spielzeug" (teaching-toys) starting in infancy. Mothers in particular, and fathers or others less often, are held responsible for the child's success in knowledge acquisition. If a child does not know enough, it is concluded that the mother has not taught enough or has failed to give the child sufficient learning opportunities. In this sense, the Kindergarten (preschool) with a structured teaching program is more highly valued than "just playing with other children." Parents who do not send their child to Kindergarten are almost considered neglectful and have to defend their decision. Even the German school system relies heavily on parents as co-teachers. Classes end at mid-day and the children get a lot of homework to do in order to practice the presented material. But if the child has not understood the material in class, no school teacher is available as an informant in the afternoon. Thus, the parents have to sit with the child and try to co-teach. In the mind of the German public, a child's school failure has long been – and may still be – associated with the parent's unwillingness or inability to co-teach the child properly.

Because of this general cultural attitude, the parents of our study were not at all surprised to be asked to play with their child during a home visit, when the child was about 24 months old. We had asked the parents to participate in a study of the development of children in their families when the focal child was born. During all home and laboratory visits, the parents were eager to talk about their children's new accomplishments and would try to demonstrate them to us. At the time of this reported part of the study, the mothers and fathers were asked to play with some new material with their toddler. They realized that their role as teacher was scrutinized so that much of their concern centered around the appropriateness of their child's handling of the given material. Many were even afraid that their child and they themselves would not perform as well as with a familiar toy. This was especially true for the fathers. Some of them were not very experienced playing with their toddler because of their somewhat lower involvement in child care, but all of them readily accepted the task and tried to present a picture of a good play-partner to their child.

Are Parents Equally Good/Poor in All Their Roles?

Studies on whether the various aspects of the parent–child relationship are interrelated or independent in their interactional quality are still largely missing (Cicchetti, Cummings, Greenberg, & Marvin, 1990). In order to understand the attachment construct as well as the concept of family functioning, it is important to study the various shared dyadic parent–child programs separately and then to compare their qualitative functioning. Some studies include cognitive and social-emotional aspects of the mother–child interaction, such as Denham, Renwick, and Holt (1991) in their observational study of preschoolers and their mothers "working and playing together." They looked at the task-oriented demands of the mother, the autonomy/dependency needs of the child, and the affective content of their interaction. They aimed at predicting the children's friendliness, assertiveness, aggression, and sadness in preschool. But the various aspects of the mother–child relationship, as well as the mother's performance in her various roles, were evaluated from the same set of interactive situations. Combining emotional, social, and cognitive variables into one set may obscure the different roles each of these aspects plays. It also precludes seeing any differences in emphasis that parents put on these domains.

Geneticists and sociologists have posited the interrelatedness of the various parental roles based on the observation that young adults seem to choose partners for procreation who are in many ways similar to themselves, that is, come from the same class or have a similar background education. Scarr and McCartney (1983) used the term *genotype-environment interaction* for the development of cognitive competence providing evidence that children not only receive their genes from their parents but they also experience their parents' interactive stimulation. And the parents' intellectual offerings are a good match for their children's genetic endowment. They see the family environment as a unit in its influence on the child. Their evidence concerns mainly the intellectual domain, but data for the emotional domain are still lacking. The discussion about the priority of sources (genes, temperament, and environment) influencing a child's behavioral makeup, and which of the sources predict what aspect of the child's subsequent behavior best, has been heated between the advocates of temperament and researchers in attachment theory (Stevenson-Hinde, 1991). Thus, in order to enhance our knowledge of what influences a child's behavior, independent data from various behavioral and interactive domains of children and their families need to be connected.

In our longitudinal study of 47 families in Bielefeld, in northern Germany, we were able to combine data on child, mother, and father from various sources. We assessed the children's attachment quality to both parents, the educational status of the parents, their social class, and the child's developmental quotient. Through these diverse data sets we wanted to see whether we could find parents who performed well or poorly in every role or whether parents could be good in one role but not so good in another, and what might account for their competence in that role.

For this presentation, data sets from the first year of the infants' life and from a home visit to the 2-year-olds were used to support the argument for separating the qualitative functioning of parents in different parent–child relationship domains. The families have been followed up since then, and two more data sets from later assessments will also be included in this report: the IQ scores of the 10-year-olds and the attachment representation of the mothers and fathers, which were obtained with the Adult Attachment Interview (George, Kaplan, & Main, 1985) when the children were 6 years old (Grossmann, Fremmer-Bombik, Rudolph, & Grossmann, 1988).

METHOD

The Families

During the years 1976–77, a total of 54 mothers were approached in the hospital as they entered to give birth. The study was explained to both parents in terms of the communicative competence of newborn babies and preverbal children, and the mothers or fathers were asked for their consent prior to the birth of the child (Grossmann, Grossmann, Spangler, Suess, & Unzner, 1985). Forty-nine of these families agreed to home visits during the first year, and 47 still participated when the child was 2 years old. (The sample is described in Table 2.1.) All families lived in stable conditions, and all parents were married and lived as nuclear families, although many grandparents lived nearby. The predominant socioeconomic class was lower middle class. The majority of parents had received the basic education, which in Germany means nine years of school plus three years of apprenticeship in a vocation.

The amount of the two parents' education in these families was significantly related ($r = .376$, $p \le .004$). In all but one family, the mother was the primary caretaker during the first year. In two more families, both parents were on shift work, and they shared child-care responsibilities. In the second year of their child's life, nine mothers held a part-time position, and ten mothers worked sporadically.

The Father's Role in This German Sample

In 46 of the 47 families of the sample, the father was the main breadwinner. The division of labor in all families was quite traditional, with 98% of the

Table 2.1.   Data on the Families of the Bielefeld Longitudinal Study

		n
Socioeconomic status of family	I (highest)	5
(German Scale by Infratest,	II	8
considering income, father's	III	19
education, and occupation)	IV	16
	V (lowest)	6
Age of mothers	Mean= 25.9, range 18–42 yrs	
Age of fathers	Mean= 30.5, range 25–45 yrs	
Schooling of the mothers/fathers	Basic education	27/26
	Realschule	16/15
	Gymnasium	1/4
	University	2/2
Gender of the children	Girls	22
	Boys	25
Number of older siblings	None	24
	One	17
	Two to four	6

mothers responding in repeated interviews that they did most of the house-hold chores.

Most mothers considered it already a great help if the father spent some time with the child or children in the evening and on weekends. About 20% of the fathers accepted regular duties like bathing the toddler or taking responsibility for the bedtime routine. Asked what the fathers liked to do best with the child, mothers ranked "going out and play" as highest. One-third of the fathers regularly roughhoused with the child, 40% read to their child at night, and 15% included the child in their hobby, if it was a manual skill, or introduced the child to his or her own sporting preference. Fathers of boys proved to be more involved in parenting than were fathers of girls.

In terms of emotional closeness, all except two mothers reported that the toddler liked to cuddle with her or his father, one toddler even exclusively with his father. But when asked who could comfort the crying toddler, only half of the fathers were mentioned by the mother. Thus, the father's primary role in these families seemed to be that of a play partner, especially on week-ends.

First-Year Parental Interactive Measures

During the first year of the infants' lives, the families were visited three times at home – at 2, 6, and 10 months. All home visits took place during the day, and some fathers took time off work to be present. Maternal sensitivity, cooperation, and acceptance according to Ainsworth's scales (Ainsworth, Blehar, Waters, & Wall, 1978) were rated from narrative reports (Grossmann et al., 1985). If the father interacted with the baby, the empathic quality of his interactions was rated in a similar way as maternal sensitivity. *Paternal empathy* had to be differentiated from *maternal sensitivity* because a father would frequently hand the baby over to the mother as soon as the infant cried or smelled bad. Thus, the father's ability to soothe the infant by himself could be observed in only 26 fathers. The variable *paternal empathy* was a rating of the attunement of all observable father–child interactions whether they were play-, caretaking, or comforting behaviors. In addition, the father's amount of participation in child care, that is, the amount of time spent in infant care and the variety of activities he did with the infant as reported by the mother, was rated on a seven-point scale. Paternal empathy – if the father was present – and participation were rated for each home visit and averaged over the first year. Within-first-year-comparisons showed that neither maternal sensitivity, cooperation, nor acceptance during infancy was related to either paternal empathy or to paternal participation in infant care.

Attachment Measures

The quality of the children's attachment to each parent and, correspondingly, the parents' quality as a secure attachment figure for the child were classified according to Ainsworth's Strange Situation when the children were 12 or 18 months old. In this standardized procedure, the focus of observation is the infant before and during separation and especially during reunion. The parent's behavior is largely restricted by the instructions to be responsive but not active. The most critical time points in assessing the quality of an infant's attachment are the moments when the parent returns to the room. These moments are thought to show the infant's expectation of the parent's availability as a source of security. The infants of our sample were rated and classified by Mary Main according to the standard procedure into the major groups A, B, and C and their subgroups. At that time the concept of disorganization was not yet used (Grossmann, Grossmann, Huber, & Wartner, 1981).

Infants are classified as secure in their attachment to that parent if they openly express their negative and positive feelings, seek comfort when upset, and return to play when settled. If an infant shows no separation distress, especially when all alone, and does not seek bodily proximity when upset, the infant is classified as avoidantly attached. Home observations have shown (Ainsworth et al., 1978; Grossmann & Grossmann, 1981; Grossmann et al., 1985; Main, 1981) that mothers of avoidantly attached infants tend to discourage the infant's attachment behaviors at home while encouraging the infant's independent play. They are not generally rejecting, but they specifically seem to dislike the infant's expression of attachment needs. In the

Strange Situation, the deactivation of attachment behaviors seems to stress the infants, as can be seen by the increase in their cortisol level after the assessment as compared to the stability of the cortisol level of secure infants (Spangler & Grossmann, 1993).

Infants who overemphasize their attachment behaviors in the Strange Situation are classified as insecure-ambivalently attached. They demonstrate their preoccupation with the attachment figure at the expense of their exploratory behavior by an unwillingness to separate, a heightened separation distress with no readiness to be diverted by the stranger, and a great difficulty to be comforted after reunion. Separation seems to confirm their fear of abandonment. They seem to distrust their attachment figure, and thus she cannot function as a secure base. At home the mothers of these infants have been quite insensitive, thereby nurturing the infant's expectation of an unpredictable availability of the attachment figure (Ainsworth et al., 1978; Grossmann et al., 1985).

The distribution of attachment qualities of the infants to both parents is shown in Table 2.2 (see also Grossmann et al., 1981). In this sample we found an unusually low percentage of securely attached infants, 33% to mother and 41% to father. Cultural and longitudinal implications have been discussed (Grossmann & Grossmann, 1981). The infants' attachment qualities to both parents were independent of each other. In our study, 20 (43.5%) infants had the same classification to both parents, but 26 (56.5%) received different classifications.

Fox, Kimmerly, and Schafer (1991) found in their large meta-analysis a statistically significant relation between the attachment qualities of infants to both parents, but they had a total sample of 672 infants. For this large sample, the emerging 58.5% concordance was significant. But for small samples, as in most studies, the independence of attachment qualities to mother and father

Table 2.2. Infants' Attachment Quality to Their Mothers at 12 Months and Their Fathers at 18 Months

	Attachment to Father				
		Insecure			
Attachment to Mother	Secure	Avoidant	Ambivalent	Not Classifiable	n
Secure	6	8	0	0	14
Insecure					
Avoidant	9	14	0	0	23
Ambivalent	4	1	0	1	6
Not Classifiable	0	2	1	0	3
n	19	25	1	1	46

indicates individualized attachment relations between an infant and each of his parents.

In addition, not only were the children's attachment quality to one parent independent of their attachment quality to the other, but so were the two parents' attachment representations independent of each other. When the children were 6 years old, mothers and fathers were given the Adult Attachment Interview and their attachment representation was classified according to the Regensburg method (Grossmann, Fremmer-Bombik, Rudolph, & Grossmann, 1988). For 38 couples both interviews were available. Concordance was 42%, 16 couples received the same classification, but in 22 couples one parent was classified secure and the other insecure in their attachment representation. It seems that the quality of attachment representation was not a mate-selection factor.

Procedures and Interactive Measures at Two Years

Around the toddlers' second birthday (range = 23 to 26 months, mean = 24.4 months), 47 families were visited in their homes. The visits included interviews with both parents, three short, videotaped parent–child play sessions, an observation of the child's intellectually valuable experiences during an unstructured one-hour time period, and the assessment of the child's cognitive ability with the Bayley Scales of Mental Development (Bayley, 1969). Only the Mental Developmental Index (MDI) was used. In this group of healthy children, the mean MDI was 110.12 (SD = 17.27), range between 80 and 150.

All visits started with interviewing the mother. When the child became impatient because he was not the center of attention, the visitor asked mother and child to sit at a small table that was of convenient height for the child. Most families had such a table. The visitor gave both a bag of colored, wooden, flat shapes and asked them to play with it. The pieces were of five different colors and four different shapes, had a very slippery surface, and were the size of about the children's palms. The material was chosen because it was not obvious to the toddlers what they should do with it, so that they needed some guidance from their mothers. The father–child pairs were given a package of play-dough, a material that most 2-year-olds had never played with. The toddlers needed instructions on how to use it. The parents were asked to engage the child for 10 minutes. No specific instructions were given. A video camera, mounted on a tripod so that the visitor could sit apart from the camera, recorded the sessions.

The play materials were chosen because they gave the parents a choice of either taking on a teacher role or a play-partner role aimed at just having fun together with the material. As we will see, not all parents felt the need to teach. A few mothers, especially those who also had older children, said that they rarely played with the child because the siblings would play together.

Analyses of the Parent–Child Interactions

The video recordings were analyzed in three ways: (1) coding the degree of joint activity during the play sessions, (2) coding the cognitive level of the child's play, and (3) rating the interactive style of mother/father and child during the whole session.

Degree of Joint Activity. The interactive play behaviors were coded on a real-time basis. The number of seconds (minimum 5 sec) in one of three mutually exclusive categories of dyadic activity was recorded:

1. "Joint Activity" was defined by two kinds of activities: (a) joint play as in cooperation, helping, teaching, and compliance, and (b) joint activity besides play, like reciprocal conversation, mutual social games, and squabbles over pieces or goals.
2. "One-sided Interest" was coded when one partner observed or talked to the other while the other played.
3. "Separate Interests" was recorded when there was parallel play, or one or both were diverted without concern for the other.

Intercoder reliability was assessed in the following way: For the categories Joint Activity, One-sided Interest, and Separate Interests the differences in percentage of observed time ranged from 0 to 3.5% with a mean of 1.6%. The most unreliable category was Parallel Play with a mean difference of 11%, because most mothers and fathers talked a lot, and it was often difficult to differentiate between a monologue, comments on the child's play, or explaining their own play, when no response of the child could be observed.

Cognitive Level of the Child's Play. When the child manipulated the play material, the cognitive level of this play and its duration were coded. Level 1 was just handling without an obvious goal. Level 2 was exploratory behavior such as producing noises, tasting the material, and experiencing its quality, that is, slippery or sticky, using it for throwing or scratching, and so forth. Level 3 was labeled "functional play": The material was used according to its purpose, that is, making patterns or towers with the wooden plates or forming the play-dough. Level 4 was coded when abstract thinking was observed, that is, sorting shapes or colors, naming patterns (flower, street) or forms (ball, plate). Level 5 was reserved for symbolic play or counting: A dough-man would want to eat or was labeled snowman by the child, one shape was a "car" using the "street" made by squares, and so on. Some children could differentiate between one and many and would use these concepts during play or during cleanup. If the child was clearly disinterested in the play material, this was also recorded as a separate category. Intercoder reliability was assessed again for the percentage of time each category was observed. For the play levels the coders differed at most by 10% (Level 1) with a mean of 4.2%. For disinterest the mean difference was 2.5%.

Mothers', Fathers', and Toddlers' Interactive Styles in the Play Situations. The videotapes of the mother–child and father–child play sessions were rated on interactive and personality characteristics by student observers using separate rating forms. Some items were taken from the Teaching Strategies Q-Sort (Harrington, Block, & Block, 1978) and some from the California Q-Set for adults (Block, Jennings, Harvey, & Simpson, 1964). They were selected for their appropriateness for this play situation. A 31-item rating form was completed for each mother and father by 10 independent student observers, but no observer rated the mother *and* the father within a couple. The 10 ratings on each of the 31 items for each parent were averaged. Subsequently, the average ratings of the 31 items for the mothers and separately for the fathers were factor analyzed using Varimax Rotation to group the single ratings into factor dimensions. Four factors for each parent met the criterion of eigenvalues exceeding unity. The items defining the four factors for mothers and fathers are shown in Tables 2.3, 2.4, and 2.5 together with their factor loadings. By adding up the mean ratings of the items in a factor, each parent received a score on that factor dimension.

The first factor dimension was labeled Leniency (Table 2.3). A parent receiving a high score on this dimension was rated high on: lets the child take a lead in the play interactions, waits for the child's ideas, does not compete with the child, is patient and lenient, and has no high standards for the child.

Table 2.3. Mothers' and Fathers' Interactive Style During Play: The Factor Dimension Leniency with the Factor Loadings of the Scales

	Factor Loadings	
Descriptive Scales of the Dimension Leniency	**Mother**	**Father**
Waits for child's ideas	.91	.95
Surrenders control	.89	.79
Does not compete	.86	.85
Accepts child's decisions	.77	.63
Is patient	.77	.73
Shows unselfish play	.75	.78
Is lenient	.74	.73
Does not have high standards for child's play	.73	.77
Does not quarrel with child	.72	.56
Exhibits prompt perception of child's emotions	.69	—
Apologizes for self	.60	—
Percent explained variance	45.0	22.2

For mothers – but not for fathers (see Table 2.3) – sensing promptly the child's emotions and needs and excusing themselves for not playing very well inter correlated with the above items. A parent scoring high on this dimension gave the general impression of remaining in the background while unobtrusively supporting the child's play. By contrast, a parent receiving low scores on this factor was best described as bossy, impatient, and strict.

Table 2.4 describes the factor dimension Playfulness with the factor loadings of the scales. The respective percentages of explained variances by this factor dimension was 22.4% for the mothers and 62.5% for the fathers. A parent scoring high on this factor dimension created a happy atmosphere during the play time, was affectionate and enjoyed the child, was supportive, and had good play ideas. If fathers were rated high on Playfulness, they were typically also quite expressive, a good conversation partner, helpful, and prompt in their reactions. The Playful mother also supported the child's self-esteem. Such a parent seemed to enjoy his or her role as the child's playmate in this situation. A parent who received a low score on this dimension was seen as gloomy, withdrawn, unsupportive, and disliking the play situation.

The third factor dimension, described in Table 2.5, was labeled Educational Orientation. It explained less variance than the others – 6.7% for mothers and 8% for fathers. It characterizes a parent as being focused on explaining things and teaching, but also attentive, helpful, and cooperative. Parents scoring high on this factor dimension took on the role of teacher during the session, whereas parents receiving low scores did not seem to be inter-

Table 2.4. Mothers' and Fathers' Interactive Style During Play: The Factor Dimension Playfulness with the Factor Loadings of the Scales

	Factor Loadings	
Descriptive Scales of the Dimension Playfulness	**Mother**	**Father**
Is cheerful	.77	.95
Creates a positive atmosphere	.80	.91
Has expressive face and gestures	—	.91
Is tender, affectionate	.54	.84
Enjoys child	.86	.76
Keeps a good conversation	—	.76
Is helpful	—	.70
Has good play ideas	.71	.66
Reacts promptly	—	.63
Is supportive	.67	.57
Is proud of child	.75	—
Supports child's self-esteem	.61	—
Percent explained variance	22.4	62.5

Table 2.5. Mothers' and Fathers' Interactive Style During Play: The Factor Dimension Educational Orientation with the Factor Loadings of the Scales

Descriptive Scales of the Dimension Educational Orientation	Factor Loadings	
	Mother	Father
Explains, reasons	.72	.77
Is cooperative	.65	.72
Teaches, focuses on cognitive aspects	.70	.71
Is attentive	.65	.68
Exhibits prompt reactions	.64	—
Is solicitous of child's failures	—	.63
Is helpful	.77	—
Keeps a good conversation	.75	—
Is talkative	.75	—
Percent explained variance	6.7	8.0

ested in the cognitive potential of the play session. The fourth factor explained less than 5% of the variance for both parents and was described by only three scales for the mothers and three for the fathers, and none of these scales overlapped. So the fourth factor was not included in further analyses.

The personality and interactive characteristics of the children during the play session were assessed in the same way as for the parents. For the children a 23-item rating form was used, including some of the scales developed as "super items" by Block, Block, and Morrison (1981) and some singleton items from their California Child Q-set – again as they appeared appropriate for a play session of 2-year-olds with a parent. The same computational procedure for giving each child a score on the factor dimensions was used as already described for the parents.

In contrast to the comparable dimensions for mothers and fathers, the children were described quite differently by the raters in the session with their mothers as compared to the session with their fathers. Therefore, the dimensions describing the children's interactive behavior had to be labeled differently with respect to each parent. Table 2.6 lists all child scales and the dimensions are described by the specific scales. The first factor dimension was called Cheerful-with-Mother, and the scales cheerfulness, expressiveness, attention seeking, liveliness, and showing pride showed the highest factor loadings. The first and strongest factor dimension for the child with father was labeled Eagerness-with-Father, and the scales that describe this dimension best were reacts promptly, seeks information, is cooperative, enjoys being taught, seeks closeness to father, and wants to be a "good child." In addition, the scales cheerfulness and expressiveness also showed high loadings on this

Table 2.6. Child Factor Dimensions in Play with Mother and Father According to Factor-Analytic Groupings of the Describing Scales with their Factor Loadings

	Child Dimensions					
	Cheerfulness with Mother	Eagerness with Father	Compliance with Mother	Extroversion with Father	Persistence with M/F	Strangeness with M/F
1. Is lively, energetic	.76			.78		
2. Seems strange, odd						.89/.66
3. Speaks clearly						-.47/-.51
4. Is cheerful	.82	.75				
5. Is emotionally expressive	.89	.73				
6. Displays specific mannerisms						.85/.95
7. Is persistent					.89/.82	
8. Is proud of his or her products						
9. Is easily frustrated			-.60			
10. Is concentrated					.73/.70	
11. Initiates interaction				.64	.71/.39	
12. Seeks distance to parent	-.53	-.82				
13. Reacts promptly		.88	.62			
14. Wants to be a "good child"		.77	.79			
15. Expresses anger openly			-.74	.67		
16. Is attention seeking	.77	.66	.63			
17. Seeks information		.88				
18. Bosses parent			-.77	.66		
19. Enjoys play session		.74			.76/.60	
20. Is camera & observer centered						
21. Is cooperative	.61	.83				
22. Enjoys being taught		.86				
23. Is shy, anxious, quiet	-.60			-.93		
Percent explained variance	39.4	59.6	19.5	23.5	11.6/9.2	7.2/7.4

dimension. This factor explained almost 60% of the variance and seemed to characterize a child that enjoyed playing with her/his father in many respects or did not enjoy it when receiving low scores on this dimension.

The second factor dimension was summarized as Compliance-with-Mother. This dimension combined characteristics such as wants to be a good child, is not bossy with the mother, does not express anger, and enjoys being taught. The second child–father factor dimension described a behavioral style of a child with his or her father which was marked by extroversion, energy, bossiness, and open expression of anger.

Two dimensions were found to be similar for the children with both parents, Persistence and Strangeness. A child rated high on Persistence would have been characterized by being persistent in play, enjoying the session, being concentrated, and having initiative. A child rated high on Strangeness did not seem "normal," had mannerisms or stereotypies, and uttered his or her verbal expressions rather unintelligibly.

To summarize, mothers and fathers were rated by 10 judges on 31 scales and the children on 23 scales for their interactive behaviors during the play session. Factor analysis was applied to organize these ratings into factor dimensions, separately for mothers, fathers, and the children with mother and with father. Three factor dimensions emerged for both parents – Leniency, Playfulness, and Educational Orientation. For the children, the factor analysis yielded various different dimensions. For the children with mother, the dimensions were labeled Cheerfulness and Compliance, as compared to the dimensions for the children playing with father, labeled Eagerness and Extroversion. The factor dimensions Persistence and Strangeness were found for the children independent of the interacting parent. By using the factor analytic method to create the dimensions, the scores on the dimensions were not interrelated. Thus, a high score on the dimension Leniency, for example, can be seen as a predominantly lenient, accepting, patient style of interacting with the child, and no other dimension would describe that parent's interactive style more precisely. These dimensions of parenting behaviors during a play session with the child and the children's corresponding interactive dimensions can now be related to socioeconomic variables of the family and attachment qualities within the families.

RESULTS

The results are presented here as answers to the question posed above: Do parents function differentially well in their different roles? Does the quality of their functioning in the various roles have different precursors and correlates? At first, it should be pointed out that the scores of the parents and children on the various dimensions were unrelated to the child's gender or position in the sibling order or to the parent's age. These demographic variables did not explain any predominant interactive style.

1. *Is the Behavior of 2-year-old Children Consistent Across the Play-partners or Rather Play-partner Specific?*

It has to be kept in mind that the play sessions with mother and father were done on the same afternoon. Comparisons of the children's degree of joint activity with each parent revealed more consistencies than differences. The amount of joint activity of a child with each parent correlated significantly (r = .55, $p \le .001$), as did the amount of disinterest of the child in either material (r = .54, $p \le .001$). But the cognitive level of the child's handling of the two different materials, that is, the amount of time the child played at Level 4 or 5 (abstract concepts and symbolic play) was not related between the two sessions. High-level play seemed to depend on that parent's intellectual support while he or she was interacting with the child.

As for the interactive ratings, across the two play situations, Table 2.7 shows the correlations between the children's scores on the dimensions when playing with their mothers as compared to their playing with their fathers. A child rated high on Eagerness with father tended also to be rated high on Compliance with mother but on Cheerfulness with mother as well. In addition, persistence and strangeness was either generally characteristic or not characteristic of a certain child, as it was rated similarly in both play sessions. These findings could be explained by the fact that both sessions were filmed within a couple of hours.

On the other hand, a child who was rated high on the dimension Extroversion with father did not show a similar expressiveness when playing with mother. Three of the contributing scales to this dimension – being bossy with parent, expressing anger openly, and being extroverted and noisy – did not correlate between the two sessions. It seems that at 2 years bossy, noisy

Table 2.7.   Interrelations Between the Dimensional Scores of the Children When Playing with Mother and Father

Interactive Child Dimensions with Mother	Interactive Child Dimensions with Father			
	Eagerness with Father	Extroversion with Father	Persistence with Father	Strangeness with Father
Cheerfulness with mother	.41**	.18	.49***	−.14
Compliance with mother	.41**	−.19	.44***	−.15
Persistence with mother	.19	.25*	.48***	.13
Strangeness with mother	−.43***	−.17	−.11	.38**

*** $p \le .001$; ** $p \le .01$; * $p \le .05$.

behavior characterizes a relationship to a parent that tolerates such behavior rather than already being a personality trait of the toddler.

Thus, our answer to the first question: "Is the behavior of 2-year-old children consistent across the play-partners or play-partner specific?" would be as follows: A child's observable willingness to join efforts in play with the parent or to be disinterested in such play seems to be an early personality feature. It was similar in the play session with mother and with father. Many of the observational ratings presented a consistent picture of the children rather than a situation-specific one. A child was usually characterized as persistent and concentrated in both sessions or in none; eagerness and compliance was overlapping; and even making a strange and unintelligible impression on the raters was rather child-specific than partner-specific.

On the other hand, clearly dyad-specific was the child's performance with respect to the amount of time the child played on a high cognitive level and the child's extroversion toward that parent. These cognitive and expressive behaviors were found to be more partner-specific than child-specific.

2. *Are the Different Predominant Parental Interactive Styles Related to Different Precursors?*

The following variables were tested for their associations with the three parental interactive styles: parental education, maternal sensitivity, paternal empathy and participation in the first year of the infants lives, and attachment quality of the infant to each parent. Table 2.8 shows that there are different correlates for the three interactive styles and that the correlates are similar for both mothers and fathers.

The family's socioeconomic status (SES) and the level of education of mothers and fathers were positively and similarly related to high scores on Educational Orientation during the play session (see Table 2.5). For mothers, SES and level of education were also related to the dimension Playfulness, that is, their quality of being a good play-partner. The close relation between Playfulness or Educational Orientation in mother's and the family's socioeconomic status is remarkable because the socioeconomic status measure of a family relies on *paternal* education, occupation, and family income. As reported in the method section, however, maternal education and paternal education was significantly interrelated ($r = .376$, $p \leq .004$)

On the other hand, neither parental education nor the family's socioeconomic status was related to the dimension Leniency in either fathers or mothers. Based on the descriptive scales in Table 2.3, these parents seem to have no teaching intentions, they wait for ideas from the child, they do not set high standards of performance, they are lenient, and they surrender their control. These mothers and fathers seem to find it more important that the children explore the material on their own terms rather than imposing goals and standards on the child.

Table 2.8.   The Three Parental Interactive Styles during the Play Session as Related to Earlier Parent–Infant Variables and Parental Education

	Maternal Dimensions		
A. Maternal Variables	Leniency	Playfulness	Educational Orientation
Socioeconomic status of the family	*ns*	.46***	.40**
Maternal education	−.33**	.54***	.29*
Maternal sensitivity	*ns*	*ns*	*ns*
Child–mother attachment			
Secure vs. avoidant (*t*-tests)	*T* = 3.08**	*ns*	*ns*
	Paternal Dimensions		
B. Paternal Variables	Leniency	Playfulness	Educational Orientation
Socioeconomic status of the family	*ns*	*ns*	.36**
Paternal education	*ns*	*ns*	.32**
Paternal empathy	*ns*	.41***	.38**
Paternal participation in child care	.24*	*ns*	.24*
Child–father attachment			
Secure vs. avoidant (*t*-tests)	*T* = 2.67**	*T* = 2.17*	*T* = 2.50*

*** $p \le .001$; ** $p \le .01$; * $p \le .05$.

ns = not significant.

The only strong relation to the dimension Leniency was the child's attachment to that parent. If a mother or father was characterized as accepting, lenient, patient, and noncontrolling, the child had shown a secure attachment to that parent at 12 or 18 months. This factor seems to capture the parent's role as a secure base *in contrast* to a play partner or a teacher. If a mother or father received a low score on that factor and thus was described as strict, competing, impatient, quarrelsome, and imposing high standards on the child, then the child had shown an insecure-avoidant attachment to that parent.

Interestingly, the quality of the child–father attachment related significantly to all three paternal dimensions. Fathers who had been a dependable, secure base to their 18-month-olds seemed to behave more optimally in all aspects of their play. Paternal empathy during the first year was related to the father's Playfulness and Educational Orientation at 2 years, whereas maternal sensitivity was not significantly related to any interactive dimension. The father's amount of participation in infant care during the first year was reflected in his Leniency as well as in his Educational Orientation toward his toddler. Table 2.8 reveals yet another interesting finding: The behavioral measures of the fathers toward their infants and toddlers interrelate much more than those measures for the mothers. It suggests that fathers who are willing to participate more in infant care and who are more empathic and a secure attachment figure also perform better on all interactive dimensions toward their toddlers. For the mothers, the attachment variable was related solely to the dimension Leniency. Looking at the different roles of parents as described in the introductory section, we can now interpret the dimension Leniency as a descriptor of a secure attachment figure: these parents give priority to the child's exploration of the play material in the sense of a secure base and are themselves very supporting and noninterfering.

The five children who showed an insecure ambivalent pattern to their mothers at 12 months could not be grouped with respect to any one dimension, nor were their mothers overrepresented in any interactive style. In fact, the insecure–ambivalently attached children differed significantly from the secure and the insecure-avoidant children on only one rating scale; they received significantly higher scores on "expresses anger openly" versus "keeps anger to himself."

In sum, the quality of child–parent attachment was strongly associated with the dimension Leniency in each parent. In contrast, the family's socioeconomic status and the education of both parents were related to the other two dimensions, Playfulness and Educational Orientation.

3. *Whose Child Plays at a Cognitive High Level and Has a High Mental Developmental Index (MDI)?*

Although the amount of time a child played at a high cognitive level (Level 4 or 5) was not related between the play sessions with mother and father, the child's MDI was related to each separately ($r = .28$ to Level 4/5 in mother–child play and $r = .29$ to Level 4/5 in father–child play, both $p \leq .05$). As found by other researchers as well, the children's MDIs were significantly higher in families of higher socioeconomic status ($r = .37$, $p \leq .01$). Fathers, but not mothers, who had more years of education had toddlers with higher MDIs ($r = .35$, $p \leq .01$). The socioeconomic status of the family (1 = highest status, 5 = lowest) was even directly significantly related to the child's amount of play at a high level ($r = -.33$, $p \leq .02$ for mother–child play and $r = -.27$, $p \leq .05$ for father–child play). As additional information, the children's cognitive performance turned out to be quite stable over the next eight years. The correlation between the MDI at 24 months and the IQ as assessed at 10 years with the Wechsler Scales was $r = .549$ ($p \leq .001$, $n = 44$).

But in our study, the child's MDI was *not* significantly related to his or her attachment quality to mother or father, although securely father-attached children tended to obtain a somewhat higher MDI score than children who were insecurely attached to their fathers ($p \leq .118$).

In Table 2.9 the two measures of cognitive functioning of the children, the MDIs and the amount of their high-level play, as well as the amount of joint

Table 2.9.   The Children's Cognitive Performances at 2 Years as Related to the Three Parental Interactive Dimension

Interactive Dimensions for the Parents	Cognitive Measures of Child		
	MDI	Amount of Play at Levels "Abstract" (4) and "Symbolic" (5)	Amount of Joint Activity
Mother's educational orientation	.52***	.33**	.62***
Father's educational orientation	.45***	.37**	.61***
Playfulness of mother	.36**	.28**	.55***
Playfulness of father	.25*	.31**	.51***
Leniency of mother	ns	ns	ns
Leniency of father	ns	ns	ns

*** $p \le .001$; ** $p \le .01$; * $p \le .05$.

ns = not significant.

parent–child activity are shown in relation to the three parental dimensions. Parents scoring high on Educational Orientation and Playfulness, regardless of whether it was the mother or the father, had children who showed high levels of cognitive performance on the Bayley Scales of Mental Development *and* in their handling of the play material during interaction with their parents. On the other hand, for the dimension Leniency of a parent, no such relation emerged, which implies that some of the children scored high and some low on the two cognitive measures. In the true sense of the word Leniency, these parents seemed neither to encourage nor to discourage the individual way in which the child handled the material whether it was intellectually valuable or plain handling. They acted as a supportive secure base for the child's exploratory activity.

If the child's MDI was partialed out, the children of the Playful mothers and fathers were still playing for longer times at a high level, and for fathers this relation remained also true for the Educationally Oriented fathers. Even if the father's education *and* the child's MDI were controlled for, children of Playful and Educationally Oriented fathers showed significantly more high-level play than children of fathers who were not rated high on those interactive dimensions. For mothers, no significant relation remained after partialing out the mother's education and the child's MDI.

The actual transmission of cognitive contents was observable on the videotapes, as seen also in Table 2.9. The Educationally Oriented mothers and fathers were more successful in achieving Joint Activity with their 2-year-olds ($r = .62$, $p \le .000$ for mothers, $r = .61$, $p \le .000$ for fathers) than their nonexplaining, bored counterparts. Similarly, the Playful parent succeeded in more

Joint Activity than the grouchy, disappointed parent ($r = .55$, $p \leq .000$ for mothers, $r = .51$, $p \leq .000$ for fathers). But the interactive dimension Leniency showed an almost zero correlation with the amount of their Joint Activity with their child ($r = .03$, *ns*, for mothers, ($r = .08$, *ns* for fathers).

The findings regarding the cognitive performance of the children can be summarized in the system proposed by Scarr and McCartney (1993): An intelligent parent has a child that is receptive for intellectually valuable information, that is, a child that is mentally advanced. This parent also plays in an intellectually stimulating way, and the child's responsiveness for this kind of information reinforces the parent for the effort. Thus, it seems to be rewarding for both partners to use their cognitive abilities.

In contrast, this "cognitive loop" seems to be independent of the attachment-related parental dimension Leniency. A very lenient parent most likely has a securely attached child. Neither the degree of Leniency nor the child's attachment quality was significantly related to any of the cognitive variables, the socioeconomic status of the family, the education of either parent, or the child's MDI. This leads to the last question of whether the family should be seen as one single system or as a system of separate but interrelated parent–child pairs.

4. *Which Kind of Mother is Married to Which Kind of Father?*

As we have shown already in Table 2.2, in this study a child's attachment quality to one parent was independent of the child's attachment quality to the other parent. Second, the qualities of the attachment representations of both parents as assessed by the Regensburg method when the children were 6 years old (Grossmann et al., 1988) were also found to be unrelated. Third, maternal sensitivity toward the infant's communication during the first year was unrelated to paternal empathy during the same period. As Table 2.10 shows, the couples were indeed differentially matched according to their interactive styles. A father scoring high on the dimension Educational Orientation was very likely married to a mother also scoring high on Educational Orientation

Table 2.10. Intercorrelations Between Interactive Dimensions of the Married Couples During Play with Their 2-Year-Olds

Maternal Interactive Dimensions	Paternal Interactive Dimensions		
	Educational Orientation	Playfulness	Leniency
Educational orientation	.476***	.384**	.006
Playfulness	.430***	.370**	−.188
Leniency	−.018	.038	.203†

*** $p \leq .001$; ** $p \leq .01$; * $p \leq .05$; † $p \leq .10$.

and Playfulness; and Playfulness in fathers was highly correlated with Playfulness and Educational Orientation in their wives.

When we dichotomized the extent to which a parent could be characterized by one dimension, 17 of the 23 Educationally Oriented fathers were married to an Educationally Oriented mother. On the other hand, it was only at chance level that a parent high in Leniency was married to an Educationally Oriented spouse. A similar picture emerged when we looked at the spouses of the fathers scoring high on Playfulness, that is, the good play-partner fathers. Their wives were also described as a good play-partner or as Educationally Oriented, but again, only by chance was a Playful father married to a mother scoring high on Leniency or vice versa. The interactive style of the spouses of a Lenient parent was largely unpredictable. Only 9 of the 23 mothers who were rated higher than average on Leniency ware married to a similarly rated father. This reinforces the hypothesis that the attachment-related secure base behavior of an adult toward his child is not a mate-selection criterion.

When looking at cognitively related parenting dimensions, our data show that a family can be viewed as one system, but regarding the attachment-related system, a family appears to be a group of independently functioning parent–child pairs.

DISCUSSION

In the North German Longitudinal Study, we found evidence for independent qualitative functioning of parents with respect to their roles as attachment figures and play-partners. We assessed different aspects of the families from the birth of the child onward. Caretaking qualities of the mothers and fathers were rated, and the attachment variables and cognitive competencies of the child and both parents were measured. We tried to view the family as a whole as well as in their various domains of functioning. The families were followed up for 16 years (Grossmann & Grossmann, 1994), so that for specific questions we could supplement earlier data sets by later assessments.

Here, we present multiple analyses of a parent–child interactive situation in the homes of the families when the children were 24 months old. Different qualitative aspects of their joint play were assessed. The explicit instruction to each parent was to play with the toddler for 10 minutes, but many parents seemed to have felt that the implicit goal of observation was their teaching of the child. Students with no information about the families, 10 for each mother–child pair and 10 for each father–child pair, rated their interactive behaviors on 31 scales for the parents and on 23 scales for the children. Parent and child interactive styles were obtained by two separate factor analyses in terms of scores on factor dimensions. The dimensions can be viewed as largely independent of the other. In the present analyses, this means that an individual who had high scores on one dimension, and is thus well characterized by this dimension, is less well described by any other dimension.

The analysis yielded three well-defined parental interactive dimensions which were remarkably independent of the parent's gender. Dimension 1, Educational Orientation, describes the extent to which a parent sees the teaching aspect of the play as most important, who takes his or her teaching role seriously but is also quite sensitive so that the child enjoys being taught. Dimension 2, Playfulness, describes a parent's tendency to see the fun part as most important and who performs as a good play-partner. Dimension 3, Leniency, describes a parent's tendency to be nondemanding and noninterfering and who behaves as a secure base, ready to accept the child's definition of the play situation, whether or not it is cognitively challenging.

The main finding of the analysis of the three interactive dimensions of the parents showed that the qualitative functioning in the different parental roles were fairly independent of each other. A good play-partner or good teacher father/mother could or could not be a noninterfering secure base as well. The typically lenient, accepting parent waited for the child to come up with ideas and followed the child's lead. Thus, some of these children were creative and cognitively resourceful, whereas others played largely in exploratory, repetitive ways. The child's level of cognitive performance was not associated with the parental dimension, Leniency. On the other hand, highly playful parents and highly educationally oriented parents had children who played for a longer time on cognitively higher levels and whose MDI was higher than that of children whose parents scored low on these dimensions.

Performance of the Children in the Two Interactive Situations

The 2-year-olds were rated as having a different interactive style with their mothers as compared to their fathers. Mostly different descriptive scales were loaded on the first two factors. In playing with mothers, the children's positive emotional expressiveness together with wanting attention dominated the first factor. With fathers, children who were cheerful were also attentive and eager to be taught, and wanted to be "good children." Looking at the first factor of the children-with-father, 11 of the 23 descriptive scales were intercorrelated. It seemed that in playing with the father, a child showed either all the positive or all the negative aspects of his or her personality. We had the general impression that it was a very special event for the toddlers to have their father's time and attention for such a long time. Some toddlers obviously wanted to give their fathers a good time, being less oppositional and more cooperative than with their mothers. On the other hand, other toddlers seemed determined to give their fathers a hard time by being demonstratively noncompliant. We will be able to see longitudinally whether these relationship qualities have predictive value.

In playing with the mother, eight positive interactive behaviors of the children described the first factor dimension and six the other, so one dimension was less general than in interaction with the father. In contrast, in terms of

Concentration and Strangeness, the children were judged very similarly with both parents.

The children's cognitive level of play, that is, the number of seconds playing on a symbolic or abstract level, was largely partner-specific. The amount of play on such a high level in the session with the mother did not correlate with this amount in the session with the father, although both figures were significantly related to the child's MDI and education of the parents. This finding suggests that during a specific play session the parent, like a good teacher, elicits or stimulates the child's cognitive performance.

Some Differences between Mothers and Fathers in Their Longitudinal Consistency

For fathers, all three interactive dimensions were significantly related to their child's attachment quality to them. For mothers, only the lenient, accepting style showed this concordance. Similarly, maternal sensitivity during infancy was unrelated to her play styles, but fathers, who scored high on two of the three dimensions, that is, who enjoyed playing with their 2-year-old, had already been more involved in child care during the infancy period.

This larger consistency in the fathers' behavior should be interpreted in view of the German culture. A father in German society can decide how much he wants to get involved with his child because he is not forced to do so. It seems that if a father decides to be close to his child, he will become a secure base in infancy *and* a good play-partner to the toddler. Mothers in this culture have less of a choice. Tradition demands of them the caretaking role for the child, whatever their emotional attitude toward caring may be (Grossmann et al., 1988). The present finding suggests that maternal sensitivity to the infant's signals in the first year can predict the infant's attachment quality to the mother (Grossmann et al., 1985) but not the interactive play style of the mother with her 2-year-old. Because the mothers' quality as an attachment figure was unrelated to her scores on Playfulness or on Educational Orientation, for some children attachment insecurity was counterbalanced by a good play/learning mother–child relationship. Longitudinal findings will show in which domains of the child's life the quality of the attachment relationship to mother and in which domains the quality of the play relationship will be most influential.

The Cognitive/Play System and the Attachment System of a Family

Comparing the three parental interactive dimensions – Playfulness, Educational Orientation, and Leniency – with the child's cognitive level of play and the parental educational variables, we found manifestations of essentially two types of shared dyadic parent–child programs. The good teacher–parent tended also to be a good play-partner, but being a good teacher or play-partner to the child had nothing to do with the quality of that parent in terms of the attachment relationship.

The network of interrelations shows that the definition of a good parent has to be made domain-specific; that is, parents can fulfill their various roles differentially well. Parents of higher education and higher socioeconomic status were more inclined to teach and play well with the child, and their child was mentally more advanced and played on cognitively higher levels. In addition, parents scoring high or low on these two dimensions were likely to be married to each other. The model suggested by Scarr and McCartney (1983) of the genotype–environment interaction with its passive, active, and evocative pathways seems to be holding up for the cognitive/play dimension of the family as one unit.

Independent of the variables that define the cognitive dimension of a family are the dyadic qualities of the two attachment relationships between child and mother and child and father. A mother or father scoring high on the dimension of Leniency behaved as a secure base during the play situation. They left the initiative to the child, and they accepted the quality of the child's exploration of the material on whatever cognitive level. This interactive style was highly related to the child's attachment quality to that parent but not to any of the cognitive or family background variables. This accepting, lenient style was highly dyad-specific. The scores on the dimension of Leniency did not correlate between married couples.

Conclusion

The child's experience in his or her family with respect to attachment does not seem to be a family style but rather a way of relating to mother and a way of relating to father, which can be very different from each other. On the other hand, a child's experience with respect to cognitive stimulation was found to be rather homogeneous with both parents and embedded in the family's socioeconomic status, the parents' education, and the child's mental ability. Bowlby made a good prediction that these shared dyadic parent–child programs function separately. In this study, we could show for a parent–child interactive play session that some parents function well in all roles, but others are either a good teacher, a good play-partner, or a secure base for the child. Each role could be assessed separately. In the meantime, we have pursued the issue of parent's roles further. In putting the secure base function of attachment in a dialectic juxtaposition to exploration, we found different predictability for the different domains for mothers and fathers. The longitudinal findings strengthen our stance on the separate qualitative functioning of the play and attachment system, but eventually, both systems contribute to the quality of relationship representation at age 22.

CHAPTER THREE

Parent–Child Synchrony of Interaction

GRAZIA MARIA FAVA VIZZIELLO,
CRISTINA FERRERO, AND MARINA MUSICCO

INTRODUCTION

Background

A great many terms are used in the psychological literature to describe the ingredients of good interaction between mothers and children. All, however, imply reciprocity and mutual pleasure, beyond the unique features that each mother and baby bring to the relationship (Brazelton, 1961; Brazelton, Koslowski, & Main, 1974; Isabella, Belsky, & von Eye, 1989; Osofsky & Connors, 1979; Ritvo & Solnit, 1958). The focus of the present study is parent–infant synchrony, with an emphasis on the contribution of both partners with one global index. To summarize the global quality of the interactions, we derived a measure of dyadic synchrony from the CARE-Index of Crittenden (1988b).

Because children learn techniques for social interaction from early interactions with their mothers, these interactions have not only short-term, functional consequences, but also long-term effects. Different sorts of dyadic interactions have been identified and compared to the social competence of children with their peers to identify a link between synchrony of parent–infant interaction and the way children open themselves to new relations with others. The mother's contribution to the parent–child interaction, however, is determined not only by the child as a partner, but also, and possibly to a greater extent, by the internal representation that she has of the child and of her relationship with the child. This representation is influenced, in turn, by the transgenerational "working through" of her own attachment to her parents (Main, Kaplan, & Cassidy, 1985; Stern, 1989, 1992; Stern-Bruschweiler & Stern, 1988; Zeanah & Barton, 1989). This consideration leads to an interest in a further level of analysis related to the quality of the mental representation of the parent. Such representation can be inferred from the content of narrative speech.

The research reported here was carried out in a day-care setting in a little village near Padua, Italy. This context was chosen in order to make the observation unintrusively in an environment familiar to both the parents and the children. In addition, we sought a setting where children could be observed with their peers. Our research addressed the following questions: How does the relationship with parents influence children's relationship with peers at the day-nursery? Why do some parents and children easily cope with the commitment to the nursery whereas others do not? What role can the nursery play in each different situation?

Italian Culture and Its Influence on Children's Adaptation to Day Care. In spite of the fact that, for 30 years, public day-care nurseries for children under age 3 years have been available in Italy, there is still some resistance to sending children to day care. Some parents feel guilty about it and prefer grandmothers or babysitters as day-care providers. Moreover, many mothers try to arrange long leaves from their job (thus losing income) in order to take personal care of their child.

Especially in the countryside, parents usually spent their own infancy in large families, being taken care of by relatives while their mothers worked in the fields, and some of them attended, after age 3, parochial care. An important cultural change of the last 25 years, with profound implications for these children, is that public care service has been totally accepted for children after age 3 years (97% attendance). Nevertheless, it is still not widely accepted for children under 3 years of age. Often the economic necessity of women working is seen as a heavy burden among the lower and middle classes. Mothers who do not have an extrafamilial job and who choose day care frequently do so based on their ideological orientation, and this choice may reflect ambivalence toward the child. We presume that all parents give some mixed messages (which could influence children's adaptation to day care) at the beginning of care. Day-care providers, however, do a very persuasive job with parents such that, following the parents' two-week attendance at day care, as they are requested to do at the beginning, parents usually feel reassured. A different situation is the one of mothers who do not work because they usually deny their child has any problem of adaptation; they send the child to day care for "his benefit." Usually these children have more difficulties adapting.

Hypotheses

Our working hypotheses were that:

1. Parent–child interactive synchrony would be independent of the age of the children.

2. Different levels of interactive synchrony would correspond to different kinds of parental representation of the child and the relationship.
3. The level of interactive synchrony would be directly tied to children's competence with peers.
4. Different interactive synchrony levels would correspond to children's patterns of attachment.

METHOD

Sample

The subjects were 28 children ranging from 9 to 30 months of age (mean = 19.7, *SD* = 7.7). There were 17 boys and 11 girls. All attended a day-care nursery in the surroundings of Padua. Twenty-one of the observations were made with the mother (75%) and seven with the father (25%); the choice of parent depended on whichever parent was available. Although we are aware of the differences in interactive style between mothers and fathers and their children, we treated the dyads as similar because the observed parent was the one who usually took the child to the nursery each morning.

The size of the sample was determined by the nursery in which the study was carried out. Of a total of 36 children attending this nursery, 8 did not participate because their parents chose not to be involved in the research. (Two were sons of the attending day-care providers; the other six were reported by the day-care providers as "special problems.")

The Day-care Nursery. The day-care situation was chosen in order to observe parents and children in an unobtrusive but ecologically valid manner. Nevertheless, the context, the part that the nursery itself plays for the parent–child dyad, cannot be overlooked. When we consider interactions and representations, we always have to consider that the nursery is present, in both the physical and the psychological sense. The impact of the nursery environment (which is different for every dyad) include the way that parents experience the separation from their child, their commitment to the institution, any blame they may be taking upon themselves, any conflict (more or less denied) with a rival parental figure, and the flexibility of this triangulation.

From the child's perspective, as Lazzarini and Rissone (1982) note, the nursery offers a great opportunity for new attachment figure choices that force a reorganization of the child's personality which coexists with previous organizations. In addition, the nursery offers new and interesting social stimuli. Nevertheless, it can also become a substitute and mediating "secure base," with a positive (or negative) effect on the relationship between parent and child.

In conclusion, the nursery receives, contains, and influences both interaction and representation. The behavior of children and their social abilities are influenced by the nursery from the moment of separation and all day long until their reunion with their parents. Moreover, the nursery setting represents an alternative that probably influences not only observable behavior, but also the parent–child relationship itself.

Procedure

The experimental situation included both the videotape recording of several periods during the day at the nursery and a semistructured interview we made with the parent. During the interview, a bipolar perceptive representations scale was administered to the parent.

Observation of Child Behavior. The videotaped observation included:

1. The first two minutes of play interaction after arrival at the day-care nursery. The parents were asked to play some minutes with their children in the hall where a carpet was laid out with toys on it. The toys chosen were suitable to the children's developmental stage. The parents were told that they could leave their children whenever they felt it was the right moment. For every dyad, we rated the first two minutes of the videotaped interaction. We chose this length because it was the length of the shortest interaction in the sample.
2. The first 40 seconds after the separation, starting from the moment the parent closed the door when leaving. Previous studies (Fava Vizziello, Palacio-Espasa, & Cassibba, 1992) showed that this was the period of time during which most of the children completed the reorganization process in order to be able to start a new activity or interaction.
3. From the fortieth second to the fifth minute after the separation, when the child had the opportunity to become involved in some activity, joining in with his peers, or starting an interaction with them.
4. The two minutes preceding lunchtime. We counted the time "backwards" from the moment the child could see the serving trolley entering the room. During this time, all the children were waiting around the table while engaging in short interactions and games with each other.
5. The three minutes after the end of the lunch, from the moment the children left the table and their bibs were taken off.
6. The reunion: from the moment the children realized that their parent had come to take them home until the moment the dyad went out the door. We rated the first three minutes of the videotaped reunion because this was the length of the shortest unit of interaction in the sample.

The Interview. The semistructured interview was carried out with the parent at the end of the video recording. Embedded within it was a bipolar adjectives scale in which the parents were asked to characterize their children by putting a mark on a scale (from 0 to 100) that linked each adjective to its reverse.

Variables

The data were coded through 81 discrete variables, drawn both from existing literature (Ainsworth, Blehar, Waters, & Wall, 1978; Crittenden, 1981, 1988b, 1990, 1991; Fava Vizziello & al., 1992; Sroufe, 1983; Zeanah & Barton, 1989; Zeanah, Keener, & Anders, 1986) and discussion within our working group. We chose to reduce the data from the videotaped interactions of the child with the parent and with peers through cluster and interpretative analysis in order to get the essence of the interactive exchanges, believing, with Crittenden (1985b), that interactions cannot be reduced to single aspects isolated from their context. A total of 36 variables were selected for analysis from the videotapes. Six of these variables relate to the parent–child interaction, 26 to the interaction of the child with peers at the day care, and 4 to the child reaction to separation. We did the same for the contents of the interview with the parent. From the narratives of the parents' interviews, we derived seven specific characteristics of parental representations of their children and of their relationships with them. In addition, 29 variables concerned the experiences, expectations, and meanings tied in the parents' minds to the commitment of their children to the nursery. We also derived nine demographic variables from the parents' interview.

The CARE-Index. The coding of the videotaped interactions was based on the CARE-Index by Crittenden (1981, 1988b). The CARE-Index assesses the quality of parent–child interaction by unifying qualitative and quantitative approaches. This instrument was suitable to our research because it takes into account the behavior of parent and child, each in the context of the other (Crittenden, 1988b). Moreover, it was suitable across the period of infancy. The CARE-index focused on seven aspects of the interactive behavior of the two partners, leading to a final score that sums the individual scores in terms of three maternal scales (sensitivity, control, and unresponsiveness) and four child scales (cooperation, compulsive-compliance, difficulty, and passivity). From this instrument, we derived a score of dyadic synchrony to represent the global quality of the interaction; the connection between the parent's sensitivity and the child's cooperation in the seven behavioral aspects led to the dyadic synchrony score. We gave a score of 2 for a total connection and a score of 1 in the case of partial connection (see Crittenden, 1988b). We gave no score when there was no connection. The sum of the seven partial scores yielded a global score of dyadic synchrony. We divided this score into three levels: low synchrony (0 to 4), medium synchrony (5 to 9), and high synchrony (10 to 14). Thus, from the CARE-Index, we derived six variables that we used for the analysis (three for the child, two for the parent, and one for the synchrony of the interaction).

The coders were trained during a workshop held by Crittenden (1991). All the videotape codings were made by three independent coders who were blind to all other data regarding the subjects. The coding was compared item by item; intercoder agreement was 90%.

Working Model of the Child Interview. The parents' representations were inferred from the narrative descriptions that they gave of their children and of their relationships with them during the interview. We used the Working Model of the Child Interview or WMCI (Zeanah & Barton, 1989; Zeanah et al., 1986) to rate both content aspects of the representation, that is, what was said (the three variables were Infant Difficulty, Caregiver Sensitivity, and Acceptance, each with three levels – none, medium, and considerable), and content-free aspects, that is, how the narration was made (the three variables were Richness of Perception, Intensity of Involvement, and Coherence, each with three levels – none, medium, and considerable). We also rated the place that the representation had with respect to the representational stream (Global Feature of the Representation, with three levels – balanced, disengaged, and distorted [Zeanah & Barton, 1989; Zeanah et al., 1986]).

According to this chapter's authors, a "balanced" representation conveys the feeling that the caregiver is involved in the relationship with his or her child and considers it a determinant of the child's behavior and development. A "detached" representation denotes the caregiver's lack of involvement; the details that he or she gives to characterize the child are sparse, and the parent cannot support these descriptions with specific examples. The main characteristic of "distorted" representations is a strong sense of estrangement from the child; the caregivers may be deeply involved and have a lot to say, but they find it difficult to stay focused on the description of the child and the relationship, they seem to be confused and anxiously involved, or they are focused on themselves and are unable to recognize the child as an individual.

The coders were trained by Fava Vizziello (1990, 1991). All the codings were made by three independent coders and compared item by item. The intercoders' agreement was 90%.

Quality of Attachment. The reunion at the end of the day was rated with Ainsworth's original Strange Situation classificatory procedure with A, B, and C major classifications (Ainsworth, Blehar, Waters, & Wall, 1978). The criteria applied to the classification included only those that we thought we could evaluate in all cases. Our situation was similar in many aspects to the Strange

Situation, as conceived by Ainsworth and her colleagues (1978), with our situation being different primarily in its natural ecological context. However, we cannot consider the day-care provider a stranger; in fact, most of the time the child counted on her presence. Thus, there was no evidence that the stress due to the parents' absence grew during the day. This transposition is justified by the expectation that an internalized behavioral pattern emerges in daily situations of separation and reunion. Coders were three undergraduate students trained by Zeanah (1990, 1991). They had a mean reliability of 89% (range 82%–95%) on the reliability test at the completion of training. Twenty-five of the cases in this study were coded by two coders. On these cases, there was 88% agreement for the three major classifications; disagreements were resolved by conference. The coders were aware of the hypotheses of the study but blind to the subjects' identity. The same coders were used for all the classifications.

Statistical Analysis

For the analysis we used the Log-linear Multiple Analysis Model. The dyadic synchrony variable was crossed with all other variables. Significance was estimated with alpha value $= 0.1/(\text{rows} - 1)(\text{columns} - 1)$ for the cross cells and with alpha value $= 0.05/(\text{rows} - 1)$ or alpha value $= 0.05/(\text{columns} - 1)$ for marginal values. Data from the adjective scale were analyzed using T-tests ($p < .05$).

RESULTS

Demographic Variables. As shown in Table 3.1, the sample consisted mainly of first-born children (Sibship, $z = 2.894$), who were taken to the nursery by their mothers (Parent carrying on the interaction, $z = 2.283$) and who first came to the nursery at between 7 and 9 months of age. These factors, as well as the gender of the child and the parent's age, were unrelated to dyadic synchrony. Marital status and maternal education, however, were related to dyadic synchrony. Parents married more than five years had more synchronous interactions than other parents (Years of marriage, $z = 1.776$). In addition, low synchrony was associated with high education of the parents (Parental schooling, $z = 2.200$).

Child Age. Congruent with the first hypothesis, synchrony of the interaction was statistically independent of child age. See Table 3.1.

Dyadic Synchrony. The dyadic synchrony variable ($p < 0.1$) was analyzed with the other variables drawn from the CARE-Index (see Table 3.2 and 3.3) in order to determine more clearly the interactive modalities peculiar to parents and children at specific global levels of synchrony.

Table 3.1. Personal Data Variables

Synchrony	Age of Child					Sex of Child		Sibship		
	9	13	19	25	30	Male	Female	Only Child	One Sibling	Two Siblings
Low	1[a]	4	1	3	2	7	4	6	4	1
	-0.985[b]	1.61	-1.204	0.813	-0.293	0.241	-0.241	-0.73	-0.203	0.613
Medium	2	1	3	3	3	7	5	9	3	0
	-0.385	-0.512	0.157	0.6	0.157	-0.15	0.15	0.946	-0.025	-0.554
High	2	0	2	0	1	3	2	3	2	0
	1.282	-0.683	1.089	-0.933	0.122	-0.08	0.08	-0.283	0.192	0.051
	5	5	6	6	6	17	11	18	9	1
	0.138	-0.596	0.449	-0.195	0.449	0.994	-0.994	2.894**	0.992	-2.445**

Synchrony	Age of First Entrance to Day care				Parent		Years Married			Problem Situation
	Within 6 Months	From 7 to 9 Months	From 10 to 12 Months	After the 12th Month	Mother	Father	1 to 2	3 to 5	More Than 5	
Low	1	4	4	2	7	4	4	5	0	2
	-0.872	-0.681	1.946*	-0.898	-1.188	1.188	1.341	0.787	-1.909*	0.788
Medium	2	7	0	3	9	3	1	5	4	2
	0.473	1.056	-0.999	0.281	-0.45	0.45	-1.356	0.188	0.902	0.327
High	1	2	0	2	5	0	1	1	3	0
	0.388	-0.346	-0.406	0.56	1.068	-1.068	0.12	-0.789	1.776*	-0.811
	4	13	4	7	21	7	6	11	7	4
	-0.528	2.251**	-1.379	0.733	2.283**	-2.283**	-0.016	1.475	-0.204	-0.868

(continued)

Table 3.1 (continued)

Synchrony	Parental Schooling				Age of Mother			
	Primary School	Secondary School	High School	University	18–25	26–32	33–38	Over 38
Low	0	9	1	1	1	7	2	1
	-0.799	2.2**	-0.444	-0.444	-0.144	0.097	-0.826	0.649
Medium	1	7	2	2	2	8	2	0
	-0.026	0.903	-0.433	-0.433	0.891	0.656	-0.559	-0.632
High	1	0	2	2	0	2	3	0
	1.01	-2.072*	0.879	0.879	-0.549	-0.619	1.304	0.102
	2	16	5	5	3	17	7	1
	-1.298	1.192	0.175	0.175	-0.907	3.258**	1.065	-1.714

Synchrony	Age of Father			
	18–25	26–32	33–38	Over 38
Low	0	7	3	0
	-0.08	0.998	-0.699	-0.08
Medium	0	6	6	0
	-0.209	0.485	0.275	-0.209
High	0	1	4	0
	0.286	-1.256	0.473	0.286
	0	14	13	0
	-1.09	1.034	1.146	-1.09

a Frequencies.

b Z points.

* Tendency to significance at alpha value = 0.05/(rows − 1) or alpha value = 0.05/(columns − 1).

** Significant at alpha value = 0.1/(rows − 1) (columns − 1).

Table 3.2. Parental Interactive Modalities

Synchrony	Controlling Parent			Unresponsive Parent			
	LC	MC	HC	LU	MU	HU	
Low	4	6	1	3	2	6	Frequencies
	−2.156**	1.503*	0.248	−1.637	−1.411	2.440**	Z points
Medium	12	0	0	5	7	0	
	1.864*	−1.21	−0.08	0.284	1.738*	−1.228	
High	4	1	0	4	1	0	
	−0.128	0.248	−0.116	1.105	−0.35	−0.445	
	20	7	1	12	10	6	
	3.38**	−0.341	−1.935	1.791	0.556	1.587	

LC = low control; MC = medium control; HC = high control; LU = low unresponsiveness; MU = medium unresponsiveness; HU = high unresponsiveness.

* Tendency to significance at alpha value = 0.05/(rows − 1) or alpha value = 0.05/(columns − 1).

** Significant at alpha value = 0.1/(rows − 1)(columns − 1).

Low synchrony was associated with parental control (Controlling parent: medium, $z = 1.503$; low: $z = −2.156$) and, even more strongly, with high unresponsiveness (Unresponsive parent: $z = 2.440$). On the child's side, we can see passivity (Passive child: high, $z = 1.613$; low, $z = −2.224$), a tendency to opposition (Difficult child: low, $z = −1.453$), and some compliance and adaptation to the parent's will (Compulsive compliant child: low, $z = 1.6$). The two partners could not carry on a smooth, mutual exchange; they seemed to follow two parallel paths, without being able to find a way to achieve for effective contact.

The medium-synchrony dyads were characterized by parents' tendency to alternate sensitivity with unresponsiveness and detachment from the interaction (Unresponsive parent: medium, $z = 1.738$). Children in medium-synchrony dyads tended to be compulsively compliant (Compulsive compliant child: medium, $z = 1.738$).

The high-synchrony dyads were characterized by high levels of parental sensitivity matched by the child's cooperation. The empirical observation points out that although these dyads could show control from the parent's part or slight compliance or difficulty in the child, they were likely to be low with regard to child passivity (Passive child: low, $z = 1.986$). Thus, synchrony was not an idyllic interaction but was based on the capacity of both partners to fit and modulate their behavior to smooth the course of the interactive exchanges.

Parental Representation. This level of analysis investigated the link between what was observed in the interaction and what related to the internal world of

Table 3.3. **Child's Interactive Modalities**

	Compulsive Compliant Child			Difficult Child			Passive Child			
Synchrony	LCC	MCC	HCC	LD	MD	HD	LP	MP	HP	Frequencies Z points
Low	6	2	3	5	3	3	1	5	5	
	−0.655	−1.411	1.6*	−1.453	0.449	0.678	−2.224**	0.719	1.613*	
Medium	5	7	0	7	3	2	5	4	3	
	−0.172	1.738*	−1.002	−0.559	0.465	−0.005	0.179	−0.347	0.154	
High	4	1	0	5	0	0	4	1	0	
	0.683	−0.35	−0.178	1.475	−0.591	−0.437	1.986**	−0.285	−1.156	
	15	10	3	17	6	5	10	10	8	
	2.505**	0.556	−1.998**	2.809**	−0.893	−1.153	0.483	0.483	−0.779	

LCC = low compulsive compliance; MCC = medium compulsive compliance; HCC = high compulsive compliance; LD = low difficulty; MD = medium difficulty; HD = high difficulty; LP = low passivity; MP = medium passivity; HP = high passivity.

* Tendency to significance at alpha value = 0.05/(rows − 1) or alpha value = 0.05/(columns − 1).

** Significant at alpha value = 0.1/(rows − 1)(columns − 1).

the parent and, therefore, was not directly observable. That is, we sought to investigate the connection between the parent's internal representation and the way the parent acted in the observed interaction with his or her child. The representation measures were Richness of Perception, Intensity of Involvement, Coherence, Infant Difficulty, Acceptance, and Global Features of the Representation (WMCI) (Zeanah & Barton, 1989; Zeanah et al., 1986).

The analysis revealed a significant association of different interactive modalities to different types of parental representation. Specifically, a difference was found among the types of interactions, a difference that was proper not only to what was observed but also to what could be an underlying characteristic of the relationship.

Interactions characterized by high synchrony and reciprocity were linked to balanced global representations (Global feature of the representation: balanced, $z = 2.089$). In greater detail, sensitivity of the caregiver to the child's needs, affective experiences, and individuality (Caregiver sensitivity: considerable, $z = 1.542$) and parental acceptance of the role of caregiver (as well as the acceptance of the child) were all associated with balanced representation (Acceptance: considerable, $z = 1.754$). On the adjectives scale, the parents characterized their child in a flexible and varied way, even if no statistical significance emerged. See Table 3.4.

Interactions characterized by medium synchrony were associated with detached representations (Global feature of the representation: disengaged, $z = 2.111$). Again, in greater detail, although the parents' narratives appeared to be quite varied and full of details (Richness of perception: moderate, $z = 1.579$), they were still limited in recognizing children's individuality and needs, especially from the affective point of view (Caregiving sensitivity: no sens., $z = 1.816$). In addition, there was psychological and emotional detachment from the relationship (Intensity of involvement: no involvement, $z = 1.507$) unlike the whole of the sample (Intensity of involvement, $z = 2.085$). On the adjectives scale, these parents tended to give scores at the extremes of the scale, especially the positive extreme (see Figure 3.1). The characterizing adjectives were beautiful, attentive, loving, calm, and independent; these fit a pattern of child characteristics with aspects of both cooperation and compulsive compliance that has emerged in other research studies (e.g., Crittenden 1988). Giving extreme positive scores seemed in line with having a detached representation, where the perception of the real child is rigid and inflexible and any negative affect of the child is minimized or denied (Zeanah & Barton, 1989).

For the low-synchrony dyads, the tendency was toward the distorted representation (Global feature of the representation: distorted, $z = 1.892$), characterized by strong involvement in a relationship so difficult to manage that there was often a sense of estrangement from the child. These parents seemed to be in conflict with their role (Acceptance: considerable, $z = -1.962$)

Table 3.4. Features of Parental Representation

	Content-free Features of the Representation								
	Richness of Perception			Intensity of Involvement			Coherence		
Synchrony	N	M	C	N	M	C	N	M	C
Low	3	3	5	0	5	6	1	3	7
	0.108	−0.571	0.497	−0.871	0.223	1.179	−0.155	−0.133	0.374
Medium	3	7	2	3	6	3	3	3	6
	0.13	1.579*	−1.589*	1.507*	−0.609	−1.453	1.122	−0.745	−0.697
High	1	1	3	0	3	2	0	2	3
	−0.194	−0.746	1.078	−0.229	0.257	0.097	−0.643	0.705	0.223
	7	11	10	3	14	11	4	8	16
	−0.656	0.221	0.483	−2.118**	2.085**	1.178	−1.815*	0.271	2.363**

	Content Features of the Representation								
	Infant Difficulty			Caregiving Sensitivity			Acceptance		
Synchrony	N	M	C	N	M	C	N	M	C
Low	4	5	2	4	4	3	2	6	3
	−1.855*	0.28	1.08	0.558	−0.103	−0.537	0.558	1.073	−1.962**
Medium	9	3	0	7	3	2	1	5	6
	1.056	0.207	−0.776	1.816*	−0.686	−1.28	−0.374	0.734	−0.356
High	4	1	0	0	2	3	0	0	5
	−0.527	−0.394	0.048	−1.509	−0.63	1.542	−0.109	−1.137	1.754*
	17	9	2	11	9	8	3	11	14
	2.742**	0.629	−2.178**	−0.429	0.416	0.129	−1.655	0.086	2.189**

	Global Features of the Representation			
Synchrony	Balanced	Disengaged	Distorted	
Low	3	2	6	Frequencies Z points
	−1.451	−0.632	1.892*	
Medium	3	8	1	
	−1.222	2.111**	−0.89	
High	5	0	0	
	2.089	−0.922	−0.564	
	11	10	7	
	1.548	−0.289	−0.893	

N = no; M = medium; C = considerable.

* Tendency to significance at alpha value = 0.05/(rows − 1) or alpha value = 0.05/(columns − 1).

** Significant at alpha value = 0.1/(rows − 1)(columns − 1).

and described their child as quite difficult to care for and to relate to (Infant difficulty: no difficulty, $z = -1.855$). On the adjectives scale (see Figure 3.1) the perceptive profile described children in low-synchrony dyads as less loving, sociable, and constant and as more restless. This finding reflects the difficulties found at the interactive level. In addition, parents reported that these

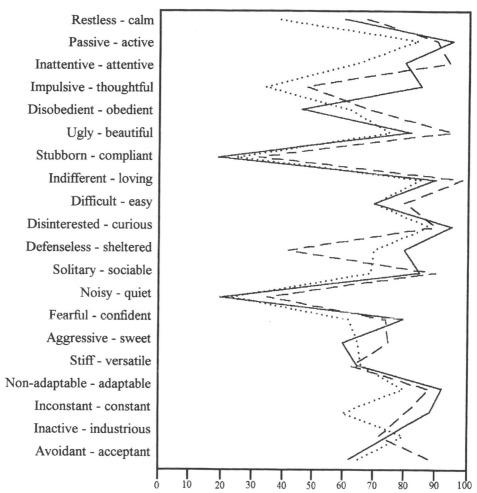

Restless - calm
Passive - active
Inattentive - attentive
Impulsive - thoughtful
Disobedient - obedient
Ugly - beautiful
Stubborn - compliant
Indifferent - loving
Difficult - easy
Disinterested - curious
Defenseless - sheltered
Solitary - sociable
Noisy - quiet
Fearful - confident
Aggressive - sweet
Stiff - versatile
Non-adaptable - adaptable
Inconstant - constant
Inactive - industrious
Avoidant - acceptant

0   10   20   30   40   50   60   70   80   90   100

Figure 3.1. Parent-child synchrony and children's perceptive profile. — high synchrony; - - - medium synchrony; ⋯ low synchrony.

children were less attentive. This finding is consistent with interactive passivity and highlights the complex interplay of influences between the parents' perception of his or her child and the behavior of the child.

Other Aspects of the Interview. Analysis of the interviews showed that parents justified the commitment to day care by both necessity and personal choice (19 cases out of 28; $z = 2.845$; $zcrit = 1.96$), while on the other hand, 11 cases out of 28 ($z = 1.863$; $zcrit = 2.12$) contradicted themselves by asserting that they would not bring the child to the nursery if their work did not force them to do so. This suggests strong conflict in parents, who felt guilty for "abandoning" the child. Consequently, they thought it necessary to reassure them-selves, to assert the importance of their personal decision to both themselves and others. Furthermore, the personal decision was often made because they did not want the child to stay with the grandparents, as they affirmed in the interview, in order to avoid too strong a bond with these "rival" caregivers (Montoli Perani, 1985).

Behavior with Peers. We explored the connection between dyadic synchrony and the social behavior of the children with their peers (after the separation from the caregiver). Children who differed in the level of synchrony of their interaction with caregivers differed in the behavioral and interactive modality that they used during the day. This pattern was in accord with existing studies of quality of attachment (Arend, Grove, & Sroufe, 1979; Matas, Arend, & Sroufe, 1978).

Within the first 40 seconds after the parent left, we found that most of the children withdrew, as though mourning, and underwent a period of solitude and detachment (16 cases out of 28; $z = 2.409$; $zcrit = 2.12$), without resorting to any particular self-calming behavior (18 cases out of 28; $z = 3.67$; $zcrit = 2.12$). In this state of isolation, the children set themselves apart as observers of what was going on around them (Involvement and use of personal energy: diffuse, $z = 2.263$). See Table 3.5.

Later on, from the fortieth second to the fifth minute, the situation changed. Although most children readily approached their peers (Modality used to initiate contact or social interaction; $z = 2.371$; see Table 3.6), low-synchrony children were not able to turn to others in a positive way (Modality used to initiate contact or social interaction: positive, $z = -1.668$). Medium-synchrony children tended to adopt a negative modality, crying or using angry or bullying gestures (Modality used to initiate contact or social interaction: negative, $z = 1.703$). There was no significance for high-synchrony children.

Two minutes before lunch, this division was still confirmed (see Table 3.6). The low-synchrony children remained negative with respect to peers (Modality used to initiate contact or social interaction: positive, $z = -2.223$). There was no significance for medium-synchrony children. The high-synchrony children showed their skill in getting into contact with others in a more positive way (Positive contact, $z = 2.596$).

The "self-involvement in social activities" aspect also discriminated differ-ent categories of children (see Table 3.5). There was no significance for low-synchrony children. Five minutes after the separation, the medium-synchrony children were still unable to engage in organized activities (Involvement and use of personal energy: productive involvement, $z = -2.027$). We could sup-pose that, in this moment, the depressive feelings related to the separation were still present or that they were just now appearing, after a previous

Table 3.5. Involvement and Use of Personal Energy

Synchrony	Within 40 Sec			From the 40th Sec. to the 5th Minute			Two Minutes Before Lunch		
	VI	DI	PI	VI	DI	PI	VI	DI	PI
Low	4	5	2	1	7	3	1	9	1
	0.159	-0.082	0.48	-0.328	0.606	-0.143	0.812	0.441	-1.342
Medium	4	6	2	3	8	1	0	10	2
	0.015	-0.522	0.366	1.279	0.827	-2.027**	-0.575	0.976	-0.019
High	1	4	0	0	1	4	0	2	3
	-0.128	1.044	-0.584	0.643	-1.054	2.072**	-0.089	-1.255	1.351
	9	15	4	4	16	8	1	21	6
	0.217	2.263**	-1.733*	-1.544	1.788*	0.273	-2.214**	3.254**	0.187

Synchrony	Three Minutes after Lunch			
	VI	DI	PI	
Low	3	6	2	Frequencies
	-0.345	-0.564	0.689	Z points
Medium	2	10	0	
	0.028	1.769	-1.113	
High	2	2	1	
	0.282	-1.31	0.79	
	7	18	3	
	0.142	2.527**	-1.862**	

VI = vacant involvement; DI = diffuse involvement; PI = productive involvement.

* Tendency to significance at alpha value = 0.05/(rows − 1) or alpha value = 0.05/(columns − 1).

** Significant at alpha value = 0.1/(rows − 1)(columns − 1).

Table 3.6. Modality Used to Initiate Contact or Social Interaction

Synchrony	Within 40 Sec			From the 40th Sec. to the 5th Minute			Two Minutes Before Lunch		
	NoC	PC	NC	NoC	PC	NC	NoC	PC	NC
Low	9	0	2	4	4	3	5	1	5
	0.983	-1.468	1.063	1.294	-1.688*	0.048	0.745	-2.223**	1.495
Medium	6	4	2	0	7	5	7	3	2
	-1.464	1.141	-0.014	-1.664*	0.626	1.703*	1.182	-0.802	-0.398
High	4	1	0	1	4	0	0	5	0
	0.231	0.798	-0.829	0.897	0.776	-1.293	-1.206	2.596**	-0.7
	19	5	4	5	15	8	12	9	7
	3.225**	-1.125	-1.196	-1.27	2.371**	-0.468	0.212	0.577	-0.683

Synchrony	Three Minutes after Lunch			
	NoC	PC	NC	
Low	3	3	5	Frequencies
	-0.218	0.02	0.214	Z points
Medium	3	4	5	
	-0.453	0.486	-0.037	
High	2	1	2	
	0.586	-0.4	-0.147	
	8	8	12	
	-0.267	-0.561	0.907	

NoC = no contact; PC = positive modality of contact; NC = negative modality of contact.

* Tendency to significance at alpha value = 0.05/(rows − 1) or alpha value = 0.05/(columns − 1).

** Significant at alpha value = 0.1/(rows − 1)(columns − 1).

negation expressed by impassivity soon after the separation. The high-synchrony children were self-involved in goal oriented productive activities (Involvement and use of personal energy: productive, $z = 2.072$), as if mourning of the separation having been achieved, they were free to turn their attention and energy to activities.

The time before lunch appeared to be a social moment of reunion and sharing that was not suitable for particularly intense and complex activities (Involvement and use of personal energy, $z = 3.254$).

Five minutes after the separation, the low-synchrony children appeared to withdraw from activities that could bring them into contact with others (Skills in leading and joining the peers' group: absence, $z = 1.658$; see Table 3.7). We found no significant results for the medium-synchrony group. On the other end, the high-synchrony children revealed a capacity for getting productively involved in some activity (see Table 3.5). This capacity was associated with leadership toward the other children and participation in the group of peers (Skills in leading and joining the peers' group: active participation, $z = 2.369$; see Table 3.7). Similar tendencies for the high-synchrony group were again found in the moment preceding lunch time.

After lunch, it appeared that all children felt free to pass some time in enjoyable activities, giving free play to their physical energies or just relaxing on a comfortable carpet. There were no group differences in interactive behavior. In particular, the children in the low-synchrony group could not be differentiated from other children. At this point, they appeared to seize the opportunity to get involved in some activity with their playmates (Skills in leading and joining the peers' group: passive $z = 1.79$; see Table 3.7).

Null Effects. We considered a number of variables indicative of unusual child behavior and inappropriate display of positive or negative affect; the absence of significant results was quite reassuring, given their importance to the development pathology. The observation period may have been too short, however, to pick up important effects. Moreover, the exclusion of the six troubled children from the sample may have reduced the variance too much to find a significant effect.

Although we expected differences in the children's reactions to frustrations, we observed few such differences. Moreover, we did not identify any relationship to level of synchrony.

Quality of Attachment in the Reunion. The attachment, rated at the reunion at the end of the day, did not reveal significant associations with dyadic synchrony (see Table 3.8). The context in which we carried out the research is very important at this level of analysis. In addition, our ability to identify patterns of individual difference may have been jeopardized by inclusion of both the youngest children (less than 11 months) and preoperational children

Table 3.7. Skills in Leading and Joining the Peer Group

Synchrony	Within 40 Sec			From the 40th Sec. to the 5th Minute			Two Minutes Before Lunch		
	AP	PP	AI	AP	PP	AI	AP	PP	AI
Low	0	0	11	0	3	8	2	2	7
	−0.733	−0.244	1.442	−1.357	0.429	1.658*	−1.553	0.6	0.907
Medium	2	2	8	1	5	6	4	2	6
	0.142	0.76	−1.296	−0.511	0.568	0.113	−0.519	0.301	0.134
High	1	0	4	3	1	1	4	0	1
	0.774	−0.323	−0.477	2.369**	−0.885	−1.63	1.771*	−0.627	−0.748
	3	2	23	4	9	15	10	4	14
	−1.054	−1.667	3.967**	−1.57	0.463	1.61	0.905	−1.689*	1.289

Frequencies
Z points

Synchrony	Three Minutes after Lunch		
	AP	PP	AI
Low	1	6	4
	−1.358	1.79*	−0.432
Medium	3	4	5
	−0.032	0.461	−0.535
High	2	0	3
	1.296	−1.467	0.769
	6	10	12
	−0.685	−0.492	1.439

AP = active participation; PP = passive participation; AI = absence of involvement.

* Tendency to significance at alpha value = 0.05/(rows − 1) or alpha value = 0.05/(columns − 1).

** Significant at alpha value = 0.1/(rows − 1)(columns − 1).

Table 3.8. Attachment[a]

Synchrony	Three Minutes after Lunch			
	A	B	C	
Low	5	6	0	Frequencies
	0.901	1.017	−1.208	Z points
Medium	4	5	2	
	−0.582	−0.384	0.726	
High	2	2	1	
	−0.412	−.701	0.873	
	11	13	3	
	1.181	1.621	−1.981	

A = anxious-avoidant attachment; B = secure attachment; C = anxious-ambivalent attachment.

[a] For one case, it was not possible to get the classification.

* Tendency to significance at alpha value = 0.05/(rows − 1) or alpha value = 0.05/(columns − 1).

** Significant at alpha value = 0.1/(rows − 1)(columns − 1).

(over 18–20 months) and the application of Ainsworth's method equally to them all.

DISCUSSION

Age and Synchrony. The independence of these two factors shows that both partners of the dyad go through a developmental pathway in which different stages call for peculiar developmental tasks that affect both parents and children. To manage development successfully, they must cope together with the developmental process. Each time the quality of the interaction could possibly be influenced; these variations are, therefore, peculiar to each dyad and can only be deterred by a longitudinal study.

Parental Couple and Synchrony. The situation of the parental couple seemed to influence synchrony; parents married at least five years had better relationships with their children, showing that a certain stability and maturity of the relationship between the parents might have an influence on what passes from parent to child and vice versa. Parents with only secondary education had less synchronous relationships. These parents might be seen as more concerned by the problems of everyday life, problems that distract their attention from the relationship with their children – that is, problems that necessitated the commitment to day care.

Reciprocal Influence. From the interactions that are the preferential focus of analysis, we tried to "reconstruct" the relationship and to look into its importance in the development of the child's "social personality." The results pointed out links between the quality of the children's social behavior toward their peers, the level of interactive synchrony with their caregivers, and parental representations. These findings confirmed our hypotheses. A model emerges in which the parent represents the context in which the first elements of sociability are sketched out; later, when meeting others, they are modeled and broadened. A good interaction is built by parents who are able to convey to their children the positive representation they have of the children themselves and of their relationships with them. There also are children who constantly shape their representations of themselves, thus further reinforcing their self-esteem, self-confidence, and autonomy.

The intrapsychic level of the parents influenced the interpersonal level with children and the replies parents gave to them. On the basis of parental responses, children appeared to form an image of themselves, as more or less competent in interacting with other people.

Quality of Attachment and Day Care. Attachment, as Ainsworth classifies it, is observed in unusual and unexpected situations, certainly more distressing than the daily and predictable situation of separation and reunion at day care. Moreover, the day-care provider is not comparable to the Stranger as conceived by the American authors, because not only is she familiar to the children but also she is affectively invested and full of maternal substitute features. We could explain these results on the basis that our situation, quite different from the Strange Situation, is not suitable for the emergence of attachment behavior, but probably measures something that is influenced by the bonds the child has already established with the day-care structure and by his or her adaptation and anticipation capacities.

Similarly, the context of the day care, that is, the person who receives the child and their manner of care, can influence the level of the interaction. In such a localized observation, we cannot differentiate steady situations from shifting ones. The dialectic between behavioral level and the level referring to the internal model of the relationship directly influences the quality of the relationship. The relation is also influenced by any variation that occurs at the behavioral level. Day care certainly represents a possible factor of variation. Nevertheless, we think that an internalized pattern can emerge in a less distressing situation too, even if in a less sensational way.

Use of the Strange Situation and the CARE-Index together, keeping an eye on the individuality of "who's doing what," can indeed provide more interesting information about the complexity of the question. The prognostic meaning of these instruments, then, is to be read within the specific context.

The Ameliorative Function of the Day-care Nursery. Children with very low or medium synchrony were able to organize, during certain moments of the daily routine, positive interactions with their peers. This situation confirms the day-care nursery's ability to offer a context where children can experience new and positive interactions. It also suggests the possibility of active preventive strategies. Nevertheless, we do not think that we can consider lack of synchrony as an indicator of psychopathology, because of the complexity of the elements involved, from the maturation elements to the influence of external systems.

The day-care nursery can be an opportunity for enrichment for both child and parent. The influence of this "third element" and the growth opportunities that it can offer depend on the quality of the interaction and the child's flexibility and capacity to assimilate new behavioral and interactive models, so as to bring new and fruitful rearrangements in the relationship. For instance, in some medium or medium-high synchrony dyads, there could be room for a positive, stabilizing, and enriching intervention of the day-care nursery. Behavioral differences and synchrony between playmates at different moments could be a very important "indicator" for adapting activity programs to special-needs children. This presence certainly may have an influence on the parental representation level: not only the decision to entrust the child to the nursery, but also, later on, the comparison with the caregiver's figure, imposes on the parent a review of the representation of her/himself as mother/father and of her/himself with the child. It is in these intermediate situations that parents tend to encounter more conflict and to blame themselves for the decision they make. Offering them the opportunity to get some help in integrating and understanding this experience could also have positive ramifications on the representation level.

In the more difficult cases of low-synchrony interactions, the day-care nursery could serve as a supportive and relieving alternative for both partners. It could become the place where the child could learn new patterns of interaction and build new relationships. Moreover, with the distance of the day-care nursery, the parent can sometimes better visualize the child. These findings merit further study.

Only during the last decade has psychosocial development in infancy been carefully considered as a basic resource for preventing psychopathology. Because large families are disappearing (and also because of the very high costs of both nursery and private baby-sitting), day care for infants has become a basic social problem. The problem of optimizing the resources includes consideration of longitudinal development of children who attend nursery school and of factors that can facilitate positive issues.

Widespread use of day care is both a cause and an effect of a slow change in parents' acceptance of nurseries. Training nursery personnel to deal with parents and observe the relationships of children with their parents, their peers, and themselves seems to be a basic milestone in developing the positive factors of extrafamilial education.

Since 1977, Italian laws have mandated that every child, including those with any kind of handicap, has the right to attend regular schools and classes. This right has been fully applied in compulsory school and in a widespread way in nursery school, especially for children with major physical and relational problems. Our study highly supports the positive effects and therapeutic function of day care when the staff (day-care providers, child, psychiatrist, and psychologist) are supportive of the family.

CHAPTER FOUR

Maternal Sensitivity and Attachment in East German and Russian Family Networks[1]

LIESELOTTE AHNERT, TATJANA MEISCHNER, AND
ALFRED SCHMIDT

INTRODUCTION

Different Perspectives on the Sensitivity-Attachment Association

Attachment patterns are conceptualized within the Bowlby/Ainsworth framework (Ainsworth, Blehar, Waters, & Wall, 1978; Bowlby, 1969; 1973) as constructs that interpret properties of dyadic mother–child relationships. At the same time, empirical findings have designated sensitive mothering as the key determinant of different qualities in attachment (Ainsworth et al., 1978; Bornstein, 1989; Grossmann, Fremmer-Bombik, Rudolph, & Grossmann, 1988; Grossmann & Grossmann, 1991; Grossmann, Grossmann, Spangler, Suess, & Unzner, 1985; Isabella, 1993; NICHD Early Child Care Research, 1997). Several domains related to sensitive mothering such as stimulation, positive attitude, mutuality, synchrony, and emotional support were recently identified by De Wolff and van IJzendoorn (1997) as playing an important role in the development of attachment. Ratings of maternal sensitivity had been originally designed to capture the promptness and appropriateness of maternal responses to the young (Ainsworth, Bell, & Stayton, 1974) and revealed high correlation to attachment patterns in the Baltimore study (Ainsworth et al., 1978). However, in later studies this strong sensitivity-attachment association could not be replicated (see meta-analysis done by De Wolff

[1] Acknowledgment: We thank Gerhard Lehwald (University of Leipzig, East Germany) and Marianne Riksen-Walraven (University of Nijmegen, The Netherlands), who smuggled "Patterns of Attachment" through the "iron curtain" in 1986 and organized the first workshop on attachment in Leipzig/East Germany. Since the political changes in 1989 Karin Grossmann (University of Regensburg) taught us to code attachment and discussed the most difficult and controversial "Strange Situations" with us. We also thank Fabienne Becker-Stoll and Katrin Seltenheim for assisting her in coding, and Ines Müller for her help in assessing maternal sensitivity. This research has been supported by grants from the German Science Foundation (Deutsche Forschungsgemeinschaft) to Lieselotte Ahnert (Az: Ah 55/7-1).

& van IJzendoorn, 1997). Some authors thus stressed the possibility that care-givers are influenced by their infants (Goldsmith & Alansky, 1987; Goldsmith, Bradshaw, & Rieser-Danner, 1986; Lewis & Feiring, 1989; Sroufe, 1985; Susman-Stillman, Kalkoske, Egeland, & Waldman, 1996; Vaughn et al., 1992). Consequently, such sensitivity ratings might capture dyadic mother–child relationships as bidirectional constructs that had been explored in only a one-sided manner. Other authors argued that even the basic ratings of sensitivity belong to a multidimensional construct that might represent contradictory information, and thus have to be reviewed with regard to their components, such as negative versus positive affective evocation (Belsky, Fish, & Isabella, 1991; Fox & Davidson, 1987), protection providing versus intimacy mainte-nance (MacDonald, 1992), or proximal versus distal interaction (Keller, Völker, & Zach, 1997) caretaking behaviors.

Furthermore, the development of Bowlby's theory has been unfortunately restricted to the individual and dyadic levels rather than being expanded to the total environment of the infant, even though caretaking behaviors might not be independent of the care setting where the dyad is embedded (Marvin & Stewart, 1990). Studies on social support for mothers (Crockenberg, 1981) as well as on marital conflicts (Cummings & Davies, 1996; Davies & Cummings, 1994) have shown an essential impact on mother–child attach-ment. In addition, even in present-day Western societies, infants have more than one caretaker in the majority of families and are thus accustomed to var-ious caregiving experiences that might alter the parameters in the dyad. Therefore, it appears to make a difference in the socioemotional develop-ment whether the child has developed none, one, or more secure attach-ments (Oppenheim, Sagi, & Lamb, 1988; van IJzendoorn, Sagi, & Lambermon, 1992).

This chapter thus deals with the sensitivity-attachment association in which we explore maternal sensitivity as well as components of maternal caretaking behaviors that are applied while interacting with an infant and referring to him. Because there is a need to think of attachment within a larger context, we will explore the coupling of sensitivity-attachment association with the environment such as different family care settings. We then ask whether influ-ences in different care settings change the impact of caretaking on the mother–infant dyad and on attachment patterns.

The Attachment Issue in Russian Infant Research

When we first reviewed the literature on attachment in East Berlin and Moscow in 1986, we learned about the predictive validity of maternal sensitiv-ity and how it might significantly differentiate secure and insecure attach-ment qualities (Ainsworth et al., 1978). We felt encouraged to prove how appropriate the model might be when transferred to the cultural context of a socialist society where different child-rearing concepts were introduced. The application of attachment theory to research also challenged our studies on mother–infant communication in the Vygotskijan framework (Dubrovina, & Puzskaia, 1990; Vygotskij, 1982, 1983). Within this framework, children's relationships are the result of sociocultural experiences rooted in various forms of communication. Research was done in order to differentiate emotional reactions in infancy during the first year of life (Lissina, 1985; Mazitova, 1977, 1979; Messerjakowa, 1979; Sorokina, 1987). Studies of different situations, such as caressing, encouragement, rejection, and indifference provided by familiar (e.g., mother), well-known, and unfamiliar adults evoked individual affective ties that led to channeling communication with different adults in different situations. Caressing, encouragement, and even affectively neutral stimulation seemed to be generally perceived as subjectively pleasurable by the child and engaged him in affective sharing, enjoyment of communication, and physical contact that is considered typical in interactions of secure mother–child dyads (Izard, Hayes, Chisholm, & Baak, 1991; Main, Tomasini, & Tolan, 1979; Roggman, Langlois, & Hubbs-Tait, 1987). Whereas hostile and rejecting environments were perceived as aversive, indifferent care was said to provoke highest irritation. Thus, the attachment theory seemed to feed into Lissina's model of affective patterns, though the narrow focus on a sensitive caretaker in order to predict the emotional development of a child might restrict the application of the theory.

This is especially true for societies where a too-close mother–infant relationship was considered to be primarily negative in socialization (Hille, 1985) and dyads were forced to facilitate the child's transition away from the relationship. Overall, the "readiness of other persons to replace the mother temporarily ... (was) ... very great" (Bronfenbrenner, 1972, p. 24), and multiple caretaking was a matter of course in socialist societies. Because maternal care could be quite different in such societies, we began to include different care settings systematically into the studies undertaken in East Berlin and Moscow. We assessed maternal sensitivity and other caretaking features during a free-play session as well as attachment quality in Ainsworth's Strange Situation in East German and Russian samples from different families. We attempted to clarify whether and how attachment, sensitivity, and interaction differ according to different family care settings.

Different Family Settings in East Germany and Russia

Although socialist propaganda emphasized that a new type of family had come into being with socialism, in reality the "socialist family" remained more or less fictitious. In line with communist doctrines, the family was defined as a "socialist collective" unit in the focus of the public (Makarenko, 1983). The "nationalization" of child care and of family life was considered to be typical for the future family (Engels, 1966). Consequently, societal norms were continuously aimed at limiting privacy in family life. However, these ideas were too extreme and did not reflect common attitudes. Investigations that focused on contrasting developments in the two sectors of Germany, following the fall of the Berlin wall in 1989, have proven the East German family to be relatively "ideology-resistant" and successful in defending privacy and autonomy (Ahnert, Krätzig, Meischner, & Schmidt, 1994). In his comprehensive study comparing American and Russian child-rearing practices, Bronfenbrenner (1972) also concluded that communist ideology did not eliminate the traditional structure in Russian families.

Family structures in Eastern Europe might differ considerably from family models in Western societies as a result of different social histories rather than of ideology. For example, in the wake of the industrial revolution in the first half of nineteenth century, the nuclear family emerged strikingly in Central Europe (Weber-Kellermann, 1987). During the socialist era, this pattern was also accepted as the family model in East Germany. In Russia, however, where industrialization processes began much later and only in a few relatively secluded centers, large, patriarchally structured family networks remained intact until today when mothers have begun to exercise a monopoly on family organization and child care (Bridger, 1987; Brugger von Nesslau, 1991).

Family Care and Maternal Roles in Infancy in East Germany and Russia

Nevertheless, some contrasting developments have taken place in child-rearing practices in socialist societies. Whereas in Western Europe the role of the family has always been strongly emphasized in child development, socialist countries rejected exclusive care in the family and even denounced it as a petty-bourgeois attitude (Schmidt-Kolmer, 1962). Consequently, public day care was increasingly offered, and attachment issues were seen as not applicable to care in as much as the concept of maternal deprivation (Bowlby, 1951) was not supposed to be discussed in conjunction with day care.

It is mostly unknown, however, that paid maternity leave for at least one year had been introduced in those countries, so that the infant, as a rule, was reared under the exclusive care of the mother during his or her first year of life. This maternity leave period had become necessary especially in East Germany because of the high infant morbidity in day-care centers, resulting in great irregularities on the labor market when working mothers were often forced to stay home. On principle, this maternity leave contradicted the socialist ideas of maternal roles and was also atypical for the socialist ideas of rearing children in general. However, the fact that the East German sociopolitical offers enabled mothers to stay at home longer, but kept them in isolated positions and relatively unprepared for motherhood, constitutes sufficient evidence that nonmaternal care was considered.

In addition, Russian investigations on communication in infancy have explicitly concluded that the infant's pronounced attachment to the mother might be associated with the infant's increasing inability to establish adequate social contacts with others. These ideas were supported by analyses of the biographies of famous and infamous personalities from politics, art, and science whose social inadequacy and maladjustment could be traced back to secluded mother–infant dyads accompanied by rarely involved fathers (Pilgrim, 1993). When too-close infant–mother relationships were discovered, especially after entering into day care, qualified multiple social interventions were considered to guarantee the balanced social development of infants (Vatutina, 1983).

Furthermore, because maternal roles under socialism were based on the doctrine of self-realization in the sphere of labor, only employed members of the society met the Marxist image of a "totally developed individuality" (Marx, 1981, p. 512). Consequently, working mothers of infants were well-accepted, although a model did not really exist for them (Ostner, 1990). An extended public day-care system and many social benefits was supposed to help those mothers master work and family, which, paradoxically, could maintain traditional roles. The burdens for mothers differed considerably, however, depending on the support given by family members and others within their social networks.

In this chapter we explore the association between maternal sensitivity and attachment qualities in societies where too close mother–infant relationships were interpreted primarily as negative for infant development and dyads were forced to facilitate the infant's transition away from it in order to establish further social contacts. In this study, we assume that greater association of maternal sensitivity and attachment would be found in small families, in which the dyad might develop in a more secluded, traditional way. In larger and more heterogeneous family structures, maternal caretaking influences might become weaker as the infant is more likely to develop relationships with people other than the mother. Thus, the more heterogeneous and larger the family structure is, the less predictable is the relation between maternal sensitivity and attachment quality. Therefore, small nuclear families must be contrasted with large family networks.

METHOD

Subjects

A total of 60 families were simultaneously studied in East Berlin ($n = 38$) and Moscow ($n = 22$) in September 1989, a period before the Berlin wall came down and the critical political changes began in Moscow. The infants were between 11 and 12 months old, healthy, and born at full-term. Eighteen of the 38 infants in the German sample and 13 of the 22 in the Russian sample were girls. German infants averaged 11.5 months old (SD = .6), with Bayley (1993) Mental Development Index/Psychomotor Development Index (MDI/PDI) scores averaging 99.7/88.1 (SD = 17.8/15.0), whereas Russian infants averaged 11.9 months old (SD = .8), with Bayley MDI/PDI scores averaging 114.5/121.3 (SD = 15.5/14.7). Up to that time, all infants had been reared exclusively in families, with their mothers as primary caretakers. According to the age, parents' age, training, and income, the sample represented middle-class families exclusively. The mean ages of East German mothers/fathers were 24.4/25.8 years (SD = 3.1/4.2), whereas the mean ages of Russian mothers/fathers were 23.4/26.9 years (SD = 4.0/6.7). Despite the different cultures, the samples showed similarities in terms of sociopolitical and socioeconomic background. The majority of family members, often even the grandparents, were involved in political and community associations and boards. Also typical for the samples was that mothers were as highly educated as their spouses and were just preparing to resume new professional activities that were considered to be of great significance for them after maternity leave. As a consequence, the infants were destined to be taken to public daycare centers.

Procedure

Each family was visited several times and interviewed. In addition, 30-minute play sessions of mother and infant were videotaped in the home, thereby excluding any other persons. Furthermore, Ainsworth's Strange Situation (Ainsworth & Wittig, 1969) was for the first time carried out outside of the homes in both East Berlin and Moscow.

Assessments

Inquiries. We inquired about the size of the family, that is, the number of persons organizing their life along common patterns as a family, as well as living conditions and daily routines of the family life. To focus on the question of which family structure was psychologically relevant, mothers were asked to identify the additional caretakers of the infants. Thus the number of intrafamilial caretakers as well as the number of acquaintances and neighbors serving as extrafamilial caretakers were surveyed, and the frequency and type of their activities were listed.

Attachment. Ainsworth's Strange Situation classificatory procedure was used to classify attachment quality. The tapes were classified by Grossmann

(University of Regensburg) with a reliability of over 90% as done by Main in 1976 and rechecked in 1993 with a reliability set of Sroufe's team with 86% agreement.[2]

Maternal Sensitivity. Thirty-minute play sessions were coded with Ainsworth's Sensitivity scale (Ainsworth, Bell, & Stayton, 1974; German translation by Grossmann, 1977). The seven units of this scale were transformed into a five-point scale, with the scale ranging from 5 ("highly sensitive") to 1 ("insensitive"). Two research assistants blind to Strange Situation behavior rated the play sessions with an agreement of 78%. Disagreements in ratings were discussed in order to reach agreement.

Interactional Features. Thirty-minute play sessions were explored for the types of interaction situations they contained. After interrater agreement in determining every interaction situation reached 98%, a coding system was applied that focused on maternal interaction styles, such as guidance structure, and organized mutuality in each interaction situation. The coding system included the following codes:

1. *Introduction,* that is, information and demonstrations of play. (Example 1: "Do you want to play? … There is the train." Example 2: "Today we'll have much fun! The train is already whistling!")
2. *Creative extension,* that is, accepting the infant perspective, accentuating, and giving suggestions and commentaries in order to continue the play and to elaborate its content. (Example 1: The infant plays with the train. "Stop! The teddy wants to go along, too." Example 2: "The teddy is at the station crying. What is the matter with him?").
3. *Confirmation* and encouragement of infant activities. (Example 1: "Yes. That's right. The train is just stopping." Example 2: "The train is very nice to take us home".)
4. *Restrictions,* correction, and negative evaluation of infant activities. (Example 1: "Stop! That is not possible. You have to go back!" Example 2: "That is very bad. Poor teddy! He can't go by train.")

---

[2] It should be noted that 23 German and 12 Russian infants were also classified by P. Crittenden. Her classifications matched Grossmann's by major classification in approximately half of the cases (Cohen's kappa .31). Crittenden identified substantially fewer Type B infants in both samples than Grossmann. Specifically, all of Crittenden's B classifications were considered B by Grossmann, too, whereas approximately one-third of Grossmann's B classifications were classified A and the remaining one-third C by Crittenden. We are convinced this is due to different classification attitudes and priorities. These differences should spark special discussions aimed at revealing and overcoming the basic differences. This, however, cannot be the aim of this chapter. *Editor's note:* See discussion in chapter 19, p. 667.

5. *Facilitation* in order to help the infant reach a toy or complete a difficult activity.

The examples show that maternal interaction styles could be realized by very different tools of interaction. Some mothers might orient concretely and pragmatically toward the situation in a clearly structured way (see all examples 1); others might emotionalize the situation, anthropomorphize, or over-generalize instances and facts (see all examples 2).

Two research assistants blind to Strange Situation behavior and to the sensitivity scores rated the play sessions. Interrater agreement ranged between 78% and 92%.

RESULTS

Different Family Settings in East Germany and Russia

Despite the similarities in the political environment of the German and Russian samples, large differences were found with regard to the size, structure, and living spaces of the families. In East Berlin, one room of an apartment was available for an average of 1.5 persons ($SD = .52$), whereas in Moscow an average of 2.5 persons ($SD = 1.04$) had to live in one room – Mann-Whitney $z_{(N = 60)} = 4.13$, $p < .01$. There were even two families in the Russian sample that shared an apartment with other families; each family settled in one room of the apartment. Highly significant differences were also found in family sizes – Mann-Whitney $z_{(N = 60)} = 4.97$, $p < .01$. Whereas the average German family did not comprise more than five family members, the Russian family included up to nine members. Moreover, only 79% of the grandparents were integrated into the German families, but 81.8% of the Russian families included grandparents. For later statistics, we differentiated the samples according to family size in subgroups I to IV (Table 4.1), where we succeeded in getting two subsamples (II

Table 4.1. Subgroups According to Family Size in East Berlin and Moscow ($n = 60$)

Subgroups		Family Size	
	Small/2–3 members	Middle/4–5 members	Large/6–9 members
East Berlin I	$n = 25$		
East Berlin II		$n = 13$	
Moscow III		$n = 7$	
Moscow IV	($n = 3$)		$n = 12$

Note: In some further analyses, the three Russian infants in subgroup IV/Small family size were excluded.

and III) equivalent for a culturally overlapping approach. Subsamples I and IV, however, were each to be found in only one of the two cultures.

Comparing the relation of intra- to extrafamilial caretakers, a distinct dominance of intrafamilial caretakers in the Russian sample in contrast to extrafamilial caretakers in the German sample was evident – Mann-Whitney $z_{(N = 60)} = 3.51$, $p < .01$. Overall, intrafamilial caretakers were more frequent, more consistently available, and characterized by genuine caretaking arrangements that included basic care, support when distressed, and all kinds of stimulation, play, and distractions. In contrast, extrafamilial caretakers were only intermittently available, and they mostly watched and played with the child during a short absence by the mother.

Maternal Sensitivity and Attachment Qualities in Different Family Settings

Comparing the distribution of attachment patterns in the East German and Russian sample revealed no significant difference, $\chi^2_{(6, N = 60)} = 3.69$, $p > .05$. However, secure patterns tended to appear more often in the Russian sample than in the German sample, whereas in the German sample there was a marked appearance of the insecure A patterns (Figure 4.1). This was certainly true, when secure (all B patterns) as opposed to insecure patterns (all A and C patterns) in subgroup II were compared with those in subgroup III, where the family sizes were equivalent, $\chi^2_{(2, N = 20)} = 8.69$, $p < .05$ (Figure 4.2).

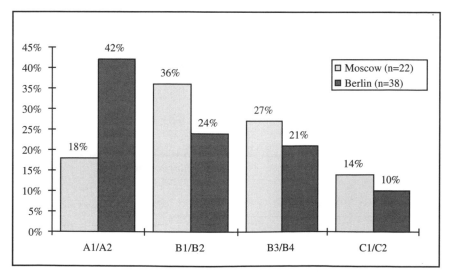

Figure 4.1. Attachment Patterns in the German and Russian Samples ($n = 60$). Two infants in the German sample and one infant in the Russian sample were unclassifiable.

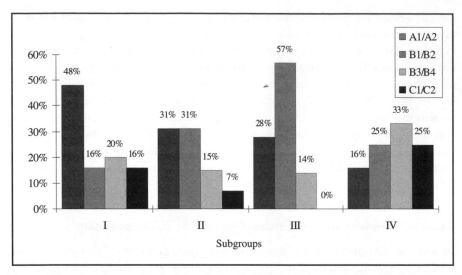

Figure 4.2. Attachment Patterns and Family Size in Subgroups I to IV. Subgroup I and II are German samples. Subgroup III and IV are Russian samples. Family sizes increase from I to IV with equivalent sizes in II and III (see Table 4.1).

Furthermore, the larger the families in both cultures, the less likely were the A1–A2 patterns, χ^2 $_{(3, N = 60)}$ = 7.05, p < .05. The insecure A patterns decreased from 48% to 31% in the German sample and from 28% to 16% in the Russian sample (Figure 4.2). In addition, Russian infants in the largest families showed the highest rate of C pattern of the subgroups. In contrast, the means of maternal sensitivity ranging from 3.16 to 2.69 in the subgroups revealed no differences as one would now expect by theory (Table 4.2). On the contrary, correlation between family size and maternal sensitivity was neg-

Table 4.2. Ainsworth's Mean Sensitivity Scores in Subgroups I to IV Referring to Family Size (*n* = 57)

		Sensitivity Scores		
Subgroups	*n*	*M*	*SD*	95% Confidence Interval for Mean
East Berlin I	25	3.16	.90	2.79 to 3.53
East Berlin II	13	2.69	.85	2.18 to 3.21
Moscow III	7	2.71	1.38	1.44 to 3.99
Moscow IV	12	2.83	1.03	2.18 to 3.49

Note: Applying the Student-Newman-Keuls test, no two groups are significantly different at the .05 level.

ative, $r = -.18$, $p < .10$, showing that with increasing family size maternal sensitivity tends to decrease.

Overall, securely attached infants had a significantly higher proportion of sensitive mothers (82%) than insecurely attached infants, $\chi^2_{(3, N = 60)} = 8.41$, $p < .05$. Nevertheless, up to 52% of the insecurely attached infants had mothers who could be described as highly sensitive or sensitive. Applying the WILCOXON RANK SUM Statistic, it became significant that the higher proportion of sensitive mothers (score 5 and 4) versus insensitive mothers (score 1 to 3) was associated with family size, $U_{(60)} = 338.5$, $p < .05$. The proportion of sensitive mothers was unusually high in subgroup I with 82% but decreased in the larger families to about 60% (subgroup II and III) and 75% (subgroup IV). Thus B patterns marked by highly sensitive mothers were evident only in small nuclear families. In larger families, the B patterns were nearly as frequently to be found in unstable or less sensitive mothers. Furthermore, C patterns appeared in very small and very large families rather than in middle-sized families (Table 4.3).

Interaction Patterns, Sensitivity, and Family Size

We factor analyzed maternal interaction patterns during play after determining that the correlation matrix had an adequate test for sphericity (Measure of Sample Adequacy, MSA, $> .9$). A principal component analysis with Varimax rotation explained 87% of the variance with a three-factor solution. (Factor loadings are shown in Table 4.4) Factor 1 explained 55% of the variance and comprised *Confirmations* and *Creative extensions* of infant activities. Factor 2 resembled *Introductions* and *Restrictions* and explained 28% of the variance, whereas Factor 3 replaced *Facilitations* and explained only 4% of the variance. Factor 1 was especially typical of sensitive mothers, shown by its highly significant correlation with maternal sensitivity, $r = .45$, $p < .05$. However, its correlation with the family sizes that embedded the dyad even increased with $r = .62$, $p < .05$. In contrast, correlations of Factor 2 with maternal sensitivity, $r = -.28$, $p < .05$, and its correlation with family size became even more strongly negative, $r = -.48$, $p < .05$. Factor 3 did not

Table 4.3 Numbers of Mothers Assessed on the Sensitivity Scale ($n = 60$)

Subgroups	n	Sensitivity Rates				
		5 Highly	4 Sensitive	3 Unstable	2 Less	1 Insensitive
I	28	12	11	3	2	0
II/III	20	5	7	5	3	0
IV	12	3	6	1	2	0

Table 4.4. Rotated Factor Matrix of Mother's Interaction Behavior

Mother's Interaction Behavior	Factor 1	Factor 2	Factor 3
Confirmations	.88	.11	
Creative extension	.87	.10	.19
Restrictions	.20	.79	.18
Introductions	.22	.77	.17
Facilitations			.97

correlate significantly either with sensitivity, $r = -.001$, or with family size, $r = -.02$.

Analyzing the interaction tools, such as emotionalizing the situation, anthropomorphizing, or overgeneralizing instances, Russian mothers used such tools three times more often then German mothers. Partial correlations excluding culture revealed weak associations with sensitivity, $r = .32$, $p < .05$.

SUMMARY AND CONCLUSIONS

The aim of our study was to explore the association between maternal sensitivity and attachment in different care settings within two socialist societies. Before the great political changes in East Germany and Russia, extended social contacts away from mother–child dyads were considered to be the most important experience in infancy. Although the mother–child dyads were investigated at the end of maternity leave in the families, we expected ideologically based impacts on attachment and sensitivity. Unfortunately, we were able to visit only small samples in both societies and got short impressions of the functioning in the mother–child dyads at home. As De Wolff and van IJzendoorn (1997) revealed in their meta-analysis of 66 studies with over 4,000 dyads, the duration of home observation was not related to the magnitude of the sensitivity-attachment association. We were able to gain important insights in those associations under rearing conditions that differed remarkably from those that had already been investigated.

We observed different caretaking situations depending on family size, assuming that the impact of ideology might be greater under non-family-centered caretaking arrangements. Primarily in East Berlin, we visited mother–child dyads that were quite isolated without any support from other family members, or those in nuclear families where the child's father was absent throughout the day. Those mothers accepted maternity leave as an interim time before their own reintegration into the work setting and the child's integration into day care. However, it turned out not to be an ideal mother–child situation, as shown by the mediocre developmental scores of the infants and by the mothers' complaints during the interviews. The situation improved for mothers who were supported by other family members or even friends. In contrast, the Russian mother–child dyads appeared to be embedded in larger than nuclear families that tended to involve mostly grandparents. Those reliable and constant available caretakers appeared to ease the situation.

Attachments in the East German sample indicated 42% A patterns, 45% B patterns, and 10% C patterns, and they reflected the same distribution of attachment patterns as compared to the studies carried out in Bielefeld in West Germany (Grossmann et al., 1985). Although no overall differences as opposed to the attachment distribution in the Russian sample were found, clear movements among the patterns depending on family size and culture were revealed. The East German attachments showed a tendency toward A patterns, especially marked in small families, whereas the Russian attachments showed a tendency toward B patterns, more marked in middle-sized families. Differentiating the German and Russian samples by different family care settings on a scale ranging from small to large sizes, we were even able to identify two equivalent family patterns in a culturally overlapping context. Again, comparing those equivalent family patterns in both cultures, we found that the Russians revealed more B patterns. Many studies (Belsky, Fish, & Isabella, 1991; Fox, & Davidson, 1987; Goldsmith & Campos, 1990; Lissina, 1985; Mazitova, 1977, 1979; Messerjakowa, 1979; Sorokina, 1987) provided an approach to understanding the formation of attachment security by affectively tuned interactions. In assessing the interaction patterns in the present study, Russian mothers, indeed, tended to emotionalize and anthropomorphize in the play sessions, whereas German mothers were oriented more toward the essential facts and utilized mainly rational-pragmatic means and concepts. However, those interaction tools were only weakly correlated with maternal sensitivity, and they seem to result from very traditional and culture-specific caretaking concepts as shown in an earlier study (Ahnert, Meischner, Schmidt, & Doskin, 1994) rather than from individual maternal caretaking styles.

Overall, it appeared that increasing family size made the appearance of attachment security more likely. However, that was true as long as the caretaking arrangements were limited in size; in the largest family samples insecure–ambivalent attachment patterns became more prominent. Thus, one has to look for principles within the care setting in order to explain positive influences aside from mother–infant dyads. Indeed, it is generally agreed that attachment patterns are rooted in the reality of social interaction and that infants identify the invariant aspects of interactions and form mentally constructed representations, of which the "internal working model" (IWM) (Bowlby, 1980) of the attachment figure is only one specific pattern intertwined with others (Stern, 1989). However, one might speculate that infants generalize the IWM of the attachment figure in large family networks to those family members who dominated family interactions. However, studies on marital conflicts (Cummings & Davies, 1996; Davies & Cummings, 1994) reveal that infants generalize the dominant caretaking behaviors that become typical for the family. In addition, Crockenberg (1981) argued that by providing the infant with a responsive substitute, insensitive mothering in large family networks might be more or less compensated, so that it will have little impact on the child's everyday functioning.

The known correlation between attachment security and maternal sensitivity was generally preserved in our study. As the sensitivity-attachment associations decreased with growing family size, the direct relation between maternal sensitivity and attachment seems to be special for dyads restricted to nuclear families. We detected a relatively higher proportion of insensitive mothers in larger family networks without identifying any loss in the general quality of caretaking. In small families, however, insecurity and ambivalence seem to correlate directly with maternal behaviors when the mother manifests fragmented behavior, sometimes even ignoring the infant. In these families there is no one to compensate for this behavior, whereas the interaction style of a larger family might mediate the sensitivity of an individual mother. The fact that insensitive mothers in large families tended to have more securely attached infants than those in smaller ones raises the question regarding what regulation mechanisms are at work as effective superior principles of the family system. The present study revealed that an interaction pattern was more likely in larger families that were child-oriented, confirming and extending the child's ideas. A more thorough understanding might be attained by observing interactions among all family members, which would allow us to understand the functional outcomes in establishing and maintaining the family's coherence as well as in formatting its attachment patterns.

CHAPTER FIVE

Behavior Problems in Swedish Four-year-olds

The Importance of Maternal Sensitivity and Social Context[1]

GUNILLA BOHLIN AND BERIT HAGEKULL

INTRODUCTION

Developmental and clinical psychology has long attempted to understand how socio-emotional problems and competencies develop. Equally long-standing has been the assumption that important mechanisms are to be sought in the parent–child relationship.

The attachment paradigm, as formulated by Bowlby (1969), Ainsworth (1973, 1982), and many followers, has become attractive in this context because it provides both theoretical mechanisms and research tools to connect early relationship experiences with later socio-emotional outcomes. The Strange Situation (Ainsworth, Blehar, Waters, & Wall, 1978) offers a view of crucial aspects of the parent–infant relationship during the first year. The availability of such a methodological device has stimulated research in this area, and there is a growing body of empirical findings relating attachment quality to various socio-emotional outcomes.

Maternal Sensitivity as a Basis for Attachment Security and Socio-emotional Outcomes

Maternal Sensitivity and Attachment Quality. Attachment theory states that maternal sensitivity to infant signals and communications is the primary antecedent of attachment quality (e.g., Ainsworth, 1982). This premise implies that observed associations between insecure attachment and negative outcomes reflect the fact that maternal insensitive interactive behavior during the infant's first year is an important source of deviant socio-emotional development. Two sets of findings support the view that socio-emotional functioning during preschool or school years has its roots in the sensitivity encountered by the

[1] The research presented in this paper was made possible though grants from the Swedish Council for Research in the Humanities and Social Sciences and from the Bank of Sweden Tercentenary Foundation.

child from his or her primary caregiver during their early interactions. The first set concerns the relation between maternal sensitivity, as shown in early interactions with the infant, and quality of attachment as assessed in the Strange Situation. The empirical evidence supports the existence of such a relationship (e.g., Ainsworth et al., 1978; Belsky, Taylor, & Rovine, 1984; Bohlin, Hagekull, Germer, Andersson, & Lindberg, 1989; Grossmann, Grossmann, Sprangler, Suess, & Unzner, 1985). There is disagreement, however, as to how strong, consistent, and specific these effects are and what the differential antecedents are for insecure-ambivalent and insecure-avoidant attachment (Goldsmith & Alansky, 1987; Lamb, Thompson, Gardner, & Charnov, 1985).

Attachment Quality and Later Outcomes. The second set of empirical findings deals with the relation between quality of attachment and later outcomes. Again the main impression from the data is that insecurely attached infants run a higher risk for negative socio-emotional outcomes than securely attached infants (e.g., Erickson, Sroufe, & Egeland, 1985; Suess, Grossmann, & Sroufe, 1992). However, some studies have failed to show this relation (Bates, Maslin, & Frankel, 1985), and the positive results are not conclusive as to the specific outcomes or the importance of child gender and type of insecure attachment (Fagot & Kavanaugh, 1990; Lewis, Feiring, McGuffog, & Jaskir 1984). Both Lamb (1987) and Field (1987) question the conclusion, even from positive findings, that outcomes can be said to be a function of early interactive experiences; it might be the current mother–child relationship that carries the association. Lamb's and Field's idea rests on the assumption that there is a certain longtime stability in relevant aspects of the mother–child relationship.

Maternal Sensitivity and Later Outcomes. Aside from the weaknesses in the empirical foundation, the indirect link between early interactive experiences and later outcomes – via attachment classification – constitutes a weakness in the evidence for early caregiving behavior as an antecedent of future socio-emotional functioning. Although there is some support for a direct relationship between early maternal sensitivity and later socio-emotional outcomes (Jacobvitz & Sroufe, 1987; Mitchell, Bee, Hammond, & Barnard, 1985), evidence is to a great extent lacking. This study aims at connecting early relational experiences directly to later behavior problems and evaluating attachment security as a mediating variable in such relations.

Context and Culture

Sociodemographic Variables. In approaching these research issues, two of the themes of the present monograph – those dealing with the effects of context and culture – are highly relevant. It is well known that socio-emotional outcomes, as expressed, for example, in behavior problems, are related to sociodemographic variables such as gender and social class (e.g., Achenbach, Verhulst, Edelbrook, Baron, & Akkerhuis, 1987). There is also some evidence for parity differences in socio-emotional functioning (Hagekull & Bohlin, 1992). Therefore, the role of early interactive experiences should be explored within the perspective of such contextual variables.

Effects of Nonparental Care. An even more intricate issue concerns the effect of early interactive experiences for infants who have received varying amounts of nonparental care of varying care quality. Relying primarily on attachment classification data as the outcome, Belsky (1988a) has argued that a link exists between experiences of substantial amounts of nonparental care during the child's first year and "elevated rates of insecurity, aggression and noncompliance" (Belsky, 1988a, p. 403). He has also posed the question of whether nonparental care acts as a third variable, with certain family characteristics (presumably including maternal insensitivity) being a common cause of early initiated nonparental care and insecure attachment.

Findings in sharp contrast to Belsky's conclusion were reported by Andersson (1989) from a study of Swedish families: children entering public day care before the age of 1 received better ratings from their teachers at 8 years with regard to both socio-emotional functions and school performance. The positive effects of day care have also been reported from another Swedish study (Gunnarsson, 1978), which raises the question of the importance of day-care quality and the general cultural context in which nonparental care is provided. The general inconsistency of findings in this area and the controversy concerning their interpretations are displayed in the paper by Scarr, Phillips, and McCartney (1990). This area of research makes clear that the contextual factor of nonparental care cannot be forgotten when the long-term consequences of early interactive experiences are discussed.

The Swedish Culture. In Sweden, since the 1930s, social policy has put great emphasis on family issues, based on the view that child welfare is a public responsibility. A child-centered attitude has imbued governmental legislation, exemplified by the law against physical punishment of children, the right to paid parental leave for 12 months, the free attendance in maternal health and well-baby clinics, the formulation of detailed guidelines to guarantee the high quality of day-care centers, a monthly family allowance for each child, and the right to subsidies for single parents (e.g., Hwang & Broberg, 1992). By giving mothers and fathers equal rights to parental leave during the child's first year, society has emphasized the importance of fathers and the need for a close father–child relationship to start developing during early infancy.

During the 1980s, when the present study was conducted, a fourth of the Swedish fathers stayed home for at least a month; only a small percentage of the fathers stayed home on paid parental leave for three months or more.

A child-centered attitude in Swedish society is also conveyed through the media and various professionals working with children and families. For women this message may become conflicting because of the equally strong emphasis on women's need and right to earn their own income and to realize their own potential outside the home. Because of this, and also in many cases because of economic necessity, most women go back to work when their paid parental leave runs out. The conflicting ambitions for the woman between her role as mother and as professional are often solved by working part time. Female employment in Sweden ranks among the highest in the industrialized countries; 87% of mothers of children under 2 years of age are enrolled in the labor force, but as many as 38% of these mothers are on leave from work due to child care (Hoem & Hoem, 1987). Thus, many Swedish infants enter external day care during their second year of life, although they may then return home again when a sibling is born.

External child care is provided in centers, by child minders (often employed and trained by the municipality to give good care in her own home to small groups of children), or in private arrangements with a sitter, relative, or friend as the caregiver (Hwang & Broberg, 1992). In the international literature, Sweden has often been referred to as offering child care of excellent quality (e.g., Scarr & Eisenberg, 1993). However, in Swedish studies variation in quality has been reported (Ekholm & Hedin, 1987; Hagekull & Bohlin, 1995; Lamb, Hwang, Bookstein, Broberg, Hult, & Frodi, 1988).

Aims of the Study

The primary aim of the present study was to evaluate the influence of early interactive experiences with the primary caregiver, as viewed from attachment theory, on socio-emotional functioning, expressed in behavior problems at age 4 in a Swedish middle-class sample. The mediating role of quality of attachment, as observed in the Strange Situation, was also assessed. The importance of contextual factors was addressed by assessing two sets of such factors: first, sociodemographic variables such as socioeconomic background, parity, and gender, and second, exposure to nonparental care.

Finally, the question of stability of maternal interactive behavior was addressed and related to the issue of the predictive power of the child's early interactive experiences. The contextual theme was applied to this question by comparing the contribution from specific early interactive experiences, as viewed from the attachment perspective, with the contribution from the contextual factor constituted by the general quality of the home environment provided by the family during the early preschool period.

METHOD

Subjects

The present longitudinal sample of 105 families was followed from infant age 6 weeks to child age 4 years. Eligible for inclusion were all families with an infant born during 11 specified weeks in 1985 at the Academic Hospital in Uppsala, Sweden, which serves the entire county of Uppsala. Further inclusion criteria were that the family have a Swedish family name, be found in the official telephone directory, and be accessible by public transport within the commune of Uppsala. Twins and infants born prematurely (> six weeks before term) were excluded, as were families planning to move out of the area. Out of a total of 200 mothers, 123 (61.5%) agreed to participate, and 63 male and 60 female infants were included. Reasons for refusal were shortage of time (15.5%) and lack of interest in research/research seen as intrusion of privacy (23%).

The attrition rate over the four years has amounted to 14.6% (18 families). The reasons for attrition encompass moving out of the county during the first months, illness/death in the family, travels abroad, objections to interview/questionnaire contents, and time shortage. During later phases of the project, several families moved out of the area; nevertheless, some contact has been kept via questionnaires and, when possible, visits to them for observations. Complete information has not been obtained from all families at all points of data collection. Nonparental care quality, for example, could only be obtained for the subsample ($n = 50$) that had such care at the time of data collection. Occasional missing data at various ages were due to much the same reasons as those given for attrition.

Maternal age ranged from 19 to 44 years ($M = 29.8$, $SD = 4.7$) at inclusion in the study. Mothers' educational level was comparatively high; 24% had a university degree, and 38% had completed other more or less advanced post-high school training. The rest, 38%, had no post-high school training; 9% had majors in theoretical subjects; and 22% had a two-year high school education with majors in practical/work-related subjects. Seven percent of the mothers had only the nine years of compulsory schooling. All but two of the mothers were living together with the infant's father. Thirty-seven percent of the fathers had a university degree, 21% had other post-high school education, 12% had finished high school in three-year theoretical programs, 15% had practical high school education, and 16% had nine years of basic schooling. Two-thirds of the families lived in suburbs or the outskirts of Uppsala, 21% lived in the central parts of the city, and 13% in rural areas. The focal child was the firstborn in 48 families; in the other 75 families, there were one to three older siblings. When the infants were 10 months old, fathers were invited to participate in the project, and 104 fathers agreed to do so.

Procedure

Data for the present study were gathered at six time periods: 6 weeks; 4, 10, 15, and 29 months; and 4 years. Following an introductory letter and a telephone call with information about the study (the general purpose was described as gaining information about early social and emotional development), a first home visit was made when the infants were 6 weeks old ($M = 6.5$, $SD = 0.6$). As in all other data-collection periods, several types of instruments were used (interviews, questionnaires, direct observations); only those directly relevant to the present study are described here. At the age of 6 weeks, pencil-and-paper registered observations of mother–infant interaction in a care situation (change of diapers) and a social situation (face-to-face; 5 minutes) were performed at the infants' home.

When the infants were 4 months old ($M = 17.5$ weeks, $SD = 0.8$ weeks), the pencil-and-paper registered observations were repeated during a second home visit. Maternal sensitivity data were obtained at the visits at 6 weeks and 4 months.

At infant age 10 months ($M = 44.1$ weeks, $SD = 1.2$ weeks), mothers and infants were videotaped in three free-play situations in the departmental laboratory in order to secure maternal sensitivity data. In the first situation (3 minutes), mothers were given a basket with several age-appropriate toys and an instruction to play with the infant as if at home. During the following 2×2 minutes, the basket was removed, and mothers were told to show the infant, first, a form board with three different forms, and second, a toy farm with animals.

When the children were 15 months old ($M = 15.5$, $SD = .67$), attachment data were obtained from the Strange Situation procedure (Ainsworth et al., 1978) which was performed (and videotaped) in the standard fashion in the lab.

At 29 months, 50 children had nonparental day-care arrangements. Quality of care in both the external environment and in the child's home environment was studied by means of direct observations and interviews with day-care personnel ($n = 48$, $M = 29.3$, $SD = 1.03$) and with parents ($n = 104$, mean child age $= 29.4$, $SD = .99$) Research assistants made 1.5-hour home visits and 3-hour visits to the child's day-care setting (when applicable).

At the age of 4 years, a questionnaire about behavior problems was filled out for each child independently by the mother (mean child age $= 51.0$ months, $SD = 2.1$), the father ($M = 51.3$ months, $SD = 2.2$), and a person in charge of a children's group in which the child participated regularly ($M = 52.8$ months, $SD = 2.3$). In the group setting, three research assistants (one had participated in the 29-month data collection, the others were new) directly observed each child in social interactions with adults and other children during three hours.

Also at child age 4 years, video recordings were made of the families during a main meal (lunch or dinner) at home. Maternal sensitivity was assessed in maternal-child interactions during the meal. The camera was set up before the start of the meal, and the research assistant stayed out of sight in another room. Of the 83 families who consented to the filming, 76 could be assessed (seven tapes were of bad technical quality); in 74 of the films mothers were present. The meals lasted between 6 minutes and 56 minutes ($M = 20.4$, $SD = 8.9$); in five families less than 10 minutes of interaction could be analyzed. From the rest of the films, 10 minutes were chosen for analysis. The second five minute-period, when the family presumably had adjusted to the camera, was chosen together with the last five minutes of the meal, which contained several interactive events. Finally, a retrospective report about the child's daycare situation each month from birth until 48 months of age was secured from the mothers.

Instruments and Measures

Maternal Sensitivity. The Ainsworth conceptualization of maternal sensitivity (e.g., Ainsworth et al., 1978) was used in all ratings of interactive maternal behaviors. The scale developed by Ainsworth was originally intended for observations of much longer duration. However, experiences from pilot studies supported our assumption that significant/meaningful maternal differences were also captured with semistructured observations of short duration.

During the mother–infant face-to-face and diaper change interactions at 6 weeks and 4 months, maternal sensitivity was rated according to a slightly modified version of a method developed by Vaughn, Taraldson, Crichton, and Egeland (1980). In the present context, the overall judgment of maternal sensitivity to infant signals (as defined by Ainsworth, Bell, & Stayton, 1971) was used as well as a measure of a more specific aspect of sensitivity, that is, physical contact (averaged ratings of amount and quality of physical contact). All ratings were made directly after the observation period on verbally defined five-step scales. The two measures used in the analyses were based on averaged ratings across the two situations and the two ages (see Bohlin et al., 1989, for details and interobserver reliability).

At the 10-month lab visit, a female observer, who had not participated in the home visits, rated general sensitivity from videotapes on Ainsworth's nine-step scale (cf. Ainsworth et al., 1978) in each of the three play situations. Interobserver reliability, based on two independent female observers' ratings of 20 mothers in each of the three situations, amounted to .99, .87, and .99 (product moment correlations) with no significant observer mean differences. The measure used here was an average of the three ratings. The three sensitivity assessments from the infant's first year will be referred to as early sensitivity.

The videotaped interaction during a meal from the four-year home visit was rated for sensitivity in maternal responses to child initiatives and for sensitivity in maternal commands with the intent of changing child behavior. A scale with nine steps (verbally defined for each type of interaction), developed by van den Boom, Leiden University, The Netherlands (personal communication, April 1990), was used. All films were assessed by one male observer; interobserver reliability was obtained with an independent observer who rated 20 tapes. The Pearson correlation for sensitivity in child-initiated responses amounted to .44 (70% exact agreement), and for sensitivity in maternal commands, the correlation was .72 (75% agreement). The modest agreement for the first type of interactions led to exclusion of this sensitivity measure. Sensitivity in maternal commands will be referred to as late sensitivity.

Attachment The videotapes from the Strange Situation were rated for attachment behaviors, and classifications of attachment quality were made by one of the authors (G. B.), who has received training and established reliability (on the Minnesota Reliability Tape) under the supervision of Professor L. Alan Sroufe, University of Minnesota. The coder was aware of study hypotheses but was blind with regard to individuals' scores on other variables in the study. Other trained raters were consulted for 26 cases (20 of which were considered difficult by the main rater); agreement for the A B C classification was 80%. Disagreements were resolved by consensus decisions. In group comparisons, the A B C (insecure-avoidant, secure, and insecure-ambivalent) classification of attachment quality was used. In correlational analyses, amount of avoidant and resistant behaviors (aggregated data from both reunions scored on seven-step scales) was utilized (cf. Ainsworth et al., 1978).

Context Variables

Socioeconomic Background. As an estimate of the family's social status (SES), the father's educational level was chosen and measured on a scale consisting of six levels of education (1 = nine years of schooling to 6 = university degree).

Exposure to Nonparental Care. Experience of nonparental care was studied in terms of both quantity and quality. Two measures of amount of external care were created: (1) amount of early care was estimated as the average number of hours per week that the child had spent in care during the first 15 months of life; and (2) amount of later care was the same type of estimate during the period from 16 to 48 months of life.

Quality of care was rated at child age 29 months in the external day-care setting. A scheme for direct observations and a structured caregiver interview were developed, with the Home Inventory (Caldwell & Bradley, 1979) as a model. Four areas were covered: structural aspects (such as adult/child ratio, caregiver education, security aspects, available space), stimulation (indoor and outdoor facilities, visits to libraries, theaters, sports centers, shops, etc.), emotional tone between caregivers and the child and between the child and other children, and finally, adjustment to and success of fulfilling the set goals for the development and upbringing of the focal child. Immediately after the direct observations and the interview, global ratings of care quality on five-step scales were made. Before the data collection started, three female assistants (one had participated in the first two home visits, two were new in the project) were trained to a criterion of 90% agreement.

Home Environment. The quality of the child's home environment was rated following the same procedure and using the same instruments as in the assessment of day-care quality. After observation and interview with the mother, a global five-step assessment of home quality was made.

Outcome Variables

Behavior Problems. Behavior problems at the age of 4 years were studied with the Preschool Behavior Questionnaire (PBQ), (Behar & Stringfield, 1974). The instrument has been developed and psychometrically evaluated as regards dimensionality and homogeneity on another sample of 4-year-olds (Hagekull & Bohlin, 1992, 1994). In the Swedish version, the original PBQ was modified in that a five-step response scale (end points "does not apply at all to my child – applies very well") was used for each item instead of three-step scales. Seven items were excluded because they do not pertain to the behavioral syndromes of externalizing (aggressive and hyperactive/inattentive) and internalizing (fearful, socially withdrawing) behaviors.

In the present study, the PBQ items formed four scales: aggressive behaviors (ten items), concentration problems (five items), internalizing problems (seven-items), and finally, a total problem scale. Following the advice by Epstein (1979, 1980) about aggregation of data to increase generalizability and reliability, an individual's scale score in each of these four measures consisted of the average of the ratings by mother, father, and a child group leader. Interrater agreement ranged from none to modest (.10 – .53; Md = .35), with higher values for parent agreement and for outgoing problems. The first three scale scores were averages of the five-step ratings of the items. In calculating the total problem score, a rating of 4 or 5 was considered to indicate the existence of a problematic behavior (cf. Hagekull & Bohlin, 1992); the total problem score was the average number of such ratings in maternal, paternal, and group leaders' reports.

Social Interaction Behaviors. Two other outcome measures were based on direct observations of child–peer and child–adult interactions in a group setting at age 4 years. A behavior checklist developed from White and Watts (1973), covering positive and negative behaviors (13 behaviors relevant to peer interactions and 13 behaviors applicable to child–adult contacts), was used. During outdoor and indoor free play and during organized activities, all interactive behaviors with adults and other children were observed and registered as they occurred during five-minute periods. The mean active observation time was 35.15 minutes (SD = 7.81 min.). The recordings consisted of ratings of duration of the observed behaviors on six-point scales with verbally defined steps, ranging from 0 = has not occurred to 5 = has lasted during the full five minutes. An individual's score for a certain behavior was based on the sum of all ratings divided by number of observation periods.

In a factor analysis of the observed child–adult and child–child behaviors, two meaningful behavior problem dimensions appeared. The first contained three externalizing problem behaviors (disobedience, negative peer contact behaviors, and negative emotions directed to adults), yielding an alpha of .67; the scale was named "negative social behavior." The other factor described social withdrawal with a slight aggressive component in six items (e.g., nonparticipation in organized activities, solitary play, competition for adult attention, rejection of peer contacts, and negative emotions directed to peers). The scale was named "withdrawal/obstruction," and the homogeneity coefficient amounted to .56. The interobserver agreement for the nine items in the scales ranged from .60 to 1.00 (product moment coefficients; Md = .83, n = 13).

Statistical Analyses

A series of hierarchical multiple regression analyses were executed to answer questions about the predictive value of early interactive experiences and context variables for the four-year outcome variables. The main effects of early experience variables and of the different context variables were first extracted through forced entry, and interaction terms were then entered stepwise (cf. Cohen & Cohen, 1983). To avoid the problems caused by multicollinearity in the intercorrelation matrix, the main effect variables were centered as suggested by Cohen and Cohen (1983, p. 238). All analyses were performed using SPSS – X (SPSS, Inc., 1983). Two-tailed tests were used except for theoretically motivated relations with sensitivity and attachment variables.

RESULTS

Descriptive Statistics

At 15 months, 62.4% (n = 68) of the infants were classified as securely attached, 16.5% (n = 18) as insecure-avoidant, and 21.1% (n = 23) as insecure-ambivalent. Descriptive data for maternal sensitivity and demographic variables are shown for the three attachment groups (Table 5.1) to facilitate comparisons with other studies in this monograph. No significant differences between groups were found with regard to socioeconomic status (SES), par-

Table 5.1.   Means/Percentages for Early Sensitivity and Demographic Context Measures for the A, B, and C Attachment Classification Groups

	Attachment Classification		
	A $n = 18$	B $n = 68$	C $n = 23$
Early Sensitivity			
Physical contact (1.5 + 4 mo.; means)	2.86	3.15	3.22
General sensitivity (1.5 + 4 mo.; means)	3.54	3.53	3.73
General sensitivity (10 mo.; means)	4.91	4.85	5.30
Demographic Context			
SES (means)	3.44	4.09	4.65
Parity (% firstborns)	44	43	26
Gender (% males)	56	56	35

ity, and sex. Among maternal sensitivity variables, only physical contact differed significantly between groups, $F_{(2,106)} = 3.35$, $p < .05$.

Means and variability measures for maternal sensitivity, attachment, context, and outcome variables for the entire sample are shown in Table 5.2. The maternal sensitivity ratings were approximately normally distributed, as were the day-care and home environment quality distributions. Avoidant and resistant attachment behaviors were positively skewed; 46.3% and 45.5% of the infants, respectively, did not show such behaviors. Amount of early care was also positively skewed, with 55% of the infants having had no such care during the first 15 months; only 5% had received a mean of 12 hours per week or more. The amount of later care was more normally distributed. Fourteen percent of the children had no nonparental care after the age of 15 months, and 41% were cared for by someone other than their parents for an average of 20 hours or more per week.

The distributions for the outcome variables showed the means to be toward the lower end of the scales; this was especially marked for the frequency of total problems. Only a fifth of the sample showed five or more problematic behaviors. The other three questionnaire-based variables, rated on five-step scales, had approximately normal distributions. Of the observation scales, reflecting duration of behavior per five-minute period, the negative social behavior scale was positively skewed, with 48.5% of the subjects not showing any such behaviors. The withdrawal/obstruction scale showed an approximately normal distribution: about 15% of the children had emitted such behaviors during almost half of the observation periods.

The skewed distributions of behavior problem variables attest to the normality of the sample. Some selection of participants with regard to acceptance to participate and attrition might also have contributed to the skewness.

Table 5.2. Descriptive Statistics for Sensitivity, Attachment, Context, and Outcome Variables

Measures	Child Age	M	SD	Range	N
Maternal Sensitivity					
Physical contact	1.5 + 4 mo.	3.11	0.48	1.88–4.50	123
General sensitivity	1.5 + 4 mo.	3.55	0.60	1.67–4.67	123
General sensitivity	10 mo.	4.99	0.90	1.67–7.00	115
General sensitivity	4 yrs	5.14	1.08	2.84–7.00	72
Attachment Behaviors					
Avoidance	15.5 mo.	2.07	1.31	1.00–5.00	114
Resistance	15.5 mo.	2.08	1.46	1.00–7.00	114
Context					
Father education (SES)	1.5 mo.	4.00	1.93	1–6	123
Amount of early NP[a] care	0–15 mo.	2.65	4.61	0–30.00	100
Amount of late NP care	16–48 mo.	16.74	11.33	0–42.73	100
NP care quality	29 mo.	3.33	0.98	1–5	48
Home environment quality	29 mo.	3.34	0.82	1–5	104
Socio-emotional Outcome					
Questionnaire data					
Total problems (freq.)	4 yrs	3.50	3.01	0–15	105
Aggressive behaviors	4 yrs	2.20	0.58	1.20–3.93	105
Concentration problems	4 yrs	2.10	0.64	1.00–4.00	105
Internalizing problems	4 yrs	2.02	0.43	1.00–3.21	105
Observation data					
Withdrawal/obstruction	4 yrs	1.65	0.34	0.97–2.65	99
Negative contact	4 yrs	0.06	0.11	0–0.75	99

NP = nonparental.

Stability of Maternal Sensitivity

The correlations among the four measures of maternal sensitivity are shown in Table 5.3. Sensitivity of physical contact was only correlated with general sensitivity observed at the same time period, that is, at 1.5–4 months of age. The two observations of general sensitivity at 4 and 10 months showed significant but low stability, and general sensitivity rated at infant age 10 months was related to sensitivity seen in mealtime commands when the children were 4 years old.

Prediction of 4-year Outcomes from Maternal Sensitivity and Quality of Attachment

Early Maternal Sensitivity. The predictive bivariate relations between the three measures of early maternal sensitivity and outcomes at 4 years are shown in

Table 5.3. Stability of Maternal Sensitivity

	1	2	3
1. Physical contact (1.5 + 4 mo.)	—		
2. General sensitivity (1.5 + 4 mo.)	.35***	—	
	(123)[a]		
3. General sensitivity (10 mo.)	.13	.21*	—
	(115)	(115)	
4. General sensitivity (4 yrs)	.06	−.01	.27*
	(61)	(61)	(60)

* $p < .05$; *** $p < .001$; one-tailed.

[a] *Ns* are given in parentheses.

Table 5.4. Both total problem load and aggressive behavior (averaged adult reports) were significantly predicted from physical contact (observed at 6 weeks and 4 months) and from 10-month general sensitivity; low sensitivity and less physical contact were associated with more problem behaviors. Concentration problems and observed negative social behavior were more pronounced when ratings of maternal sensitivity at 10 months had been low (borderline significance for concentration). For internalizing problems there was a tendency ($p < .05$) for more problems to be associated with low general sensitivity observed at 6 weeks and 4 months. For the observer-rated child–peer and child–adult interactions general sensitivity at 10 months was related to negative social behavior.

Attachment Quality. The relation between attachment quality and 4-year outcomes was assessed both by one-way analysis of variance (ANOVA), using attachment quality as an independent variable, and by bivariate correlations between resistant and avoidant reunion behavior and the various outcomes. Using planned contrasts within the ANOVAs, significant effects were found for aggressive behaviors and for total problems with avoidant infants showing more problems than secure children. The bivariate correlations, using reunion behavior as attachment indicators, showed significant associations between avoidant behavior and aggressive behaviors as well as total problem load ($r(103) = .21$, and .17, both $p < .05$).

Multiple regression analyses were employed to assess whether the insecure avoidant relationship at 15 months captured salient aspects of the mother–infant relationship other than early maternal sensitivity in predicting total problems and aggressive behaviors. Amount of avoidant reunion behaviors was entered in the regression after the three early sensitivity measures. The independent contribution of avoidance was not significant.

Table 5.4. Bivariate Relations Between Maternal Sensitivity Measures and 4-Year Socio-emotional Outcomes

	Total Problems	Aggressive Behaviors	Concentration Problems	Internalizing Problems	Withdrawal/ Obstruction	Negative Social Behavior
Early Sensitivity (n = 99–105)						
Physical contact (1.5 + 4 mo.)	-.18**	-.20*	-.06	-.05	-.10	.01
General sensitivity (1.5 + 4 mo.)	-.26***	-.12	.07	-.16+	.06	-.01
General sensitivity (10 mo.)	-.23**	-.16*	-.16+	-.08	.04	-.19*
Late Sensitivity (n = 72)						
General sensitivity (4 yrs)	-.26*	-.39***	-.28**	.07	.08	-.17+

+ $p < .10$; * $p < .05$; ** $p < .01$; *** $p < .001$; one-tailed.

Early Versus Late Maternal Sensitivity. Maternal sensitivity observations at 4 years bore relations to much the same outcome variables as early sensitivity (see Table 5.4). To assess whether the early and late sensitivity observations accounted for the same variance in the explanation of behavior problems, regression analyses were performed with initial entry of the early measures followed by the late measure. Aggressive behavior was the only variable for which 4-year sensitivity gave a significant unique contribution (F for R^2 change = 10.69, $p < .01$; $R^2 = .44$, $p < .01$).

Prediction of 4-year Outcomes, Combining Maternal Sensitivity and Contextual Variables

SES, Parity, and Gender. The effects of context variables and interactive effects between maternal sensitivity and context variables were explored in hierarchical regressions. Early sensitivity measures were entered first as one block, followed by forced entry of each of the context variables (in the order of SES, parity, gender), and finally stepwise inclusion of the products. Main effects of context variables were found (for bivariate correlations, see Table 5.5), but no interactive effects. As can be seen in the first part of Table 5.6, effects independent of maternal sensitivity were found on all outcome variables except the withdrawal/obstruction scale (relations with the sensitivity measures are shown in Table 5.4). SES contributed significantly to the prediction of aggressive behaviors, concentration problems, and total problem load. Parity contributed to the explanation of total amount of problems ($p = .06$), concentration problems, and internalizing problems. Finally, gender contributed to the explanation of total amount of problems, concentration problems, and observed negative social behaviors. In all instances the direction of effects was that low SES, being firstborn, and being male were connected with more problems. Table 5.6 also shows that the regression equations were significant for all outcome variables except one, withdrawal/obstruction.

Nonparental Care. The bivariate relations between amount of nonparental care and outcomes are shown in Table 5.5. In regression analyses, the three sensitivity measures were first entered as a block; then early and late nonparental care were entered in that order; and finally the interactions were included by stepwise entry (middle part of Table 5.6). Amount of early care contributed significantly to the prediction of concentration problems and withdrawal/obstruction, in both cases in the direction of increased problems with more nonparental care during the first 15 months (see middle part of Table 5.6). Amount of late care had the opposite effect for total amount of problems, aggressive behaviors, and internalizing problems. There were no significant interactions with sensitivity measures.

Table 5.5. Bivariate Relations Between Context Variables and 4-Year Socio-emotional Outcomes

	Total Problems	Aggressive Behaviors	Concentration Problems	Internalizing Problems	Withdrawal/ Obstruction	Negative Social Behavior
SES (n = 99–105)	-.23*	-.28**	-.32***	.11	-.17+	.07
Parity (n = 99–105)	-.25*	-.13	-.24*	-.36***	-.15	-.23*
Gender (n = 99–105)	-.22*	-.17+	-.23*	.09	-.03	-.23*
Early nonparental care (n = 93–97)	.02	.10	.26*	-.04	.22*	-.04
Late nonparental care (n = 93–97)	-.23*	-.19+	.01	-.18+	.13	.02
Nonparental care quality (n = 45–46)	-.28*	-.16	-.07	-.33*	-.20	.02
Home environment quality (n = 93–98)	-.24*	-.30**	-.19+	-.17+	-.04	-.25*

+ p < .10; * p<.05; **p<.01; ***p < .001; two-tailed.

Finally, the importance of nonparental care quality was addressed as bivariate relations (see Table 5.5) and in regression analyses in which the quality measure was entered after the block of early sensitivity measures and interactions were included stepwise (Table 5.6, bottom). The quality of nonparental care as observed when the children were 29 months old contributed to the prediction of total problem load (statistical tendency) and internalizing problems; high quality was associated with few problems. For aggressive behaviors, the interaction between general sensitivity at 6 weeks and 4 months and care quality gave a significant contribution. The interaction resulted from the fact that for children whose mothers had been sensitive, high quality in nonparental care was associated with low aggressiveness, while this was not true for children whose mothers had been rated as average or low in sensitivity.

Home Environment. The contextual variable home environment quality was significantly related to total problem load, aggressive behaviors, and observed negative social behaviors (Table 5.5). It was then asked whether the maternal sensitivity variables contributed to the explanation of outcomes independently of the contextual variable home environment quality. For each outcome variable, two regression analyses were performed: in the first one, early sensitivity variables were entered after home environment quality; in a second analysis, the 4-year sensitivity was entered after home environment quality. For aggressive behavior and total problem load, both early and late sensitivity contributed (Fs for R^2 change were between 2.97, $p < .10$ and 7.80, $p < .01$). Thus, specific interactive experiences with mother contributed to the explanation of problem behavior over and above the general home environment quality.

DISCUSSION

Maternal Sensitivity and Attachment Security as Predictors. The present findings support the assumption of attachment theory that early maternal interactive behavior is related to later child behavior problems. The interpretation of these findings is strengthened by the fact that outcomes were not confined to maternal ratings but were obtained through several sources.

Information about attachment security was of little additional predictive value. Infant avoidance, as observed in the Strange Situation at 15 months, captured much the same variance in total problem load as early maternal sensitivity, thus supporting the theoretical proposition that insecure attachment is a developmental phenomenon mediating between early maternal interactive behavior and later outcomes. However, the support can only be seen as partial, because insecure attachment in the form of ambivalence was not significantly related to any of the problem areas.

Table 5.6. Predictive Value of Three Sets of Context Variables, After Inclusion of Early Sensitivity, for 4-Year Socio-emotional Outcomes. The R and β Values in Each Section Are Taken from the Final Equation

Predictors	Total Problems				Aggressive Behaviors				Concentration Problems			
	R^2 Change	F Change	β	R	R^2 Change	F Change	β	R	R^2 Change	F Change	β	R
SES	.04	4.79*	−.21		.06	6.81**	−.25		.08	8.75**	−.29	
Parity	.03	3.61*	−.18		.01	.59	−.05		.04	4.56*	−.20	
Gender	.04	4.38*	−.19	.45***	.03	3.39+	−.18	.42**	.06	7.58**	−.26	.49***
Early NP[a] care	.04	.14	.20		.01	.97	.27		.07	6.66*	.35	
Late NP care	.06	7.27**	−.30	.45**	.07	7.46**	−.32	.38**	.02	2.05	−.17	.36*
NP care quality	.011	1.39	−.18	.46**	.01	.63	−.16		.00	.01	−.02	.20
NP care quality x sensitivity					.14	6.77*	−.41	.46+				

Predictors	Internalizing Problems				Withdrawal/Obstruction				Negative Social Behavior			
	R^2 Change	F Change	β	R	R^2 Change	F Change	β	R	R^2 Change	F Change	β	R
SES	.02	1.50	.11		.01	.47	−.08		.03	2.59	−.16	
Parity	.11	11.74***	−.35		.03	2.92+	−.18		.03	3.47+	−.19	
Gender	.01	.70	.08	.44**	.00	.00	−.02	.23	.05	5.58*	−.23	.39*
Early NP care	.00	.12	.09		.05	4.72*	.20		.00	.24	−.08	
Late NP care	.04	3.69+	−.24	.26	.00	.14	.05	.27	.00	.18	.05	.20
NP care quality	.11	4.97*	−.34	.37	.04	1.68	.21	.25	.01	.19	.07	.20

[a] NP = nonparental.

+ $p < .10$; * $p < .05$; ** $p < .01$; *** $p < .001$.

Insecure Avoidant Versus Insecure Ambivalent Attachment. Previous studies differentiating insecure-avoidant and insecure-ambivalent children in terms of development of behavior problems have given a mixed picture. Erickson et al. (1985) concluded that both kinds of insecure attachment were predictive of negative outcomes, but regarding the behavior-problem scales it was the avoidant group that differed significantly from the secure children. The results by Lewis et al. (1984) yielded a complex picture; both avoidant and ambivalent boys received higher maternal ratings of psychopathology at 6 years than secure children did, while among girls ambivalent infants were later rated as showing the lowest degree of psychopathology. Two studies (Fagot & Kavanaugh, 1990; Suess et al., 1992) used samples in which all insecurely attached infants were of the avoidant type. While Suess and co-workers found avoidant children to show more behavior problems, Fagot and co-workers concluded that only for girls was there any indication that avoidant attachment would be related to later problem behaviors. Although the picture conveyed by these studies is scattered, it appears that there is more support for avoidant attachment to be associated with later behavior problems than there is for ambivalent attachment. Our own results fit this conclusion also in the sense that the maternal variable that has been considered a specific antecedent of avoidance, insensitivity in physical contact (Ainsworth, 1982), predicted both aggressive behaviors and the total amount of problems.

The failure of ambivalent attachment to predict later outcomes in the present study should also be viewed in the context of the Swedish culture. Because of the 12 months' right of paid parental leave, many Swedish children experience a shift from parental to nonparental care during the first half of their second year. The group of infants classified as ambivalent in the present study was large, 21.1%, as compared to the average of 6% reported for West European samples by van IJzendoorn and Kroonenberg (1988) in their meta-analysis. The question may be raised whether the resistance we observed at 15 months to some extent reflected a temporary condition due to a recent shift from parental to nonparental care (cf. Hårsman, 1984). Of the infants classified as ambivalent, 50% had started nonparental care between their's first birthday and 15 months, while this was true for 26% of the other children ($\chi^2 = 31.61$, $p < .001$). The total amount of nonparental care before 15 months did not differ significantly between groups.

Stability of Maternal Sensitivity. The results gave evidence for low, but significant, stability of maternal interactive behavior between 10 months and 4 years. The very early measures of sensitivity, however, were not significantly related to 4-year sensitivity, and the specific component of sensitivity, dealing with physical contact, was not related even to the 10-month general sensitivity rating. The fact that predictive relations to behavior outcomes were obtained for measures from all three ages, in spite of low or nonexistent stability, has several implications. A first suggestion is that maternal sensitivity should be seen as encompassing several aspects, which might be more or less observable in different situational contexts (cf. Bohlin et al., 1989; Bridges & Connell, 1991) and which might be of differential importance during the various phases of child development. The late sensitivity measure, which was obtained in a very different situation as compared to the early measures, a situation where the mother tried to control the child's behavior, contributed independently to the explanation of aggressive behavior. Together, these results yield some evidence against the idea that, due to stability of maternal behavior, associations between attachment quality and later behavior actually reflect the influence of the current mother–child relationship on child behavior (Field, 1987; Lamb, 1987).

Late Maternal Sensitivity. The relations between late maternal sensitivity and behavior problems showed much the same pattern as those for early sensitivity. These findings could be seen as strengthening the conclusion that the sensitivity aspect of maternal interactive behavior is a salient aspect of mother–child interaction. It is not, however, necessarily the same mothers who are able to meet the needs of the very young infant who are also able to cope with the needs of a maturing child for whom a certain amount of behavioral control is necessary. It appears that both early and concurrent relationship experiences are important (cf. Suess et al., 1992).

Although the contextual variable of home environment quality was related to several outcomes, both early and late sensitivity gave independent contributions to the explanation of problem behaviors. Thus, there is evidence for the specific importance of the mother–child relationship as compared to the effect of general home conditions.

Demographic Context. The results showed clear main effects of demographic context variables on the 4-year outcomes. There was little support for the assumption that behavioral differences among children associated with demographic factors would be mediated by differences in the early mother–child relationship. The question that then remains is: which mechanisms connect demographic variables with child behavior? Although genetic differences might be responsible for some results, for example, some gender differences, other effects, like those of parity, should be of environmental origin. Regarding parity, a possible mechanism is the social training provided by older siblings. It is notable that the most pronounced parity effect was observed for internalizing problems; having older siblings around as models in various situations might be of particular importance in counteracting the development of that type of behavior. The parity results could also be related to Dunn's (1984) findings concerning effects on the first-born child of the arrival of a sibling; increases in behaviors of the internalizing kind tended to remain.

SES effects, associating negative outcomes with low SES, are commonplace in the literature, especially as regards externalizing problems, which were also the variables associated with SES in the present study. Presumably, the SES effects are of multiple origin, some of which ought to be related to parental behavior. While none of the early measures of maternal sensitivity was significantly related to SES, as measured by father's educational level, a significant relation was found at 4 years ($r(71) = .31$, $p < .01$). When SES was entered after maternal sensitivity at 4 years in regression analyses, SES did not give any significant contribution to the explanation of problem variance. Thus, it appears that part of the SES effect has to do with aspects of parenting style, which develop differently in different subcultures. The situational context used in the 4-year sensitivity observation, maternal attempts to control child behavior, might be particularly suitable for identifying such differences. It appears, then, that there are cultural influences on maternal sensitivity after infancy.

Nonparental Care. The findings prove the importance of separating early and late exposure to nonparental care. The findings for early care were to some extent in line with Belsky's (1988a) contention that negative child behaviors bear a relation to substantial amounts of early nonparental care. From the perspective of attachment theory and research, it is interesting to note that such effects appear to occur independently of the quality of the early mother–child relationship.

For nonparental care after the first 15 months, the data indicate a positive influence on several aspects of socio-emotional functioning. In this respect, the present results corroborate the conclusion about positive effects of nonparental care drawn by Andersson (1989). However, when outcomes were related to the age at which the child first entered nonparental care, there were no significant relations except for concentration problems, in which case more problems were reported for those starting early ($r = -.23$).

Andersson's findings (1989) have been discussed in terms of the high quality of nonparental care in the Swedish society. Our findings contribute to that discussion by showing that, even within this cultural setting, quality of care was important for behavioral development, especially with regard to internalizing problems. Our data further suggested that for certain outcomes there might be interactive effects between quality of nonparental care and the mother–child relationship; an association between high nonparental care quality and low aggressiveness was obtained only for children who had experienced sensitive mothering. The cultural context in which these results were obtained should be considered in interpreting the results. Swedish society allows parents to stay home for a substantial period of time during infancy without losing income, provides generally high-quality nonparental care, and has a governmental policy for child-care institutions in which the importance of social and emotional development is stressed as much as, or more than, intellectual development. It appears that, in such a context, the possibility of interacting with children and adults outside the family has beneficial effects on the socio-emotional functioning of preschool children.

Conclusion. The present study draws a picture of children's socio-emotional development where influences stem from a variety of sources. The mother–child relationship stands out as an important source throughout early childhood, but different aspects of maternal sensitivity appear to be relevant during different developmental phases. The contextual aspects of the child's living situation, such as interactive experiences with other social partners, provide opportunities for changed developmental pathways.

CHAPTER SIX

Patterns of Attachment in Young Egyptian Children

ANNA VON DER LIPPE AND

PATRICIA McKINSEY CRITTENDEN

INTRODUCTION

In the 25 years since Ainsworth identified three qualities of attachment in a small sample of American children, investigators have explored the validity and meaning of these patterns in an increasingly wide range of children. At this point, it seems clear that patterns of attachment identify infants and children on developmental pathways that differ in important ways. The distribution of the patterns across cultures is less well understood. As noted by Kagitcibasi and Berry (1989), cross-cultural studies permit us to test the generalizability of theories about caregiver–child relationships.

Although one meta-analysis of studies of infant attachment demonstrated that within-culture differences exceeded between-culture differences (van IJzendoorn & Kroonenberg, 1988), this does not close the issue. There may still be subtle aspects of the display and function of the patterns that differ from one culture to another; strict use of the original Ainsworth A B C classificatory system might not identify these. Furthermore, mean differences in patterns among countries will not divulge possible differences in the meaning of behaviors, which the study of intracultural covariations may give. In addition, because all human societies are expected to contain the full range of human possibility, within-culture differences will necessarily be greater than between-culture differences. On the other hand, any given culture may still show a more restricted range of potential caregiver patterns than the variability shown over many cultures (Sigman & Wachs, 1991). The real question is whether there are systematic differences in distribution among different societal groups. If there are, it becomes important to understand why these occur – that is, what function they serve in the interaction of person and context. Finally, because cultural adaptation increases as children develop, it would be expected to affect behavior least in infancy. During the preschool years, on the other hand, children emerge from their families to begin taking their place in society. At the same time, they begin to acquire a verbal understanding of who "we" are; that is, preschool-aged children begin to be enculturated with the history and customs of their people. Consequently, they may show differences in distribution of quality of attachment that infants do not.

Further, a particular limitation to conclusions regarding the application of attachment theory to all humans has been the near-exclusive focus on Western children developing in Judeo-Christian cultures. Although there are exceptions, particularly with regard to studies of Japanese children, the pool of existing data is heavily influenced by Western culture. Moreover, the non-Western data contain indications that the methods, distributions, or meanings of the data may not be the same as for Western societies.

Among the least studied groups are children from Middle Eastern countries. This chapter focuses on young children growing up in Cairo, Egypt. Our interest is in exploring the relevance of the Ainsworth patterns of attachment for children developing in an Islamic culture whose traditions and environment are quite different from those of Western Europe and North America. Our intent is to place attachment in the social context experienced by children growing up today in urban, poor, lower class Egypt.

Danger, Protective Strategies, and Culture

According to Bowlby, attachment behavior functions to promote the protection of the children by their attachment figures, usually the child's parents. Studies using the Ainsworth patterns have demonstrated that, based on individual differences in mothers' responses to infants' signals, infants organize their attachment behavior in ways that maximize the mother's probability of providing protection (or, conversely, reduce the probability of her rejecting or harming her infant). The protective function of attachment under threatening conditions becomes even clearer in the preschool years (Crittenden, 1992a). In addition, there is evidence that aspects of a mother's own early experience are reflected in her parenting behavior, which, in turn, greatly influences her child's pattern of attachment (Benoit & Parker, 1994; Fonagy, 1991).

A critical variable in both mothers' and children's experience is threat or experience of danger. Children threatened with the uncertain outcome of danger tend to organize as Type C (coercive attachment strategy), whereas children experiencing predictable danger, including psychological rejection, tend to organize as Type A (avoidant attachment strategy). In addition, preschool-aged children have been shown to adapt the basic Ainsworth strategies in ways that both reflect their distress and function to further reduce their danger (Crittenden & Claussen, 1996; Fagot & Pears, 1996; Teti, Gelfand, Messinger, & Isabella, 1995). Severe threats with unpredictable outcomes are associated with C3-4 (aggressive and feigned helpless, respectively), whereas severe and predictable dangers are associated with A3-4 (compulsive caregiving and compulsive compliance, respectively); the most severe conditions are associated with A/C and AD (anxious depressed) organizations. In interpreting the cross-generational effects, one might say that mothers take what they have learned about staying safe and apply it to rearing their children. In interpreting the data on child–mother attachment, one might say that children adapt the model provided by their mothers to fit their own experience.

Less attention has been directed to the question of whether cultures, that is, generations of parent–child transmissions, differ in the distribution of the patterns and whether such differences reflect cultural differences in experienced danger and the best means to protect oneself from these dangers. Although culture has many components, none is more important than knowing how to live safely in one's environment. Furthermore, parents' most important obligation, in all cultures, is to keep their children alive and safe. Therefore, one of their responsibilities is to transmit to the child what people in a certain society have learned about safe ways to live.

Demography of Modern Egypt

According to an international Human Development Index (HDI), Egypt is a country of medium human development (MHD) and ranks 107th among 174 countries, excluding China (UNDP Report, 1996). The specific components of the HDI are life expectancy, educational attainment, and purchasing power. The basic idea is that, if people have these three opportunities, they are empowered to attain others. Egypt's situation may be described through some demographic figures. GDP national income is $33.6 billion. Exports are low compared to the average for the middle HDI group. Forty-four percent of the population lives in cities, and 51% of these live in large cities, the largest being Cairo. Urbanization in Egypt is on the same level as that in other countries with MHD, and crowding is the rule. Criminality is exceptionally low. The labor force is 29% of the total population, and women comprise 10% of the adult working force. This 10% figure is very low, as the average for MHD countries is 30%.

With regard to the nutritional and health situation, daily calorie supply per capita is somewhat higher than the average MHD. For toddlers, however, daily calorie intake is lower than recommended (Recommended Dietary Allowance, 1989), but the children are not malnourished (Sigman & Wachs, 1991). Compared to average MHD, maternal and infant mortality rates are high; mortality for children under age 5 is .009%, which is considerably higher than that in high human development (HHD) countries. Hoodfar (1995) found 16% mortality in a low-income sample of Cairo children (21 mothers). The proportion of underweight children below age 5 years is 10 percent, which is the same figure as HHD. Eighty-three percent of children are reported to be breastfed for more than six months (see also Hatem, 1987).

In other words, once children survive birth, they seem to receive reasonably good nourishment, and their mothers nearly always care for them. Neither UNDP nor UNICEF gives gender breakdowns in their statistics for Egypt on infant mortality, deaths before 5 years, or state of malnutrition, making it difficult to evaluate if girls are cared for as adequately as boys. From the perspective of intraculture competition, however, it is noteworthy that Egyptian mothers living near Cairo (the site of the present study) tend to withdraw personal/psychological resources (verbal interaction and responsivity) from less well-nourished children, while better fed children are given more developmentally facilitative interactions (Sigman & Wachs, 1991). Although no analyses were made of gender and nutrition, other investigators note that Egyptian boys are given preferential treatment as they grow older (but not as babies) such as being given better food (Hatem, 1987). According to Hoodfar (1995), mothers are considerably more careful with the health of sons (they say boys are weaker) and so spend more money on nourishing food for sons.

The Family Context of Egyptian Childrearing

Although there is very little psychological literature on Egyptian families and none on attachment, what there is, together with the sociological literature, forms a basis for several specific hypotheses. Barakat (1985) describes Arab societies as family centered and the Arab family as the socioeconomic unit of production and the center of Arab social organization, especially among the rural population and the urban poor. All members of the domestic unit cooperate to secure its livelihood and community standing, with the success or failure of individuals becoming that of the family as a whole. In this context, large numbers of children enhance the family's power and prestige. Discontinuity of caregiving is seen as children grow older (Sigman & Wachs, 1991). As the mother withdrew to care for younger babies, Sigman and Wachs observed that older siblings did not replace her caregiving. This pattern of caregiving could give rise to higher than usual rates of anxious attachment.

Egyptian families are patriarchal and hierarchically structured according to gender and age, with fathers holding absolute authority. Nevertheless, mothers function as the real authority because of the fathers' near constant absence from the home. Because openly challenging men's authority leads to unacceptable marital and family disharmony, mothers' power tends to be concealed and is often underhanded. Indeed, fathers often become distant threats of discipline, while mothers are the affection center of the family (Barakat, 1985; Hatem, 1987).

Control is a major socialization tool, with obedience as the goal (Hatem, 1987; Lippe, in press; Wikan, 1982). Physical closeness and verbal interaction were not found to be usual responses for relief of distress in the Sigman and Wachs study, but rather were used for control purposes. Downward communication (from husbands to wives and from mothers to children) often takes the form of orders, instructions, threats, and shaming, accompanied by anger and punishment, whereas upward communication uses obedience, pleas, appeals, and apologies, accompanied by crying and covering up (Barakat, 1981). Again, the evidence suggests the possibility of anxious attachment, particularly coercive strategies (Type C) and, in some cases, compulsive compliance (subtype A4).

With regard to gender differences, Barakat evaluates the mother–son relationship as verging on morbidity. This could well be reflected in coercive, enmeshed Type C relationships. Girls, on the other hand, are clearly the less favored sex (Hatem, 1987), being more frequently beaten by the mother, more restricted, given far less freedom outside the home, and forced to obey their brothers (El Safty, 1979). It was our expectation that the A type pattern, including the compulsively compliant subpattern (A4), would more often be demonstrated in girls.

The relation between Egyptian girls and their mothers is complex. The birth of a girl fails to bring approval to the mother, if it happens prior to the birth of sons. On the other hand, a daughter can function as a help to the mother with household chores and the care of siblings and give her emotional support (Hoodfar, 1995). Finally, in the gender/age-based hierarchy of Egyptian society and in the context of women's confinement to their homes, daughters represent the only opportunity for women to exercise power. Of course, mothers and daughters also share the unique bond of gender.

Attachment and Maternal Behavior

Child development has been demonstrated to covary with the sensitivity, social skill, empathy, and decentration of the primary caregiver(s). In this study of Egyptian children, we have already demonstrated that the quality of mothers' mediation of children's learning experiences (through decentered attention, sensitivity, and empathy) was related to the children's educability and intellectual development beyond what could be accounted for by the mothers' own intelligence (Lippe & Hartmann, 1996). An issue raised in this chapter is whether maternal behaviors leading to child educability and intellectual development can also be shown to facilitate development of secure attachment.

Although the consequences for children of maternal behavior have been widely noted (Bruner & Bornstein, 1089; Feuerstein, 1980; Klein & Feuerstein, 1985; Richman, Miller & LeVine, 1992; van IJzendoorn & Kroonenberg, 1988), this question has received little attention in either the Egyptian psychological literature or the scientific literature at large. In a study of Israeli children, Tal and Klein (1996) found that mediated feelings of competence (one of five criteria of mediational skills) significantly improved children's quality of attachment. It will be important to determine whether mothers' skills in mediating children's learning experiences are the same skills that mediate experiences of psychological safety. We believe that mothers' decenteredness, empathy, and identification with their children are related mental processes that are both cognitive and emotional in nature. Furthermore, such mediational skills enable mothers to take their children's perspective and understand their needs. Consequently, we expect them to be relevant across situations.

In this chapter, we explore (1) whether individual differences in quality of attachment among Egyptian children are correlated with other variables in ways that suggest that attachment has the same meaning in Egyptian society as in Western cultures (the transcultural validity of constructs issue), (2) what the distribution of qualities of attachment in Egyptian children was (the cross-cultural differences issue), and (3) whether there were distinctive patterns or differences in the display of the patterns as compared to Western children (the issue of expansion of the array of human patterns). We set these three questions in the context of Egyptian culture, seeking answers that might help us to understand why Egyptian mothers and children behave as they do. Specifically, among young Egyptian children, we expected to see (a) gender differentiation, particularly in patterns that reflect power, (b) relatively few Type B children, (c) more Type A children, especially in girls, with possibly some A4s, and (d) a larger proportion of Type C patterns, particularly in boys, than is usually found in Western populations. We also expected (e) "subdued" patterns as compared to Western children. Finally, we anticipated (f) that attachment patterns in children would be related to mothers' decentered teaching style, with Type B children having mothers who demonstrated a decentered style of mediating learning experiences.

Children of 5–8 years of age were studied, specifically because these years coincided with the initiation of formal education. Such children are still heavily dependent on the home but are beginning to prepare to spend time away from home. As a consequence, pressure should be put upon them to conform to culture-specific rules about comportment, particularly cultural guidelines regarding safe conduct. Given our small sample size and the scarcity of previous literature on this issue, this study is exploratory and the findings will at best be tentative. If the hypothesis of a positive relationship between maternal mediation and attachment were empirically supported, it would also suggest the validity of the present measurement of attachment in a new cultural setting.

METHOD

Subjects

The data for this chapter were collected as part of a more extensive study on cultural mediation of competence among the working-class poor in Cairo (Lippe, in press; Lippe & Hartmann, 1996). The subjects were 30 children aged 5–8 years (M = 6.7 years, SD = 1.37), their mothers, and 28 of their siblings (M = 7.78 years, range = 1–11 years). There were 19 focal boys and 11 focal girls; of the siblings 17 were boys and 11 were girls. The mothers ranged in age from 24 to 44 years in age (M = 33.33 years, SD = 5.09). Twenty-seven of the mothers lived with husbands who ranged in age from 30 to 60 years (M = 39.14 years, SD = 6.06). The average education of the mothers was 8.7 years with a range from 0–16 years (SD = 5.3). Including all children in the 30 families, there were 33 girls and 59 boys; the sex ratio approached almost two to one for both focal children and their siblings. About half of the families lived in an inner-city, low-income area of Cairo, and the other half lived in more recently urbanized and densely populated areas, with low-quality housing erected to meet the demands of the rapidly growing city.

The families were recruited through the social networks of a set of inner-city families previously studied by Wikan (1980). Families with children of the desired age were located primarily through family networks and to a lesser extent through neighborhood acquaintances. Because the larger study was concerned with the effects of maternal education on socialization and maternal teaching, the education of the mothers was systematically varied but within the same families and neighborhoods to control for environmental differences.

Procedure

The families were seen during three to four home visits. As the households were usually crowded two- to three-room apartments, there was little space for shielded test conditions. We were usually ushered into the little-used living-room or combined bedroom. The curiosity of the siblings, other adults, and neighbors insured the presence of five to ten onlookers who made comments freely and helped or criticized the subjects as they saw fit. Although somewhat deviant from Western standards for conducting psychological research, the scene was characteristic for how the Cairene families live their lives. Indeed, we suspect that they would have felt ill at ease in the isolated quiet of standard data-gathering conditions.

Measures

The reported data for this chapter came from three sources: (1) free play with mother, focal child, and siblings, used to code *attachment* with the Preschool Assessment of Attachment (PAA) (Crittenden, 1988–1995); (2) Running Horse Game Test (RHGT), used to assess *mediation of learning experience* and *child educability* (Hartmann & Haavind, 1981; Lippe & Hartmann, 1996); and (3) Raven Progressive Matrices (Raven, Court & Raven, 1992), used to assess intellectual level. For the siblings, we only had attachment data.

Attachment. The focal child and mother were placed on the floor, together with a number of toys. The toys were a carriage with colored wooden blocks, some cars, a doll, a ball, a plastic zoo, kitchen utensils, and small adult and child human dolls. The mothers were instructed "to do something together" with the child. Ten minutes of play were video recorded from an aerial position, which gave a good view of the participants. The family rooms were small with beds around the walls where onlookers placed themselves. Siblings under 4 years of age would invariably join the play, and sometimes a mother asked an older sibling to help if she felt uncomfortable. A few mothers chose to sit with their backs to the camera, wrapped in a large headshawl for religious reasons. None of the mothers refused to be video recorded for religious or other reasons. Although it would have been desirable to use an unfamiliar setting and possibly a separation, this was not feasible in Cairo. Instead, we hoped that the presence of two foreign women (the first author and a translator) as well as the unfamiliar videotaping procedure and the new toys would create a mild stressor. In this regard, we believe that the mothers were substantially more stressed by the procedure than were the children.

Quality of attachment was coded by the second author from nonverbal[1] behavior using an adaptation of the procedure defined for the PAA. Because the PAA had already been used successfully in homes (see Chisholm, Chapter 10 this volume) and with 5- to 7-year-olds (Head & Williams, 1995), we felt its exploratory use in this sample was warranted. The procedure was, however, more difficult to code than a standard Strange Situation, and our findings should be considered exploratory, pending replication and expansion with other procedures. For the analyses of attachment patterns, siblings were included. As noted earlier, we expected gender differences in the distributions of patterns of attachment and fewer Type Bs than in North American and British samples.

Maternal Teaching Style and Child Educability. The Running Horse Game Test is a children's board game constructed to assess maternal teaching styles of different mediating quality and children's cognitive competence and learning style (Hartmann & Haavind, 1981). In order to win the game, players must plan carefully how they should best move two horses along a route with many obstructions and shortcuts. The game is constructed for children around 6 years of age. The mother is taught the game by an examiner, and she then teaches the game to a child other than her own. The

---

[1] English translations of the dialogue were read by the second author without reference to the videotapes. Because the dialogue was quite irrelevant to attachment issues, the dialogues were not used in the classification of attachment.

examiner teaches the game to her child to ensure that all the children are taught the game in the same pedagogical manner. The behaviors of mother and child are audiotaped, and their moves are recorded (Hartmann & Haavind, 1981). The variables scored for the mother were: (a) informing about rules, (b) anticipation, helping the child to plan ahead, (c) demonstrating alternatives, (d) seeking feedback from the child, (e) obtaining imperative feedback, giving the child orders without explanations when uncertain, (f) spontaneously commanding the child without explaining, (g) limiting the child with incorrect information, (h) referring to the competitive element of the game (divided into decentered and self-centered competing), and (i) giving emotional support. The child's game behavior was coded for (a) rule mastery, (b) decision making, (c) planning, (d) irrelevant attention, (e) adequate interest, (f) inadequate reaction, (g) competing, and (h) appropriate emotion.

In this study, it was hypothesized that pattern of attachment and decentered maternal teaching style would be related. We anticipated that the mother's mediational competence (i.e., her decentered and sensitive awareness of the learning needs of her child) would also reflect decentered and sensitive awareness of the child's emotional needs for psychological safety. No hypothesis was posed regarding children's educability and attachment. However, because related maternal behaviors may facilitate development in apparently independent child domains, we explored the relation (Lippe & Hartmann, 1996).

Intellectual Functioning. Because attachment was expected to be related to maternal mediation of learning tasks, it was desirable to include a measure of intelligence in the analyses. Children were administered the Raven Colored Progressive Matrices. The scores were percentiles for the age group, using British norms. The mothers were administered the Standard Progressive Matrices. For mothers, raw scores were used because age norms were not at issue and scores quite often were too low for percentile norms. Lippe and Hartmann (1996) have reported a strong covariation in this sample between decentered teaching and intellectual functioning in both the mothers and children.

Analyses

Categorical data were analyzed with a Chi-square. Analysis of variance (ANOVA) was used for the analysis of attachment with the continuous cognitive variables. When specific hypotheses could be made, one-way ANOVAs with contrasts or linear trends were used. In addition, principal component analyses were used for data reduction of the cognitive data.

RESULTS

Validity of Our Assessment of Quality of Attachment

Demographic and Cognitive Data. The attachment patterns were first tested for possible relations to demographic or cognitive variables using one-way ANOVAs. Attachment was not related to child or maternal age or to parental education. Mothers of Type B children, however, scored significantly higher on the Standard Progressive Matrices than mothers of Type A and Cs ($F_{(2,27)} = 4.90$, $p < .02$). Type B children, therefore, seemed to come from somewhat more resourceful homes than the rest. Although the analysis was not significant, fathers' education was 9.2 years for Type C and 11.6 years for the remaining children. There were no gender differences on Raven scores for children.

Maternal Mediation and Attachment. The mother and child variables were subjected to separate principal component analyses with Varimax rotation, yielding two factors for each of the two analyses. The two factors for the mother differentiated positive mediating variables (emotional support, informing, anticipation, seeking feedback, and demonstrating alternatives) and negative mediating variables (self-centered competing, imperative feedback, restriction, and spontaneous commands). The two factors were named positive and negative (see Table 6.1).

When the factor scores were entered into a one-way ANOVA, positive maternal mediation differentiated the attachment groups, but the negative mediation factor did not ($F_{(2,27)} = 4.46$, $p < .05$) (see Table 6.2).

The Duncan post hoc test indicated that Type B children had mothers with significantly higher positive mediation scores than Type A children had. The

Table 6.1. Principal Component Analysis of Mothers' Decentered Mediation of Learning Experience (Running Horse Game Test. Varimax Rotation)

Variables	Positive Mediation (Variance: 51.7%)	Negative Mediation (Variance: 13.0%)
Emotional support	.83	−.12
Informing	.74	−.55
Anticipation	.73	−.07
Seeking feedback	.72	−.25
Demonstrating alternatives	.71	−.27
Self-centered competing	−.02	.77
Imperative feedback	−.37	.76
Restriction	−.51	.71
Spontaneous commands	−.08	.65

Table 6.2. Patterns of Attachment and Mothers' Decentered Mediation of Learning Experience

Group	N	Positive Mediation Means	Negative Mediation Means
A	11	–.5938	–.2547
B	8	.6783	–.0658
C	9	.1487	.3760

mothers of Type C children scored in between. These analyses suggest that, in this sample, the salient maternal behaviors for attachment were mothers' helpful behaviors, both pedagogically and emotionally, whereas maternal confusing and constraining behaviors were not related to the quality of children's attachment to their mothers. The results also show that Type A children tended to have mothers with the poorest quality of teaching skills.

The principal components analysis of the child's Running Horse Game Test variables yielded two child factors: the first was related to degree of decentered educability (rule mastery, planning decision making, irrelevant attention, and inadequate reactions), and the other to vitality (competing, appropriate emotions, and adequate interest). The factor loadings are presented in Table 6.3.

Table 6.4 shows that although child educability was not related to pattern of attachment, vitality was ($F_{(2,27)} = 6.53$, $p < .01$). In this case, the Duncan post hoc test of differences among groups showed that the Type B children had significantly higher vitality scores than children classified as either Type A or Type C. Separate analyses could not be carried out for the sexes because the ns were too small. Not surprisingly, pattern of attachment was related to the more motivational and affective aspects of educability and not to the more cognitive aspects. Type B children showed more vitality in a learning situation.

Table 6.3. Principal Component Analysis of Children's Decentered Educability (Running Horse Game Test. Varimax Rotation)

Variables	Educability (Variance: 44.4%)	Vitality (Variance: 22.6%)
Rule mastery	.85	.19
Planning	.79	.38
Decision making	.77	.16
Irrelevant discerning	–.70	.40
Inadequate reactions	–.76	–.13
Competing	–.05	.87
Appropriate emotion	.16	.74
Adequate interest	.36	.73

Table 6.4.   **Attachment Patterns and Children's Decentered Educability**

Group	N	Educability (Means)	Vitality (Means)
A	11	.1359	−.4074
B	8	−.1228	1.0660
C	9	−.2128	−.2128

We also tested gender differences, using *t*-tests. There were no gender effects in child educability scores. Positive maternal mediation did, however, favor the focal boys ($t = 2.63$, $p < .02$).

Gender and Attachment. There was a significant effect of gender on attachment ($\chi^2_{(2)} = 9.47$, $p < .01$) such that the focal boys were more often classified as Type B (42%) and C (37%), whereas the focal girls were more often classified as Type A (73%). Because the number of focal girls was relatively low (11 out of 39), we looked at the distribution of siblings by gender. The same differences were found as for the focal children ($\chi^2_{(2)} = 10.45$, $p < .01$). The results are presented in Table 6.5 and Figure 6.1.

Exploring the absence of girls further, we found that only two families had no sons (one with seven girls) while nine families had no daughters. There were five families with several boys and a single girl, but only three families with several girls and a single boy. Eight families had a similar number of boys and girls. Considering birth order, only 10 of 30 families had a first-born girl.

Finally, we considered the patterns of attachment of boy/girl sibling pairs by gender. In 10 of the 16 pairs, the boy was favored (i.e., B vs. A & C; C vs. A; and A1-2 or C1-2 vs. A3-4 or C3-4).

Table 6.5.   **Patterns of Attachment in the Two Sexes**

Patterns of Attachment	Girls	Boys	Row Totals
Focal Children			
A	8 (73%)	4 (21%)	12 (40%)
B	0	8 (42%)	8 (26.7%)
C	3 (27%)	7 (37%)	10 (33.3%)
Column totals	11 (36.7%)	19 (63.3%)	30 (100%)
Siblings			
A	7 (64%)	2 (12%)	9 (32.1%)
B	3 (27%)	4 (24%)	7 (25%)
C	1 (9%)	11 (64%)	12 (42.9%)
Column totals	11 (39.9%)	17 (60.7%)	28 (100%)

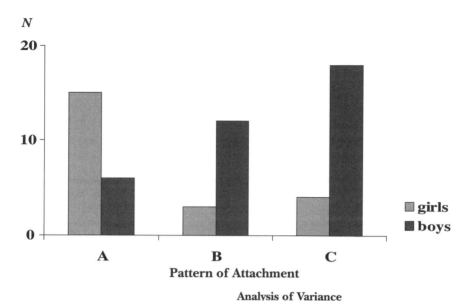

		Analysis of Variance			
		Sums of	**Mean**		
Source	*df*	**Squares**	**Squares**	*F* **Ratio**	*p*
Between groups	2	3.29	1.64	8.85	.005
Within groups	53	9.84	.20		

Figure 6.1. Sex and Attachment

In five pairs, the children were classified the same, and in only one pair, the girl was favored (C vs. A for the boy). These data suggest that, in our sample, girls tended to be rejected, often severely rejected, by their parents, and 86 percent were anxiously attached to their mothers. In addition, these families had fewer girls than should be born by chance, and they rarely had girls when there was not already a boy. This finding is corroborated by Hoodfar (1995) who reports that fathers want sons, whereas mothers want at least one daughter. Mothers also want sons, however, as an economical guarantee for their old age.

Distribution. The distributions of classifications in these Cairene children have several interesting features. First, among both boys and girls the proportion of extreme classifications (i.e., A3-4, C3-4, and AD) that are indicative of risk was quite high (24% of the sample). Not surprisingly, given the gender effect, the proportion of at-risk girls was more than double that of boys (71%). Second, the overall distribution of the patterns was typical for distrib-

Table 6.6. The Distribution of Subpatterns of Attachment in Egyptian 5- to 8-Year-Olds by Gender

Gender	N	AD	A3-4	A1-2	B1-2	B3	B4	C1-2	C3	C4	A/C
					Subpattern of Quality of Attachment						
Boys	33	0	1	5	5	1	6	15	1	2	0
Girls	22	3	5	7	3	0	0	2	0	2	0

utions using the PAA, that is, about a third in each pattern (with possibly a slight underrepresentation of Type B: 26%). In this sample, however, boys were more often (79%) classified as Types B and C, whereas girls were far more often (73%) classified as Type A. In fact, only 9% of girls were classified as Type B (see Table 6.6).

New Patterns and Differences in Presentation of Patterns. In this section, we present a more subjective view of young Egyptian children's play behavior. Rather than describing our observations in terms of variables, we offer our impressions of the play sequences themselves.

Compared to Western European and North American samples, even samples of at-risk children, these 5- to 8-year-old Egyptian children "played" very little. That is, they showed little exploratory behavior, excitement, or interest in storylike or sequential patterns of play. Instead, they picked up and put down objects, followed maternal requests regarding where to place objects, and frequently watched their mothers' play. The mothers' play, however, was of the same sort: the mothers made fences and put all the animals inside, lined blocks up, and so on. Mothers' speech to children was a constant flow of commands, "Put it there! Hurry! Put it there!" Although they occasionally referred to children by name, mothers more often used descriptors, such as "little father" and "sweetheart." In addition, quite a few of the descriptors were openly derogatory, such as "you donkey" or "you dog." Finally, the attachment strategies were less intensively used than in Western samples. However, whether this is an Egyptian characteristic or an artifact of our methodology cannot be determined.

Girls' play, in particular, was extremely contained; that is, most girls did not move about at all during their play, did not often reach for toys they wanted, held their hands still (sometimes almost frozen) in their laps for long periods, and vocalized infrequently. Although the most frequent (resting) expression on their faces was inscrutable neutrality, they gave evidence of being aware of being observed. For example, they rarely looked up and when they did, they looked coyly disarming if they were classified B, C, or A1-2, and empty if classified as A4 or AD. Similarly, they were constantly pulling their skirts down over their knees. They also checked frequently, but obliquely, for approval from their mothers; their mothers were rarely looking at them and almost never gave evidence of approval. In addition, girls often helped their brothers, giving them toys they wanted, and so on. Mostly, however, girls sat quietly at a distance and (often with faint shadows of desire or wistfulness on their faces) watched their mothers or mothers and brothers play. The girls appeared passively rejected but without surprise, resentment, or protest. When they did play, girls most frequently enacted cooking sequences and occasionally held or rocked a doll. In every case, they played alone and at a greater distance from the mother than the boys.

Boys, on the other hand, moved about the room freely, occasionally even disruptively. They handled the toys freely and grabbed them from each other, from their mothers, and from girls, rather than asking for them. Except when they grabbed from their brothers, the toys were yielded readily, and in no cases were there extended fights among male siblings. Many boys spoke freely, some almost continuously, and many initiated comments to their mothers. Several of the boys, however, seemed frail, sensitive, and uncertain of themselves. They leaned against their mothers and made ineffective attempts to reach things that were then provided by the mother or sister. In a few cases, one boy in a large sibling group would withdraw to sit in a corner looking pitiful. In these cases, a sibling (boy or girl) would invite the forlorn child back into the group, where he would again engage actively with the others. (No withdrawn girl was ever invited back, nor did the girls use nonverbal signals to draw attention to their withdrawal.)

DISCUSSION

Before discussing the meaning of our findings, the limitations of our data should be emphasized. Our critical variable is quality of attachment, and it is this variable that was assessed in a nonstandard manner. Our play setting was familiar to the child (unlike the usual laboratory setting of the Strange Situation). Furthermore, there was no separation of mother and child. In addition, usually other children and adults were present. Finally, our subjects were older than those for whom the Preschool Assessment of Attachment was developed. Each of these conditions reduces our certainty that the assigned attachment classifications are consistent with other uses of the PAA.

On the other hand, the validity of the Strange Situation depends on its relevance to behavior outside the Strange Situation (both before and after). Moreover, quality of attachment has been found to be a powerful variable specifically because it is developmentally relevant across the life span and across many aspects of relationship. Thus, it seems reasonable that a home play situation would elicit behavior indicative of underlying attachment strategies, although it might not do so as clearly as a stress-inducing laboratory procedure.

Our data are also limited by the investigators' lack of "insider" cultural knowledge. Neither of us is Egyptian, nor has either of us lived in Egypt (or any other Arab country.) The first author, however, has traveled several times to Egypt and assisted in the home visits for data collection (for about half of the sample). Our lack of an insider's view of the culture could have either of two effects. On the one hand, it could enable us to apply the patterns of attachment without the distortion that can come from seeing one's own culture as familiar, expected, and (normally) secure. On the other hand, we might, through cultural ignorance, misinterpret the dyadic meaning of behavior. Furthermore, even if we correctly understood the dyadic meaning, we might misunderstand its function in the whole of the culture. These issues require that we treat our data and our interpretations as exploratory.

Within our data, however, there is variability with regard to the extent of uncertainty. We cannot be certain that the patterns of attachment that we have assigned are accurate. We can be certain that boys were treated very differently than girls, that there were many fewer girls than boys, and that bouts of play for all children tended not to be long, reciprocal, or playful. It is around these relatively firm findings that we base most of our interpretations.

Validity. The analyses of the relation of our validating variables to quality of attachment suggest that our classifications are operating in expected ways. That is, maternal intelligence differentiated the attachment groups such that children classified as Type B had more intelligent mothers. However, parental education (which was reliably related to maternal intelligence) was not significantly related to attachment, although Type C children had parents with the least education. The moderate effects favoring Type B children most and Type C children least are consistent with previous findings, but their minimal effect suggests the specificity of our assessment of attachment to attachment issues.

Data drawn from the Running Horse Game Test provide a test of the validity of the assessment of quality of attachment. We have previously found support for the hypothesis that decentered maternal mediation and decentered educability show the same structure and interrelationship in Egypt as in Norway. In this study, we found support for the hypothesis that the quality of maternal mediation of learning experience is related to attachment patterns. The relation between the children's emotional vitality and secure attachment also supports the validity of the attachment data. These findings lend credibility to the assumption that the meaning of attachment in Egypt may be similar to that in Western cultures.

Gender, culture, danger, and strategies. Gender differences are an unusually important finding in our study. Although the entire range of patterns of attachment was found for both boys and girls, the distributions were noticeably different. Moreover, *all* the differences favored boys. Specifically, boys enjoyed the freedom of the balanced Type B strategy far more often than did girls; they seemed playful and at ease with both their mothers and, in the absence of their mothers, with their sisters. Further, more boys seemed comfortable taking a coercive role with regard to their mothers than did girls. Girls, on the other hand, were more often quiet, inhibited, and obedient. They seemed less free in their actions to the point of often not engaging in playful activities with their mothers and/or brothers. They were also far more inhibited in their display of affect. Because our sample is small, we cannot feel confident that these observations apply to Egyptian children or even to low income Egyptian children in general. But our observations do suggest the importance of exploring the role of gender in Egyptian children's development. Further, we cannot say whether these patterns will be maintained over time, especially as these children reach puberty with its emphasis on gender roles and functions and its maturational opportunity for change. Further research is needed to explore the validity of our findings for the school years and to assess their impact on gender patterns at later ages. Our data, however, suggest that this issue is worthy of exploration from an attachment perspective.

In our Egyptian sample, the underrepresentation of girls (33 girls and 59 boys in 30 families) is notable. The skew may be accidental. In a later expansion of the study, the distribution of the genders was less skewed, although boys were still predominant.

Cultures may reflect what social groups have learned over generations about the nature and how to prevent it or protect oneself from it. We think our data may, in fact, be interpreted in this manner. Boys' patterns of secure or coercive attachment that reflect their focus on other people and on negotiating relationships suggest the importance to boys of a social world in which there are friends and foes. The relatively large number of Type C boys suggests their preparation for the struggle for resources among men. On the other hand, girls focus on deflecting attention from themselves and complying with the demands of powerful people and their failure to turn to their mothers for help or comfort suggests the relative omnipresence of danger to girls.

Is there any light in all of this? Indeed. In every case, after the play sequence with the mother, the children were left to play alone while still being videotaped. In these episodes, the differences between boys and girls melted away. Sibling groups played like children everywhere with a free give-and-take among siblings of both genders. Gentle and protective behaviors were seen on the part of the boys, especially toward the younger siblings of both sexes. Moreover, all of the children seemed more at ease, as the tension tied to the mother and performance was removed. Thus, even at seven and eight years of age, boys seemed to have a context-based double standard for their sisters, one that provided occasions where their company could be enjoyed in equality and mutual satisfaction. Also, we found no gender differences on any of our cognitive variables, neither on the Raven nor on the child educability scores. This increases the potential for psychosocial change in a culture that is already undergoing rapid demographic, educational and technological change. These may gradually change the social situation for women.

CHAPTER SEVEN

Maternal Sensitivity

ANGELIKA HARTL CLAUSSEN AND
PATRICIA MCKINSEY CRITTENDEN

Sensitivity to children's signals, an important construct in attachment theory, is presumed to be the central predictor of pattern of attachment (Ainsworth, 1973, 1978; Bowlby, 1980). Although this concept is supported by research, measures of sensitivity have not been as powerful predictors of attachment as expected (Goldsmith & Alansky, 1987). In their recent meta-analysis, De Wolff and van IJzendoorn found an effect size of only $r = .24$ for the association between sensitivity and infant pattern of attachment (De Wolff & van IJzendoorn, 1997). This finding may reflect limitations in both theory and the measures that operationalize theory. Specifically, the exact definition of sensitivity is not clear: what exactly are good attachment figures sensitive to, and, methodologically, how does one know if they are sensitive?

THEORETICAL CONSIDERATIONS

Sensitivity as a Multistep Communicative Process

All communicative efforts depend on two components: interpreting signals and implementing suitable responses. Conceptually, "sensitivity" refers primarily to the parent's ability to decode the child's signals. However, when studying sensitivity, the ability to read signals appropriately is usually deduced from the response of the parent rather than investigated directly (De Wolff & van IJzendoorn, 1997). Therefore, the concept of sensitivity often also implies the second component of communication: the ability to provide an appropriate response. In other words, responsiveness frequently is not differentiated from sensitivity (De Wolff & van IJzendoorn, 1997). For example, in Ainsworth's original rating scale, "sensitivity" incorporated the ability both to perceive and to interpret the infant's signals accurately as well as the ability to respond to these signals appropriately and promptly (Ainsworth, Bell, & Stayton, 1974). Conceptually, this is problematic because these are different steps in the processing of information. (See Crittenden, 1993a for a discussion of information processing of child signals as a multistep process.) Consequently, sensitivity and responsivity are not necessarily linked. Some parents may read the child's signals and yet not respond appropriately. For example, a parent may interpret a signal accurately but decide a response is not needed, or a parent may identify the need for a response but not know what response to offer. On the other hand, parents may have selected an appropriate response but be prevented from implementing it – by other children, by a phone call, and so on. At a minimum, identifying which components of the process of interpersonal communication are being included in the construct of "sensitivity" would help to clarify both data and the results of studies.

Sensitivity as an Intrapersonal versus a Dyadic Construct

Sensitivity is often treated as a characteristic of the parent, that is, as an intrapersonal variable. However, because sensitive parents are those who accurately read their child's sometimes unique signals (Seifer & Schiller, 1995), sensitivity is better described as a dyadic construct. Focusing on the dyadic nature of sensitivity permits temperament and unique characteristics of both children and caregivers (Belsky & Isabella, 1988), as well as aspects of the context, to be acknowledged as influences. It also makes clear that parents' sensitivity to one child may not be the same as their sensitivity to another.

Parental sensitivity is also influenced by the child's skill in signaling to the parent (van den Boom, 1997). Parents have an easier task with a child who communicates desires clearly than with a child who sends mixed or subtle signals. Some researchers, therefore, have focused more on the concept of synchrony, which explicitly involves the characteristics of the dyad rather than the parent alone (e.g., Isabella, Belsky, & von Eye, 1989). Fava Vizziello et al. (this volume) used a measure of dyadic synchrony in their study of parent–child interaction in order to capture the contribution of both parent and child to the interaction.

Sensitivity as a Multicriterion Construct

Research on parental sensitivity has been criticized because it often emphasizes the warm and supportive aspects of parenting rather than the skill of reading and responding to children's signals (Mangelsdorf, Gunnar, Kestenbaum, Lang, & Andreas, 1990; Seifer & Schiller, 1995). Seifer and Schiller point out that sensitivity is not equivalent to warmth and affection because it also involves the technical aspect of skillfully reading the child's sometimes unique signals. Whether or not one agrees, the critical point is that few investigators are explicit in identifying the criterion definition of sensitivity embedded in their use of the construct. Without an explicit statement, observers are left to apply their own criteria, and these criteria may differ from one person to another, one study to another, and even one culture to another. For example, sensitivity can be defined affectively as a sensitively warm response. On the other hand, synchronous temporal contingencies can be deemed the defining feature of sensitivity. Alternatively, the intellectually stimulating qualities of parental behavior might be considered central to parental sensitivity. Still other investigators might be most interested in the adaptiveness of parental responses. Because any of these and other criteria could define sensitivity, it is essential that investigators who use the construct of sensitivity be explicit about the meaning intended.

From the perspective of attachment, sensitivity may best be defined as the ability to determine when protection and comfort are needed. In line with this thinking, Ainsworth's original studies emphasized sensitivity to attachment behavior, assessed over many months, naturalistically, in the child's home. However, as in the studies in this volume, parental sensitivity is more often assessed in brief and nonthreatening circumstances, such as parent–child play or teaching situations where protection is a minor issue. These contexts may require a different definition of sensitivity and another set of parental responses. When applied to nonthreatening situations, instruments that focus on sensitivity to attachment needs may not be directed toward appropriate behavior, whereas assessments directed toward other aspects of parental sensitivity may not capture those that are most relevant to pattern of attachment.

Sensitivity as a Role-Defined Construct

This suggests the importance of noting explicitly the many roles parents assume in relation to their children. Within the dyadic relationship, children's behavior may signal many different things, and, in response to these signals, parents function in different roles, for instance, as protector, teacher, and playmate. For example, Grossmann and Grossmann (chapter 2 in this volume) assert that parental sensitivity can help children become developmentally advanced. Specifically, German culture is described as emphasizing the educational aspect of the parental role. In keeping with the cultural goal of advancing the child's cognitive and academic advancement, German parents may display more sensitivity to children's exploratory signals than will parents in cultures where teaching is not emphasized. Because global definitions of sensitivity do not differentiate these roles, they may not adequately capture the numerous components that constitute good parenting (Ahnert, Meischner, & Schmidt, chapter 4 in this volume; Seifer & Schiller, 1995).

Although each of these roles is important for the child's development as a full member of society, the central evolutionary function of caregiver sensitivity, as related to attachment, is to promote children's need for safety (Bowlby, 1982). There is considerable research that shows an association between the children's pattern of attachment and aspects of parent–child interaction in other types of interactions (e.g., Lippe & Crittenden, chapter 6 in this volume; Grossmann & Grossmann, chapter 2 in this volume). Nevertheless, it is not known to what extent parental sensitivity towards attachment behavior is correlated with sensitivity in other roles (Cicchetti, Cummings, Greenberg, & Marvin, 1990). Grossmann and Grossmann found that in German mothers, sensitivity as an attachment figure was not directly predictive of the ability to foster children's development as teacher or play-partner (see chapter 2).

The studies in this volume confirm that parental sensitivity is key to understanding the parent–child relationship. Nevertheless, it often is more related to other aspects of child development than to infants' pattern of attachment. Bohlin and Hagekull found their measure of parental sensitivity to be more relevant to child behavior problems than to classifications of infant attachment. Fava Vizziello, Ferrero, and Musicco found that interactive synchrony was related to parental factors and child functioning, but not to their assessment of pattern of attachment. Thus, parental sensitivity may vary across roles, and, depending on the definition of sensitivity used, it will be associated with different aspects of child functioning. These aspects will not always emphasize the protective role of attachment figures.

Sensitivity to the Child versus the Fit of the Child to the Context

Adult caregivers need to be sensitive both to the child and to the context to which the child must adapt; that is, they mediate the nature of the context and the unique features of the child. Attachment research has focused primarily on immediate sensitivity to children's signals. However, from a social ecological perspective, optimally sensitive parenting functions to promote children's overall adaptation rather than only their comfort or happiness at specific moments in time. For example, parents who wish to teach a toddler self-soothing skills at bedtime may choose to minimize their response to the child's distress signal. In the immediate context, the child's desire is to be comforted; therefore, such parents may be described as acting insensitively. In the long term, however, the child's needs for self-regulation and independence may be fostered more effectively when parents create opportunities for the development of self-soothing skills. Put another way, attachment figures function in the child's zone of proximal development (Vygotsky, 1987); when this zone changes, sensitive parents modify their behavior (Crittenden, 1995). Furthermore, protection may even at times require behavior that, in the immediate context, is clearly insensitive to the child's signals. For example, the parent who quickly and roughly pulls a child back from danger is sensitive to the child's need for protection while, nevertheless, behaving in a manner that is intrusive and uncomfortable to the children. Again, it is necessary to be explicit about the manner in which sensitivity is being evaluated.

Sensitivity to Needs versus Desires

The example of crying at bedtime illustrates another issue: distinguishing between children's needs and desires. Children display attachment behavior when they feel they are in danger. However, the children's perception of danger may not be accurate. In fact, children often feel anxious when there is little danger, and they may feel secure when danger is imminent. Consequently, children may desire protection in situations when they do not need it or need protection when they do not desire it. In situations where children inaccurately perceive danger, parents have the task of both responding to the child's desire for comfort to alleviate feelings of anxiety and modulating the child's interpretation of the level of threat. A potential conflict is the fact that parents who respond with comfort may at the same time reinforce the child's feeling that protection was necessary. For example, a child who is left by a parent in an unfamiliar environment (e.g., Strange Situation, preschool) may interpret the situation as potentially dangerous and may signal for protection. If the parent stays with the child, he or she may reinforce the child's association of separation from the parent with danger. If parents signal safety by verbally reassuring the child and then leaving, they may not be responsive to their children's immediate desire for protection but, in the long term, may teach the children, through their own modeled response, to interpret the unfamiliar place as a safe environment. A crucial issue becomes the parent's ability to determine whether the situation is dangerous or safe. If there is danger, the parent must decide whether it is best to protect the child or to promote the child's ability to protect him- or herself. If it is safe, the parent must determine whether the child needs information about the safety of the situation or needs comfort. In either case, the parent must then determine the best means of providing the information (or helping the child to discover it) or providing comfort (or helping the child to learn self-comforting skills).

Defining Sensitivity

Ultimately, the question of how to define sensitivity comes down to the function of sensitivity. From an evolutionary perspective, promoting the child's survival is the central function of parenting (Stern, 1995). In research, however, children's happiness is often used as an indicator of parental sensitivity, as in the study by Bohlin and Hagekull. Similarly, Fava Vizziello et al. emphasize mutual pleasure as an indicator of positive interactions. The measure developed by Crittenden defined sensitivity as any behavior that increased a child's comfort or decreased discomfort (1988b, 1998a). However, particularly in the transition to toddlerhood, discipline and limit setting to protect children become a major developmental issue that is often at odds with children's immediate happiness. Neither is closeness a universal indicator of parental sensitivity. Ahnert et al. (chapter 4, this volume) state that, in socialist Russian and East German society, parents were encouraged to prepare children for transition into society to the extent that closeness between mothers and infants even had a negative connotation. The questions for attachment theory are: (1) What is the effect of this cultural value (presuming that it is reflected in less close behavior with infants) on infants' pattern of attachment and (2) presuming that it does affect pattern of attachment, what is the effect on children's safety in their developmental context?

As Lippe and Crittenden point out, even children's safety is affected by the cultural characteristics of their environment. For example, in Egyptian culture, different conditions for survival may affect girls as compared to boys. Because sensitive parenting must shape the child's behavior in such a way that adaptive functioning in the larger society is promoted, sensitive behavior toward Egyptian girls is probably different than that toward Egyptian boys. Caregiver sensitivity, in other words, should reflect sensitivity both to children's signals regarding protection and comfort and to the context in which the signals are given.

Operationalization of Theory

Because sensitivity must be deduced from observed behavior, its measurement becomes a major issue. In attachment research, a large body of evidence for patterns of attachment has been gathered using the same method, that is, Ainsworth's Strange Situation (Ainsworth, Blehar, Waters, & Wall, 1978). This makes it possible to compare findings from different studies. Studies of maternal sensitivity, on the other hand, use a variety of instruments that differ in many ways. For example, each study in this volume that assesses parental sensitivity uses a different method. Furthermore, because the coders are members of the observed culture, culture-specific standards and expectations may be applied uniformly by all the coders but in ways that would not be used by coders from outside the culture. In such cases, the investigators could accurately report high intercoder reliability without identifying sensitivity as observers from outside the culture would see it. Put another way, the theory, constructs, and guidelines underlying the operationalization of sensitivity are usually not stated explicitly. When left implicit, they promote misunderstanding.

Underlying Dimensions. Many studies use or adapt Ainsworth's scale of maternal sensitivity, which consists of a unidimensional, linear scale of sensitivity. This approach both defines sensitivity as a global construct rather than as a set of specific parental characteristics or skills and presumes that the effects of different forms of insensitivity are similar.

There are, however, at least two ways in which parents can be insensitive to children's signals: specifically, parents can be over- and underresponsive. This suggests the need to consider multiple negative endpoints of a sensitivity scale. For example, the CARE-Index (Crittenden, 1998a) allows sensitive parenting to be contrasted to both controlling-intrusive and unresponsive parenting.

Explicit Coder Guidelines. Tied to the identification of criteria for defining sensitivity is the specification of guidelines for meeting these criteria. Without clear behavioral guidelines, determination regarding the quality of a response relies entirely on the judgment of observers. Consequently, parents are considered sensitive when they respond to the child in a way that the observer finds appropriate. Without an explicit definition of sensitivity and guidelines for meeting the definition, the usual difficulties in establishing reliable observations are compounded by the possibility of observer variation in definition and application of the definition. On the other hand, explicit morphological definition of "sensitive behaviors" would interfere with applying functional definitions to the wide variety of human interpersonal organizations that could serve a single function.

Developmental Issues. Another often overlooked issue is the effect of maturation on the meaning of parental behavior. Sensitivity can be treated as behavior-specific, meaning that sensitive parenting behavior is similar in appearance across child developmental stages, or as age-specific, meaning that sensitive parenting behavior may take quite different forms depending on the child's developmental needs. As pointed out by Lippe and Crittenden, cultural adaptation becomes increasingly important after infancy.

Indeed, if one considers attachment figures to operate in children's zone of proximal development, parents must constantly adjust their behavior to fit their children's increasing ability to protect themselves from familiar dangers and provide guidance as children are exposed to new dangers. Consequently, parents who are sensitive to the needs of a young infant are not necessarily equally able to respond sensitively to the needs of a preschool-aged child and vice versa (Vereijken, Riksen-Walraven, & Kondo-Ikemura, 1997). Bohlin and Hagekull's research points to the issue that the role and effects of parental sensitivity may change during the course of child development. They found that maternal sensitivity showed only limited stability over time, but that measures of early and later sensitivity independently predicted children's behavior problems. Sensitivity in each of the developmental contexts yielded both independent and meaningful information regarding aspects of the parent–child relationship (Bohlin & Hagekull, chapter 5 in this volume; Vereijken, Riksen-Walraven, & Kondo-Ikemura, 1997).

Conclusions

Sensitivity is an important component of the communicative process between parent and child. To understand it, particular attention must be paid to the immediate and long-term contexts in which the interaction is taking place. As discussed in the previous chapters, parental roles vary in terms of their function in different cultures and at different points in time (Grossmann & Grossmann, chapter 2; Bohlin & Hagekull, chapter 5). Thus, it appears that sensitivity must be defined explicitly within the social and cultural context (Ahnert, Meischner, & Schmidt, chapter 4; Lippe & Crittenden, chapter 6; LeVine, 1977) as well as with children's immediate needs and the functional role of their parents in mind. This implies careful consideration of the directions investigators give to parents when interaction is being observed for research. The problem that arises from including context in defining sensitivity is that if sensitivity is defined in culture-specific ways that are not stated explicitly, then we cannot compare studies across cultures. If it is not defined contextually, some cultures will look very insensitive, even when their children are well adapted and made safer (in that context) by the parents' "insensitive" behavior.

It is important to consider that in her original studies, Ainsworth was discussing sensitivity as it pertained to mothers' response to children's attachment behavior. The attachment component of the parent–child relationship has as its goal protection of the child from danger. Because of its meaning for survival, it is a universal and necessary aspect of sensitivity and applicable to all humans. Nevertheless, danger varies from one context to another (see chapter 13) and from one development period to another (see chapter 18). This implies that appropriately protective behavior may also vary.

Given these issues, it is not clear that an absolute consensus on the meaning of sensitivity can ever be reached. However, such a consensus may not be necessary. Rather, an open discussion of the issues, combined with explicit statements regarding the meaning of constructs and the process of operationalizing these constructs in each study, can further our understanding, particularly when it is nonjudgmental.

PART TWO

CONTEXT

CHAPTER EIGHT

Attachment in Finnish Twins

IRMA MOILANEN, ANNE KUNELIUS,

TIINA TIRKKONEN, AND

PATRICIA McKINSEY CRITTENDEN

INTRODUCTION

This study focuses on attachment in Finnish twins, particularly the possibility that rates of secure attachment may be affected by twin status, biophysiological risk, and seasonal depression. Because these phenomena have particular relevance to circumstances in Finland, we begin with a discussion of twinning, then turn to a discussion of Finnish culture, and conclude with our hypotheses regarding attachment in Finnish twins.

The Context of Twins

In Finland, as in other developed countries, the proportion of twins among newborn babies is increasing because of the increasing age of mothers and the use of hormonal therapies. In addition, various treatments of infertility increase the probability of multiple pregnancies. Thus, twins' status in families is also changing: they were more often the last-born children of elderly, multiparous mothers, and nowadays they are more often first-born children of couples who previously suffered from infertility.

Special risks are involved in a twin pregnancy and delivery. About one-third of all twins are born prematurely, with about one-third of first-born and 40% of second-born twins receiving treatment in the neonatal ward. The risk of neurological handicap is fivefold in twins and eighteenfold in triplets as compared to singletons. However, the great majority of those who are free of disabilities have equal or only slightly delayed locomotor development (Bryan, 1992; Moilanen, 1979, 1987).

Twins' verbal development is known to be slightly delayed, which has been attributed to the risk situation of pregnancy as well as to the fact that twins who have to share the mother with the other twin have reduced dyadic verbal communication with adults. Another explanation might be the intertwin relationship, which does not necessarily need words and which can lead to construction of a private language. In addition to quantitative differences between twins' and singletons' early verbal communication, some qualitative differences have been found: Because mothers generally address both children at once, they may offer their twins a less "conversationally responsive" linguistic environment. This three-way verbal communication involves one speaker and two potential listeners. Thus, twins acquire language under more complex conditions than singletons (Robin & Casati, 1994).

Differences are also found in twins' social-emotional development, especially the infant–mother relationship. The differences in parenting twins begin during pregnancy. On the one hand, there is a feeling of privilege and, on the other hand, an awareness of the special risks involved in a twin pregnancy and delivery. During the first months of the infants' life, the burden of material tasks in baby care leave little time for starting relationships based on pleasure and play. The impossibility of responding simultaneously to the needs of two babies and the difficulty of forming relationships on an individual basis foster early concerns of egalitarianism (Robin, Josse, & Tourrette, 1988). Maternal attachment to one twin may differ from that to the other one, with the future of the "left-alone" twin containing risk of developmental problems, including anxious attachment (Minde, Corter, Goldberg, & Jeffers, 1990; Yokoyama, Shimizu, & Hayakawa, 1995). On the other hand, in one small study (Szajnberg, Skrinjaric, & Moore, 1989) parental preference did not significantly affect infants' quality of attachment, or mothers' attunement.

According to Robin, Kheroua, and Casati (1992), the mothers' attitudes can range from "early twinness," where the two babies are treated as though they were a single unit, to attempts to create two dyadic relationships. More highly educated mothers are more differentiating in bringing up their twins. Western countries have emphasized individuality for years, and emphasizing individual treatment of twins is recommended in handbooks for parents of twins (Bryan, 1992).

Because of the amount of work involved in raising two infants and because of the parents' desire to treat their twins individually, many families come to the solution of "sharing twins": a mother's twin and a father's twin may develop. This solution has been found to promote individual development of the twins and to relieve mutual rivalry between them, for now each of them has his or her own parent as an object of identification and attachment (Moilanen, 1987). Moreover, the recent egalitarian Scandinavian culture has increased the fathers' opportunity to be involved in taking care of their children.

In Conclusion. To be born as a twin is a special situation, including perinatal risks and risks for development. Parents' communication with twins is more often three-way communication, with fewer opportunities for dyadic communication with an adult. This sometimes results in parental sharing of the care of twins. Twins are, therefore, a good population for infant psychiatric research of certain special situations:

1. *Perinatal risks.* Are the infants who have experienced perinatal complications differently attached because of possible brain damage, because of distance from the mother during treatment in the neonatal ward, or because of parental concern?
2. *Amount of parental attention.* Twins share parental attention with a co-twin. Does this lead to lower percentages of securely attached twins, when compared to singletons?
3. *Parental favoritism between twins.* Are "mothers' twins" differently attached as compared to "fathers' twins" or those who are primarily treated by the mother and the father equally? Might an anxious attachment to one parent be compensated by a more secure attachment to the other parent?

Finnish Culture

Historical View on National Culture, Parental Roles, and Child Care. Finland was under the rule of the Kingdom of Sweden for centuries, but in 1809 after the Finnish War it became part of the Russian Empire. Independence was achieved in 1917. Thus, Finland has been on the interface between a Swedish empire that reached its greatest extent during the seventeenth century and a Russian one that was gradually acquiring more power and influence over part of northeastern Europe. As a concept, however, Finland began an independent existence while still under Swedish rule, and even more so after incorporation into Russia as a relatively autonomous grand duchy in 1809. One cause for this special situation might be the Finnish language. It may also have been attributable to a perception that Finns were neither Swedes nor Russians and did not want to be either. Thus, Finland's declaration of independence on December 6, 1917, was relatively unproblematic. Finland was a geographical territory and had a dominant language, a largely similar culture, a predominant religion (Protestant), and the long-standing perception that its people were neither Swedish nor Russian. As a result, during the Second World War, Finland was able to avoid foreign occupation and thwarted both Hitler and Stalin.

Yet the Second World War was a difficult period for Finland. Refugees from the easternmost parts of Finland, Karelien, had to be evacuated to other parts of the country, and, after the loss of those areas to the USSR, these people, comprising about 10% of the whole population, had to be integrated into other parts of Finland. Large areas were destroyed during the war. In addition, war debts to the USSR forced rapid industrialization and urbanization. Moreover, many mothers had to work outside the home. A spirit of solidarity was typical, and high-quality nursery schools were started for preschool children in order to give mothers the opportunity to work. Women's position became rather equal to men's, even if it had been nearly so before: Finnish women were second in the world to get the right to vote and the first to obtain the right to be members of the Parliament (1906). Finnish women's opportunity for education and employment has changed society and even men's position in families: fathers often take considerable responsibility for care of their children.

Several years of development and growth have made it possible to achieve high social security, including free primary health care services, low-price hospital care, and low-price, high-level kindergartens, guaranteed by a law to be available for all children under school age. Maternity leave with almost full economic compensation lasts altogether 11 months, 1 before and 10 after the expected birth of the baby (in multiple pregnancies, 2 months more), after which the mother has the right to be at home up until the child reaches 3 years of age without losing her job. A considerable part of the maternity leave payment can alternatively be paid to the father if he is the parent who gives care for the child at home. Parents who bring up their children at home receive a moderate monthly sum, depending on the mother's previous salary, for up to three years. In addition, monthly economic support is given for every child from birth to 18 years.

However, the international economic depression that followed the 1987 stock market crash affected Finland in the 1990s, and unemployment grew rapidly to the current 17%. The government provides unemployment benefits. This, along with a lowered income tax, has made it difficult for the government to maintain the social security program, which, among the other Scandinavian countries, is among the highest paying in the world. In 1993, social security expenditure in Finland made up 36.3% of the country's gross domestic product; this percentage was the second highest in Europe (after Sweden with 40.3%). The previous spirit of solidarity is decreasing, and employed adults often regard their taxes as too high.

The Present. The population of Finland is 5.1 million, giving an average density of only 17 per square kilometer and an annual growth rate of 0.4. The demographic pyramid resembles that of most other industrial countries, with the middle-aged groups predominating. Average household size is 2.4 persons. Fifty-five percent of the population live in single-family homes and 42% in apartments. Three quarters are urban dwellers, with almost one million living in Helsinki area. Half of the population has completed post-primary education, and 11% has a university degree or its equivalent. Seventy percent of women are employed outside the home.

Land and Climate. Ten percent of Finland is water, in the form of 188,000 lakes. Eight percent of the land is under cultivation, and forests cover 69% of the country. The arctic circle crosses Finland about 70 miles north from Oulu, the city from which the material of the present study has been collected. Thus, during the darkest time of the year, in December, the sun is visible only 3 $1/2$ hours per day, while during the lightest months, May, June, and July, no dark period is seen. In June a slight dimness lasts one and a half hours, and it is possible to read a book at night without extra light. The mean temperature ranges from –11° Celsius in January to +16° Celsius in July.

Among adults, Seasonal Affective Disorder (SAD) has been described as depression during winters; it is most probably caused by desynchronization between the solar clock and the human biologic clock during seasons of short photoperiods (Chung & Daghestani, 1989). The supplemental bright light of phototherapy resynchronizes disturbed rhythms, and many Finns are helped by this treatment (Nagayama et al., 1991; Partonen, 1994). The action of melatonin and serotonin and the photochemical effect of light have been intensively studied among adults (Hawley & Wolfe, 1994) but not yet among children. In addition to light, however, many everyday practical factors might have impact, especially among families with infants. During the dark winter, there are other stressful factors: clothing infants is more troublesome, incidence of respiratory infections is higher, and parents work more and are more tired than in summer, when they often have summer holidays.

In Conclusion. The Finnish culture is rather uniform, and its special features have helped this nation to achieve rather high autonomy under foreign rule and then independence; Finland has been a sovereign parliamentary republic since 1917. The Finns have endured hard days, which have been overcome with the spirit of solidarity, and a high-level social security program has been available for all citizens. During the last few years, unemployment has become prevalent. Women's position is one of the best in the world, and along with maternal employment, the fathers have become more involved in the primary caretaking of children. The environment also has special features of a long, dark winter and a short, very light summer.

These circumstances make it possible to study several aspects of the children's attachment and development:

1. *Social-cultural values*
   a. A safe society with rather equal social status of mothers and fathers: Are attachment patterns different in those infants who are reported to be cared mainly by mothers, when compared with those cared mainly by fathers or by both parents equally?
   b. Attitudes toward childrearing which support mother–infant separations due to maternal employment. Does separation enhance the development of independence?

2. *Effect of darkness or light.* Is infants' attachment different when assessed during the dark season? Do infants who have experienced more light months during their lifetime more often demonstrate secure attachment?

HYPOTHESES

1. Because of Finland's Scandinavian culture and policy of maternal employment, we expected normative Finnish children to display a distributional bias toward Type A, relative to other cultures. On the other hand, the special needs of twins might elicit the compensatory attention of conscientious Finnish parents. This would result in fewer Type A twins than singletons.
2. Because of egalitarian values of Finnish culture, we expected no gender differences.
3. "Overt" risk factors are predicted to increase parental attention to infants such that the greater the risk, the greater the probability of security (where Type C was viewed as intermediate between A and B). Risk factors included twin status, premature birth, and hospital treatment.
4. Darkness was not treated as an "overt" risk variable because there is no evidence that parents saw it as such. Therefore, darkness was expected to adversely affect security of attachment in both twins and singletons.

METHOD

Subjects

The present analysis of twins' development and attachment is part of a longitudinal twin study that was begun during pregnancy and is intended to continue at least to the beginning of school. The present study consists of twin pairs and singletons born in the University Central Hospital of Oulu and living in Oulu or nearby. All children were first born in their families. During delivery, the ages of the mothers of twins ranged from 22 to 37 years (mean 29.9), and mothers of singletons from 22 to 35 years (27.8). One of the twin pairs was living with their divorced mother; all the other twins and all the singletons were in original full families with both their biological parents.

Procedure

The subjects were identified by the Obstetric Department of the Central University Hospital of Oulu; 30 consecutive twin deliveries were selected, and the mothers were primiparae and living in Oulu district. For the controls, 30 consecutive first-born singletons were selected. Thus, altogether the original sample consisted of 60 families and 90 toddlers.

Hospital records were gathered concerning pregnancy and delivery and possible neonatal treatment. At 18 months of age, corrected by the degree of prematurity, a questionnaire was sent to both parents about their children's health, development, and temperament, asking about their own education and employment, as well as some facts of family life – for example, family pattern, the primary caretaker of the child, and whether the parents have shared caretaking responsibility for their twins.

At the same time, the parents and their children were invited to participate in the Strange Situation at the Child Psychiatric Outpatient Clinic of Oulu University Central Hospital. Altogether 85 toddlers came (58 twins and 27 singletons). The Strange Situation was performed with each child with each parent (except one pair with one twin with mother and the other with father) in order to analyze attachment to each. Thus, each child participated in two Strange Situations. Because many of the families of twins had to travel long distances to the laboratory, it was often necessary to complete all four Strange Situations on one day. Although this arrangement was not ideal, it gave us an opportunity to explore the possible effect of retesting. We expected this to lead to quantitative changes in reactions, not qualitative ones.

The order of parents was varied. For the present analysis, only the Strange Situations with the mother as the first studied parent are presented: 47 twins (20 twin pairs, 6 members of twin pairs such that the other's Strange Situation was first performed with father, and the one twin whose Strange Situation was performed with mother only and the co-twin's Strange Situation with father only) and 18 singletons. Because they were not able to separate from the co-twin, 3 twin pairs of these 20 were assessed at the same time, together with the mother.

Assessment of Attachment

The Preschool Assessment of Attachment (Crittenden, 1992) uses the modification of the Ainsworth infant classificatory procedure to fit the more complex mental and interpersonal functioning of preoperational children. The classificatory system differs from the infancy system in that (1) the ambivalent infant pattern is viewed as becoming organized as a coercive strategy and (2) those Type A (avoidant) infants who are threatened by parental hostility or unresponsiveness are viewed as developing new compulsive subpatterns – that is, compulsive caregiving (A3) and compulsive compliance (A4). The coercive strategy is particularly suited to inconsistent or unpredictably available parents. With these changes, the distribution of the A B C patterns is expected to change as compared to infancy. In American and German samples, this has led to fewer secure Type B children (around one-third of normative samples), together with a substantial increase in Type C children (about 40 to 50%), especially among young preschoolers (21–24 months) versus older (4–5 years) preschoolers. Some children cannot be fitted into any of these main categories A, B, or C, and they are coded as outside the normal range (i.e., "insecure other").

Finnish attachment data are not yet available for any age period. The fact that our children are 18 months of age presents special problems because they clearly show more complex organizations than 12-month-old infants. Nevertheless, many do not show the full preschool organization. This is especially true for emerging Type C (coercive) children. Our sample, therefore, is best viewed as being in transition from infancy to the preschool years.

Attachment was scored by the third author, who was blind to twin status, according to the PAA method developed by Crittenden (1992). T. Tirkkonen had 91% interrater reliability on the standardized reliability test and 94% with Crittenden on 16 tapes randomly selected from this data set.

RESULTS

Attachment in Twins versus Singletons and in Boys versus Girls

Twins seemed to be more often Type B, but most probably because of the small samples, there was no significant difference between twins and singletons in the distribution among the patterns of attachment (Tables 8.1 and 8.2). Forty-two percent were classified as Type A (defended), 37% as B, and 18% as C. Two of the 65 children were outside the normal range. Comparing first-born and second-born twins, a nonsignificant trend was found of first-born being more often Type A and second-born Type B (44%, 32%, 20%, and 4% of first-born ones were classified as A, B, C and outside the normal range, while the corresponding figures for second-born ones were 32%, 54%, 14% and 0%, respectively, nonsignificant). The attachment in boys and girls also

Table 8.1. Subclassifications of Attachment Type in Finnish Twins and Singletons

	Subclassifications										Total
	A4	A3	A1-2	B1-2	B3	B4	C1-2	C3	C4	Insecure Other	
Twins	0	0	18	14	2	4	7	0	1	1 (D,A/C)	47
Singletons	1	1	7	4	0	0	2	0	2	1 (D,A/C)	18
Total	1	1	25	18	2	4	9	0	3	2	65

Table 8.2. Quality of Attachment in Finnish Twins and Singletons, in Boys and Girls

Twin Status	Category of Attachment				Total
	A	**B**	**C**	**IO**	
Twins	18 (38%)	20 (43%)	8 (17%)	1 (2%)	47 (100%)
Singletons	9 (50%)	4 (22%)	4 (22%)	1 (6%)	18 (100%)
Gender					
Twins					
Boys	9 (47%)	6 (32%)	4 (21%)	–	19 (100%)
Girls	9 (32%)	14 (50%)	4 (14%)	1 (4%)	28 (100%)
Singletons					
Boys	5 (50%)	3 (30%)	2 (20%)	–	10 (100%)
Girls	4 (50%)	1 (12%)	2 (25%)	1 (12%)	8 (100%)

IO = insecure other.

seemed to be quite similar; a slightly higher proportion of boys was classified as Type A and of girls as Type B, but the numbers are small and not statistically significant (see Table 8.2).

Effects of Risk Factors: Prematurity, Perinatal Morbidity, and Darkness

Prematurity. The infants' attachment was analyzed in relation to prematurity by dividing the study group into two subgroups: preterm (36 or fewer weeks of gestation) and full-term (37 or more weeks of gestation). Preterm twins were slightly more often of Type B and full-term twins of Type A in quality of attachment (Table 8.3). Because of the high-level maternity care, most singletons were full term in spite of our efforts to get as many preterm singletons as preterm twins. A combined analysis with both twins and singletons showed that the prematurely born ones were more often Type B and the full-term ones Type A.

Thirty-six percent of twins (17/47) and 17% (3/18) of singletons had been treated in a hospital. Those who had experienced hospital treatment seemed to be more often classified as Type B when compared to those without such problems, as 59% of the hospital treated twins and one-third of hospitalized singletons, but only 29% of the healthy ones were securely attached (see Table 8.4).

Darkness. The effect of darkness was analyzed in two different ways: (1) looking at the date of performing the Strange Situation and (2) counting the total number of dark or light months the particular child had lived; in extreme cases, some have lived two dark winters and one summer, and the others, two light summers and one winter. In these evaluations, the five months from

Table 8.3.   Attachment in Preterm and Full-term Children

	Category of Attachment						
	A	**B**	**C**	**IO**	**Total**	*df*	*p*
Twins							
Preterm	5 (24%)	10 (48%)	5 (24%)	1 (5%)	21 (100%)		
Fullterm	13 (50%)	10 (39%)	3 (11%)	–	26 (100%)		
						3	*ns*
Singletons							
Preterm	1 (33%)	–	1 (33%)	1 (33%)	3 (100%)		
Full term	8 (53%)	4 (27%)	3 (20%)	–	15 (100%)		
						3	*ns*
All							
Preterm	6 (25%)	10 (42%)	6 (25%)	2 (8%)	24 (100%)		
Fullterm	21 (51%)	14 (34%)	6 (15%)	–	41 (100%)		
						3	0.063

Fisher's exact test.

IO = insecure other; ns = not significant.

Table 8.4.   Attachment and Perinatal Hospital Treatment

	Category of Attachment						
	A	**B**	**C**	**IO**	**Total**	*df*	*p*
Twins							
Healthy	12 (40%)	10 (34%)	7 (23%)	1 (3%)	30 (100%)		
Hospital							
treatment	6 (35%)	10 (59%)	1 (6%)	–	17 (100%)		
						3	*ns*
Singletons							
Healthy	8 (53%)	3 (20%)	4 (27%)	–	15 (100%)		
Hospital							
treatment	1 (33%)	1 (33%)	–	1 (33%)	3 (100%)		
						3	*ns*
All							
Healthy	20 (44%)	13 (29%)	11 (25%)	1 (2%)	45 (100%)		
Hospital							
treatment	7 (35%)	11 (55%)	1 (5%)	20 (100%)			
						3	0.084

Fisher's Exact Test.

IO = insecure other; ns = not significant.

September to January were seen as dark months and the five months from April to August as light months. Lightness begins early in spring because of snow, and darkness in turn begins early in fall because of the dark ground.

Assessment of attachment during the dark winter months or intermediate months of the year seemed to result most often in Type A attachment, while assessment during the light months resulted slightly more often in the Type B category (see Table 8.5).

Comparisons between those having experienced mostly dark months and those the mostly light months revealed a slight, nonsignificant association of light months and Type A attachment (Table 8.6). The possible interaction of both having lived more light months and having the assessment performed during light time versus the opposite, lifetime more dark months and assessment during dark season, also did not reveal statistically significant differences.

Parental Preference

The questionnaire asked: *"Which parent is the primary caretaker of the child?"* Among singletons, the mother was reported to be the primary caretaker in

Table 8.5. **Effect of Darkness on Attachment I: Date of Performing SS**

	Category of Attachment						
	A	B	C	IO	Total	*df*	*p*
Twins							
Dark months	7 (35%)	9 (45%)	3 (15%)	1 (5%)	20 (100%)		
Light months	8 (36%)	9 (41%)	5 (23%)	–	22 (100%)		
Intermediate	3 (60%)	2 (40%)	–	–	5 (100%)		
						6	*ns*
Singletons							
Dark months	9 (56%)	4 (25%)	3 (19%)	–	16 (100%)		
Light months	–	–	–	–	–		
Intermediate	–	–	1 (50%)	1 (50%)	2 (100%)		
						3	.052
All							
Dark months	16 (44%)	13 (36%)	6 (17%)	1 (3%)	36 (100%)		
Light months	8 (36%)	9 (41%)	5 (23%)	–	22 (100%)		
Intermediate	3 (43%)	2 (29%)	1 (14%)	1 (14%)	7 (100%)		
						6	*ns*

Fisher's Exact test.

IO = insecure other; ns = not significant.

Table 8.6.   Effect of Darkness on Attachment II: Which Type of Months the Child Has Lived In

	Category of Attachment					df	p
	A	**B**	**C**	**IO**	**Total**		
Twins							
Dark months							
more	6 (38%)	8 (50%)	2 (12%)	–	16 (100%)		
Light months							
more	9 (38%)	9 (38%)	6 (25%)	–	24 (100%)		
Equally	3 (43%)	3 (43%)	–	1 (14%)	7 (100%)		
						6	ns
Singletons							
Dark months							
more	2 (40%)	1 (20%)	2 (40%)	–	5 (100%)		
Light months							
more	7 (58%)	3 (25%)	2 (17%)	–	12 (100%)		
Equally	–	–	–	1 (100%)	1 (100%)		
						6	ns
All							
Dark months							
more	8 (38%)	9 (43%)	4 (19%)	–	21 (100%)		
Light months							
more	16 (44%)	12 (33%)	8 (22%)	–	36 (100%)		
Equally	3 (37%)	3 (37%)	–	2 (26%)	8 (100%)		
						6	ns

Fisher's Exact test.

IO = insecure other; ns = not significant.

44%, both equally in 56% and father never, and the corresponding figures among twins were 20%, 73%, and 7%, respectively. Among twins, 52% of those being equally cared for by both parents were Type B. Among singletons those primarily cared for by the mother were in this category B most often (see Table 8.7).

Cumulative Effects of Risks

In order to evaluate the cumulative nature of risks, a new variable was counted for each child: the number of perinatal risks, which were defined as twinship, prematurity, and neonatal hospital treatment. Thus, this new variable of cumulative risk varied in singletons between 0 and 2 and in twins between 1 and 3. Children having no risk were most often Type A, while increasing number of risks led to an increasing percentage of children Type B (see Table 8.8).

Table 8.7. Parental Preference and Attachment Type

	Category of Attachment						
	A	**B**	**C**	**IO**	**Total**	*df*	*p*
Twins							
Mother's							
favorite	4 (50%)	2 (25%)	2 (25%)	–	8 (100%)		
Both equally	11 (38%)	15 (52%)	2 (7%)	1 (3%)	29 (100%)		
Father's							
favorite	2 (67%)	–	1 (33%)	–	3 (100%)		
						6	*ns*
Singletons							
Mother's							
favorite	2 (29%)	4 (57%)	1 (14%)	–	7 (100%)		
Both equally	6 (67%)	–	2 (22%)	1 (11%)	9 (100%)		
Father's							
favorite	–	–	–	–	–		
						3	0.048
All							
Mother's							
favorite	6 (40%)	6 (40%)	3 (20%)	–	15 (100%)		
Both equally	17 (45%)	15 (39%)	4 (11%)	2 (5%)	38 (100%)		
Father's							
favorite	2 (67%)	–	1 (33%)	–	3 (100%)		
						6	*ns*

Fisher's Exact Test.

IO = insecure other; ns = not significant.

Table 8.8. Cumulative Risk and Attachment: Combined Risk Factors Twinship, Prematurity, and Hospital Treatment as Number of Risks

	Category of Attachment					
	A	**B**	**C**	**IO**	**Total**	*p*
No risk	7 (54%)	3 (23%)	3 (23%)	–	13 (100%)	
One risk	11 (42%)	10 (39%)	4 (15%)	1 (4%)	26 (100%)	
Two risks	6 (46%)	4 (31%)	3 (23%)	0 (0%)	13 (100%)	
Three risks	3 (23%)	7 (54%)	2 (54%)	1 (8%)	13 (100%)	
						ns

IO = insecure other; ns = not significant.

Table 8.9.   Number of Risk Factors in Each Category of Attachment Type: Mean Values of Risk Factors and 95% Confidence Limits

	Category of Attachment			
	A	B	C	IO
Risk factors				
–mean	1.19	1.62	1.33	2.0
–95% CL	.80–1.56	1.18–2.07	.65–2.02	–10.7–14.7

IO = Insecure other.

Calculation of risk factors in each category of attachment revealed the same finding: children of Type B had the highest mean of risk factors, and Type A the lowest (see Table 8.9).

DISCUSSION

The present analysis is part of a more comprehensive followup of Finnish twins and singletons, started during pregnancy in order to follow the children's early human relationships, development, and mental health at least up to the beginning of school. Because of the international makeup of the researchers, cross-cultural comparisons were also possible.

When compared with reference groups classified using the PAA from the United States, the Finnish twins' attachment seems more often to be Type A, called avoidant or defended. Looking at this result through "Finnish eyes" causes some discussion about the naming of this kind of behavior. Since the Second World War, Finnish culture has emphasized the children's development of independence, as so many children are brought up in kindergartens. For the family to function in these circumstances, it is much easier if the children do not cling to their parents and mix easily with their peers. Finnish society is also very safe; thus, independence can also be encouraged. Bringing up children is often the responsibility of fathers, who are known to be less binding and to encourage more independence than do mothers (Minde et al., 1990). Thus, the finding of a higher proportion of Type A Finnish toddlers fits our observation and understanding of Finnish society, but the descriptive terms do not. Type A independent might be better.

When comparing Finnish twins with singletons, no statistically significant differences could be found in the categories of attachment. However, twins seemed to be slightly more often in category B, whereas singletons more often exhibited Type A attachment behavior. The obligation to share the parents' attention with the co-twin seems to activate more active seeking of the mother's comfort after separation, when compared with the singleton situation where no competition is needed. Thus, the singleton preschoolers can safely go on examining their surroundings without the fear of losing their place on the mother's lap. Finnish girls, especially twin girls, seem to be slightly more often of Type B attachment.

Those infants who had received treatment in the hospital seemed to be more often in category B. At first glance this finding could be surprising. This result is probably explained by the fact that these infants elicit more concern and attention from their parents, who are worried about their babies.

In view of the previous literature on Seasonal Affective Disorder, attachment of infants might be expected to be more secure when scored during the light and more livable time of the year, but this was not found to be true. Twins scored during the dark months were most often in category B, whereas intermediate months seemed to produce more Type A attachment. Perhaps the lighter and warmer circumstances without thick clothing together with the parents' reduced stress, give the child better opportunities to explore the outside world and become independent. Regrettably, the singletons' Strange Situations were not evenly performed throughout the year, and no conclusions can be drawn from so uneven a distribution. Gathering more data and followup, including repetition of PAA at 36 months of age, may reveal more about this issue.

Usually, normal nighttime melatonin rhythm in newborns is developed at the age of 3 months (Attanasio, Rager, & Gupta, 1986; Hartman, Roger, Lemaire, Massias, & Chaussain, 1982), and it is not known whether this development is different between dark and light seasons. In adults only slight, though significant, changes are registered in serum melatonin levels between seasons (Kauppila, Kivel, Pakarinen, & Vakkuri, 1987). Thus, the role of melatonin in the attachment of toddlers born in different seasons is not evident.

The Finnish woman's position in regard to education, career, and politics is one of the most advanced in the world. So it is not surprising that the primary caretaking of children was often reported to be both parents' equal responsibility. When parents of twins reported having a favorite child, the child was less likely to be Type B than if the parents reported enjoying the children equally. For singletons the effect seemed to be the opposite, so that equally enjoyed children were far more likely to be classified as Type A than the mother's favorites.

The accumulation of the three risk factors – twinship, prematurity, and treatment in the hospital – increased the probability that the toddler would be classified as Type B. This result is in accordance with our hypothesis that the worry and extra attention given by conscientious parents because of the risks was experienced by the infant as consistent and predictable parental availability.

In conclusion, Finnish twins and singletons' attachment is more likely to be of Type A, if all circumstances are optimal. Typical Finnish parents encourage their toddlers' independence, which seems to lead to independent behavior in the Strange Situation even after reunion of the child and mother. If the infant has suffered from perinatal risks, the parents attend more constantly to the infant and the attachment is more often classified as Type B. Thus, in an international view, the names of the attachment types are perhaps misleading; in some cases, Type A could be renamed "independent" and B "tight bond."

CHAPTER NINE

Characteristics of Attachment Behavior in Institution-reared Children[1]

STANISLAWA LIS

INTRODUCTION

Studies exploring the developmental effects of institutionalization on young children have indicated numerous delays and disturbances in development. Disorders have been found in (1) physical development (Aubry, 1955; Bakwin & Bakwin, 1972; Bielicka & Olechnowicz, 1967; Gelinier-Ortiques & Aubry, 1955), (2) mental development (Ainsworth, 1962; Aubry, 1955; Przetacznikowa, 1967; Spitz, 1945, 1958; Yarrow; 1961, 1964), and (3) social-emotional development (Aubry, 1955; Gewirtz, 1965; Lis, 1978; Matejćek, 1962, 1964, 1967; Olechnowicz, 1957; Przetacznikowa, 1967; Rutter, 1981; Tizard & Hodges, 1978; Tizard & Rees, 1974; 1975; Wolkind, 1974). Progress in medical care and changes in organization of institutions have reduced the threat to development to such an extent that children raised in institutions are more likely to display normal physical and mental development (Tizard, 1977; Tizard & Tizard, 1974). Several important studies have shown that, although substitute mothering did not solve all the developmental problems of children brought up in institutions, it did provide a chance for relatively normal psychomotoric development (Aubry, 1955; Fox, 1977; Lis, 1978; Spitz, 1945; Spitz & Wolf, 1946). Nevertheless, research has consistently shown disorders of social-emotional development and personality formation both in children residing in institutions and in children living in adoptive families for many years (Baran, 1985; Bohman & Sigvardsson, 1979; Jurga, 1985; Klominek, 1981; Lis, 1992; Tizard & Hodges, 1978; Tizard & Rees, 1975).

[1] *Acknowledgment:* The author would like to thank Dr. Patricia M. Crittenden for critical and encouraging comments on earlier versions of the manuscript and for her help in preparing the present version of the chapter.

The author is grateful to Prof. Izabela Bielicka and Prof. Alicja Blaim, psychologists: Dr. Hanna Olechnowicz, Mgr. Zofia Kowalska, Mgr. Rosita Giryńska, and Mgr. Irena Czajka, doctors and nurses who worked at the Department of Social Pediatrics of the Warsaw Medical Academy in Warsaw, Poland, as well as children and their parents who made this research possible.

These studies considered the influence of institutional life on children's development. However, the results of one study indicated that some features of infants could influence the course of their development (Schaffer, 1966). Schaffer's work raises important questions regarding the influence of the quality of central nervous system functioning on the development of young children reared in institutions and particularly on the process by which their attachment to caregivers develops. This issue is explored for Polish children living in institutions from 1965 to 1975.

Effects of Polish Culture on Institutionalized Children

After World War II, a totalitarian system was imposed on Poland following the Conference at Yalta. From that time until 1989, all political, economic, and social matters were subordinated to an idea of building a system based on Marxist theory. This purpose was realized in many ways, including reducing private ownership to a minimum, submitting as many aspects of social life as possible to the rule of the Communist Party and state authorities, and striving to eliminate all forms of traditional Polish socioeconomic life. The most dramatic changes occurred in the years 1945–1956. Among them were restraints (and even liquidation) of human and civilian rights, repression, a strong press toward institutionalization of all aspects of social life, and its subordination to obligatory ideology.

One of the ways of strengthening the system and indoctrination was through limiting and taking over family functions by institutions. This aim was realized by (1) setting up institutions such as crèches (day or week care of infants), nurseries, kindergartens, orphanages (called children's homes), day rooms for school children, and children's and youth organizations, (2) propagation of opinion that specialists working in the institutions were well prepared to take care of the health and development of infants, children, and teenagers and that institutional care could better prepare them to live in modern society than families, and (3) economic pressure on women to work.

Although the forms and intensity of pressure used to promote the socialistic system changed over 50 years, the purpose did not. During World War II, the number of children who lost their parents increased enormously. Some lived in orphanages, whereas others were informally adopted. (Formal adoption could mean death for children and parents – for example, children deported from Zamosc or Jewish children.) After the war, orphanages continued to exist, and new ones were established, but no organizations were set up to help people to adopt children. Only in 1950 was an institution founded to qualify supervisors of orphanages to direct candidates for adoptive parents to a child's curator (Bielicka, Stelmachowski, & Sztekiel, 1966).

With time, the political and economic situation of the state changed, and more was known about the negative consequences of living in institutions. As a result, efforts were made to improve institutional care. Although the first Adoptive Center of the Society of Children's Friends came into existence in 1960, the Center did not carry out all adoptions. Many children were adopted directly from children's homes or from hospitals. Therefore, the exact number of adopted children in the years 1965–1975 is unknown. Official statistics indicate that from 1965 to 1970 about 40,000 children (in a population of 31 to 34 million) were raised in institutions per year (Rocznik demograficzny, 1976). Among them were about 8,000 to 8,500 infants (Rocznik statystyczny MziOS, 1976). However, only 11 to 15% of the infants and children living in children's homes were freely available for adoption (Rocznik statystyczny MziOS, 1976). The majority had at least one parent (usually an unmarried mother) with limited parental rights. Because neither parents nor children's relatives relinquished these rights, few of these children could be adopted. In the 1970s, the state officially promoted the (scarce) possibility of fostering in private homes.

The attitude of Polish people toward adoption has traditionally been positive; indeed, some eminent people in Polish history were adopted. The institutions that arranged adoption always had more parental candidates than available children. But many people were anxious about the physical and mental health of the children and about their character, especially those children whose parents were alcoholics, dysfunctional, criminals, and prostitutes.

Couples sought adoption primarily to have a child. Young children and females were preferred because people trusted that they could form stronger and more persistent ties and function more nearly as "biological" children than older and male children. The most important issues, however, were the children's prognosis for normal mental and emotional development and, sometimes, good looks or similarities in appearance to the parents. But risk children were also adopted if parents trusted that, under their care, the child's development would improve. For some people, a child's developmental delays or disturbances posed a challenge. In such cases, parents' emotional ties with the adopted child were especially strong. Nearly all adoptive parents wanted to keep the adoption secret and to assure the child, themselves, and other people that the child was "their own" son or daughter.

Institutionalized Children in the Department of Social Pediatrics in Warsaw

The research described here was carried out at the Department of Social Pediatrics (DSP) of the Warsaw Medical Academy. Since the 1960s, the Department has cooperated with the Warsaw Center for Adoption of the Society of Children's Friends in diagnosing and predicting the psychophysical development of infants before making the decision to place a child in adoption. Infants admitted to the DSP for preadoptive evaluation were brought from the newborn units of obstetrical hospitals in Warsaw, usually in the first or second month of their lives. Their biological mothers were usually young and unmarried.

Conditions at the DSP. The DSP was made up of two units, one intended for infants less than 12 months old, and the other for those who could walk. The younger infants were kept in large rooms with four to eight beds depending on room size and number of patients. The floor was covered with sheet-dressed mattresses. During waking periods, the infants were placed on the mattresses to play. Colorful and noise-producing toys were hung on ribbons so that those infants who had not yet learned to grasp objects could look at them and listen to the sounds. Older infants could reach out to grasp and manipulate the toys. One child's touching of a toy set other toys in motion, thus stimulating other infants to look at them and try to grasp them. The children also had rubber toys such as animals, plastic toys, balls, and boxes of different colors.

While on the mattresses, the infants were stimulated to interact and play with an adult, usually a nurse, and with their peers. The adult took the infants in her lap one by one, encouraged them to look, listen, and reach out, and to enter in vocal and emotional interaction with her. Each infant had approximately 7 to 10 minutes of contact daily with the adult, although the exact amount of time devoted to each infant differed and was dependent on the infants' health and level of development, social reactivity, attractiveness, and emotional bonds formed between infant and adult. Infants were usually placed on the mattresses twice daily and in good weather were taken to a little garden near the DSP building.

The older children stayed in their rooms only during naptime and at night. Their waking hours were spent in the hall or garden. The hall was equipped with the necessary furniture, a small ladder, toys, and books for children. From time to time, members of the staff took the children on walks outside the DSP. In addition, they could occasionally visit the offices and kitchen. The child–staff ratio was never lower than 5:1, with an average of 4:1. The children had many social contacts in the morning and early afternoon with different people: doctors, nurses, psychologists, students, and practitioners. The department was also visited often by pediatricians and other specialists participating in specialized courses. In the afternoons and at night, the children were in the care of the pediatrician and nurses on duty.

Although an effort was made to provide each infant with individual care, an infant was not always assigned to the exclusive care of one person. Almost all of the infants and children were on friendly terms with several persons who showed them sympathy and tried to find occasions for interaction with them, although professional duties usually limited these interactions to 20 minutes or less. Nevertheless, these contacts were repeated over the course of a day.

The majority of the infants resided at the DSP for about three months, undergoing a multitude of specialized medical procedures, including neurological and psychological examinations. All were systematically observed day by day in their regular environment through large windows separating the patients' rooms from corridors and other parts of the department. In rare cases, because of problems with health and diagnosis or because of formalities regarding the children's legal status, the infants stayed at the DSP for more than three months.

Forming Attachments. Because the infants staying in the DSP for longer than five months could be adversely affected in their psychophysical development or experience a worsening of existing developmental disturbances, care was taken to provide constant and individual substitute mothering by a particular person. This person was acknowledged as a child's substitute mother when she verbally declared her emotional engagement; clearly spent as much time as possible with "her" infant; or presented behaviors characteristic of an emotional tie with the child. Such behavior included favoring the child, picking up and cuddling him or her more often than other children, taking obvious interest in the child, being able to observe and inform the physicians and psychologists about the child's achievements and problems, trying to solve such problems, and interpreting facts as positively as possible for the child. On the infant's part, the behaviors that indicated attachment constituted differentiating the particular person and directing attachment behavior to her. When these conditions were met, a substitute mother was recognized as such, and the fact was recorded in the patient's medical and psychological case history. If, however, no spontaneous ties developed, a member of the staff (a physician, psychologist, or nurse) was asked to take individual care of a child.

Because the substitute mother's time was limited by her professional duties, she could offer "her" child half an hour to three hours a day. But during that time, the visual, auditory, tactile, and play interactions were intensive and accompanied by strong, usually positive, emotions. Nevertheless, substitute mothering was not constant, being interrupted by holidays, days off, night duties, vacations, and absences caused by illness and other reasons. As time elapsed and the ties between substitute mother and child developed, visits to "her" child during her free time became more common, and even excursions to the substitute mother's home were possible. Excursions of this kind were rare, however, and were limited to children with well-established walking skills. The presence of a substitute mother gave children the opportunity to explore more actively and intensively. Consequently, the children were better able to develop their psychomotor and psychosocial skills.

Aims of This Study

The specific aims of the present study were to:

1. Assess the characteristics of attachment behavior toward substitute mothers among children reared in institutions.
2. Seek differences in patterns and development of attachment to substitute mothers between children with CNS damage and those without such damage.
3. Evaluate the attachment to adoptive parents shown by children reared in institutions.
4. Assess the rate of psychomotor development and patterns of behavior of children in institutions (a) before forming attachments to substitute mothers, (b) in the course of development in the institution, and (c) later in the adoptive home.

METHOD

Sample

Twenty institutionalized, longitudinally observed children were selected from 285 who were evaluated between 1965 and 1975. The criteria of selection were residence in the DSP during all of the first 18 months of life and the stable care of a substitute mother. Only 20 children met these criteria because most children stayed at the DSP for less time and most had no individual care. The mean age at admission was 9.4 weeks; the mean age upon departure was 20.3 months.

Ten of the 20 children (4 girls and 6 boys) had CNS damage as determined by pediatric, neurological, and EEG examinations (Group I). Paresis was found in four infants, epileptic seizures and abnormal EEG tracings in two children, generalized hypotension syndrome and microcephaly in one girl, mental deficiency and inborn heart defects in one girl, Hercules syndrome in one boy, and abnormal EEG curves and suspected inborn deafness in another boy. Seven infants in Group I were born with low birth weight, either prematurely or at term.

The 10 remaining children (3 girls and 7 boys) showed no signs of CNS damage (Group II). All were born at term with birth weight adequate to their fetal age.

Procedure

Data were gathered at two time periods: during institutionalization and following adoption. Two methods of data collection were used: naturalistic observations of children's behavior and formal testing.

Observations during Institutionalization

Naturalistic Observations. Infants and children were observed independently by three specialists in developmental and clinical psychology. Observations were made in different social contexts: when the infant was (a) alone, (b) with one or more adults, (c) with other children, and (d) with children and adults including both familiar and unfamiliar people. The psychologists focused on naturally occurring, unconstrained, and spontaneous behaviors that were part of children's everyday situations: sleeping, eating, grooming, undergoing medical treatment, psychological testing, and play. Occasionally there were specially arranged situations, for example, presenting a stranger, male or female, with well-known persons present or absent.

Observation periods differed depending on the situation, activity, child age, and amount of time a psychologist had available. Periods of observation lasted from two to three minutes to one hour or longer. Usually, younger infants had shorter observations. Most often, infants' behavior was observed by one or two psychologists, but from time to time they were observed by all three researchers. Because the infants were accustomed to the presence of well-known psychologists, their presence did not interfere with children's activities. The observations were as detailed as possible. Neither the children nor the caregivers knew who or what was being observed at any given time.

Formal Testing. Infants were tested using the Gesell Developmental Schedules every four weeks during the first year of their life and every three months in their second year. The testing was done by the psychologist who cared for the infant and was responsible for updating records. But from time to time testing was done by the two other psychologists.

Coding of the Observational Records

Phase of Attachment. Records were kept regarding three phases of attachment based on Bowlby (1969) and Ainsworth (1967). Phase 1 (orientation and signals without discrimination of figure) occurs during the first three months of life. During this stage, infants show interest in people, prefer interaction with persons to simple contact with objects, attain skills necessary to discriminate people and the signals coming from them, and become able to signal specific needs. The characteristic behaviors of Phase 1 include inborn reflexes (rooting, suckling, clinging, grasping) and behaviors formed on the basis of inborn reactions, for example, focusing on and following objects with the eyes, listening and being able to signal needs with the help of a social smile, crying, or vocalization. Phase I development was assessed to be adequate to age when (a) an infant showed all the behaviors, with the exception of two, by the age of 3 months and (b) the behaviors were observed by two persons at least three times on different days.

Phase 2 (orientation and signals directed toward one or more discriminated figures) normally occurs between 4 and 7 months of age and is characterized by the ability to recognize specific individuals and to behave toward them in differentiated ways. Typical behavior includes: entering and maintaining interactions with people, influencing adult behavior by differentiated crying or protesting against being left by the adult, differentiated greeting, showing preference for the main caregiver by a general body excitement, social smiling and/or vocalization, and discrimination of unfamiliar persons by taking on serious facial expressions when an unfamiliar person comes near, frowning, taking a deep breath, looking or turning away. An infant was considered to be in Phase 2 if (a) he or she was able to discriminate between familiar and unfamiliar people and show preference for particular persons by all modalities but one, and (b) such behaviors were observed and recorded three times on different days by at least two observers. The infant was considered to be age-appropriate if this occurred prior to being 7 months old.

In Phase 3, which usually lasts from 7 to 8 months to 3 years, children form strong, lasting ties with at least one person. Attachment in Phase 3 was indicated by (a) following, approaching, greeting, hands-up gesture, touching, embracing, kissing, burying face in attachment figure's lap, calling, talking and smiling; (b) more differentiated and longer lasting exploration in the attachment figure's presence; (c) protest and/or distress upon separation from attachment figure; and (d) reluctance in making contacts with strangers, including protest and fear when unfamiliar people interact with the child. Children were assigned to Phase 3 when their behavior pertinent to these four categories was observed and recorded three times or more on different days. They were deemed age-appropriate if this occurred prior to 18 months.

Quality of Attachment. Children in Phase 3 were also assigned a quality of attachment based on the pattern of their behavior (a) with the attachment figure, (b) during both short (1–2 days) and long (2–4 weeks) separations from the substitute mother, and (c) upon reunion with the attachment figure, according to Ainsworth (1967), Ainsworth and Wittig (1969), and Ainsworth et al. (1978). Obviously, however, modifications were needed because a formal Strange Situation was not used and because the children had more numerous contacts with unfamiliar people than home-reared children.

Attachment was classified as *secure* if in the relationship with the substitute mother there were (a) a predominance of positive feelings, (b) emotional reactions that were adequate to the stimuli, (c) toleration of short periods of separation from attachment figure (not longer than two days), (d) greeting the attachment figure on her return, (e) undisturbed patterns of interaction with her, (f) toleration of short delays in having biological needs met by the attachment figure, (g) engagement in play while having distal contact with the attachment figure, and (h) exploration of the environment.

An attachment was classified as *insecure* when the child (a) demanded permanent presence and reassurance from the attachment figure, (b) avoided close or distal contacts with the attachment figure, or (c) preferred toys to the attachment figure. Insecure children demonstrated inactivity, helplessness, and disorientation. Four subclassifications of insecure attachment were defined.

Insecure-ambivalent attachment was assessed when the child's behavior indicated an inability to tolerate short periods of separation from the attachment figure, with simultaneous contrasting or mixed feelings about the attachment figure. (For instance, the child demanded to be picked up but was not comforted and quickly wriggled away in order to be put down; he or she clung tightly to the attachment figure and then immediately afterward turned away for no particular reason; and so on.)

Children were considered *insecure-ambivalent with aggressive features* when they performed patterns of behaviors characteristic of the insecure-ambivalent patterns and also directed aggression against other children and adults (including their substitute mothers or themselves).

Avoidant attachment was assessed when children appeared to be oblivious to a short separation by ignoring, turning away from, or avoiding contact with the attachment figure. Such children demonstrated independence from their substitute mothers and willingly left them to approach unknown adults, especially men, smiled at them, and demanded to be picked up by them.

The fourth pattern was *avoidant with autistic features*. This pattern was shown by only one child.

Behavior Disturbances. Seven aspects of behavior were analyzed. Disturbances in *psychomotoric drive* included hyperactivity, hypoactivity, and difficulties in concentrating. Disturbances in *manipulative and play activities* comprised brief interest in toys, poverty of manipulative and play operations, and stereotypies. Disturbances in *visual and auditory perception* included irregularities in position and in eye movements, and motionless staring into a distance (combined with no reactions to visual and auditory stimuli). Disturbances in *social contacts* covered delayed and restrained reactions to social stimuli. Disturbances in *emotional development* included irritability, clamorousness, moroseness, aggression toward adults (including substitute mothers) and toward children, auto-aggression, strong negative reactions, temper tantrums, and intensified fears of people and things. Disturbances in *eating* comprised rumination, long-term sucking of the lips, tongue, or thumb, poor or voracious appetite, or pica. *Sleep* disturbances included difficulties in falling asleep, light sleep, excessive need of sleep, and eyelids partly open during sleep.

Followup Examinations after Adoption

Followup. When children left the DSP, their natural, adoptive, or foster parents were asked to return for followup evaluation. These evaluations were carried out by a pediatrician and psychologist, usually the same specialists who had previously been in charge of the child. The aims of followup examinations were to (a) investigate the persistent developmental consequences of children's staying in the institution during the first months of their lives, (b) study the process of children's adaptation to familial environment, and (c) give children medical and psychological consultation and help, if needed. Few adoptive parents accepted this opportunity and then only for a short time. This was mainly because they wished to keep the fact of adoption secret from the child and other people. Some parents even moved to another district or town altogether. Sixteen children were evaluated in the third year of life. The child's behavior was observed, the Gesell Developmental Schedules were carried out, and one or both of the adoptive parents were interviewed.

Child Behavior. Children's behavior was observed before testing, with one or both parents present, during testing with the psychologist and parents absent, and after testing with the parents present. Attention was paid to children's verbal and nonverbal behavior toward their parents both before and after separation from them.

Interview Data. During the interview, the parents were asked who was the main object of the child's attachment, with whom he or she preferred to stay and play, to whom he or she turned most often for consolation and help in case of trouble or danger, who gave him or her a sense of security and comfort, how the child behaved with unfamiliar persons and in unknown places, how he or she interacted with other children, and whether or not he or she was willing to leave the home alone. The present study only covers the results of the examination made nearest the children's third birthday.

Observer Agreement

Psychological observations were supplemented and compared with the data recorded by pediatricians and nurses. The team of pediatricians, psychologists, and nurses working at the unit evaluated all the data concerning each child once a week. Special attention was paid to interaction with people. Interobserver agreement of evaluations of child development and behavior was high but was not formally calculated. Each infant was observed an average of 10 times per month by the psychologists. It should be emphasized that the official recording of the formation of substitute mothering bonds with a child in his or her case history was considered as the beginning of such relationship. In reality, the ties between substitute mother and "her" child started developing much earlier than that (Bronfenbrenner, 1979). In addition, the team prepared a comprehensive evaluation when the patient left the DSP. Recorded information included the level, rate, and rhythm of the child's psychomotor development and interpersonal relations, with special emphasis on the ability to form emotional ties with one or more adults.

The development of the infants' attachment to their substitute mothers was evaluated independently by three psychologists (specialists in developmental and clinical child psychology). Interrater agreement ranged from 80% to 90% (Phase I: 90%, Phase II: 80%, Phase III: 85%).

RESULTS

The data analyses are both descriptive and comparative. For the comparative analyses, children with CNS disorder were compared to children without such disorder. At each time period, that is, institutionalization and followup, the results are presented for three kinds of functioning: attachment, behavior disturbances, and psychomotor development.

Institutionalization

Attachment

Phase Development. Phase 1: Achievement of Phase 1 attachment was adequate for their age for only seven infants (two from Group I and five from Group II). By 9 months of age, six infants from Group I and all but one from Group II had developed attachments that were adequate to their age to their substitute mothers.

Phase 2: All the infants from Group II and all except for two from Group I had the individual care of substitute mothers during Phase 2. These two infants, a boy and a girl, were very unattractive. They showed serious delays in psychomotor development, and their social-emotional reactions were atypical. The girl was very slim and quiet only when she was alone; she cried and shouted loudly any time somebody approached and touched her. The sound of her voice was so unpleasant that the personnel of the DSP usually refrained from interacting with her, especially when contact was not essential. In addition, when she was 8 months old, she contracted a contagious disease and moved to the Clinic of Children's Contagious Diseases for nine weeks. The boy was cross-eyed but tall and strong. He showed hypertension of muscles, and his movements were uncoordinated and clumsy. His reactions to social-emotional stimuli were weak and delayed, and his social contacts were impersonal and superficial. Both infants obtained individual care of substitute mothers during the last trimester of the first year of their lives. The differences between number of children with attachment adequate to their age at

Phase 1 and Phase 2 were statistically significant (Group I: $\chi^2_{(1)}$ = 5.2083, p <.05; Group II: $\chi^2_{(1)}$ = 4.9864, p <.05).

Phase 3: Observational records confirmed that each child had at least one attachment figure. Six children (three from each group) had only one attachment figure, whereas the remaining 14 children had from two to five attachment figures. Substitute mothers were the principal attachment figures in all the cases. Toward the others, the children showed attachment behavior only under special circumstances (in the absence of substitute mothers or during feeding for instance, etc.)

The groups differed in two ways: (1) time elapsed before the child received proper and constant care from a substitute mother and (2) motivation of staff members to become substitute mothers. A mean of 15.2 weeks was necessary for infants from Group I to form an attachment to a substitute mother, whereas a mean of 5.5 weeks characterized infants from Group II ($t_{(18)}$ = −4.06, p <.01). Spontaneous involvement of adults with infants was the case of all the infants from Group II, but a member of the staff was specifically asked to accept individual care in the case of three infants from Group I.

Patterns of Child Behavior with the Attachment Figure. The patterns of children's behavior with their substitute mothers depended on the situation and the forms of interaction preferred by the attachment figure. Two types of situations were distinguished: (1) only the substitute mother and "her" child were present, and (2) the substitute mother and "her" child were in the company of others. Interaction between substitute mothers and "their" children when alone was usually very intense. Often the child would be in the arms of the substitute mother or playing close by with toys (see Fig. 9.1). While playing or manipulating objects, the children tended to maintain close contact with their attachment figure, showing her the toys, looking at her, talking to her or vocalizing, gesturing, and grimacing for her benefit. These dyadic interactions were satiated with emotion, reflected in smiles, laughter, sometimes crying, caresses, hugs, rarely kisses, touching each other's faces, hands, and other parts of the body, and singing (see Fig. 9.2). Playing with toys was encouraged more often by persons with university education (physicians, psychologists), whereas substitute mothers with secondary education (nurses) were more likely to interact directly with the children talking to them, caressing them, feeding and washing them, and changing their clothes. In the presence of substitute mothers, the children demonstrated the richest and most differentiated forms of interpersonal interaction and diverse forms of emotional experiences.

In situations when the substitute mothers and "their" children found themselves in the company of other people, the children rarely explored their surroundings. Almost all of their time was spent watching their substitute mothers and controlling other children's behavior. They tried to attract the substitute mothers' attention in all possible ways, occupying attachment fig-

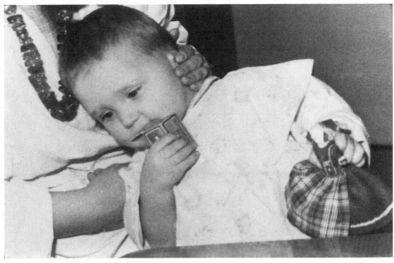

Figure 9.1. Joasia (1 year 6 months). The girl manipulates an unknown object while standing with her back close to her substitute mother.

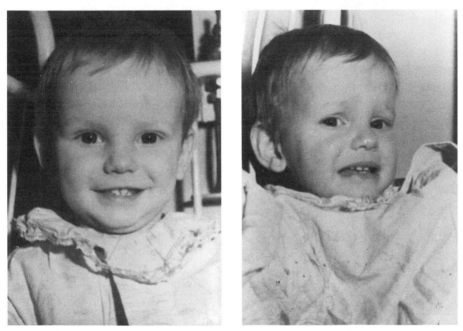

Figure 9.2. Piotruś (1 year 1 month). A sequence of pictures illustrating a situation that lasted about 2–3 minutes: Substitute mother approaches the boy who is looking at her and smiling. She stands next to him motionless. After the moment, the boy turns away and then shows his disgust and fury.

ures with themselves and interfering with "rivals." The most frequently
observed ways of attracting the attachment figure's attention were screaming,
trying to leave the room, having "accidents," attacking others (including substitute mother), and auto-aggression. In the company of peers, children spent
as much time as possible sitting in the laps, or held in the arms, of their substitute mothers (see Fig. 9.3); in this position, they explored their surroundings with their eyes and ears.

Exploratory behavior was most often demonstrated by children in the presence of their subsidiary attachment figures or during rest periods when the
children were lying alone in their beds. It was then that they concentrated on
manipulating objects and discovered varied ways of playing with them.

Reaction to Strangers. All the children in the study discriminated strangers,
and all but three showed negative reactions when unfamiliar people tried to
interact with them; they cried, escaped, avoided the strangers, or turned away
from them (Table 9.1; see Fig. 9.4). Two girls from Group I (one with autistic

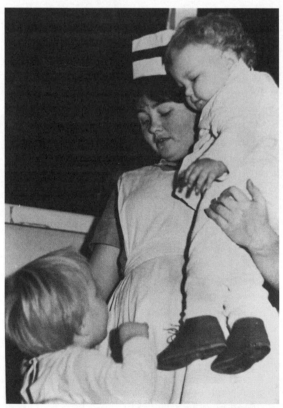

Figure 9.3.   Buba (1 year 4 months). The girl spent
as much time as possible in her substitute mother's
lap.

Table 9.1. Contacts with Unfamiliar Persons and Objects

	No. of Children	
Kind of Reaction	Group I	Group II
Negative reactions in contact with strangers (fear, crying, refusing contact)	8	10
Willingness to approach strangers and even demanding to be picked up by them	6	7
Fear of unfamiliar things and surroundings	6	2

features and the other with delayed psychomotor development, hypoactivity, and weak emotional reactivity) failed to show obvious negative reactions in contacts with strangers. At the same time, however, 13 out of 18 children demonstrated at 12–15 months of age willingness to approach strangers and even demanded to be picked up by them. No specific factors determining

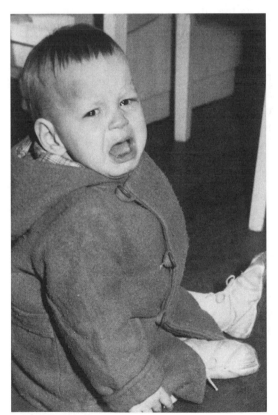

Figure 9.4. Marcus (1 year). With an unfamiliar man in absence of his attachment figure.

such almost simultaneous contrasting behavior could be found. Gender of the unfamiliar person is a possible factor. Children were more willing to interact with unfamiliar men, although there were exceptions, too, with some of the children showing more intensive negative reactions or fear of male strangers. Interestingly, all the children from Group I and a couple from Group II who interacted willingly with strangers reacted with obvious fear to unfamiliar objects and situations.

Behavior During Separation. One of the important criteria in evaluating attachment is their behavior during separation from, and upon reunion with, attachment figures. Seventeen children (seven from Group I and ten from Group II) experienced longer (2–4 weeks) separations from their substitute mothers at the age of 9–18 months. All the children were disturbed emotionally during the separation. The predominant behavior included crying, mournfulness/clamorousness, aggression, and/or auto-aggression. Disturbances in motor ability or play were found in most of the children. Stereotypic movements such as rocking, spasmus nutans, and tapping with hands appeared or intensified. Five children had sleeping and eating disorders (see Table 9.2).

Separation from substitute mothers highlighted the complexity of the children's interpersonal relationships. More intensive contacts with the DSP staff were demonstrated by 14 out of 17 children separated from their substitute mothers. The children seemed to be trying to compensate for the lack of access to their primary attachment figures by seeking other people who were lower in their hierarchy of attachment figures. It was from these persons that the children demanded specific nursing activities such as feeding and washing. Some of the children even demanded to have special privileges during the separation; for instance, they had to be fed first, or they refused to eat at all.

Reunion after Short Separations. During their stay at the DSP, all children experienced weekly short (1- to 2-day) separations from attachment figures. In eight children (six from Group I and two from Group II), no obvious differences in behavior before and after separation were observed. Twelve children demonstrated behavioral disturbances of a predominately socio-emotional character after reunion. Negative reactions predominated, with three children from Group I being morose and sad, and five (three from Group I and two from Group II) being apt to cry or scream. Aggression was demonstrated by three of the children from Group II, and three showed auto-aggression. Other kinds of disturbances were observed sporadically. Symptoms of emotional reserve, such as the predominance of negative feelings and tearfulness, usually disappeared during the first meeting with the substitute mother after separation, but aggression and/or auto-aggression tended to last longer. These disturbances appeared or were augmented in spite of the stability of the child's environment.

Reunion after Longer Separations. Repeated short-term separations resulted in temporary emotional disorders. Longer separations (two to four weeks)

Table 9.2. Behavior Disturbances Observed During Separation with Substitute Mothers and Upon Reunion with Them

		No. of Children								
	After Short Separation			**During Long Separation**			**After Long Separation**			
Kind of Disturbances	**Group I**	**Group II**	**All**	**Group I**	**Group II**	**All**	**Group I**	**Group II**	**All**	
Disturbances in manipulative and play activity	—	—	—	8	5	13	3	4	7	
Difficulties in concentrating	—	—	—	1	—	1	—	—	—	
Stereotypies	—	—	—	2	4	6	4	5	9	
Disturbances in emotional functioning:	5	7	12	7	10	17	7	10	17	
Dejection, sadness	3	—	3	1	1	2	1	1	2	
Tearfulness, crying	3	2	5	5	10	15	5	7	12	
Alternate clinging and drawing away from substitute mother or aggression toward her	—	—	—	—	—	—	—	5	5	
Aggression toward adults and/or children	—	3	3	4	3	7	6	9	15	
auto-aggression	—	3	3	1	2	3	2	4	8	
Reserve toward substitute mother (pretending not to see or recognize her but despairing upon her trying to leave)	—	2	2	—	—	—	4	4	8	
Particular disobedience in substitute mother presence	—	—	—	1	1	2	2	—	2	
Fears	—	—	—	1	1	2	4	5	9	
Behavioral disturbances connected with meeting a child's biological needs:	1	—	1	2	3	5	7	6	13	
Sleep	—	—	—	1	1	2	1	3	4	
Eating	1	—	1	1	2	3	8	5	13	

from attachment figures led to multiple and differentiated disorders: emotional disturbances, motor and/or play sensitivity, and biological functioning (sleep and food intake). The typical pattern included (a) predominant negative emotions (dejection, sadness, or tearfulness), (b) acts of aggression toward children, adults, or self, and (c) disturbed relationships with substitute mothers comprised of ambivalent and avoidant behaviors. Ambivalent behavior was exemplified by clinging to the attachment figure and then pushing her away, hugging and then unexpectedly biting, pulling her hair, or butting her with the head. Avoidant behavior included retaining a physical and mental distance from the attachment figure. Such children kept their distance and appeared not to notice the presence of their substitute mothers or to recognize them. Nevertheless, when the mothers tried to leave the room, the children burst into tears and later spent as much as an hour huddling in the mothers' laps. The seven children who demonstrated this kind of disorder willingly left their substitute mothers to approach unfamiliar persons. Five of these children asked to be picked up while simultaneously observing the reaction of their substitute mothers. This syndrome was frequently accompanied by fear of unfamiliar objects and situations, stereotypic movements, disturbances in motor or play activity, and eating and sleeping disorders (six children had poor appetites and two ate voraciously). Pica was observed in five children of Group I and coprophagia in two boys (Table 9.2). The disorders became less intense when the substitute mother returned to take care of the child, but only stereotypic movements disappeared completely. The majority of disturbances persisted through the end of the child's stay at the DSP. Only four of the children did not demonstrate intensified attachment behavior toward persons other than their substitute mothers.

Patterns of Attachment. An analysis of children's behavior in different situations revealed that all of the children had formed insecure attachments toward their substitute mothers. The majority of children from both groups (16) formed ambivalent attachments (see Table 9.3). Children considered insecure-ambivalent recognized their substitute mothers, followed them, and demanded to be picked up and hugged by them. In addition, they longed for their attachment figures and became depressed, less active, demonstrated a lack of appetite, and had troubles falling asleep when their substitute mothers were absent for a longer time. After their attachment figures returned, they behaved as if offended; they refused to recognize their attachment figures or even notice their presence. In addition, they did not approach them, and they pretended not to hear when they called. Some ambivalent children were demonstrably disobedient and directed misbehavior toward their attachment figures. Thirteen of the children who were ambivalently attached demonstrated acts of aggression or auto-aggression and were considered insecure-ambivalent with aggressive features.

Table 9.3.   Patterns of Attachment in Children from Group I and Group II During the Third Phase

Patterns of Attachment	No. of Children	
	Group I	Group II
Secure	—	—
Insecure-ambivalent	2	1
Insecure-ambivalent with aggressive features	6	7
Insecure-avoidant	1	2
Insecure-avoidant with autistic features	1	—
All	10	10

Children with avoidant attachment ignored, turned away from, or avoided contact with the attachment figure. They demonstrated independence from their substitute mothers and willingly left them to approach unknown adults, especially men, smiled at them, and demanded to be picked up by them.

One child was considered insecure-avoidant with autistic features. This child was a pretty girl, almost like a doll, with huge, sparkling, intelligent blue eyes. But her mimicry was not typical for her age. Her interactions with people were limited, with definitely greater interest in objects. Reactions to human voices were delayed, but she reacted readily to mechanical and animal sounds. In addition, she demonstrated a tendency to stare motionlessly into the distance or at her hands with oddly bent fingers. She seemed not to notice when the psychologists tested her responsiveness by covering her eyes with their hands or waving their hands before her eyes. During contacts with people, she often seemed to look right "through" a person.

Behavior Disturbances. All the children from both groups were found to have numerous behavioral disturbances while at the DSP. The frequency of behavior disturbances in the seven areas is shown in Figure 9.5, with most children showing evidence of disturbance in four of the seven areas. In all the areas except two (psychomotoric drive and emotional development), the number of children with behavior disturbances decreased during the stay at the DSP, especially when under the care of substitute mothers. A change toward normal behavior was particularly evident in the case of visual and auditory perception, social contacts, sleep, and food intake. In Group I analyses failed to reveal any statistically significant differences other than (1) in *visual perception* at the beginning and at the close of stay at DSP ($\chi^2_{(1)} = 10.2083$, $p < .01$) and at the beginning of bonds with the substitute mothers and at the close of stay at the DSP ($\chi^2_{(1)} = 10.2083$, $p < .01$), and (2) in *eating* at the beginning of bonds with substitute mother and at the close of stay at the DSP ($\chi^2_{(1)} = 7.849$, $p < .01$). However, the differences in the number of children with *manipulative*

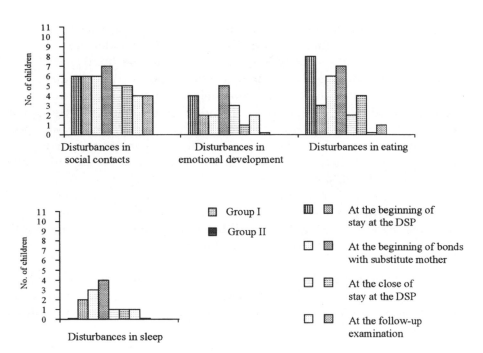

Figure 9.5. Frequencies of Behavior Disturbances in Each of the Seven Aspects During Four Periods in Children from Group I and Group II.

and play activity disturbances approached statistical significance at the beginning of stay at the DSP and at the beginning of bonds with substitute mother ($\chi^2_{(1)} = 3.5164$, $p < .05$).

The statistics for Group II were similar. There were significant differences in the frequency of disturbances in *social contacts* between the beginning of stay at the DSP and the beginning of bonds with substitute mother ($\chi^2_{(1)} = 5.9523$, $p < .02$); and in *sleep* in two periods, between the beginning of stay at the DSP and the beginning of bonds with substitute mother ($\chi^2_{(1)} = 5.0$, p <.05), and between the beginning of bonds with substitute mother and the close of stay at the DSP ($\chi^2_{(1)} = 5.2083$, $p < .05$).

No quantitative changes in the number of children with *psychomotoric drive* disturbances were found, although some clear qualitative changes were noted. Individual care was linked with qualitative changes in psychomotoric drive; children under the care of substitute mothers most often demonstrated growing behavioral dynamics, and hypoactive subjects with concentration difficulties became hyperactive with concentration difficulties. In three children (one from Group I and two from Group II), psychomotoric drive became normal during their stay at the DSP.

Emotional development was different. The number of children with emotional disturbances increased considerably while the children were under the care of substitute mothers. By the end of their stay at the DSP, nearly all the children had such disturbances. The comparison of the number of disturbed children at the beginning of their stay at the DSP and the number at the start of their contacts with substitute mothers was statistically meaningful ($\chi^2_{(1)} = 3.516$, $p = .05$), although the effect was greater for children in Group I ($\chi^2_{(1)} = 5.952$, $p < .02$).

Thus, the results of the analysis indicate that, among children under the care of substitute mothers, the number and level of behavior disturbances diminished but did not disappear completely, whereas irregularities in emotional development increased.

Psychomotor Development. Psychomotor development in the children was compared in four periods: before forming bonds with substitute mothers, at the beginning of bonds with substitute mothers, at the close of their stay at the DSP and during followup examinations. The data were analyzed using Multiple Analyses of Variance (MANOVAs) with repeated measures.

A MANOVA indicated that during the stay at the DSP, the Developmental Quotients (DQs) of the children increased steadily in all the spheres so that the differences in mean DQs in all spheres at the beginning and end of their stay at the DSP were statistically significant. Also statistically significant were the differences between the mean DQs in all the areas in Group I at the beginning of the relationships with substitute mothers and at the close of the children's stay at the DSP; in Group II this was true for fine motor only. But between the beginning of the stay at the DSP and the beginning of bonds with substitute mothers, there were no differences in mean DQs in Group II and in only fine motor in Group I. Thus, the rate of psychomotor development in children accelerated only when they were under the care of substitute mothers. As a result, the children's development in some spheres became normal. However, in other spheres, particularly speech, the children did not attain the norm, in spite of a faster rate of development.

Group I and Group II were compared in five spheres of the Gesell Schedules in four periods in the MANOVA series. The results of the analyses, presented in Table 9.4, indicate that, at the beginning of the stay at the DSP, there were statistically significant differences in three spheres between the mean DQs of infants from Group I and those from Group II: gross motor ($t_{(7)}$ = 2.39, p <.04), fine motor ($t_{(7)}$ = –3.08, p <.02), and adaptive ($t_{(18)}$ = 2.28, p <.04). At the beginning of bonds with substitute mothers, mean DQs increased in both groups, with statistically significant differences observed in only two spheres: gross motor ($t_{(18)}$ = –4.57, p <.003) and adaptive ($t_{(18)}$ = 2.37, p <.04). At the close of the stay at the DSP, there were no group differences between mean DQs of children.

Followup after Adoption

All the children except one accepted their adoptive parents easily and quickly grew into their new surroundings (see Fig. 9.6). Only one girl from Group II did not fully accept her new family for a period of two weeks; afterward, however, her relationship with her parents was good.

Attachment. Fifteen children (7 in Group I and 8 in Group II) were followed up as 3 year olds. All had at least two attachment figures – usually the mother and the father. Fourteen of these presented secure attachment patterns. Only one girl from Group I was considered to show an avoidant attachment pattern with autistic features (the same pattern which she represented during her stay at the DSP). See Table 9.5. The four children who did not take part in the followup examination had been considered ambivalent with aggressive features while at the DSP.

Children who were classified as securely attached at followup demonstrated caution at first and kept their distance in contacts with unfamiliar persons and unknown objects in the Outpatient Clinic at the DSP. But they adapted quickly enough to enter into contacts with strangers. Some were encouraged in this by their parents. After a short period, their behavior became unrestrained; they were cheerful, communicated with the doctor or psychologist easily, helped adults, and included them in their play activities. They were able to tolerate longer periods (even up to a few hours) of absence on the part of their attachment figures, particularly if warned about the fact. Upon the attachment figure's return, they greeted him or her cheerfully and reported everything that had happened while they had been separated. When fearful, the children returned to their attachment figures, regaining a sense of security through physical and mental closeness (tactile contact or verbal, visual, or auditory contact). If they encountered problems during play or testing, they usually tried to manage by themselves. But if they failed, they signaled their difficulties and looked for help to the attachment figures or psychologists.

Table 9.4. Comparison of Mean DQs by Children from Group I and Group II in Five Areas of the Gessel Developmental Schedule

	Mean DQ											
	At the Beginning of Stay in the DSP			At the Beginning of Bonds with Substitute Mother			At the Close of Stay at the DSP			During Followup Examination		
Area	Group I	Group II	p	Group I	Group II	p	Group I	Group II	p	Group I	Group II	p
Gross motor	55.8	77.7	.04	59.4	81.8	.003	88.4	94.7	ns	97.7	105.0	ns
Fine motor	55.8	78.5	.02	66.1	80.2	ns	85.6	99.6	ns	96.4	102.4	ns
Adaptive	50.7	81.6	.04	63.4	85.5	.04	82.6	94.9	ns	90.1	103.0	ns
Language	53.1	65.8	ns	63.7	75.9	ns	68.7	76.8	ns	81.6	99.4	ns
Social-personal	53.8	75.6	ns	64.6	85.6	ns	83.0	89.6	ns	102.4	110.8	ns

ns = not significant.

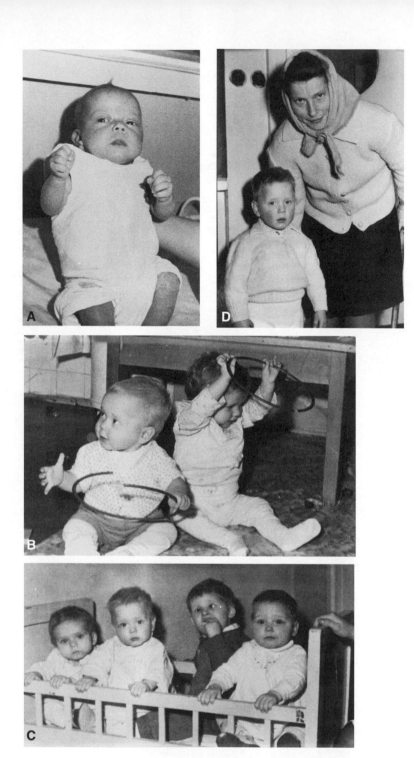

Figure 9.6. Robert (**A:** 5 months; **B:** 1 year; **C:** 1 year 3 months; **D:** 3 years). Series of pictures illustrating developmental changes in the boy during his stay at the DSP. The last in the sequence shows the 3-year-old boy with his adoptive mother.

All of the children considered as securely attached at followup had been designated as insecurely attached during their stay at the DSP. The girl considered as insecure-avoidant with autistic features showed the same pattern of attachment toward her new parents. She was a calm and cheerful child on the outside, but her visual and verbal contacts with people were rare and incomplete. She said a few single words and seemed to understand a limited range of words; she played with toys willingly, but it was difficult to persuade her to follow orders and to imitate demonstrated activities. (However, her resistance was not felt to be the result of negativity or contradiction.) Her emotional reactions were rare and weak.

Behavior Disturbances. During the followup study, the frequency and degree of behavior disturbances were found to decline considerably in all areas but drive. Some disorders disappeared, whereas others diminished (see Figure 9.1). Statistical analyses revealed significant differences in the *emotional* area in Group I at the end of the children's stay at the DSP and during followup ($\chi^2_{(1)} = 5.625$, $p < .02$). In Group II there was only a trend in a direction of statistical significance ($\chi^2_{(1)} = 3.5164$, $p < .1$). In both groups, statistically significant differences were found between intake at the DSP and followup in *visual perception* (Group I: $\chi^2_{(1)} = 8.1281$, $p < .01$; Group II: $\chi^2_{(1)} = 4.7531$, $p < .05$), *appetite* (Group I: $\chi^2_{(1)} = 4.7531$, $p < .05$; Group II: $\chi^2_{(1)} = 3.8503$, $p < .05$), and *sleep* (Group I only: $\chi^2_{(1)} = 4.7531$, $p < .05$). The difference in the number of children with *manipulative and play activity* disturbances was small and not statistically significant. Only the number of children with *psychomotor drive* disturbances was nearly the same at followup as at the beginning of their stay at the DSP. Four children from Group I and three from Group II were hyperactive and had difficulties in concentration; one boy from Group II was hypoactive. It was clear, however, that drive disturbances at followup were much less intensive than during the children's stay at the DSP.

Psychomotor Development. As indicated by Table 9.5, the rate of the children's psychomotor development when in the care of their adoptive parents accelerated. As a result of a faster tempo of development, the children attained at

Table 9.5.   Patterns of Attachment with Adoptive Parents at Followup

	No. of Children	
Patterns of Attachment	**Group I**	**Group II**
Secure	7	8
Insecure-avoidant with autistic features	1	—
No information	2	2
All	10	10

followup DQs that were in all the areas higher than at the end of their stay at the DSP. In two spheres, language ($t_{(7)} = 3.21$, $p < .02$) and personal-social ($t_{(7)} = 4.38$, $p < .01$), the differences between mean DQs were statistically significant in Group I and, in three spheres, adaptive ($t_{(7)} = 3.71$, $p < .01$), language ($t_{(7)} = 5.72$, $p < .002$), and personal-social ($t_{(7)} = 5.04$, $p < .002$), means were statistically different for Group II. Results of the followup study indicate that after a certain period of time spent in adoptive families, a year or longer, the children attained the norm or more than the norm in psychomotor development.

DISCUSSION

The present study indicates that care provided by substitute mothers enabled institution-reared children to form permanent bonds with one or a few persons. Attachment between children and substitute mothers formed in spite of the limited time substitute mothers could devote to "their" children and regardless of professionals' attitudes toward too close emotional bonds with subjects. However, all of the children formed insecure attachment bonds with their substitute mothers. Belsky and Rovine (1988) had similar results studying infants who had experienced extensive nonmaternal care in the first year of their lives. In addition, Sagi, Lamb, Lewkowicz, Shoham, Dvir, and Estes (1985) and Sagi, Donnel, Harel, Joels, and Tuvia (1989) confirmed these results in their study of children brought up in kibbutzim, as did Dontas, Maratos, Fafoutis, and Karangelis (1985) and Crittenden et al. (1992) for infants living in the Metera Center in Athens. It seems that the most important factors determining the formation of insecure attachment patterns in Phase 3 were the specific relationships between substitute mothers and children, frequent separations from attachment figures, and conditions of interaction between the children and their substitute mothers (i.e., the presence of rival children and the interest and actions of the substitute mother). This presumption is supported by Benn's (1986) and Jarvis and Creasey's (1991) studies.

The attachment pattern in the majority of the DSP children (80%) was considered insecure-ambivalent (with or without aggressive features). Ambivalent feelings and the behaviors reflecting them may result from the incessant stress experienced by the children. Their needs for physical and psychological contact with attachment figures were constantly frustrated by the shortness of their daily contacts as well as frequent short and sporadically longer separations. Even when they were with their substitute mothers, the children did not have stable contacts because the substitute mothers often divided their attention among children. Feelings of jealousy were expressed by acts of aggression that enabled children to discharge their negative emotions and to remove other children perceived as obstacles to the substitute mother's full attention. When it was the substitute mother who herself constituted an obstacle (by refusing or not being able to fulfill a child's expectations), the child directed his or her aggression at her. Aggression toward other children was often used as a means of attracting the attention of the attachment figure, who was thus forced to intervene and to hold the aggressor. Similarly, the children frequently used auto-aggression as a form of provocation. Children used diverse and sometimes quite subtle ways to attract the physical or mental closeness of their attachment figures. The child's leaving its attachment figure to approach a stranger and demand to be picked up by him or her may be taken as just such provocative behavior. This assumption was confirmed by children's simultaneous observation of their substitute mother's reactions.

Thus ambivalent behaviors may be considered the effect of emotional uncertainty on the part of children whose ties with a substitute mother were often unclear. The behavior of attachment figures was often unpredictable and could be interpreted by children as either evidence of indifference (if their expectations failed to be met) or love (if they were fulfilled). In similar situations, the behavior of substitute mothers frequently varied. The children's struggle to gain the attention and favors of attachment figures was expressed by misbehavior and disobedience to attract her attention and generate concern. In three children behavioral traits were close to Crittenden's (1992a) coercive threatening category of attachment (C1), and in two it was close to her coercive aggressive category (C3).

Because children formed insecure attachment bonds while under the care of substitute mothers, one could ask whether this kind of care is favorable or harmful to the child's further development. The question seems all the more reasonable if one considers that the number of children with emotional disturbances increased under the care of substitute mothers. Analyses revealed, however, that bonds with attachment figures accelerated the rate of psychomotor development in the children; this was particularly obvious in the fine motor and adaptive spheres. Achievements in these spheres are important for the development of sensorimotor intelligence. Psychomotoric activity in children under the care of substitute mothers increased, as did manipulative behavior and play activity; disturbances in visual and aural perception and in sleep and food intake diminished, forms of social contacts changed, development retardation disappeared, and the number of interactions with people grew and became differentiated and more diverse in form. Although no reduction in the number of children with drive disturbances was found, some changes in the pattern of disturbances were observed. Hyperactivity and concentration difficulties were substituted for hypoactivity (and even sometimes for adynamy).

The question is whether the price paid by the child and the substitute mother for this kind of individual care, which can be painful to both sides and is definitely the cause of increased emotional irregularities and disturbed social, is worth it. An affirmative response appears reasonable, considering that individual care enabled the children to preserve a developmental potential that could be realized under favorable circumstances. The study has shown that once with their adoptive families, the children were able to normalize interpersonal relations and their developmental achievements quickly reached or exceeded the norm, especially in the language and socio-personal spheres. Behavioral disturbances observed at the DSP either diminished or disappeared completely after adoption.

The present study concerns children up to 3 years old. The projected followup studies of the children taking part in the study at least into adolescence could not be carried out because adoptive parents broke off contacts with the DSP center and its staff. Parents in most cases stopped consulting DSP staff and even gave up personal contacts when the children were 3 to 4 years old and started being interested in their origins as well. In fear that the fact of adoption would be revealed, parents tried to cover all the traces. Sporadic conversations with parents indicated that they attempted to confirm to themselves (not just to the children) their parenthood in a social, and even biological, sense after a period of time. They revealed this tendency verbally, for example, speaking of traits that the child was supposed to have inherited from them.

Individual care seems particularly important for children with CNS damage. The study indicated that the rate of psychomotor and attachment development in brain-damaged children was faster than that in children without such damage. It was therefore possible to lower or even eliminate the differences in psychomotor development and attachment.

The same was true of behavioral disturbances. The study has shown that, if children are given the chance to experience substitute individual care while in an institution, there are no significant differences in the processes of forming bonds and patterns of attachment between children with brain damage and those without. The results are in concordance with Easterbrooks' data (1989), which indicated that prematurity was not a reason to affect an infant's ability to form bonds with attachment figures. Similar results concerning hearing defects were found by Lederberg and Mobley (1990). Thus, it would seem that in spite of suggestions by some authors (e.g., Ainsworth, 1990; Easterbrooks, 1989; Grossmann, Scheurer-Englisch, & Stephan; 1989; Main, Kaplan, & Cassidy, 1985) that attachment patterns formed in the first year of life remained stable in children up to 6 years of age, the children preserved the ability to change insecure attachment into secure attachment patterns once they entered a favorable family environment.

Security in Formerly Institutionalized Polish Children. The finding of secure attachment after adoption in all but one child would not be expected, based on findings using the Strange Situation. The differences between the above data and studies using the Strange Situation might be the result of several reasons:

1. Both the Strange Situation procedure and its use at 12–18 months give some problems. One question is whether the ratio of securely/insecurely attached children is the same in other countries as in the United States; it seems probable that it is not (Belsky, 1989; Belsky & Rovine, 1989; Easterbrooks, 1989; Sagi et al., 1989). Another question is whether the situation has the same meaning for more autonomous 3-year-old children whose attachment relations, attachment behaviors, and conditions eliciting these are wider and more differentiated as compared to infants.

2. The very high proportion of securely attached children in both groups may be explained by the fact that adoption radically changed the children's lives in ways that favored the liquidation of existing fears and anxieties. Specifically, the children received tender care as the parents showed a tendency to overprotection. Thus stability and quality of parental care might lead to secure attachment.

3. Mental abilities (especially internalization), interpersonal relations, and attachments develop extensively in the second and third years of life. At that time mental representations are formed. Intensity of developmental changes is usually connected with great plasticity. Consequently, positive changes in children's lives may lead to wiping out traces of earlier unfavorable circumstances, to forming new ones, and to consolidating positive mental models. Although some studies indicate the persistence into adulthood of working models (Collins & Read, 1990; Kirkpatrick & Davis, 1994; Kirkpatrick & Hazan, 1994; Main, Kaplan, & Cassidy, 1985; Shaver, 1989), a problem is whether young persons formed their attachment patterns as an effect of early, infantile experiences exclusively or whether the patterns resulted from long-lasting relationships of unchanging quality.

4. It is also possible that the children fragmentarily remembered and were able to recognize both the building and the persons at the DSP. The traces of fragmentary reminiscences might cause them to feel at ease during the followup observations.

5. It is also possible that the children's early contacts with many strangers had "hardened" them, enabling them to interact in an undisturbed manner with unknown people in everyday life situations thereafter.

It is difficult to decide which of these hypotheses is true. The solution to this problem requires more developed theory of attachment beyond infancy and more elaborated methods of assessment, as suggested by Ainsworth (1993) and Bretherton, Ridgeway, and Cassidy (1993).

The findings of this study are limited in a number of ways. First, because videotape was not used, it is difficult to verify the reliability of the observers. Second, because the standard Strange Situation was not used, the relation of the classifications in this study to Strange Situation classifications cannot be determined. The lack of difference in the distributions of CNS disordered and normative children needs further study. The addition of a normative control group would have been helpful, both for empirical comparison and for the observing psychologists. Nevertheless, the data were gathered with exceptional care and reflect development under conditions that may not be replicable. Indeed, it is the richness of the descriptive observations and the evidence of adaptation of the children that constitute the primary contribution of this study.

CHAPTER TEN

Attachment in Children Adopted from Romanian Orphanages

Two Case Studies[1]

KIM CHISHOLM

INTRODUCTION

In the early literature on institutionalized children, researchers suggested that such children were unable to form emotional bonds with their adoptive parents given the deprivation the children had experienced as a result of institutionalization (Goldfarb, 1945a, 1945b). These findings, however, were based largely on descriptive data on very small numbers of children, many of whom had experienced several foster home placements. Later work on children housed in higher quality institutions found that institutionalized children were indeed able to form attachments with their adoptive parents (Lis, chapter 9 in this volume; Tizard, 1977). Similarly, Crittenden et al. (1992) found that children housed in the Metera institution in Greece formed attachments with their primary caregivers in the institution, although such attachments were consistently insecure. Given these diverse findings, the impact of institutionalization on children's ability to form an attachment relationship remains unclear.

In 1989, when the Ceausescu regime was overthrown in Romania, the outside world became aware of thousands of children housed in deplorable conditions in Romanian orphanages. Shortly thereafter, families from all over the world, including Canada, traveled to Romania to adopt these children. These

[1] *Acknowledgment:* This chapter is part of a larger project on the Development of Romanian Children Adopted to Canada supported by a National Welfare Grant from Human Resources Development Canada. The views expressed in this publication do not necessarily reflect those of Human Resources Development Canada.

The author would like to thank Elinor Ames for her support and advice concerning this work. I would also like to thank Kim Bartholomew, Patricia Crittenden, Lianne Fisher, and Patricia Kerig for their helpful comments on earlier drafts of this chapter. Most of all, I would like to thank the families who have shared their experiences with me in the service of helping other adoptive parents. Inquiries can be directed to the author at Saint Francis Xavier University, Psychology Department, Antigonish, Nova Scotia, Canada, B2G 2W5.

adopted children and their families have provided us with the unique opportunity to study more clearly the effects of institutionalization on children's
development in general and on the development of attachment in particular.

The conditions in Romanian orphanages were similar to, or worse than,
the conditions reported in earlier studies of institutionalization (Goldfarb,
1945a, 1945b; Provence & Lipton, 1962; Tizard, 1977). Child-to-caregiver
ratios in Romanian institutions ranged from 10:1 for infants to as high as 20:1
for children over 3 years of age (Chisholm, Carter, Ames, & Morison, 1995).
Children spent as many as 20 hours a day in their cribs, and, as a result of
inadequate staffing, any human interaction they experienced was in the provision of minimal physical care (Ames & Carter, 1992). Such conditions may
jeopardize the formation of human relationships.

The ability of institutionalized children to form an attachment bond is a
particularly important issue for several reasons (Chisholm et al., 1995). First,
institutionalized children are developing an initial attachment later than is
typical, which may place them at risk for the development of attachment or
unusual organizations of attachment relationships. Developing an attachment later necessarily implies that a child has experienced some form of
extreme interpersonal deprivation in the first year or two of life. Second,
given their experience of extreme neglect, many institutionalized children
lack pre-attachment behaviors, such as smiling, making eye contact, and crying (Chisholm & Savoie, 1992; McMullan & Fisher, 1992), which are critical in
promoting and maintaining proximity to caregivers. Third, it is likely that,
prior to their adoption, most adoptees had developed internal working models of self as unlovable and of caregivers as unresponsive. The reciprocal
effects of these factors on adoptive parents and children warrant exploration.

This chapter addresses the development and organization of attachment
in two children who had spent 3 years 3 months and 4 years 5 months, respectively, in a Romanian institution prior to their adoption and move to Canada.
I had received permission to write this chapter from the parents of both children. During the writing of the chapter, both families were given drafts of the
chapter and their comments and concerns were discussed. The information
regarding the children and their families was obtained from two extensive
interviews with the parents, the first conducted when the children had been
in their adoptive homes for 11 months and 8 months, respectively, and the
second conducted approximately three years later. Attachment was assessed
during our second interview using a play interaction and separation–reunion
procedure conducted in the families' homes. This procedure was coded using
the Preschool Assessment of Attachment (PAA) developed by Crittenden
(1992a).

My description covers (a) parents' reports of the conditions of the orphanages from which their children were adopted, (b) parents' reports of the
developmental condition of their children when they first met them, (c) par-

ents' reports of the problems they initially experienced with their children, (d) problems parents were still experiencing three years after adoption, and (e) types of attachment relationships that developed between the adoptees and their adoptive mothers. Given the similarities of the two children's early backgrounds (i.e., age at adoption, length of institutionalization, delays when first adopted), it is notable that each child developed a different pattern of attachment with her or his adoptive parent.

Jill

Jill was adopted from a Romanian orphanage by her mother, Pat, a single professional woman, when Jill was 3 years 3 months old. Pat began investigating the possibility of domestic adoption 3 years before adopting Jill. Becoming impatient with this process and hearing news stories concerning the situation in Romania, she decided on international adoption.

The Institution. Little is known of Jill's birth history except that she was the fourth child in a family whose biological mother was 33 years old and whose father was unknown. She had been abandoned in the hospital at birth and was shortly thereafter sent to an orphanage. Jill was housed in an overflow building where conditions were much worse than in the main orphanage. She lived in a stark room where one or two staff members provided care for approximately twenty 2- to 3-year-old children. The room was unadorned, very hot, and crowded with children rocking in their cribs. Toys were nonexistent, and the children were dirty and covered with mosquito bites. Pat reported that there were obvious "favorite children" and that, although Jill was not a favorite, she was also "not the lowest on the pole." Jill's diet in the orphanage consisted of bread, salami, and tea, although Pat reported that the children never had enough to eat or drink.

Pat was permitted to visit Jill for one hour per day during the month that she was in Romania. She was only able to take Jill out of the orphanage for her medical exam in Sibiu. Prior to this, Jill had never been out of the orphanage compound. Consequently, the car trip to Sibiu was terrifying for her, she screamed throughout.

Jill's Condition When First Adopted. At the time of adoption, Jill was delayed in all areas of development (personal-social, fine motor, gross motor, and language). She was short in stature, had a small head, and was not toilet-trained. She was below the 5th percentile for weight. At 3 years 3 months of age her gross and fine motor skills were at the 18 to 21-month-old level. She suffered from intestinal parasites, anemia, and chronic ear infections that had produced a 40% hearing loss in one ear. Severe language delays were also apparent. Jill was echolalic and more often used gestures and noises than verbal language to let her needs be known. When she was adopted, she had approximately seven Romanian words in her vocabulary.

Jill displayed several atypical behaviors that were directly attributable to the deprivation she had experienced in the orphanage. She was silent, sullen, sucked her fingers, and continually rocked her body whether she was sitting (rocking forward and back) or standing (rocking from side to side, shifting her weight from one foot to the other). She was terrified of many things (e.g., toilets, baths, loud noise, cars, men, and animals, particularly dogs). When Jill first came home, she ate ravenously "as though she would never eat again." Everything went in her mouth without chewing, and she appeared unable to recognize when she was full. Initially, she was easily frustrated by other children and, when frustrated, she would throw temper tantrums (i.e., throwing herself on the floor, kicking, and screaming). She was also very possessive of toys, which Pat felt reflected her fear of losing them, given that she had never before had toys to play with. During these first few months together, Pat reported that she felt that what Jill needed most from her was a sense of security or "a sense that I'd always be there."

Jill's Progress 12 Months Post-adoption. We first visited Pat and Jill when Jill was 4 years 3 months old and had been in her adoptive home for almost a year. At this time, Pat discussed the difficulties she had had since adopting Jill and the progress Jill had made. In her first 10 months in Canada, Jill grew 6 inches and gained 10 pounds, which placed her at less than the 25th percentile for weight. She still experienced hearing loss, but physicians did not expect this to be permanent. At this point, she had recently been toilet-trained but was still not trained during the night. Although showing steady progress, Jill's language skills were still delayed. Her speech was difficult to understand; it was telegraphic and consisted of one- to three-word utterances. She often used noises as opposed to words to let her needs be known. During our visit Jill was distractible and very active. She appeared to have difficulty settling on any task for any length of time.

An interesting behavior that Jill had developed shortly after her adoption was her indiscriminate friendliness. Whereas initially Jill had been frightened and wary of everyone, now she eagerly approached and engaged in conversations with everyone, including strangers. Pat reported that while she and Jill were walking on a busy city street, Jill approached a stranger who was walking ahead of them and took her hand. As well as being friendly, Jill also had a tendency to wander off when out in public places. Pat expressed concern about this behavior and reported that, as a result, she had to watch Jill carefully anytime that they were out.

Such indiscriminately friendly behavior may be particularly relevant to attachment. Given that attachment by definition is a discriminating bond, such indiscriminate friendliness may be not unlike the indiscriminate behavior displayed by infants prior to forming an attachment bond.

Many of Jill's eating problems had disappeared within her first few months in Canada. She now appeared able to recognize when she was full and no longer ate with such urgency. She had a good appetite and would eat most foods that were presented to her. Her social skills with peers had also improved. She was now more willing to share toys with her peers and was less likely to be frustrated in interaction with her peers. As a result, her temper tantrums had become rare.

At one year post-adoption, many of Jill's fears had dissipated, but she was still very frightened of unexpected loud noises (e.g., fire alarms, sirens), costumes (e.g., Santa Claus), and dogs. Although her rocking had diminished in frequency, Jill still rocked when she was nervous or unsure, and sucked her fingers.

Jill's Progress 3 Years 3 Months Post-adoption. When we next visited Jill, she had been in her adoptive home for approximately 3 years 3 months and she was 7 years 6 months old. She was a bubbly, energetic girl who now weighed 41 pounds. This placed her between the 5th and 10th percentile for weight. Her gross and fine motor skills showed dramatic improvement. Pat stated that Jill enjoyed gross motor activities (swimming and playing outside) and was now able to ride a two-wheeler and was learning to skate. Jill had begun piano lessons which, though challenging, indicated the improvement in her fine motor skills.

Pat reported that Jill continued to display fear of loud noises, although she no longer rocked. She still sucked her fingers and used a stuffed toy kitten as a security object. For the first time, Pat suggested that Jill had difficulty dealing with traumatic situations. Each time that Jill was upset by something, she needed to hear about the event repeatedly. Her mother felt that this was her way of coping with trauma. For example, when Jill was present, her grandmother experienced a fall and was taken to hospital by ambulance. After that, Jill repeatedly asked to hear the story of "grandma's fall."

After having spent over three years in her adoptive home, Jill still displayed indiscriminately friendly behavior. She had recently been diagnosed with Attention Deficit/Hyperactivity Disorder (ADHD). Pat felt that Jill's indiscriminate friendliness might be the result of ADHD and not a result of her orphanage experience per se. Pat again expressed concern about this behavior, particularly Jill's propensity to engage in conversation with strangers. Given that Jill was more verbal now, Pat was more actively teaching her about the dangers of interacting with strangers. Thus far, however, such active instruction had not helped in dissipating Jill's behavior.

By the time of our second visit, Jill was in her second year of school in a regular Kindergarten-Grade 1 classroom. Pat reported that Jill's first year of school was difficult because her teacher's classroom was very structured and strict. Given Jill's short attention span and high activity level, this environment was extremely frustrating and difficult for her. During her first year at

school, Jill had had a full-time aide, and now in her second year she had an
aide for two hours per day. Pat reported that Jill loved going to school and
that her teacher was pleased with the progress she had made. For example,
for the first time Jill had begun to speak in full sentences and now knew her
alphabet and could count to 20.

Jill was still distractible, and Pat found that helping her cope in structured
situations (like the classroom) was a challenge. In order for Jill to keep up in
school, it was necessary for Pat to do a lot of academic work with her at home.
Pat stated that Jill needed to be intentionally taught, not only academic concepts, but also social skills. She found that Jill simply did not pick up such
skills on her own. Pat's solution has been to actively role play many social situations with Jill to teach appropriate social behavior. This strategy appears to
have been effective because Pat reported that Jill's social skills were improving
and that she often got along well with other children.

Assessment of Attachment. To assess attachment we conducted our separation–reunion procedure during the second visit with Jill's family. Prior to our
home visit, Pat was sent a letter describing the procedure. In this letter Pat
was instructed to interact with Jill as she normally would, and, when she was
given a signal (i.e., a cough), she was to tell Jill, "Stay here until I get back,"
and then leave the house. Two researchers made the home visit. Upon arrival,
one researcher interacted with Pat and Jill while the second researcher set up
the video equipment for the separation–reunion procedure. This second
researcher, who played the role of the "stranger/camera person," interacted
as little as possible with Pat and Jill prior to the separation–reunion procedure and did not initiate any interaction with Jill during the separation
episode. Once our equipment was set up (it was visible in the family living
room), the first researcher left the house and Pat and Jill were invited to play
on the floor with a standardized basket of toys. The play interaction lasted
eight minutes. Then the "stranger/camera person" signaled Pat to leave the
house. Pat was outside for three minutes, and upon returning she rejoined Jill
for a further three minutes of interaction.

Jill's relationship with her mother was coded as Secure (Other). Using
Crittenden's system (1992a), such a classification is given when the relationship is clearly secure, but some behaviors and strategies used by a child do not
reflect any of the usual secure patterns. Crittenden's system takes into
account children's strategies in interaction, behavior patterns, regulation and
display of affect, negotiation, exploration and affiliation, and the behavior of
the attachment figure.

Jill's interaction with her mother was very warm and relaxed, although her
mother worked hard to structure the interaction. For example, during play
with a puzzle, Pat had to work to maintain Jill's interest in the puzzle. "What
do we have to do first? Turn over all the pieces, right? Are you going to help

Mom with this? What do we do next? Let's get all the pieces together. You want to help? Let's put Barney together." It was apparent from their gentle laughter in conversation and play that they enjoyed each other's company.

In the middle of the play interaction, Jill suddenly stood up and began to leave the room, saying, "I'm going to find Sara" (the second researcher who had left the house). Pat turned to the stranger smiling and then turned toward Jill saying, "Oh, I don't think Sara's here right now, honey." Pat was in no way upset or concerned about Jill's behavior but rather appeared delighted with her daughter's "antics." Pat's comment succeeded in redirecting Jill's attention, and she quickly returned to her mother saying, "Where is she?" Pat returned to the puzzle, saying, "She had to go for a little while." Jill accepted this with "Oh" and rejoined her mother on the floor. Pat quietly said, "You wanted to play with Sara?" Jill responded in a somewhat disappointed voice, "Yeah." Pat then said, a little brightly, "Well, she'll be back a little later." With this explanation Jill shifted her attention once again to the puzzle. Although we would not expect a secure child to leave her mother in search of a stranger, the open communication about the episode and Pat's response to Jill's behavior are evidence of the openness of their relationship.

When her mother left the house, there were clear signs of open negotiation regarding her departure. Jill facially displayed her surprise at her mother's departure and verbally expressed her concern ("Are you going to go far?"). Jill watched her mother retreating and then looked to the stranger with her mouth open and her eyes wide. Her look was one of shock and disbelief. To an observer, it was clear that Jill was unaccustomed to her mother leaving with so little explanation. In her mother's absence, Jill was noticeably upset; initially, she was immobilized, sucking her finger and lying on the couch. Shortly thereafter, she recovered somewhat and moved toward the toys again. Her play, however, lacked its earlier joy and focus. Upon her mother's return Jill clearly brightened, and once again there was direct discussion about her mother's departure. Jill said, "But where did you go?" Pat responded, "Where did I go? Well, I just had to go and do a little errand." Jill persisted by saying, "Where?" Pat replied, "Where?" (laughing gently) "I had to go down the hall for a little while. OK?" They shared a long look at this point. Then Pat said, "All right?" Jill said "Yeah." It was obvious from this interaction that Jill was accustomed to communicating openly with her mother regarding the dyad's behavior and that she expected honest and open answers from her mother. Once Jill accepted her mother's explanation for her departure, she was able to resume her play. Negative feelings were both expressed and resolved.

Pat's behavior also contributed to the Secure classification. She delighted in her daughter's behavior and in their interaction together. She was unthreatened and amused by Jill's desire to play with Sara. Pat gave Jill clear answers regarding Sara's whereabouts and acknowledged Jill's desire to play with Sara. Upon reunion with her daughter, Pat put Jill's needs before the needs of the researchers by automatically following Jill to a mirror that was out of camera range to see Jill put a play mask on.

Although Jill is securely attached to her mother, she displayed some behaviors that are not typical of secure children. Secure children explore widely prior to separation episodes, and their play is typically complex. Although they may use a stranger to help them cope with separation, secure children rarely initiate interaction with the stranger (Crittenden, 1992a). Jill explored very little during the pre-separation episode. She stayed very close to her mother and relied heavily on Pat to structure the play. In addition, her play lacked the complexity and creativity expected from secure children. Like secure children, however, there was a dramatic reduction in Jill's play upon Pat's departure, and she used the stranger to gain information about her mother's whereabouts. However, unlike secure children, Jill initiated all of the overtures toward the stranger.

The behavior that notably contributed to Jill's Secure (Other) classification and set her apart from other secure children was her indiscriminate friendliness toward strangers. She initiated all interaction with the stranger during the separation episode. She moved very close to the stranger and watched her quite openly. Jill's indiscriminate friendliness was displayed even more clearly toward Sara. It is unlikely that a secure child would leave an interaction with her attachment figure to search out an absent stranger. Her indiscriminate friendliness was apparent once again when Sara reentered the house. Jill displayed obvious delight with Sara's return, jumping up from the interaction with her mother and racing toward her. Such delight upon the return of a stranger is surprising. This behavior, however, is not unusual among children with Romanian orphanage experience. Based on parents' reports from a sample of 33 Romanian adoptees, 65% of these children displayed indiscriminate friendliness (Chisholm et al., 1995).

What do displays of indiscriminate friendliness indicate? Given that attachment by definition is a discriminating bond, some researchers have suggested that indiscriminate friendliness is indicative of nonattachment (Lieberman & Pawl, 1988; Provence & Lipton, 1962). Jill's behavior during her mother's absence, however, demonstrates that she clearly discriminates between her mother and others.

For some dyads, the indiscriminately friendly displays of children may be perceived by parents as rejection. In contrast, Pat was both delighted and unthreatened by Jill's desire for the stranger, and communicated openly with Jill about Sara's whereabouts. Therefore, the mere presence of indiscriminate friendliness does not tell us about the attachment relationship. More importantly, it is how indiscriminately friendly behavior is organized, the function it serves, and the perception of such behavior by attachment figures that truly inform us.

Pat's obvious delight in Jill's behaviors, even those that may be viewed as nonoptimal, provided Jill with a responsive, safe environment wherein she could learn that she was loved and that she could trust what her attachment figure communicated to her. In this way she has learned to articulate openly her own feelings without fear of rejection. For a child who began life in an environment where few of her needs were met, Jill has come to see herself as loved and others as lovable, and this is a wonderful accomplishment.

Jamie

Jamie and his twin brother Todd[1] were adopted from a Romanian orphanage when they were 4 years 5 months old. Initially Rose and Eric, his adoptive parents, had intended to adopt an infant to complete their family but because there were a limited number of children available for adoption, they adopted two 4-year-old boys. They also had Rose's 9-year-old biological daughter at home.

The Institution. Jamie had lived in the orphanage since he was 2 months old, and his adoptive parents, Rose and Eric, had no information regarding his birth or medical history. The conditions in Jamie's orphanage were very similar to those in the orphanage from which Jill was adopted. The orphanage itself was unsanitary and unheated. The children were unclean, and two to three caregivers had the task of caring for 30 to 40 children. Although unable to visit the boys' rooms, Rose and Eric doubted that the children had any toys to play with. Rose and Eric were permitted to take the boys on outings, and in the last week before their adoption was finalized, they were able to have the boys with them in their hotel. Jamie's parents suspected that both he and Todd had been physically abused in the orphanage, given the scarring on their backs.

Jamie's Condition When First Adopted. Like Jill, Jamie was delayed in all areas of development at the time he was adopted. He was below the 5th percentile for his age on all growth parameters; he was small in stature with a small head, and he weighed 31 pounds. At 4 years 5 months of age Jamie's gross motor skills were at the 21- to 24-month-old level and his fine motor skills were at the 18- to 21-month-old level.

---

[1] The choice to profile Jamie rather than his brother Todd was an attempt to match as closely as possible two orphanage children who had a similar orphanage experience (e.g., conditions in the orphanage, length of institutionalization, physical and psychological condition at the time of adoption) and yet subsequently developed different attachment patterns. Jamie and Jill were more closely matched than Todd and Jill in terms of their condition at adoption.

Jamie displayed several atypical behaviors that were directly attributable to his orphanage experience. He was passive, did not smile, incessantly rocked and sucked his thumb, rarely cried, and did not like to be held or cuddled by his adoptive parents. He had a number of fears (e.g., animals, particularly dogs; baths; and heights), and yet he also displayed indiscriminate friendliness toward strangers. Jamie was attention seeking and demanding, which was understandably difficult for Rose, given that she also had two other children to care for. Jamie ate with a sense of urgency and drank incessantly without swallowing; according to Rose, he would simply let the liquid "pour down his throat." For months after he was adopted, Rose reported that he "never seemed to get enough to drink." His language development showed extreme delays. He called everyone "Mommy," was echolalic, and knew three to four simple words.

In addition to Jamie, Rose had to deal with Todd's many behavior problems, which she found more difficult to cope with than Jamie's behaviors. Rose reported that Todd would deliberately harm himself (e.g., he would punch himself in the nose until his nose bled and would laugh about it), was cruel and mean to other people and to animals, displayed many strange behaviors, and was easily overstimulated. For example, often at bedtime Todd would race around his bedroom, laughing hysterically. In addition, like Jamie, Todd rarely cried, was withdrawn, rocked and sucked his thumb.

Rose also voiced some concern regarding her daughter's ability to adapt to her two new brothers and their behaviors. Her daughter had been expecting an infant sibling, so she was ill-prepared for two 4-year-old brothers. Rose reported that the boys continually teased and attempted to upset their sister and "seemed to know all the right buttons to push with her."

Jamie's Progress 7 Months Post-adoption. When we first visited Jamie's family, they had moved to another town since his adoption. He had now been with his adoptive family for approximately 7 months and was 5 years of age. At this time Jamie's physical development had shown progress, but his fine motor skills were still grossly delayed (2 $1/2$-year-old level). Jamie continued to demonstrate pronounced language delays, although his receptive language was better than his expressive abilities. He was able to name some objects and was willing to repeat the names of objects he wasn't able to identify. To compound his speech problems, since his adoption he had developed a severe stuttering problem. His speech pathologist, however, was unconcerned about this until such time as Jamie could use more expressive language. Jamie continued to rock and suck his thumb and tended to get overly excited about food.

Few of Jamie's difficult behaviors had improved over time, and Rose reported experiencing considerable stress in dealing with the boy's behavior. Rose reported that parenting the boys was a more difficult task than she had anticipated. A particular concern was the tendency for Todd to physically fight with Jamie. Rose reported that Todd often "would beat up on Jamie and Jamie would not retaliate." She stated that Todd terrorized Jamie to the point that Jamie would retreat to his room, where he would stand against the wall rocking and sucking his thumb. Even though his brother often physically hurt him, Rose reported that Jamie was close to his brother and was often anxious when separated from him. If Todd was out, Jamie continually asked about his whereabouts and inquired when he would return.

Rose reported that Jamie was also prone to temper tantrums, during which he would scream, kick, and throw objects around the room. Using time-out in his room to deal with this behavior appeared ineffective, given that when placed there Jamie would simply destroy everything he could. Rose was unable to get any respite from caring for the boys. She felt she couldn't leave them with anyone because they were too difficult for anyone else to manage.

Seven months after his adoption, Jamie still displayed indiscriminately friendly behavior, which concerned Rose. She reported that Jamie often approached total strangers, and she felt that he would be willing to go home with anyone. Rose stated that she had to watch Jamie all of the time because he had a tendency to wander away without concern.

Jamie's Progress 2 Years 4 Months Post-adoption. When we visited Jamie's family for the second time, he had been in Canada for 2 years 4 months and he was 7 years 4 months old. The family had just recently moved again to another town. Rose was expecting a fourth child and had been quite ill for the last two months. Jamie was still below the 5th percentile for weight and was 46 inches tall. He enjoyed outdoor gross motor activities and had recently learned to ride his two-wheel bicycle. Although in Kindergarten he had adjusted well (with an aide), he was now struggling with the Grade 1 workload. Moreover, even though at this time Jamie had shown progress in some areas, Rose still had concerns about many of his behaviors. Jamie's rocking and thumb sucking had decreased, but he still displayed these behaviors when he was upset. He maintained his fear of dogs and was often startled by loud noises. Jamie's language was still delayed to the point that Rose reported that children his age did not attend to him because "he doesn't talk the way they do." Jamie's speech was very difficult to understand, and it appeared that his peers simply did not take the time to decipher what he was saying. He was often teased by peers about the way he talked, but his stuttering problem had shown improvement on this second visit. Although Rose felt that other children didn't play with Jamie because he "talked funny," she also reported that he didn't play at a 7-year-old level, which undoubtedly contributed to peer rejection. Rose was concerned about this peer rejection but stated that Jamie seemed unaffected by it.

Rose stated that since moving to their new home, both Jamie and Todd had awakened in the night with nightmares, although Todd experienced more nightmares than Jamie. This had not been a problem previously, and

Rose felt, at least in Jamie's case, that such nightmares were usually the result of movies that he had watched prior to bedtime.

Another behavior that Rose had not reported during our first visit was Jamie's "need to break things." Rose said that when he was given a toy or object Jamie "seemed to have a need to step on or throw it until the toy broke." He had attempted to disassemble the swing set in the backyard and had unscrewed and removed a full-length mirror from his bedroom wall. Rose also reported extreme frustration with Jamie's inattention to rules. She reported that she had to tell Jamie rules repeatedly, and "he just doesn't seem to get it." Jamie was still prone to temper tantrums that were often either the result of frustration or in response to discipline. Rose reported little improvement in the fighting between Jamie and Todd. Such fighting often resulted in her having to separate the boys and have them play independently in separate areas of the house. Jamie continued to have problems getting along with his older sister, and Rose described this as a "personality clash" between the two.

At the time of this second interview, Jamie continued to display indiscriminately friendly behavior toward strangers. Rose felt he would be willing to go home with a stranger he had just met, that he was never shy, and that, if given the opportunity, he would likely wander off and not be distressed at separation. Rose had received little help or advice dealing with Jamie's behavior and stated that she felt isolated, given that other adoptive parents she knew did not have the same experiences. Initially, she had socialized with other families who had adopted children from Romania, but she found this quite discouraging because none of the families reported having as many difficulties with behavior problems in their children.

Assessment of Attachment. Attachment was assessed using the same procedure described for Jill. Jamie's relationship with Rose was coded as Compulsively Caregiving (A3). In Crittenden's system this is a defended strategy in which the child organizes his or her behavior to maintain access to an attachment figure while avoiding emotional involvement (Crittenden, 1992a). Such children strike a balance between keeping an attachment figure physically available while simultaneously retaining emotional distance. Caregiving children use several patterns in interaction with their attachment figure. They may soothe or give care to a withdrawn attachment figure, attempt to "cheer up" their attachment figure, or maintain the pretense of involvement with their attachment figure by carrying on a one-sided conversation (Crittenden, 1992a).

We clearly saw this strategy in Jamie's behavior. When the play interaction began, Rose appeared quiet and somewhat withdrawn. In contrast, Jamie was false bright, seemingly having a wonderful time. This asynchrony in the affective displays of mother and child persisted throughout the interaction. Jamie got extremely excited when he saw a toy in the toy basket, but once he picked it up he quickly discarded it on the floor. He got very excited about every toy he picked up, but his discarding toys without investigation indicated a lack of interest. As a result, his overbrightness appeared false.

According to Crittenden (1992a), caregiving children use false, overbright affect in an attempt to gain and/or maintain an attachment figure's attention. Jamie used this strategy throughout the interaction. His overbright, exaggerated affect succeeded in gaining and sometimes maintaining his mother's attention. When he had her attention, his caregiver was physically available to him. Jamie's false bright affect also served the function of disguising the interaction so that it appeared as though the dyad was enjoying their time together, even though each member was typically focused on different things. Such interactions could be mistaken as secure except that Jamie's affective displays were false, overdone. The monologue that Jamie conducted as he played is yet another example of a caregiving strategy. Such conversation made it appear as though Rose was involved in Jamie's play. Rose, however, mainly continued her focus on the blocks, the first toy she had removed from the basket.

Together with Jamie's overbright affect, his lack of negative affect during the interaction also suggests a defended strategy. Jamie inhibited any display of negative emotion even at times when such displays would be expected (i.e., departure and separation). Crittenden (1992a) has stated that defended children often inhibit open displays of negative emotion because such displays may lead to rejection by the attachment figure. In contrast, secure dyads openly express both positive and negative emotions.

Further evidence for a caregiving strategy is the fact that Jamie often took responsibility for keeping the interaction going. When there were silences during the interaction, Jamie became overbright and moved to another toy in a bid for Rose's attention. Jamie initiated interaction, albeit from afar, by holding toys out to his mother for her comment. When Rose made suggestions with respect to what they should do, Jamie responded with excitement, although this excitement often did not translate into his participation in the suggested activity. His mother's attention to his play was fleeting. As quickly as interaction was initiated, it was often terminated by both Jamie and Rose looking down and away from each other.

Jamie and Rose appeared awkward in interaction with each other, and there were very few times when they were close enough to touch. This behavior fits a defended strategy of "being close but not too close" (Crittenden, 1992a). Their conversation also seemed awkward because it was often out of synchrony. What one partner said was often independent of what the other had just said.

Rose's behavior also contributes to the Caregiving classification. Throughout the interaction, Rose was quiet and somewhat withdrawn. When she attempted to initiate interaction, it did not appear as though she expected

Jamie to respond. She became interested in Jamie's play with the toy house (i.e., passing him figures, pointing out the swing and the slide), but she never moved any closer to the play. She handed him toys by reaching her arm across the toy basket, which she kept between them. It could be suggested that Rose may have been unsure about moving the toy basket because of the needs of the researchers. Nonetheless, this also suggests that the demands of the particular situation take precedence over Jamie's demands. Although Rose spoke to Jamie, her gaze was often not directed toward him. More often she looked down and away from him when she spoke. This is in stark contrast to the close physical proximity and the shared, open looks characteristic of secure dyads.

Jamie's play also lacked the interactive and symbolic qualities characteristic in the play of secure children. He appeared unable to settle on any activity for very long. Rather than genuinely enjoying an activity, Jamie seemed attention-seeking in much of his play. Furthermore, as Crittenden has suggested, in defended dyads toys serve as a distraction because they draw attention away from the relationship. This was clear when Rose and Jamie played with the puzzle. During puzzle play, they were closer together than they had been throughout the interaction. Both of them kept their eyes focused downward, working busily on the puzzle together. It almost appeared as though they were feeling, "We can interact together and have fun, as long as we keep it on this superficial level."

When Rose was signaled to leave the house, she stood saying, "OK now. I'm going to go out for a minute so you can try that, OK?" Jamie nodded his head and said, "Yeah. Yeah." He kept his eyes cast downward until his mother's back was turned and she was leaving the room. He then turned and looked briefly at her retreating back. Then he shifted his attention to the puzzle he was working on, talking to himself as he tried to put two incorrect pieces together. Jamie's overbright behavior was attenuated in Rose's absence, and he appeared more relaxed and became absorbed in his play. He looked twice at the camera person with a full smile. He only looked directly at his mother twice during their interaction, and these looks were fleeting. Also absent in Rose and Jamie's interaction was the expected open negotiation regarding shared plans seen in secure dyads. As Rose left, Jamie did not inquire about where she was going and did not appear distressed by her departure. In addition, he requested no explanation concerning her whereabouts when she returned. Upon his mother's return, Jamie instantly became false bright again and was less relaxed (e.g., stammered about his progress on the puzzle).

DISCUSSION

Jill and Jamie were two children who were part of a larger study that examined attachment in children adopted from Romanian orphanages (Chisholm, 1998). In the Romanian orphanage sample as a whole ($n = 43$), approximately one-third of children were securely attached, one-third displayed rather typical insecure attachment patterns according to Crittenden's system, and one-third displayed atypical attachment patterns. So Jill's attachment pattern is representative of the one-third of Romanian orphanage children in the Secure group, and Jamie is representative of the one-third of Romanian children displaying atypical insecure patterns. Is there any evidence that might explain why Jamie and Jill have developed very different attachment relationships with their attachment figures?

Several issues must be considered in an attempt to answer this question. First, consideration of the similarities and differences in the children's pre-adoption histories is important to establish the kinds of internal working models of self and others that each child likely developed prior to adoption. Second, it is important to evaluate both the number and the kinds of behavior problems each child displayed. This is because such problems may mediate the development of attachment through the strong relationship between behavior problems and parenting stress. Third, several differences in the family systems experienced by Jamie and Jill may contribute to our understanding.

Pre-adoption Histories

To a certain extent, Jill and Jamie experienced similar histories prior to their adoption. Both had come from understaffed, unsanitary, overcrowded orphanages where there was never enough to eat or drink and where the world remained unresponsive to any of their actions. Clearly, both children were exposed to extreme neglect. Both Jamie and Jill were passive, withdrawn, and nonverbal when their parents first met them. It is important to note, however, that pre-attachment history variables in the Romanian sample as a whole did not predict children's attachment patterns. Orphanage children classified as insecure were no more likely than Orphanage children classified as secure to have spent a longer time in institution or to have come from poorer quality institutions. Orphanage children classified as insecure were also no more likely to have been dirty or soiled in the institution, or to have been a favorite child in the institution (Chisholm & Carter, 1997).

The pre-adoption histories of Jill and Jamie do differ, however, in one important respect. Although both children experienced extreme neglect, there was no evidence that Jill had been physically abused in the orphanage. In contrast, it appeared that both Jamie and his brother Todd had been abused, given the scars on their backs and some of their behaviors (e.g., Todd's self-harming behavior and aggression toward others). The abuse that Jamie experienced, concomitant with neglect, may have made it doubly difficult for him to form a secure attachment. Researchers have clearly demonstrated that abused and/or neglected children are typically insecurely attached to their caregivers (Crittenden, 1985b; Egeland & Sroufe, 1981b;

Schneider-Rosen, Braunwald, Carlson, & Cicchetti, 1985) and often display difficult interaction patterns with their attachment figures (Crittenden, 1988b). Although Jamie experienced abuse only prior to his adoption, such a history has undoubtedly made it more difficult for him to learn to love and trust others and to develop a sense of the world as safe. Compounding these feelings, Jamie continued to experience physical aggression from his brother. He has adapted to his history of abuse by allowing others "to get close, but not too close" (Crittenden, 1992a).

Behavior Problems

Behavior problems are particularly stressful for parents. In our sample of Romanian adoptees, we have found that children's behavior problems are more highly correlated with parenting stress than are their developmental delays (Mainemer & Gilman, 1992). After adoption, both Jamie and Jill continued to exhibit delays in their physical and language development. Both were distractible, and Jill had been diagnosed with ADHD. Most of Jill's behavior problems (rocking, tantrumming, fears), however, had steadily improved since her adoption. Her mother felt that Jill had made tremendous progress, and this, in itself, was encouraging to her.

In contrast, few of Jamie's behavior problems had dissipated, even after two years in his adoptive home. This was understandably disheartening for Rose. She was often overwhelmed by the behaviors displayed by both Jamie and Todd. Jamie's inattention to rules and his need to destroy things were particularly frustrating. The discipline techniques that Rose used were appropriate (e.g., time-out in his room, discussing misbehavior) but often seemed ineffective in changing Jamie's behavior. Because she experienced such frustration and had to spend an inordinate amount of time administering discipline, it is unlikely that Rose was able to be as warm and responsive to Jamie's needs as she might otherwise have been. If parents begin to feel discouraged because their parenting strategies appear ineffective, they may withdraw somewhat from their child.

It is crucial, however, to keep in mind the transactional nature of relationships (Sameroff, 1994). For example, Jamie brings difficult behaviors to the interaction with his mother, she responds, hoping to change the behavior; Jamie continues displaying the behavior; she becomes discouraged and less responsive; Jamie escalates his behavior in an attempt to gain his mother's attention. A cycle of interaction is created that is difficult to break.

Family Systems

The role of maternal sensitivity and responsiveness in the development of secure attachments in children has been strongly supported in the literature

(Ainsworth, Blehar, Waters, & Wall, 1978; Sroufe, 1985). Theory also suggests, however, that the study of attachment should be conducted using a family systems approach (Marvin & Stewart, 1990). Family systems models maintain that transitions or changes in one part of the system affect all other parts of the system. Such an approach is particularly useful when considering the different relationships that Jamie and Jill have developed with their mothers.

Jamie's family adopted two Romanian children, both of whom had numerous behavior problems. In our sample of adoptive families, we have found that families adopting two Romanian children experienced more parenting stress than families who had adopted one child (Mainemer, Gilman, & Ebbern, 1997). Compounding this stress, Rose and Eric also had an older, biological daughter at home who had some difficulty adjusting to her brothers. Even in the best of circumstances, adjustment to new siblings would be difficult for a child who had been the only child in a household for nine years. Add to this the fact that she had anticipated an infant sibling and that the boys continually terrorized and teased her, and we see the considerable stress this situation would create. Although Rose reported that Eric was supportive and helpful with the children, Rose was still managing the boys, with their myriad behavior problems, on her own during the day. In addition, at the time of our second assessment, she was expecting a fourth child and could only anticipate the family becoming more complex in the future.

Another consideration is that Rose and Eric had moved their family twice since Jamie was adopted. Moves in themselves are stressful and require a transition period for families. It takes time to find a new support system of friends and to establish new relationships. This was perhaps even more difficult because Rose was unable to get any respite from the boys given that their behaviors were too difficult for others to manage. Even though Rose and Eric had initially belonged to a support group of families who had adopted Romanian children, Rose did not find the group particularly helpful for her and felt somewhat isolated as a result. The moves must also have been stressful for the boys, given the unpredictability such moves would create in their lives. Quite clearly, Jamie's family experienced considerable stress from various sources after his adoption. The task of responsive parenting becomes formidable when a parent is exposed to such stressors. Researchers have found both parenting stress and parental lack of social support to be related to children's insecure attachment (Crittenden, 1985a; Jacobson & Frye, 1991; Jarvis & Creasy, 1991).

In contrast, Jill was adopted by a single professional woman and was the only child in her household. Although Pat worked outside of the home, she did not have other children who were experiencing problems that required her time and energy. She was able to focus considerable attention on Jill, and she also had time away from her. In addition, Pat had training in dealing with special needs children and so was perhaps more prepared and familiar with the types of problems that Jill presented than most parents would be. Although Jill had many problems (e.g., fears, distractibility) to overcome, Pat's training may have made it easier for her to cope with these problems and seek warm, responsive ways to deal with them.

Pat and Jill had lived in the same home since Jill's adoption. Jill's world was both consistent and predictable. Pat had a large support group of family and friends who were very interested in Jill and the progress she was making. Pat's own parents lived nearby, and they were a large part of Jill's life, spending a lot of time with her (e.g., taking her on outings, baby-sitting). Every Sunday her grandparents joined Jill and Pat for dinner. This provided Jill with another loving relationship and also gave Pat some respite from caregiving. In addition, Pat had a very good friend whose family had adopted a Romanian child the same age as Jill. This friendship equipped Pat with considerable social support because she was able to discuss Jill's difficulties with her friend and could share potential strategies for alleviating problems. All of these conditions contributed to effective, responsive parenting.

CONCLUSIONS

Contrary to suggestions in the early literature on institutionalized children (Goldfarb, 1945a, 1945b), it is clear that even children who have spent their first three to four years in institution are able to form attachment relationships. Both Jill and Jamie have formed attachments to their adoptive parents. The present case studies suggest the range of outcomes that previously institutionalized children may experience, the process through which attachment relationships develop, and the somewhat atypical organizations of attachment that develop.

Although Jill developed a secure attachment with her mother, she was classified as Secure (Other) because some of the behaviors and strategies she used in interaction with her mother were not characteristic of the major patterns of security. Specifically, Jill's indiscriminately friendly behavior and the lack of complexity in her play do not typically reflect secure patterns. In addition, Jill was more upset during the separation episode than most 7-year-olds who have developed a goal-corrected partnership with their caregivers (Schneider-Rosen, 1993). Jill's behavior is not so unusual, however, if we consider her developmental history; in the experience of attachment, Jill is still a young child. If parents of adoptees who had never had an opportunity to develop an attachment in the first few years of life were to view their children's behaviors through this lens, those behaviors might seem less strange. This would enable parents to cope more effectively with their children's behavior, and, as a result, parents would be warmer and more responsive in interaction with them. I would not suggest, however, that Jill's pattern of attachment simply reflects developmental delay; rather, it may reflect a somewhat different developmental pathway to security.

Given the physical abuse Jamie experienced prior to adoption, the little improvement in his behavior problems, and the stress experienced by his family, it is a comment on Rose's perseverance that Jamie has indeed formed an attachment relationship with her. Although his attachment lacks the security we would like to see, there is certainly the possibility of changing Jamie's insecure pattern in the future. If some of the stressors that Rose has experienced are alleviated, she may be better able to cope with Jamie's behaviors. If as a result, she begins to see some encouraging changes in Jamie's behavior, such changes may result in her becoming more contingently responsive to his needs. As a consequence, his behavior may improve further, which could lead to yet warmer responsive interactions with Rose. In this way Jamie could learn that his attachment figure is available to meet his needs, and we may indeed see him become more secure.

The Jamie and Jill case studies have given us valuable information concerning both the attachment process and the resiliency displayed by previously institutionalized children. These studies provide us with examples of the possibility of altering existing maladaptive developmental pathways through changing children's environments (Cicchetti, 1993).

CHAPTER ELEVEN

Maternal Depression and Child–Mother Attachment in the First Three Years

A View from the Intermountain West[1]

DOUGLAS M. TETI

INTRODUCTION

That maternal depression places children at risk for mother–child interactional disturbances is amply documented, with depressed mothers variously characterized as incompetent, insensitive, disengaged, intrusive, uninvolved, and emotionally flat, and their children as manifesting greater emotional dysregulation, gaze-avoidance, distress, and higher rates of psychiatric symptoms than children of nondepressed mothers (Cummings & Davies, 1994; Downey & Coyne, 1990; Gelfand & Teti, 1990; Teti & Gelfand, 1997a). Indeed, reports of the debilitating effects of maternal depression on mother–child relationships are quite consistent throughout the depressed mother literature, justifying the expectation that young children of depressed mothers are at higher risk for insecure attachment than are children of nondepressed mothers. This chapter addresses the impact of maternal depression on children, examines the somewhat inconsistent literature on relations between maternal depression and child–mother attachment, and specifically examines the links between maternal depression, security of child–mother attachment, and the quality of maternal behavior in an Intermountain West sample of clinically depressed and nondepressed mothers during their children's infancy and preschool years. In doing so, it also addresses the construct validity of the Preschool Assessment of Attachment (PAA) (Crittenden, 1992a, 1992b), a newly developed attachment classification system for use in the preschool years.

Acknowledgment: This chapter was supported by NIMH Grant 41474 awarded to Donna M. Gelfand and Douglas M. Teti. We wish to thank the Salt Lake Valley Mental Health Services, participating practitioners, and John E. Brockert, Director, Bureau of Vital Records, Utah Department of Health, for assistance in subject recruitment. Special thanks are given to the participants of this longitudinal project. Requests for reprints can be directed to the author, Department of Psychology, University of Maryland Baltimore County, 1000 Hilltop Circle, Baltimore, MD 21250 (e-mail: teti@umbc2.umbc.edu).

Parental Depression and Child Psychopathology: Theoretical Perspectives

Processes underlying the intergenerational transmission of psychopathology are complexly rooted in what is perhaps the "core" issue of development, that of nature versus nurture. Among depressed parents and their offspring, the context most often examined for clues in this regard is the parent–child relationship and in particular the quality of depressed parents' behavior toward their children. Several theoretical models of transmission have been advanced. Cognitive theories of depression (Abramson, Seligman, & Teasdale, 1978; Beck, 1967) suggest that depression predisposes dysphoric attributions not only about the self but also the broader social environment. Dysphoric attributions in parents can thus be expected to generalize to perceptions about one's children (see Gelfand & Teti, 1990, and Teti & Gelfand, 1997a, for reviews), which in turn can be expected to influence parental behavior. Negative perceptions about children's motives and behavior may predispose a parent's selective attention to misbehavior, verbal criticism, and aversive, coercive parent–child exchanges that set the stage for oppositional-defiant child behavior (Patterson, 1982; Teti & Gelfand, 1997ab). At a more cognitive level, a depressed parent's negative perceptions and labeling of a child may lead subsequently to the child's internalization of negative self-schemas, selective attention to and processing of negative information about the self, and subsequent vulnerability to psychopathology.

Models of faulty emotion regulation (Cohn, Campbell, Matias, & Hopkins, 1990; Emde & Sorce, 1983; Field, 1986; Tronick & Gianino, 1986) have been invoked to explain the impact of maternal depression on infant functioning, in particular citing the negative impact of parental dysphoria on the infant's emotional displays and self-regulatory capacities when exploring the environment and socially engaging others. Cohn et al. (1986) and Field (1984), for example, demonstrated that normal mothers who act "depressed" in face-to-face exchanges with their infants for short periods predispose infant gaze aversion and negative affect. Although prediction from infancy to later periods of life can be problematic (Sameroff & Chandler, 1975), emotional dysregulation has been identified as central to conceptualizations of psychopathology in both adults and children (Cole, Michel, & Teti, 1995). Poor self-regulatory capacities established early in life may be difficult to overcome, predisposing negative parent–child interactional exchanges (especially if the parent is also emotionally dysregulated), poor self-control, lack of empathy, problematic peer relations, and later psychopathology.

It is attachment theory, however, that provides one of the most comprehensive and compelling frameworks for explaining the effects of parental depression on children. Ainsworth's seminal observations of infant–mother relationships identified maternal sensitivity during the first year of life as a critically important precursor to secure infant–mother attachments, so characterized when infants displayed an ability to use the mother as a secure base from which to explore their environments under conditions of moderate stress (Ainsworth, Blehar, Waters, & Wall, 1978). In Ainsworth's now classic study, sensitive mothering, conceptualized as an empathic awareness of and appropriate responsivity to an infant's needs and desires, predicted secure (Type B) attachment at 12 months, whereas insensitive mothering (e.g., unresponsive, inconsistent, rejecting, and/or abusive parenting), predicted insecure-avoidant (Type A) or insecure-ambivalent (Type C) 12-month attachments (see Bretherton, 1985, and Teti & Nakagawa, 1990, for reviews). The significance of early attachments for later socio-emotional development is rooted in the premise that early attachment relationships are the foundation for developing internal working models of self and other, models that serve as gateways for processing and interpreting social information (Bowlby, 1969/1982; Bretherton, 1985; Crittenden, 1992a, 1992b; Main, Kaplan, & Cassidy, 1985). A secure attachment, presumably the outcome of sensitive, appropriate care, should lead to a working model in which the child views the caretaker as loving and responsive, and himself as worthy of that love. By contrast, an insecure attachment, presumably rooted in a history of insensitive care, should lead to a working model wherein the child views the caretaker as unresponsive and possibly rejecting, and herself as unworthy of love. Over the long term, individual differences in the contents of internal working models are believed to have organizational influences on children's behavior both within and outside of the original attachment relationship, and to be increasingly resistant to change (see Bretherton, 1985, for an excellent discussion of these points).

In light of data consistently associating maternal depression with inadequate, insensitive care, attachment theory would view children of depressed mothers to be at high risk for developing insecure attachments and, over the long run, faulty working models of self and other that could lead to child behavior disorder and depression, especially in the context of enduring family stressors (Lewis, Feiring, McGuffog, & Jaskir, 1984). Furthermore, given the association of disorganized/disoriented attachment patterns (Main & Solomon, 1990) with high pathognomic caregiving environments (Cicchetti & Barnett, 1991; Lyons-Ruth, Connell, Grunebaum, & Botein, 1990; Rodning, Beckwith, & Howard, 1991; Spieker & Booth, 1988), it is not unreasonable to expect disorganized attachments in infancy, and atypical attachment patterns in the preschool years, to be associated with maternal depression, especially if mothers' illness is chronic and severe. This chapter begins with an examination of available literature on maternal depression–early attachment relations, and in turn presents findings from a longitudinal study, with an intervention component, of maternal depression and child development in the first three years, based in Salt Lake City, Utah.

This study's sample is unique in having a heavy (but not exclusive) concentration of Latter Day Saints (LDS–Mormon) mothers in both the depressed and nondepressed groups, a religious and cultural group that is quite representative of the Intermountain West region of the United States. A second important feature of the sample is the age range of the children, which spanned the infancy and preschool period at the time security of attachment was assessed and necessitated the use of separate attachment coding systems for infants (Ainsworth et al., 1978; Main & Solomon, 1990) and preschoolers (the Preschool Assessment of Attachment; Crittenden, 1992b). Thus this chapter presents separate analyses of relations between maternal depression and security of attachment in two age groups of children. Attention is then directed to two questions that derive straightforwardly from the depressed mother literature and attachment theory: First, is quality of attachment related predictably to a diagnosis of unipolar depression given during the first year postpartum and to the severity/chronicity of mothers' depression during the first two to three years postpartum? Second, does attachment security and child–mother attachment relate in a theoretically predictable fashion to the quality of maternal behavior during structured observational tasks? Indeed, the Salt Lake City sample may be uniquely suited to address these questions, from the perspective of statistical power and effect size, because of the extreme variation observed in depressive symptoms across the mothers.

Featured in this chapter are two developmentally relevant attachment classification systems, the first being the well-established Ainsworth – Main classification system for infants, and the second a recently developed system for preschoolers, the Preschool Assessment of Attachment (PAA) (Crittenden, 1992a, 1992b). Thus, examining relations among maternal depression, early attachment, and maternal behavior more broadly addresses the construct validity of this newly emergent classification system. The findings presented in this chapter and future research efforts relevant to the construct validity of the PAA represent another central component of this chapter.

Maternal Depression and Early Attachment

Interestingly, associations between unipolar maternal depression and attachment security in children have been established relatively recently (Murray, 1992; Teti, Gelfand, Messinger, & Isabella, 1995), with earlier work implicating bipolar, but not necessarily unipolar, maternal depression as predictive of insecure attachments in young children. Gaensbauer, Harmon, Cytryn, and McKnew (1984), for example, reported an increasing trend toward insecure attachment from 12 to 18 months of age in a small sample of infants ($n = 7$) with at least one bipolar parent. Furthermore, although Radke-Yarrow, Cummings, Kuczynski, and Chapman (1985) reported that children of depressed mothers (unipolars and bipolars combined) were significantly more likely to be insecurely attached than were children of nondepressed, control mothers, a post hoc Chi-square analysis of these data (conducted by this author) indicated that the bipolar group primarily accounted for this difference. The attachment status of children of mothers with unipolar depression (46% insecure) was not significantly different from that of children of nondepressed controls (29% insecure; $\chi^2_{(1)} = 2.04$, $p > .10$), when secure children from the Radke-Yarrow et al. (1985) study were compared with a combined insecure group of avoidant (Type A), ambivalent (Type C), and avoidant/ambivalent (Type A/C) children. By contrast, children of mothers with bipolar depression (79% insecure) were significantly more insecure than control children ($\chi^2_{(1)} = 9.59$, $p < .005$). Similar results were reported in a followup study from the same sample of infants, toddlers, and preschoolers (DeMulder & Radke-Yarrow, 1991) in which attachment security of children over 30 months of age was re-coded using the MacArthur working group (Cassidy, Marvin, et al., 1991) classification guidelines for preschoolers. Indeed, at least four additional studies of infants and young children of mothers with *unipolar* illness report no associations between attachment security, using either the traditional Ainsworth A B C or the more recently elaborated Ainsworth-Main A B C D classification systems, and maternal depression (Campbell, Cohn, Meyers, Ross, & Flanagan, 1993; Naslund, Persson-Blennow, McNeil, Kaij, & Malmquist-Larsson, 1984; Sameroff, Seifer, & Zax, 1982; Seifer, Sameroff, Dickstein, Keitner, Miller, Rasmussen, & Hayden, 1996).

The absence in some studies of relations between insecure attachments in children and maternal unipolar depression is surprising, given evidence of interactional difficulties in mothers with unipolar depression (Gelfand & Teti, 1990) and the fact that quality of mothering and security of children's attachments have been established across a variety of contexts (Bretherton, 1985; Teti & Nakagawa, 1990). Two important factors that help to disentangle this puzzle are the *severity* and *chronicity* of maternal illness during the child's attachment-forming years, which may be more important determinants of child problem occurrence than parental diagnosis (Sameroff et al., 1982). In their study showing higher proportions of insecure attachments among children of bipolar mothers, DeMulder and Radke-Yarrow (1991) reported that their mothers with bipolar depression showed more psychiatric impairment from the Global Assessment of Severity (GAS) index of the Schedule for Affective Disorders and Schizophrenia, Lifetime Version (SADS-L) than did mothers with unipolar depression. Moreover, whereas Frankel, Maslin-Cole, and Harmon (1991) found no overall differences in maternal interactions and in the attachment security of 3-year-old children (using the classification guidelines of Cassidy, Marvin, et al., 1991) between mothers with and without unipolar depression, they did find significantly higher proportions of insecure children in a subgroup of mothers labeled as "doubly depressed" (mothers whose depression was both episodic and intermittent) relative to children of mothers with either an episodic or intermittent disorder alone.

Independent observers also rated "doubly" depressed mothers as significantly poorer parents than mothers with episodic or intermittent depression on dimensions of emotional availability and negative affect and behavior, dimensions touted by attachment theory and research as directly relevant to a child's inability to form a secure base attachment (Ainsworth et al., 1978; Bretherton, 1985). Campbell et al. (1993) also reported no associations between unipolar maternal depression and security of 12-month-infant attachment in their full sample but did find significant associations between chronic unipolar depression in mothers during infants' first 12 months of life and attachment insecurity. Importantly, these investigators found that maternal depressive symptoms in their postpartum depressed group dropped significantly from 2 months postpartum. At this time 86% and 14% of mothers met Research Diagnostic Criteria (RDC, based on the SADS interview) for major and minor depression, respectively, to 12 months postpartum, and only 15% of mothers in the postpartum depressed group met RDC criteria (Cohn, Campbell, & Ross, 1991). This drop in symptom severity may explain the lack of relations in infant attachment security between the postpartum depressed and nondepressed groups in the full sample.

The relation of maternal symptom severity and insecure infant attachment is also highlighted in Ross and Jennings (1992), who reported a significant association between depression symptom severity among mothers with unipolar and bipolar depression and insecure attachment in 11- to 36-month-old children; in Dawson, Klinger, Panagiotides, Spieker, and Frey (1992), who found depression severity to relate positively to ratings of infant disorganization in the Strange Situation; and in Spieker and Booth (1988), who found higher levels of maternal depressive symptoms when infants were 6 weeks of age among mothers of to-be-classified anxious-ambivalent (Type C) infants when compared to mothers of to-be-classified secure (Type B) infants. Finally, in one of the few studies examining relations between maternal depression and child outcome in the context of low socioeconomic status, environmental risk, and early intervention, Lyons-Ruth et al. (1990) found double the rate of insecure-disorganized attachments among 18-month infants of untreated depressed mothers, most of whom showed clinical levels of depressive symptoms over approximately the first 18 months of their infants' lives, when compared to infants of depressed mothers receiving a home-based intervention during this same time.

THE PRESENT STUDY: MATERNAL DEPRESSION AND CHILD–MOTHER ATTACHMENT IN SALT LAKE VALLEY

General Design

From 1988 to the present, my colleague, Donna Gelfand, and I have been conducting a large longitudinal study of depressed mothers and their children, based in and around Salt Lake City, Utah, a study supported by the National Institute of Mental Health (Grant no. 41474). This longitudinal study included two depressed mother–infant groups and one nondepressed group. One group of depressed mothers received a 12-month home-based intervention aimed at improving depressed mother–child relations and reconnecting socially isolated mothers with social agencies and networks in their communities. The other depressed mother group and the nondepressed group served as controls. Following recruitment (time 1, when infants were 3 to 13 months of age), a postintervention evaluation of mothers and children took place approximately 13 months later (time 2), at which point security of child–mother attachment was assessed with the Strange Situation along with a variety of additional observational and maternal perception measures. Two additional mother–child assessments took place approximately 7 months (time 3) and 18 months (time 4) after the initial postintervention visit.

Recruitment Strategy and Sample Characteristics

Of the 149 mothers with first-year infants in the initial recruitment sample, 91 were clinically depressed, in therapy at the time of recruitment, and were referred to the project by their therapists. Approximately 85% to 90% of the mothers solicited by therapists for this study were willing to participate. Excluded were any mothers with acting-out personality disorders, substance abuse, or bipolar affective disorders. Fifty-two of the 91 depressed mothers were assigned to receive a 12-month home-based intervention program, involving 29 home visits by trained public health nurses (one nurse per family), with the aim of improving the quality of the mother–child relationship via modeling and demonstration of appropriate and sensitive mothering routines, discussing specific parenting concerns, and fostering liaisons with social service and community networks as needed (see Gelfand, Teti, Seiner, & Jameson, 1996, for a comprehensive description of the intervention). The remaining 39 depressed mothers served as depressed controls. Fifty-eight nondepressed mothers were recruited with the assistance of the Utah Department of Vital Statistics from the same general neighborhoods as the depressed mothers, as a rough attempt to obtain a socioeconomic group match between the depressed and nondepressed groups. Further details about recruitment can be found in Teti et al. (1995) and Gelfand et al. (1996).

This chapter is concerned with the subsample of 104 mothers and infants for whom attachment data were collected at time 2 and for whom interactional data were collected at times 1, 2, and 3. All mothers had an infant between 3 and 13 months of age at recruitment (mean infant age = 7.16 mos., SD = 2.74). Sixty percent of the infants were male. The sample was lower-middle to middle class, with 79% of the mothers completing more than 12 years of schooling. Mothers ranged from 18.5 to 45.4 years of age at the time of recruitment, with a mean age of 30.27 years (SD = 5.42), and 95% of the sample was white, with 4% Hispanic and 1% African American. DSM-III-R (American Psychiatric Association, 1987) diagnoses of the depressed mothers were obtained from their therapists and included major depression (71%), dysthymia (16%), and adjustment disorder with depression as a major feature (13%). Attrition analyses of the 45 mothers who withdrew from the project between recruitment and the time security of attachment was assessed revealed no relations between attrition and group status, race, sex and age of infant, hours mothers worked outside the home, family income, and (for depressed mothers) diagnosis, length of previous and current depressive episode, and whether or not mothers were on medication. Mothers who dropped out, however, were more likely to be single (33% vs. 18%, $p < .05$), non-Latter Day Saints members (73% vs. 54%, $p < .05$), younger (25.87 vs. 30.29 years, $p < .001$), and less likely to have completed high school (30.2% vs. 8.6%, $p = .05$) than were mothers who remained.

The recruitment strategy for this study was unique relative to the general community screening methods employed in other studies of maternal depression in the field (e.g., Campbell et al., 1993; Radke-Yarrow et al., 1985). That all depressed mothers were already in therapy for their depression before referral to the project likely created a sample of women who were more severely depressed at recruitment, with a mean Beck Depression Inventory (BDI) (Beck, Ward, Mendelson, Mock, & Erbaugh, 1961) score among depressed mothers of 22.75. Their score reflected moderate-to-severe depression from BDI criteria set forth by Beck, Steer, and Garbin (1988), and their depression was likely to remain significantly elevated during their children's attachment forming years. Indeed, the depressed mothers in our sample were very likely to have experienced significant depression prior to the postpartum period, with 85% of the depressed mothers reporting previous bouts of depression. Furthermore, 47% of these mothers had depressive symptoms at recruitment severe enough to warrant antidepressant medication. By contrast, the nondepressed mothers in this study had low levels of depressive symptoms, with a mean BDI score of 6.81, which falls into the subclinical range (Beck et al., 1988). Thus, the present, relatively large sample was composed of mothers whose severity of depressive symptoms ranged widely. This in turn presented a unique opportunity, from the vantage point of statistical power and effect size, to examine not only the association between early child–mother attachments and the diagnosis of maternal depression in the postpartum period, but also the relation between the quality of early attachments and the chronicity and severity of maternal depression during the children's first two years.

Cultural Context

The preponderance (73%) of Latter Day Saints (LDS-Mormon) families in our sample was another unique feature of this study. There was no reason to expect the nature of relations between maternal depression, maternal–child relationships, and developmental outcomes in children to differ in this sample in comparison to others. However, the present study afforded the first opportunity ever to examine such relations in a U.S. subculture with increasing presence and influence, whose population ranges from the Rocky Mountains of Utah to the Sierra Mountains of California (including Utah, Nevada, western Colorado, northern Arizona, southern Idaho, and some parts of western Wyoming), an area termed the Intermountain West. Founded by Joseph Smith in the 1830s and first settled in Utah in 1846, Mormonism was "a radical and Utopian response to the prevailing political, economic, and sexual order … (an) answer to an America plagued by violence, poverty, slavery, and civil war; their new theocracy would accomplish what the Puritans had failed to do" (Gottlieb & Wiley, 1984, p. 13). The Mormons have since become an important conservative force in the United States, emphasizing a traditional patriarchal family structure that idealizes motherhood, eschews birth control and divorce, and views family size as determined by God. The traditional family prototype is one in which the husband is the sole provider, with the wife maintaining a supportive and nurturing role to her husband and children. It is important to note, however, that, paralleling trends in the United States as a whole, increasing numbers of Mormon women have been entering the workforce over the past four decades in response to economic realities. This in turn has created conflict among working Mormon mothers who wish to remain true to traditional Mormon values vis-à-vis women's roles in the home (Gottlieb & Wiley, 1984). The reader is referred to Shepherd and Shepherd (1984), Gottlieb and Wiley (1984), Kauffman and Kauffman (1994), Alexander (1986), and Campbell (1988) for more comprehensive treatments of LDS history, church structure and hierarchy, theology, and family life.

Measures

The larger, longitudinal study on which this chapter is based examined mother–infant functioning across a variety of domains, a complete coverage of which is beyond the scope of this chapter. All families received a series of two to three home visits, over a one-month period, at all four time points, and visited the university laboratory after home visits were completed at times 2, 3, and 4 for a series of videotaped recordings. This chapter examined relations among the following measures at times 1, 2, and 3.

Maternal Depression. The Beck Depression Inventory (BDI) (Beck et al., 1961), completed by all mothers during home visits at all four time points, served as an assessment of depressive symptom severity. At recruitment, the mean BDI score of depressed mothers was 22.81, reflecting moderate-to-severe depression (Beck, Steer, & Garbin, 1988), versus 6.81 for nondepressed mothers, a significant difference ($p < .001$).

Maternal Caregiving. Independent ratings of mothers' behavior toward their children were made in the home at times 1, 2, and 3 by trained graduate and undergraduate student raters who were blind to all other data on the mothers. These ratings were based on the theoretical contributions of Ainsworth et al. (1978) and Crittenden (1981) and were developed by Zoll, Lyons-Ruth, and Connell (1984). Four 5-point Likert-type rating scales were chosen because of their straightforward relevance to a "good mothering" construct. These scales included *maternal sensitivity* (the ability to read and respond appropriately to infant signals), *warmth* (the quality of expressed affection toward the child), *flatness of affect* (degree of impassive, expressionless affect as manifested in facial expressions and voice tone), and *disengagement* (disconnectedness from child as indexed by body positioning, pacing, and control of interaction). Mothers were rated twice on these four dimensions – once in a 10-minute observation of feeding and again in a 10-minute observation of free play using Shelcore's "Infant Soft Play Set" provided by the study. This yielded a total of eight ratings (four per observation). Interrater reliability (Pearson r) between two graduate trainers and undergraduate raters on these four dimensions ranged from .70 to .78, based on 45 mother–infant observations. Because all eight ratings related conceptually to quality of mothering and possessed high internal consistence (alpha = .90, .90, and .84 at times 1, 2, and 3, respectively), a composite *maternal behavioral competence* index was computed for each mother at times 1, 2, and 3 by summing for each mother the eight ratings at each time point. Interrater reliability on this composite was adequate (Pearson $r = .85$).

Child–Mother Attachments. Strange Situation video recordings at time 2 were used to assess quality of children's attachments to mothers. All assessments of the videotapes were conducted by this author, who was blind to all maternal identifying data. The Strange Situation procedure (Ainsworth & Wittig, 1969), in which children participate in a 21- to 24-minute series of three-minute episodes of separations from and reunions with the mother and a female stranger, has become the standard laboratory metric for assessing quality of attachment in young children. Because children at time 2 ranged in age from 11 to 31 months, two developmentally appropriate classification systems were employed. Attachment classifications for children under 21 months of age ($n = 50$) were derived with the traditional Ainsworth et al. (1978) and Main and Solomon (1990) infancy classification criteria. Attachment classifications for children 21 months and older were obtained using the Preschool Assessment of Attachment (Crittenden, 1992b).

(a) The infancy system yields one major secure classification (Type B; with subtypes B1 to B4) and three major insecure classification systems: *anxious-avoidant* (Type A; with subtypes A1 and A2), *anxious-resistant* (or *anxious-ambivalent;* Type C, with subtypes C1 and C2), and *disorganized-disoriented* (Type D). Secure (Type B) babies exhibit an appropriate balance between the attachment and exploratory behavioral systems and use the mother as a secure base to explore (Ainsworth et al., 1978; Sroufe & Waters, 1977). Secure babies typically greet their mothers during reunions, show some proximity seeking and contact maintenance, console readily on contact with mother, exhibit very low levels of avoidance and anger, and normally can move fluidly back into exploration with periodic checks on the mother's whereabouts. Differences among subtypes B1 to B4 relate to the degree of proximity seeking and contact maintenance seen (low in B1 babies, high in B4 babies). Anxious-avoidant babies (Type A) characteristically avoid the mother on reunion, as indexed by avoiding eye contact and ignoring the mother's social bids. A1 infants show very little proximity seeking and contact maintenance, whereas A2 infants mix conspicuous avoidance with some proximity seeking and contact maintenance. Anxious-resistant (or anxious-ambivalent) babies (Type C) are characteristically angry at the mother during reunion, as manifested by rejections of toy offers, pouting or whining, and/or showing prolonged distress despite the mother's efforts to console. C1 babies' anger is overt and actively directed at the mother, whereas C2 babies' anger is embedded in bouts of prolonged distress, conspicuous passivity, and helplessness. Disorganized-disoriented babies display behavior indicative of fear, conflict, or confusion vis-à-vis their mothers during reunions, which can be variously manifested (from Main and Solomon, 1990, pp. 146–140) by sequential or simultaneous display of contradictory behavior patterns; undirected, misdirected, incomplete, and interrupted movements and expressions; stereotypies, asymmetrical movements, mistimed movements, and anomalous postures; freezing, stilling, and slowed movements and expressions; and direct indexes of apprehension, disorganization, or disorientation.

(b) The Preschool Assessment of Attachment (PAA) (Crittenden, 1992b), used for children 21 months of age and older ($n = 54$), takes into account preschoolers' advancements, relative to infants, in social cognitive, linguistic, and emotional regulatory capacities in classification decisions. Based on the original Ainsworth tripartite classification scheme, it identifies one *secure* major category (Type B, with subtypes reserved, comfortable, and reactive) and insecure major categories of *defended* (Type A, with subtypes inhibited, compulsively caregiving, and compulsively compliant), *coercive* (Type C, with subtypes threatening, disarming, punitive, and helpless), *defended/coercive* (Type A/C), *Insecure Other* (Type IO), and *Anxious Depressed* (Type *AD*). Following Main (1981), Crittenden (1992a, 1992b) views all attachment behavior patterns as reflections of underlying strategies deployed by children when accessing their mothers in times of stress. Although most strategies are adaptive in the short term as children strive to cope with the demands of the social-ecological niche in which they are reared, secure children have distinct advantages over insecure children in terms of quality of adaptation over the long term. Secure children manifest an easy, intimate access to their mothers, express feelings directly and clearly, share the responsibility of affect regulation with their mothers, and openly negotiate plans for separations and reunions with their mothers.

Three subtypes are identified, based on the seminal work of Cassidy, Marvin, and the MacArthur Working Group (1991): secure-reserved (B1–2), secure-comfortable (B3), and secure-reactive (B4), with differences from B1–2 to B4 accounted for primarily by the degree of children's reactiveness to separation and of the propensity to seek out mothers on reunion (both increase from B1–2 to B4 subtypes). Defended children organize their behavior so as to limit access to their mothers by minimizing emotional displays and take primary responsibility for regulating their affect. Defended children spend a great deal of time focusing on toy play at the expense of their relationship with their mothers. Three defended subtypes are identified: inhibited (A1–2), characterized by inhibition of emotional expressiveness and proximity seeking; compulsively caregiving (A3), described by overbright affect and role-reversing, caregiving behavior patterns; and compulsively compliant (A4), identified by extreme behavioral inhibition, vigilance, and apprehension in the presence of the attachment figure. In contrast to defended children, coercive children are preoccupied with problems in their relationships with their mothers, and they maintain access to mothers by various means of coercion and manipulation (e.g., threats, anger, coy, or feigned helpless behavior) that tend to keep mothers continually off-balance as they strive to meet their children's needs. The coercive strategy is exemplified by four distinct behavior patterns: Threatening (C1) children are characterized by frequent outbursts of anger and pouty, whiny behavior; disarming (C2) children deploy sweet, coy, seemingly helpless behavior; aggressive (C3) children engage in verbal and/or physical punishment, and open rejection of the attachment figure; and helpless (C4) children engage in feigned, extremely exaggerated helpless behavior. Defended/coercive (A/C) children display a blend of defended and coercive patterns, either simultaneously or alternatingly, that appears to be contingently related to changes in the mother's behavior. Insecure Other (IO) is used to identify children without clear-cut, recognizable strategies and whose behavior does not indicate good secure base behavior, whereas Anxious Depressed (AD) is employed for children without clear, recognizable strategies but who also evince sad affect, extreme lethargy or listlessness, helpless and prolonged crying in the mother's presence, and/or panic (not anger) during mother's absence.

RESULTS

Maternal Depression, Chronicity/Severity of Illness, and Quality of Attachment

Among the 50 infants (< 21 months old, classified using the Ainsworth-Main system) in this variable-risk sample, there were 20 classified as secure (3 B1, 10 B2, 3 B3, and 4 B4), seven classified as avoidant (all A2), nine classified as anxious-ambivalent (7 C1, 2 C2), and 14 classified as disorganized. Of the 54 preschoolers (≥ 21 months, classified using the PAA), there were 14 securely attached preschoolers (1 B3, 12 B4, and 1 Secure Other), 12 defended (6 A1–2, 6 A3), 17 coercive (8 C1, 3 C2, 6 C3), 9 anxious depressed (Type AD), 1 insecure other (Type IO), and 1 defended/coercive (Type A/C). Because of very low ns obtained for the individual infancy and PAA subtypes, avoidant infant and defended preschool subtypes were combined into two, overall Type A groups (one for infants, one for preschoolers); secure infant and secure preschool subtypes were similarly combined into two, overall Type B groups; and anxious-ambivalent infant and coercive preschool subtypes were combined into two, overall Type C groups. All D infants were combined into one disorganized/disoriented infant group. Finally, because PAA classifications of AD, A/C, and IO represent atypical and problematic attachments, preschoolers so classified were combined into a single AD-A/C-IO group. Interrater reliability between this author and another trained coder on the infant classifications, based on major category (Types A, B, C, and D), was adequate (kappa = .84, using 24 mother–infant dyads, with disagreements resolved through consensus). Interrater reliability between the present author and P. Crittenden on PAA major category (Types A, B, C, and AD-A/C-IO) was adequate (kappa = .86, using 22 mother–child dyads, again with disagreements resolved through consensus).

Table 11.1 presents the association between the presence of maternal depression (depressed vs. nondepressed, from therapists' diagnoses) and the quality of child–mother attachment at time 2, separately assessed for children under 21 months and for children 21 months and older. Analysis by major attachment category showed that maternal depressive diagnosis was signifi-

Table 11.1. Attachment Security Among Infants and Preschoolers with Clinically Depressed and Nondepressed Mothers

Infants[a]		Depressed Mothers	Nondepressed Mothers
Avoidant (Type A)			
Subtype	A2	5 (16.7%)	2 (10%)
TOTALS		5 (16.7%)	2 (10%)
Secure (type B)			
Subtype	B1	1 (3.3%)	2 (10%)
	B2	4 (13.3%)	6 (30%)
	B3	0 (0%)	3 (15%)
	B4	1 (3.3%)	3 (15%)
TOTALS		6 (20%)	14 (70%)
Anxious-ambivalent (Type C)			
Subtype	C1	6 (20%)	1 (5%)
	C2	1 (3.3%)	1 (5%)
TOTALS		7 (23.3%)	2 (10%)
Disorganized (Type D)		12 (40%)	2 (10%)
Preschoolers[b]			
Defended (Type A)			
Subtype	A1-2	3 (9.7%)	3 (13%)
	A3	3 (9.7%)	3 (13%)
TOTALS		6 (19.4%)	6 (26%)
Secure (Type B)			
Subtype	B3	0 (0%)	1 (4.4%)
	B4	4 (12.9%)	8 (34.8%)
	Secure Other	0 (0%)	1 (4.4%)
TOTALS		4 (12.9%)	10 (43.6%)
Coercive (Type C)			
Subtype	C1	4 (12.9%)	4 (17.4%)
	C2	2 (6.5%)	1 (4.4%)
	C3	6 (19.4%)	0 (0%)
TOTALS		12 (38.8%)	5 (21.8%)
AD-A/C-IO[c]		9 (29%)	2 (8.7%)

[a] Depressed group significantly different from the nondepressed group, $\chi^2_{(3,\ n\ =\ 50)} = 12.92$, $p = .005$.

[b] Depressed group significantly different from the nondepressed group, $\chi^2_{(3,\ n\ =\ 54)} = 8.92$, $p = .03$.

[c] Combined group of anxious depressed (AD), defended-coercive (A/C), and insecure other (IO) preschooler.

cantly associated with insecure attachment in both groups of children ($p <$ .05), with 80% of infants and 87% of preschoolers of depressed mothers designated insecure (vs. 30% of infants and 56% of preschoolers of nondepressed mothers designated insecure). Of particular interest was that the proportion of atypical attachments (D infants and AD-A/C-IO preschoolers) was higher in maternally depressed than in nondepressed groups, with 40% of infants ($n = 12$) classified as D and 29% of preschoolers ($n = 9$) of depressed mothers classified as AD-A/C-IO (vs. 10% D infants and 8.7% AD-A/C-IO infants in the nondepressed groups). Eight of the nine AD-A/C-IO preschoolers in the depressed group were classified as AD and one as A/C. Of the two AD-AC-IO preschoolers in the nondepressed group, one was classified as AD and the other as IO. These findings were upheld when demographic variables such as maternal education, family income, and marital status were statistically controlled.

Chronicity/Severity of Maternal Depression. A subsequent set of analyses examined relations between security of children's attachment and chronicity/severity of maternal illness over the first three time points. Three subgroups of mothers were identified from BDI scores across the first three time points that represented differing degrees of chronicity/severity of depression: The first ($n = 30$), termed the *chronic/severe* group, was composed of mothers whose BDI scores were 11 or higher at all three time points. The second ($n = 42$), labeled *intermittent,* contained mothers with BDI scores of 11 or higher at least once across the first three time points but not at all three points. The third ($n = 32$), termed *nondepressed,* was composed of mothers whose BDI scores were below 11 across the first three time points. This manipulation appeared to have validity, as evidenced by the severity of depression criteria set forth by Beck et al. (1988) for the BDI. The chronic/severe group had mean BDI scores of 26.03, 25.87, and 22.07 at times 1, 2, and 3, all of which were in the moderate-to-severe range; the intermittent group had mean BDI scores of 17.93, 10.10, and 9.91 at times 1, 2, and 3, considered to be of mild-to-moderate severity; and the nondepressed group had subclinical mean BDI scores of 4.59, 3.88, and 3.19 at times 1, 2, and 3.

A Chi-square analysis was then conducted examining the association between these three chronicity/severity groups and security of child–mother attachment, using the full group of children (infants and preschoolers combined) to maintain statistical power and cell size. Conceptually analogous infant and preschool attachment classifications were grouped together, such that Type A infants and preschoolers were combined into an *avoidant/defended* (Type A) group; Type B infants and preschoolers were combined into a *secure* (Type B) group; Type C infants and preschoolers were combined into an *ambivalent/coercive* (Type C) group; and Type D infants and AD-A/C-IO preschoolers were combined into a D-AD-A/C-IO group. The 3 (chronicity/severity group: chronic/severe, intermittent, nondepressed) X 4 (attachment grouping: Types A, B, C, and D-AD-A/C-IO) Chi-square analysis was significant ($\chi^2_{(6)}$ = 18.43, p = .005). Figure 11.1 reveals a higher percentage of secure children (47.1%) in the nondepressed group than in the intermittent (29.4%) and chronic/severe (23.5%) groups, and a lower percentage of D-AD-AC-IO children (8.0%) in the nondepressed group than in the intermittent (36.0%) and chronic/severe (56.0%) groups. Indeed, as the degree of chronicity/severity of mothers' depressed increased, the percentages of secure children decreased, and the percentages of D-AD-A/C-IO increased, in linear fashion (see Figure 11.1).

Maternal Depression and Behavioral Competence

One mean maternal behavioral competence score was computed for each mother by averaging her time 1, 2, and 3 scores, and this index was used to assess relations between the quality of mothers' caregiving behavior, maternal depression, and quality of attachment. Analyses of maternal behavioral competence in relation to maternal depression revealed significant differences between depressed and nondepressed groups (from therapists' diagnoses), and between the three chronicity/severity groups derived from BDI scores at times 1, 2, and 3. Depressed mothers were less behaviorally competent overall (M = 30.37, SD = 4.26) than were nondepressed mothers (M = 33.44, SD = 3.79; $F_{(1,86)}$ = 12.12, p = .0008), and maternal behavioral competence decreased as chronicity/severity of maternal illness increased ($F_{(2,85)}$ = 5.49,

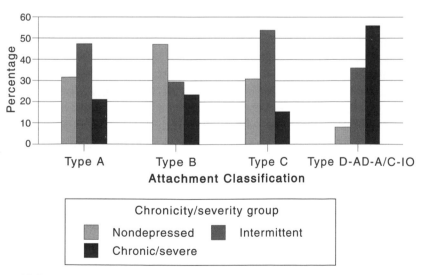

Figure 11.1. Attachment classification and mothers' chronicity/severity grouping.

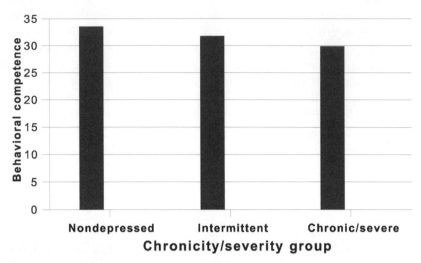

Figure 11.2.   Maternal behavioral competence and chronicity/severity of depression.

p = .006). Student Newman-Keuls post hoc comparisons revealed a significant difference between the chronic/severe and nondepressed groups (p < .05), with the intermittent group falling in between. Of particular interest was the apparent linear decrease in maternal behavioral competence as chronicity/severity of maternal illness increased (see Figure 11.2).

Maternal Competence and Child–Mother Attachment

A second set of analyses assessed relations between maternal behavioral competence and security of infant–mother attachment, using the infancy classifications for children under 21 months and security of preschooler–mother attachment, and PAA classifications for children 21 months and older. In both cases, one-way analyses of variance were significant (infant classifications: $F_{(3,39)}$ = 4.97, p = .005; PAA classifications: $F_{(3,41)}$ = 6.55, p = .001). These data are presented in Table 11.2. Contrasts revealed that mothers of securely attached infants were judged to be behaviorally more competent than mothers of insecurely attached infants ($t_{(39)}$ = 3.49, p = .001), and mothers of D infants were behaviorally less competent than were mothers in all other groups ($t_{(39)}$ = –2.09, p = .04), which is theoretically consistent with predictions from attachment theory. Mothers of A and C infants did not differ. For PAA classifications, contrasts again indicated mothers of securely attached preschoolers to be behaviorally more competent than mothers of insecurely attached preschoolers ($t_{(41)}$ = 2.48, p = .017), and mothers of atypically, more problematically attached preschoolers (Types AD-A/C-IO) to be behaviorally less competent than mothers in the remaining three groups ($t_{(41)}$ = –3.74, p =

Table 11.2.   **Maternal Behavioral Competence and Security of Attachment in Infants and Preschoolers**

	Infants			
	Anxious-Avoidant (Type A)	**Secure (Type B)**	**Anxious-Ambivalent (Type C)**	**Disorganized (Type D)**
n	7	15	7	14
M	30.88	34.80[a]	30.86	29.5[b]
	(4.43)	(2.70)	(4.04)	(4.49)
	Preschoolers			
	Defended (Type A)	**Secure (Type B)**	**Coercive (Type C)**	**AD-A/C-Io**[c]
n	10	14	11	10
M	30.43	33.43[d]	33.52[e]	27.5[f]
	(3.46)	(3.55)	(3.14)	(4.59)

Note. Numbers in parentheses are standard deviations.

[a] Significantly different from mothers of insecure children combined, *p* = .001.

[b] Significantly different from mothers of Type A, B, and C infants (combined), *p* = .04.

[c] Combined group of anxious depressed (AD), defended-coercive (A/C), and insecure other (IO) preschoolers.

[d] Significantly different from mothers of insecurely attached preschoolers combined, *p* = .02.

[e] Different from mothers of defended preschoolers, *p* = .06.

[f] Significantly different from mothers of Type A, B, and C preschoolers (combined), *p* = .001.

.001). These differences are in accord with Crittenden's (1992a) theoretical formulations. Interestingly, the contrast comparing behavioral competence between mothers of Type A and Type C preschoolers approached significance (*p* = .06), with mothers of Type C preschoolers judged as more behaviorally competent than were mothers of Type A preschoolers.

DISCUSSION AND FUTURE DIRECTIONS

Unipolar Maternal Depression and Attachment

Significant relations were established in the infant and preschooler subsamples between maternal depression and quality of attachment, and between quality of attachment and maternal caregiving, with secure attachments significantly less likely when mothers were depressed and less behaviorally competent. Given the theoretical and empirically established linkages between maternal depression and parental insensitivity and neglect (Gelfand & Teti, 1990), and in turn between maternal sensitivity and security of attachment (Ainsworth et al., 1978; Bretherton, 1985; Crittenden, 1992a), the significant associations between maternal depression and insecure attachment in the present study are fully consistent with expectations drawn from attachment theory. Maternal depression was also more likely to be associated with disorganized attachments in infants and atypical attachment in preschoolers (anxious depressed, defended/coercive, and insecure other attachments), when compared to nondepressed mothers and their children, especially when mothers' depression was chronic and severe (see later in this chapter). The majority of depressed mothers in this study were deemed by independent observers to be less sensitive, warm, and more affectively flat and disengaged than were nondepressed mothers. They were often preoccupied and absorbed with worries about issues that had little to do with their relationships with their children; thus, they appeared to tend to the needs of their children sporadically, when they had the energy reserves to do so. Indeed, the predominant theme characterizing many of the depressed mothers in this sample was inconsistency and, for mothers of older children, an inability to cope with the demands their children placed on them. It is perhaps not surprising that, as a result, the proportion of anxious-ambivalent infants was greater among infants of depressed mothers (23.3%) than among infants of nondepressed mothers (10%), and among preschoolers of depressed mothers (38.8%) than among preschoolers of nondepressed mothers (21.8%), given Crittenden's (1992a) proposition that Type C attachments function to "draw in" inconsistently attentive, insensitive attachment figures. This was especially true of children of mothers who were "intermittently" depressed, among whom the highest proportion of Type C attachments were found. These children would appear to be at risk for establishing the consistently coercive parent–child interactional patterns so well articulated by Patterson (1982).

Chronicity/Severity of Maternal Depression and Attachment

The present findings also concurred with those from earlier work emphasizing relations between chronicity/severity of maternal illness and maternal–child functioning (Campbell et al., 1993; Dawson et al., 1992; DeMulder & Radke-Yarrow, 1991; Frankel et al., 1991; Ross & Jennings, 1992). Specifically, the proportion of secure attachments decreased, and the proportion of atypical attachments (D infants and AD-A/C-IO preschoolers) increased, in linear fashion, with more chronic/severe maternal depression during children's first and second years of life. An inverse, linear association was also found between maternal behavioral competence and chronicity/severity of maternal depression. Thus, although disorganized and atypical attachments among infants and preschoolers were associated with maternal depression, they were most likely to appear in the context of severe and lasting maternal dysfunction. The present data suggest that severely and chronically depressed mothers' caregiving may be severely and chronically impaired (rather than inconsistent, which may better characterize the caregiving of intermittently depressed mothers and more likely foster Type C attachments in their children, as suggested in Figure 11.1). Mothers with chronic/severe depression were the least sensitive and warm, and the most affectively flat and disengaging, in terms of the constructs examined during structured observational contexts. More broadly, one might expect such mothers' behavior to conform to the frightened/frightening behaviors that Main and Solomon (1990) argue are central caregiving antecedents of disorganized attachments. Such frightened/frightening, emotionally unsettling behavior may be variously expressed, perhaps directly toward the child or to others in the child's presence (e.g., violent temper or crying outbursts specifically directed either to the child in response to the child's bid for comfort or to the spouse in front of the child, as might occur in a heated marital exchange that so characterizes the marriages of depressed women; see Gelfand & Teti, 1990). It is easy to see how children so reared would experience difficulty organizing their behavior toward their unpredictable, inappropriately responsive, frightening attachment figures. Previous investigators have emphasized the need to give higher priority to the chronicity/severity of parental psychopathology rather than to parental diagnosis per se, in predictions of child developmental outcome (Keller, Beardslee, Dorer, Lavori, Samuelson, & Klerman, 1986; Sameroff et al., 1982). The present findings underscore this perspective. Furthermore, given the episodic nature of depression, it is argued that any attempt to understand the mechanism of intergenerational transmission of affective disorder *must* focus on the extent to which parental depression actually compromises the parenting subsystem during the period of child development in question (rather than focusing only on whether the parent was "ever-depressed").

Cultural Context

The research project discussed in this chapter is perhaps the first to examine relations between maternal depression, child–mother attachment, and parenting competence in a predominantly LDS sample in the Intermountain West. Although this sample's composition differed from that in other reports on maternal depression's effects on children (it can be argued that no research sample is ever truly "representative" and that the best one can hope for is to recruit a sample that is reasonably representative of the local population), there was no reason whatsoever to believe that the mechanisms underlying the putative effects of parental depression on child development differed in this sample relative to others. Comparisons between the LDS and non-LDS subsamples in the present study revealed no differences in maternal education, family income, mothers' employment status, mothers' age, and marital status.

In addition, no differences between LDS and non-LDS families were found in distributions of attachment classifications, in depressive symptomatology, and in maternal behavioral competence. Thus, it is argued that despite the author-itarian and patriarchal structure of LDS family life and culture, the present findings reveal critical insights into the manner in which parental depression, especially when chronic and severe, affects early child development.

Construct Validity

The data in this chapter support the construct validity of both attachment classification systems used. The construct validity of the Ainsworth-Main clas-sification system for infants is, already well-established (see Teti & Nakagawa, 1990, for a review). The present findings contribute to that "nomological net" (Cronbach & Meehl, 1955) by demonstrating clear B–non-B and D–non-D differences in maternal behavior, consistent with predictions of attachment theory and research, and by establishing significant associations between inse-cure attachments and maternal depression. Indeed, this project demonstrates that associations can be found between *unipolar* (not just bipolar) maternal depression and infant–mother attachment, provided that mothers' illness is sufficiently chronic and severe during children's first two years.

Similar relations were established with PAA classifications, thus contribut-ing to the growing evidence in support of the validity of this system for use with preschoolers. Relevant to this point in particular were some additional analyses of attachment classifications obtained earlier on the preschool-aged sample (prior to training on the PAA) using the Ainsworth-Main system. No relations were found between these infancy-based classifications and either maternal depression (both presence/absence and chronicity/severity) or maternal behavioral competence. Thus, whereas the infancy classification sys-tem worked quite well for children under 21 months in this sample, it appeared to be developmentally inappropriate for children 21 months and older. This is not surprising, given that the Ainsworth-Main system was specifi-cally developed for use with infants, not preschoolers. Indeed, Main and Solomon (1990) expressed reservations about the developmental relevancy of infancy classification guidelines for children beyond 21 months of age. By contrast, the PAA, was specifically developed to take into account the advanced social-cognitive-linguistic capabilities of preschoolers. Its develop-mental appropriateness and validity for this age range were supported by the present findings.

Future Directions

The PAA thus appears to be a promising system for assessing quality of attach-ment in the preschool years. In addition to focusing on theoretically meaningful correlates of major PAA categories, as done in the present study, this chapter identifies some specific issues that are particularly relevant to future work with the PAA. The first is the need to examine the extent to which a range of maladaptation exists across the PAA's three defended attachment subtypes and across the four coercive attachment subtypes. For example, is the disarming (C2) child, whose coerciveness of the attachment figure is accomplished primarily by coy manipulation, as problematic as the threatening (C1) child, who deploys open expressions of angry, pouty behavior to draw in the attachment figure? Are aggressive (C3) children, who punish and openly reject their attachment figures, and helpless (C4) children, whose feigned dependence in the presence of their attachment figures leads casual observers to believe that these children can accomplish very little on their own, at greater risk for maladaptation than are disarming (C2) and threatening (C1) children? Similarly, are compulsively caregiving (A3) children, characterized by role-reversing caretaking of the attachment figure, with forced, overbright affect; and compulsively compliant (A4) children, who openly manifest fear and wariness of their attachment figures, at greater risk for maladaptation than are inhibited (A1-2) children? Such comparisons were not possible in the present sample because of very small cell sizes for individual PAA subtypes. However, individual defended and coercive subtypes may be clinically meaningful and may have antecedents and sequelae that are distinct from other subtypes within their respective major category.

Also important to the construct validity of the PAA is Crittenden's (1995) proposition that instability in attachment security from infancy to the preschool years is to be expected as a complex interaction of child maturational factors, specifically the emergence of more sophisticated social-cognitive-linguistic skills by the preschool years, and the caregiving environment. For at least some children, these developments predispose a shift from secure or avoidant attachments in infancy to coercive patterns in the preschool years. In support of the increased prevalence of Type C, coercive attachments and the decreased prevalence of Type B, secure attachments among preschoolers, several studies using the PAA with low-risk preschool samples report roughly equal proportions of Type A, Type B, and Type C attachments (between 30 and 33%) (Crittenden, 1993b; Fagot & Pears, 1996; Sakin & teti, 1995), in contrast to the typical 65–70% Type B, 20% Type A, and 10–15% Type C distribution with the infancy classification system (Teti & Nakagawa, 1990). In a particularly interesting longitudinal study of attachment stability and cognitive and emotional correlates of attachment at 30 months and 7 years, Fagot and Pears (1996) documented substantial infant (18 months)-to-preschooler (30 months) shifts from secure (Type B) to coercive (Type C), and from avoidant (Type A) to coercive (Type C) attachments. The eight children who manifested B-to-C shifts had experienced major life transitions, including parental divorce ($n = 7$)

and remarriage ($n = 1$). Analyses comparing children classified as Type A in both infancy and the preschool years with children who shifted over time from Type A to Type C revealed significantly higher incomes and educational levels, more instructional behavior, and less positive verbal behavior during home observations among mothers of children with stable Type A attachments than among mothers of children with Type A-to-Type C shifts. At 30 months, coercive children were judged by independent observers to be less prosocial toward other family members, by mothers as more oppositional and aggressive, and by teachers as more problematic than were defended and secure children. By 7 years, children classified as coercive at 30 months were seen by teachers to have higher levels of externalizing and internalizing symptomatology than children classified as either defended or secure. In addition, coercive children performed significantly more poorly than did defended and secure children on a mathematics achievement exam, whereas defended children performed better than did secure and coercive children in reading achievement. Fagot and Pears speculated that shifts from avoidance in infancy to a coercive strategy in the preschool years may be a likely coping response to a threatening, inconsistent parent with the advent of more sophisticated social-cognitive-linguistic skills in the child. By contrast, a consistent Type A strategy from infancy to the preschool years may evolve as a natural response to parents who are demanding, intrusive, but nonthreatening. Furthermore, such children are likely to successfully deploy the cognitive skills that, in Fagot and Pears's study, were emphasized by parents during interactions. Thus, there is some support for Crittenden's (1995) propositions, which broadens the conceptualization of attachment by incorporating maturation–caregiving interactions as potential predictors of attachment instability from infancy to the preschool period. Future research should delve further into specific temperamental, caregiving, and maturational processes that underlie these shifts and into why such shifts only characterize some children.

Finally, additional work is needed to establish the PAA's predictive validity. For example, it would be of interest to determine how PAA classifications predict the quality of functioning during middle childhood. Does a secure attachment in the preschool years predispose more optimal functioning in relational and instrumental competence domains in middle childhood than does an insecure attachment? Does the lack of a clearly identifiable, coherent attachment strategy in the preschool period (e.g., Types AD-A/C-IO) bode poorly for individual functioning during the school years and worse than that of children with insecure but clearly coherent and functional strategies (Types A or C)? Can one identify in parents of preschoolers who differ in PAA classifications precursors of the authoritative, authoritarian, permissive, and neglectful parenting styles that characterize parenting of older children (Baumrind, 1970; Darling & Steinberg, 1993; Maccoby & Martin, 1983)?

These are only some of the many important questions that remain to be addressed.

This variable-risk Intermountain West sample should continue to provide information critical to understanding the manner in which psychopathology is ultimately transmitted from parent to child, especially as the children move out of the preschool years into middle childhood. Quality of attachment in infancy and preschool serves primarily as a marker of the quality of relationship between parent and child. However, it may be an important mediating variable in establishing relations between early parental depression and later child development, especially in the context of other enduring familial (e.g., marital discord) and ecological (e.g., life stressors) risk factors (Lewis, Feiring, McGuffog, & Jaskir, 1984; Shaw, Keenan, & Vondra, 1994). We hope to be able to address these questions in future work.

CHAPTER TWELVE

Relations Among Mothers' Dispositional Representations of Parenting

PATRICIA McKINSEY CRITTENDEN, CLAUDIA LANG,
ANGELIKA HARTL CLAUSSEN, AND
MARY F. PARTRIDGE

INTRODUCTION

Maternal cognitions, that is, generalizations held in semantic memory, regarding parenting have been studied as a means of understanding maternal parenting behavior (Dekovik, Gerris, & Janssens, 1989; Newberger & Cook, 1983). Parental behavior, however, may be regulated by several different memory systems, including procedural, imaged, semantic, episodic, and working memory (Schacter & Tulving, 1994; Tulving, 1979, 1985), with each memory system generating one or more dispositional representations (Damasio, 1994).[1] Evidence of consistency among these dispositional representations is relevant to both predicting and changing parental behavior. A brief discussion of memory systems and representation is presented here, followed by a set of hypotheses regarding representations of parenting in maltreating families.

Procedural Memory

Beginning in infancy and continuing throughout the life span, procedural memory encodes information as sensorimotor schemata; procedural knowledge is expressed as familiar, preconscious patterns of behavior. Procedural representations (i.e., generalized procedural schemata) regulate everyday behavior. The majority of behavior, including most parenting behavior, is of this sort.

---

[1] There is a tension in both meaning and terminology between the developing neurological and the more established psychological literatures on information processing. The central differences are the emphasis (1) in the neurological literature on processing and the probabilities of different neurological pathways and (2) in the psychological literature on enduring models and stored content. Thus, attachment researchers have used the terms *working model* and *internal representational model*, whereas the neurologically based literature speaks of more transient dispositions to action that may or may not be implemented. The term *dispositional representation* is used here.

Imaged Memory

Again, beginning as early as birth, infants respond to certain kinds of incoming sensory stimulation with affective arousal that, in turn, changes their somatic state. These two sorts of sensory information (i.e., contextual and somatic) function as signals regarding the threat to the self of various contexts. This gives rise to feelings of (1) anger, fear, and desire for comfort for danger and (2) comfort for safety. Based on this affective assessment, the individual is motivated to (1) fight, flee, or approach or (2) explore, that is, attend to other things (Bowlby, 1973; Seligman, 1975). Imaged processing occurs parallel to procedural processing, and both are rapid, preconscious processes.

Semantic Memory

Semantic cognitions, on the other hand, are encoded verbally and express individuals' beliefs, in this case, beliefs about parenting. Semantic dispositional representations, derived from such cognitions, can be accessed consciously. Such representations initially develop around the third year of life (i.e., after the advent of language) and become steadily more complex and well articulated as a function of both experience and maturation.

Because of their dependence on language, semantic representations are thought to be derived initially from parentally presented models and to be readily influenced, throughout the life span, by the opinions and approval of others. In other words, semantic memory often contains information about what should be as opposed to what is. The relation of semantic generalizations to behavior is not entirely clear, with many theorists and researchers doubting that individuals' consciously expressed attitudes, generalizations, or intentions consistently reflect their behavior (Bowlby, 1980).

Episodic Memory

Episodic memory contains event-specific information regarding past experience. Episodes consist of temporally ordered information integrated with imaged information. Of all the episodes that a person experiences, only a few are retained in memory; these tend to be those associated with arousing events. Possibly because unresolved danger is extremely arousing, instances of unresolved danger tend to be retained in preference to ordinary, repetitive episodes or even happily concluded episodes. Remembered experiences relevant to parenting include both those in which parents were children and those in which they were parents interacting with their own children, particularly under dangerous circumstances.

Episodic memories are thought to develop after semantic memory, with few people having evidence of more than an occasional, partly remembered

event before age 3 (Tulving, 1979). The ability to access these memories consciously varies considerably from person to person, from memory to memory,
and from occasion to occasion (Blaney, 1986). It has been argued that children learn, on the basis of feedback, that discussion of some memories or
behavior tied to them is not permitted (Crittenden, 1995a).

Working Memory

Integration of competing dispositional representations occurs in the pre-
frontal cortex, that is, in working memory. When all reflect the same disposition, this process is rapid and rarely reaches consciousness. When there is a
precortical (imaged or procedural) assessment of substantive and impending
danger that reaches person-specific thresholds, self-protective action is undertaken immediately; cortical processing is suspended or curtailed altogether.
Under conditions of relative safety, however, competing dispositions can be
resolved in working memory. This process is affected by both prior experience and innate intelligence.

Because procedural and imaged representations are thought to regulate
daily parental behavior, semantic representations of parents' beliefs may be
accessed only when individuals are unable to act solely on the basis of preconscious representations and are experiencing sufficiently low arousal that conscious thought is possible. For instance, when an entirely new situation is
encountered, existing procedural and imaged representations may not provide a ready response. In such cases, the process of conscious consideration of
alternatives (i.e., problem solving) may include semantic processing. In other
cases, the complexity of the situation may trigger different and competing
responses; the dilemma may then come to consciousness. Alternatively, when
preconscious dispositional representations lead to behavior that does not
result in the expected outcome (as implied by the representation), the discrepancy between realized outcomes and expected outcomes may bring
behavior to consciousness, for review after the event. In cases such as these,
semantic representations may be used as a basis for problem solving.

Episodic representations contain information about specific times in the
past; accessed episodes match current conditions, more or less, in terms of
differing combinations of temporal contingencies and contextual or
somatic images. These provide information about how similar situations
have turned out in the past. When elicited arousal is too intense for conscious problem solving, individuals may respond by repeating the prior
response, drawn from the recalled episode. Although these experiences
may, or may not, be consciously remembered, through the linking of present and past they can influence current behavior. Because episodes often
reflect intense and unsuccessful experiences of danger, behavior resulting
from activation of episodic representations may be highly inconsistent with

both everyday procedural behavior and semantically generated beliefs about oneself as a parent.

Predicting parenting behavior when representations are inconsistent is a complex task, dependent in part on knowing (a) the nature of the representations associated with each memory system as well as (b) how intensely each system is likely to be activated in specific situations and how complete processing is likely to be before action is taken. That is, the extent of integration is important for understanding how competing dispositions are resolved behaviorally. When the representations from the four memory systems are consistent, evidence of differential activation will be unclear. When, however, they are discrepant, it may be possible to determine which regulates actual behavior.

Maltreatment and Self-Protective Strategies

Incomplete processing of discrepant dispositional representations seems most likely when some of the information signifies self-threatening danger. Under these conditions, the information that most rapidly identifies a substantial threat is most likely to trigger action that suspends or aborts further processing. Because danger from protective figures is particularly threatening, child maltreatment defines a population at particular risk for incomplete processing of inconsistent dispositional representations. When there is no danger, procedural representations should guide behavior. When the danger is identified by sequentially organized behavior that leads to danger, procedural inhibition of the eliciting behavior or procedural display of (compelled) self-protective behavior may be expected. When danger is identified by contextual or somatic images, anxious arousal may be expected to elicit protection seeking, aggression, or fearful withdrawal. This may prevent the full processing of information to integrative conclusions about the actual source of anxiety. When danger is identified by semantic information, that information may be distorted to increase the probability of safe responses. When parents are the source of the semantically identified danger, the distortion is likely to reflect parental perspectives as opposed to child perspectives. This enables the child to maintain a harmonious relationship with the parent. In some cases, either the sequential or imaged attributes of an event may elicit episodic recall of past experiences, which then motivates current behavior, often in a repetition of the earlier behavior. At the most sophisticated level, conscious awareness and consideration of the discrepant motivations can result in an integrative solution constructed in working memory.

The choice of which disposition to act upon – that is, which memory system will generate a self-protective strategy – may depend on which information has, in the past, been most reliable. Parents who use false positive affect misleadingly when they feel angry and who punish the display of negative affect in their children would be expected to have children who use a strategy of inhibited or compulsive procedural behavior and inhibition of behavior elicited by imaged memory, whereas parents who respond positively to children's negative affective displays and give little or inconsistent semantic information to their children are likely to have children who act in response to imaged dispositions and with little access to semantic representations (Crittenden, 1995a). The impact of these self-protective processing and behavioral strategies on parenting competence is likely to be greatest when individuals and their children experience frequent threat, especially threats that resemble painful experiences from childhood (Bowlby, 1980; Crittenden, 1990, 1992b; Crittenden, Partridge, & Claussen, 1991).

Parents who abuse and neglect their children experience precisely this set of conditions. They were often abused or neglected themselves as children, they frequently live with the stresses associated with poverty, and many experience interpersonal threats similar to those of their families of origin (Crittenden, 1987, 1988a; Egeland, Breitenbucher, & Rosenberg, 1980; Wolfe, 1985). Moreover, in spite of their aberrant behavior, few are diagnosed as mentally disturbed, and many appear "normal" and appropriate when speaking about parenting. The theory outlined here, however, suggests the possibility of subtle distortions in their daily behavior and dramatic distortions under threatening conditions when episodic representations are activated without cortical integration with procedural, imaged, and semantic representations.

The Present Study

This study explored these issues in a sample that varied in quality of parenting. Parents were observed in three settings: (1) a routine, low-stress activity, intended to activate procedural representations, (2) a contemplative interview about parenting, intended to activate semantic and episodic representations and working memory, and (3) a mildly stressful, affect-inducing experience with their child, intended to activate images in cases of contextual or somatic anxiety and procedural representations of inhibition of affect in other cases.

It was expected that adequate mothers would (1) have procedural, imaged, semantic, and episodic representations that were most supportive of children and (2) that their representations would be consistent in content, that is, integrated, across observation contexts. Neglectful mothers were expected to have (1) procedural and episodic representations that were the least supportive of children and very limited or absent semantic representations, and (2) consistency of content among their representations. Abusive mothers were expected (1) to appear supportive of children in consciously held semantic representations and less supportive in preconscious procedural and imaged representations and (2) to have substantial schisms between representation processed through different memory systems, that is, to lack integration.

The Cultural Context

The subjects of the study represent two cultural subgroups within the United States. The Appalachian families are descended from immigrants who came predominantly from Germany as mercenaries during the Revolutionary War or from Scotland during the early years after the revolution. Both groups settled in the hollows of the Appalachian Mountains. At that time, the area was isolated from the few colonial settlements; even today, the Appalachian population is among the least assimilated into, and most wary of, the larger society of the United States. Marriage to outsiders was quite limited until recently, with marriage within the kinship group being common. In addition, Appalachian families were characterized by family feuds, often continuing over generations. Although there is an increasing trend toward moving to urban areas, most such families continue to have limited education and unskilled employment. Moreover, there continues to be a pattern of early marriages, large families, and male dominance within the household.

The African-American families are largely the descendants of slaves who worked the plantations of the colonial South. Thus, their 400-year history in the Americas included having little control over their families and frequent disruption of marital and parent–child relationships. After the end of slavery a little over a hundred years ago, most African Americans in the South lived in segregated communities with overt discrimination and little protection from the legal system. Most were poorly educated and received minimal health or social benefits. In recent years, especially since the end of legal segregation, many such families have moved from rural agricultural areas to the cities in the hopes of improving their living conditions. The pattern among these families is often one of mother- and grandmother-headed households, with children who are born to unmarried adolescents being raised with the assistance of maternal grandmothers.

Both Appalachian families and African-American families have higher than average (for the United States) rates of illiteracy, crime, poverty, and child maltreatment.

METHOD

Subjects

The sample consisted of 107 maltreating and adequate mother–child dyads. The children ranged in age from 11 to 48 months (mean = 31 months) and the mothers from 15 to 38 years (mean = 24 years). There were 18 abusing mothers, 25 abusing-and-neglecting mothers, 16 neglecting mothers, 19 marginally maltreating mothers, and 29 adequate mothers (determined on the basis of child protection investigations). These figures do *not* represent normative distributions for these cultural groups; instead, maltreating families were purposefully oversampled. Of the whole sample, 44% of the children were female and 54% were Appalachian/Caucasian. Although all 78 of the maltreating mothers were under protective services supervision, only 38 were receiving specialized parenting services.

Procedure

The subjects were seen three times at home (for two to three hours each visit) and once in the laboratory. During home visits, demographic data, including participation in parenting services, were gathered. In addition, three observational procedures were carried out: a mother–child play situation, the Strange Situation (Ainsworth, Blehar, Waters, & Wall, 1978), and an interview regarding parenting.

Procedural Memory. During the home visit, mothers were videotaped for three minutes playing with their children as naturally as possible. The videotapes of the play interaction were coded using the CARE-Index (Crittenden, 1988b) which yields scores, ranging from 0 to 14, for maternal sensitivity, control, and unresponsiveness. These scores constituted the measure of maternal procedural representations, that is, preconsciously enacted parental behavior exhibited in a low-stress situation.

Mothers with high scores on sensitivity were those who attended to child signals and responded in ways that increased dyadic synchrony and shared affect. Mothers who scored high on control appeared to be mimicking the sensitive pattern of behavior without dyadic synchrony. Indeed, they seemed to be using positive affect to cover dyssynchrony in the relationship. Specifically, mothers scoring high on control were those who displayed false positive affect (especially when their children were unhappy), who attended to their children's behavior but used this information to increase their interference with the children's activity, and who expressed hostility through pseudosensitive behaviors (such as teasing) that irritated their children. Mothers who scored high on unresponsiveness were inattentive to their children and uninvolved in their play.

Imaged Memory. In the laboratory, the dyads participated in the Ainsworth Strange Situation (Ainsworth et al., 1978). Strange Situations of children less than 24 months old were classified using the standard Ainsworth infant procedure that classifies infants into categorical groups based on their (a) proximity seeking, (b) maintenance of contact, (c) avoidance, and (d) resistance.

To the standard *secure* (Type B), *anxious-avoidant* (Type A), and *anxious-ambivalent* (Type C) classifications, we added an *avoidant/ambivalent* (Type A/C) classification (Crittenden, 1985ab, 1988b).

For children from 24 to 48 months of age, the Preschool Assessment of Attachment (PAA) was used (Crittenden, 1992a, 1988–1995). This system assessed aspects of children's organization of attachment behavior in the preschool years in terms of (a) patterns of behavior as well as (b) patterns of negotiation, (c) regulation of feeling states, (d) regulation of displays of affect, (e) underlying strategy, and (f) maternal behavior. In this system, the three infant qualities of attachment were redefined as: (1) *secure/balanced* (Type B): open and direct communication of intentions and feelings, negotiation, and joint awareness with attachment figures of plans; (2) *defended* (Type A): inhibition of display of true feelings, joint awareness of intents, and an absence of communication regarding feelings or negotiation of plans; and (3) *coercive* (Type C): leveraged communication, split and exaggerated display of feelings, and frequent misinformation regarding attachment figures' intents. As with the infant system, an *A/C* classification was used.

The classifications from these two systems were combined for analysis. Each of the child classifications has been related to patterns of maternal behavior such that mothers of secure (Type B) children tend to be warm and emotionally responsive when their children are distressed, mothers of avoidant (Type A) children tend to be rejecting or withdrawn when their children most need them, and mothers of ambivalent (Type C) children tend to be inconsistently responsive (Ainsworth, 1979; Belsky, Taylor, & Rovine, 1984). Mothers of A/C children tend to be both rejecting and withdrawn as well as inconsistent, such that their children switch from using an avoidant strategy (i.e., pretending not to care about the mother's rejection) to begging for contact from an inconsistent mother (Crittenden, 1985, 1988b). Based on these relations between child classification and maternal behavior, the child patterns were used here as indicators of patterns of *maternal* behavior when children were under stress, that is, as evidence of mothers' imaged representations.

Semantic Memory. To assess semantic memory, the mothers participated in an interview about their experiences formerly as children and currently as parents. The interviews were similar to both the Adult Attachment Interview (AAI) (George, Kaplan, & Main, 1985) and Bretherton's Parent Attachment Interview (Bretherton, Biringen, Ridgeway, Maslin, & Sherman, 1989) in that mothers' perceptions of both their childhood and their parenthood were emphasized. Some of the mothers were interviewed jointly with their partners; those interviews included some discussion of the couple relationship. The interviews were videotaped and later transcribed for coding. See Crittenden, Partridge, and Claussen (1991) for a discussion of the effects of having partners present.

The interviews were coded for semantic generalizations regarding parenting using an adaptation of Newberger's parental reasoning scale (Newberger, 1980). Newberger's scale describes parental conceptions of child-rearing issues in terms of four hierarchical levels of parental reasoning: egoistic, conventional, individualistic, and analytic. Our adaptation was intended to assess parents' level of reasoning with regard to parenting decisions. To obtain finer discriminations, midpoints were identified between each of the levels described by Newberger. Parental generalizations about parenting (i.e., parental semantic dispositional representations of parenting) were rated on our Level of Parental Reasoning Scale whenever parental statements answered the (implied) question, "Why did you do what you did?" See Table 12.1. The data were the *frequency* of statements at each scale level, the *mean* scale level, and the *highest* and *lowest* level used by each mother.

Working Memory. The interviews were coded and classified a second time using the AAI coding and classificatory procedures created by Main and Goldwyn (in press).[2] These data were treated as providing information regarding mothers' integration of semantic and episodic representations.

Table 12.1.   Level of Parental Reasoning Scale (Adapted from Newberger, 1980)

Abdication
Level 0:   Parents don't know why they do what they do or are incoherent
Level 0.5:   Parents defer to others or echo their views

Egoistic reasoning
Level 1:   Parents make decisions based on self-interest
Level 1.5:   Parents behave the way they would have wanted if they were the child

Conformist reasoning
Level 2:   Parents' decisions are based on normative standards
Level 2.5:   Parents modify normative standards on the basis of some characteristic of
             the child (e.g., age or sex)

Individualistic reasoning
Level 3:   Parents select their own behavior in response to unique aspects of the
             child
Level 3.5:   Parents' reasoning includes more than one level but is not individualized

Integrative reasoning
Level 4:   Parents' reasoning is based on the integration of information from lower
             levels, including the unique characteristics of the child

---

Source: Newberger; 1980.

[2] The original Main and Goldwyn procedures were used, not the dynamic-maturational expansion.

Coders rated the adults' childhood experiences and their present state of mind with regard to attachment. The supportiveness of childhood relationships with parents was rated on five dimensions: loving, rejecting, involving, neglecting, and pressuring to achieve. The state of adults' semantic memory was rated on scales of idealization, passivity of thought, derogation, and coherency of transcript (specifically, oscillations). The state of adults' episodic memory was rated on scales of involving anger, lack of memory, fear of loss, and coherency of transcript (specifically, relevancy of long episodic digressions). Integration of information was rated on scales of metacognition, coherency of mind, unresolved trauma, and lack of resolution of mourning. Emphasis was placed on logical, coherent and fluent presentation of thoughts, and on the ability to integrate episodic and semantic memory.

There were three AAI classifications: (1) *balanced* (Type B), characterized by coherency and ability to integrate semantic and episodic memory, (2) *dismissing* (Type A), characterized by semantic idealization or derogation and lack of or unintegrated episodic memory, and (3) *preoccupied* (Type C), characterized by lack of semantic clarity and a preoccupation with affectively tinged episodic memories. A subgroup of the preoccupied pattern, "fearfully preoccupied," was used for individuals with evidence of unresolved and preoccupying trauma regarding which they had intense, but contradictory, feelings, and memories. Because we lacked sufficiently systematic data on all women, lack of resolution of loss or trauma was not classified.

Coders, Coding, and Intercoder Agreement. All assessments were coded by independent sets of coders who were blind to all other information about the dyads as well as to the hypotheses of the study. The six coders using the CARE-Index achieved 89% agreement on 31 of the tapes; disagreements were resolved by conference. There was 90% agreement among four coders on 20 of the Strange Situations using the infant system and 87% among six coders on 20 of the tapes using the PAA for preschool-aged children. Again, disagreements were resolved by conference. The two coders of levels of parental reasoning had 90% agreement on six transcripts. The data used were those of the second author. For the AAI classifications, the transcripts were coded by two researchers, trained by Mary Main on the AAI classificatory procedures, with agreement of 85% on 20 of the transcripts. The AAI codings used for data were those of the fourth author.

Parenting Intervention. Approximately half of the maltreating mothers were receiving parenting services from the local infant development project. Because this intervention could be expected to modify parental behavior and cognitions, data were gathered on length of service for each mother who received this service.

RESULTS

Before analyzing the data, we first tested for the effects of ethnic effects. Thereafter, there were three sets of analyses. The first set explored differences in representations for the five child-rearing groups as a means of validating the meaning attributed to the variables. The second set explored relations among the variables assessing dispositional representations. The third set tested the effects of parenting intervention on the representations. Because related sets of variables were used, alpha-levels were corrected by using either multivariate procedures or a Bonferroni correction.

Effects of Ethnicity. Although there was no difference in the overall distribution of the patterns by ethnicity, anxiously attached Appalachian children were more likely to be classified as Type C, whereas anxiously attached African-American children were more likely to be classified as Type A ($\chi^2_{(1)} =$ 3.80, $p < .05$). There was a nonsignificant trend for Appalachian mothers to be classified as preoccupied on the AAI (two-thirds of the anxious mothers) versus only half of the anxious African-American mothers. No other variables showed ethnic differences. For the remaining analyses, these groups were combined.

Maltreatment Group and Dispositional Representations

Each cluster of variables related to dispositional representations was analyzed by quality of parenting, that is, maltreatment status. Because this sample is drawn from a larger study from which some CARE-Index and child attachment data have already been published, only analyses using the level of parental reasoning and intervention data represent entirely new findings.

Procedural Representations (Care-Index Data). MANOVA was used to test differences by maltreatment group in maternal representations in the low-stress play situation, that is, sensitivity, control, and unresponsiveness as assessed by the CARE-Index; the observed relation supported the hypothesis (Wilk's lambda = .65; $F_{(8,190)} = 5.67$, $p < .001$). Univariate tests indicated differences on all three variables (sensitivity: $F_{(4,96)} = 4.62$, $p < .005$; control: $F_{(4,96)} = 4.18$, $p < .005$; $F_{(4,96)} = 8.63$, $p < .001$); see Table 12.2. Adequate mothers were the most sensitive, abusing-and-neglecting mothers the most controlling, and neglectful mothers the most unresponsive. The relatively high scores of abusive mothers on both the sensitivity and control scales should be noted, as should their low score on unresponsiveness. The array of scores for marginally maltreating mothers suggests a mixed pattern that is most similar to that of sensitive mothers.

Semantic Representations (Levels of Parental Reasoning Data). The association between semantic dispositional representations and maltreatment status was tested using a second MANOVA. Maltreatment status and levels of parental reasoning were significantly related as predicted (Wilk's lambda = .68, $F_{(16,303)}$ = 2.48, $p < .001$). Of the four levels of parental reasoning variables, three had significant relations with maltreatment group (mean: $F_{(4,102)}$ = 4.62, $p < .005$; lowest: $F_{(4,102)}$ = 4.18, $p < .005$; highest: $F_{(4,102)}$ = 8.63, $p < .001$). See Table 12.2.

Adequate mothers had the highest mean level (contrast for all maltreating groups versus adequate: ($t_{(103)}$ = 3.20, $p < .01$), whereas groups with neglect were the lowest (contrast for abusing-and-neglecting and neglecting versus abusing, marginally maltreating, and adequate: $t_{(103)}$ = 4.89, $p < .01$). In other words, adequate mothers tended to respond with high conventional reasoning, whereas neglectful mothers tended to be incoherent or defer to others rather than articulate a basis for their decisions. Abusing, abusing-and-neglecting, and marginally maltreating mothers tended to use conventional reasoning.

With regard to lowest level, adequate mothers were significantly higher than all but marginally maltreating mothers, the contrast between adequate and abuse being significant at $t_{(102)}$ = 2.05, $p < .05$. Neglectful mothers had lower scores than any other group, the contrast between neglect and abusing-and-neglecting being $t_{(102)}$ = 2.46, $p < .05$.

With regard to highest level, adequate mothers were scored higher than abusing-and-neglecting mothers, the contrast between adequate and abusing-and-neglecting mothers being $t_{(102)}$ = −2.36, $p < .05$. Neglectful mothers scored the lowest, the contrast between neglect and abusing-and-neglecting being $t_{(102)}$ = 3.15, $p < .005$.

Imaged Representations (Based on the Strange Situation). A Chi-square was used to test the association of maternal response under stress to maltreatment status. The results were as predicted ($\chi^2_{(12)}$ = 27.35, $p < .001$), with adequate mothers tending to be sensitively responsive to their children's distress; both abusing and abusing-and-neglecting mothers tending to be rejecting or extremely rejecting of their children; neglectful mothers tending to be rejecting or withdrawn; and marginally maltreating mothers being rejecting or inconsistently available. See Table 12.2.

Integration of Dispositional Representations from Different Memory Systems. A Chi-square was used to test the association between maternal AAI classifications and maltreatment status; the statistic was significant ($\chi^2_{(8)}$ = 27.57, $p < .01$). Adequate mothers had a normative distribution of classifications with a predominance of mothers who integrated semantic and episodic memory. None of the maltreating mothers had significant numbers of integrated classifications. Indeed, 28% of abusing, 36% of abusing-and-neglecting, 50% of

Table 12.2.   The Relation Between Maltreatment Status and Maternal Sensitivity in Play, Maternal Level of Reasoning About Parenting, and Quality of Attachment

	Maltreatment Status				
Representations	Abuse (1)	Abuse/ Neglect (2)	Neglect (3)	Marginal Maltreatment (4)	Adequate (5)
Maternal CARE-Index					
Sensitivity	7.20	5.00	4.00	6.32	8.30
Control	4.87	5.58	1.69	3.67	2.78
Unresponsiveness	1.87	3.42	8.31	3.74	2.93
Level of Parental Reasoning					
Frequency	4.22	4.48	2.69	3.95	4.35
Mean	1.65	1.37	0.91	1.62	1.77
Lowest	0.92	0.80	0.41	1.00	1.22
Highest	2.35	2.00	1.53	2.45	2.55
Quality of Attachment					
Secure (B)	1	3	3	5	17
Avoidant/Defended (A)	7	10	8	8	7
Ambivalent/Coercive (C)	3	4	2	4	3
A/C	7	8	3	2	2

neglecting, and 22% of marginally maltreating mothers were classified as fearfully preoccupied, suggesting substantial risk that these mothers would respond, under stress, with inconsistent behavior based on conflicting representations. See Table 12.3.

Relations Among the Variables

The CARE-Index mother–child play variables (i.e., maternal sensitivity, control, and unresponsiveness) were correlated using Pearson product moment

Table 12.3.   The Relation Between Maltreatment Status and Maternal AAI Classification

	Maltreatment Status				
AAI Classification	Abuse (1)	Abuse/ Neglect (2)	Neglect (3)	Marginal Maltreatment (4)	Adequate (5)
Balanced	3	1	0	1	12
Dismissing	6	10	3	9	8
Preoccupied	9	14	13	8	9
Fearfully Preoccupied	(5)[a]	(9)	(8)	(4)	(5)

[a] These are not additional cases; they are included within the Preoccupied classification.

correlations with the level of parental reasoning variables (i.e., frequency, mean, lowest level, and highest level) from the interview. The mean and highest level were positively correlated with maternal sensitivity; none was correlated with maternal control; mean, highest, and lowest were negatively correlated with maternal unresponsiveness. Frequency of level of parental reasoning statements was not related to any maternal play scales, whereas mean, lowest, and highest were. See Table 12.4.

Relations between quality of attachment and level of parental reasoning variables were tested using analysis of variance. Although the overall MANOVA did not reach significance, one-way analyses showed that for mean, lowest, and highest response, the effects were as expected; that is, mothers of secure children had higher levels of parental reasoning than mothers of anxious children, except that mothers of A/Cs (i.e., the most anxiously attached) could not be differentiated from mothers of secure children by level of parental reasoning. There were no effects for frequency of codable statements. See Table 12.5.

Relations between AAI classification and the level of parental reasoning variables were as expected (Wilk's lambda = .77, $F_{(8,200)}$ = 3.15, $p < .005$), except that there were no differences in the lowest level scored; instead, there appeared to be a floor effect. For each of the other variables, balanced mothers were scored highest on level of parental reasoning, and preoccupied mothers were scored the lowest. See Table 12.6.

AAI classifications were related to CARE-Index scores such that balanced mothers were the most sensitive, dismissing mothers the most controlling, and preoccupied[3] mothers the most unresponsive (Wilk's lambda = .90,

Table 12.4. The Relation of Maternal Sensitivity in Play to Maternal Reasoning About Parenting

Maternal CARE-Index	Level of Parental Reasoning Variables			
	Frequency	Mean	Lowest	Highest
Sensitivity	*ns*	.24[a]*	*ns*	.30**
Control	*ns*	*ns*	*ns*	*ns*
Unresponsiveness	*ns*	−.34**	−.22*	−.31**

[a] Entries represent Pearson product moment correlations.

*$p < .05$; **$p < .01$; ***$p < .001$.

[3] Many of the preoccupied mothers were almost silent during the interview; their lack of semantic responses and overt indicators of fear placed them in the preoccupied category under previous Main & Goldwyn guidelines. Nevertheless, under current Main & Goldwyn guidelines, they would be considered unclassifiable; under the Dynamic-maturational guidelines (Crittenden, 1998), they would often be classified as compulsively isolated, a Type A, dismissing classification.

Table 12.5.   The Relation Between Quality of Attachment and Maternal Level of Reasoning About Parenting

Quality of Attachment	Level of Parental Reasoning Variables			
	Frequency	Mean[a]	Lowest	Highest[b]
Secure (B)	4.24	1.69	1.02	2.52
Avoidant/Defended (A)	3.72	1.39	0.85	2.16
Ambivalent/Coercive (C)	4.25	1.32	0.72	1.97
A/C	4.18	1.60	1.02	2.25

[a] Significant for B versus A + C + A/C ($t_{(103)}$ = 1.92, p = 05). Significant for B versus A + C ($t_{(103)}$ = 2.36, p < 05).

[b] Significant for B versus A + C + A/C ($t_{(103)}$ = 1.92, p = 05). Significant for B versus A + C ($t_{(103)}$ = 2.08, p < 05).

$F_{(4,192)}$ = 2.40, p = .05). Balanced mothers had the most secure children ($\chi^2_{(6)}$ = 12.93, p < .05). Finally, mothers of secure children were the most sensitive, the least controlling, and the least unresponsive (Wilk's lambda = .78, $F_{(6,192)}$ = 4.15, p < .001). See Tables 12.7 and 12.8.

Effects of Intervention. There were no effects attributable to having received parenting intervention or to the length of that intervention on our variables.

Table 12.6.   The Relation Between Maternal AAI Classifications and Maternal Level of Reasoning About Parenting

AAI Classification	Level of Parental Reasoning Variables			
	Frequency[a]	Mean[b]	Lowest[c]	Highest[d]
Balanced	5.53	1.93	1.17	3.09
Dismissing	4.27	1.50	.90	2.19
Preoccupied	3.47	1.33	.82	1.99

[a] Significant for Dismissing versus Balanced + Preoccupied ($t_{(103)}$ = 2.52, p < .01) and for Dismissing versus Balanced ($t_{(103)}$ = 1.72, p = 08).

[b] Significant for Dismissing versus Balanced + Preoccupied ($t_{(103)}$ = 3.59, p < .001). Significant for Dismissing versus Balanced ($t_{(103)}$ = 2.72, p < .01).

[c] Significant for Dismissing versus Balanced + Preoccupied ($t_{(103)}$ = 2.16, p < .05) and for Dismissing versus Balanced ($t_{(103)}$ = 1.69, p = .09).

[d] Significant for Dismissing versus Balanced + Preoccupied ($t_{(103)}$ = 4.47, p < .001). Significant for Dismissing versus Balanced ($t_{(103)}$ = 3.62, p < .001).

Table 12.7. The Relation of Maternal AAI Classification and Quality of Attachment to Maternal Sensitivity in Play

Maternal Variables	Maternal CARE-Index		
	Sensitivity	Control	Unresponsiveness
Maternal AAI Classification			
Balanced	8.60	2.67	2.73
Dismissing	5.47	4.72	3.65
Preoccupied	6.12	3.47	4.41
Quality of Attachment			
Secure (B)	8.89	2.77	2.37
Avoidant/Defended (A)	5.42	3.42	5.15
Ambivalent/Coercive (C)	6.27	4.00	3.46
A/C	4.57	5.48	3.90

DISCUSSION

The results of this investigation support the hypotheses regarding consistency and inconsistency among dispositional representations derived from different memory systems. As expected, the relation is seen most clearly among abusing and abusing-and-neglecting mothers (whose representations were most inconsistent) and least clearly among neglectful and adequate mothers (whose representations were most consistent.)

Validating Analyses. The analyses by maltreatment group support the interpretation given to the CARE-Index, Strange Situation, and Level of Parental Reasoning variables. Specifically, maternal sensitivity during low-stress play, responsiveness to child distress during stressful separation and reunion, and high-level explanations of the rationale for mothers' behavior were all associated with adequate childrearing. Maternal control, pseudosensitivity, and covert hostility during low-stress play, rejection of child signals of needing maternal support during stressful separation and reunion, and conformist

Table 12.8. The Relation Between Quality of Attachment and Maternal AAI Classification

Quality of Attachment	Maternal AAI Classification		
	Balanced	Dismissing	Preoccupied
Secure (B)	10	8	11
Avoidant/Defended (A)	4	15	20
Ambivalent/Coercive (C)	0	6	10
A/C	3	7	12

standards of parental and child behavior were associated with abuse of children. Finally, unresponsiveness in low-stress play, distressing separation and reunion, and lack of explanation of parental behavior characterized neglectful mothers.

Among these, the cases of abuse most clearly demonstrate incongruity among representations. This suggests that abusing mothers do not respond to child distress with either a rule-based approach (such as their levels of parental reasoning scores would suggest) or an emotionally warm approach (such as their semantic AAI representations would suggest) or even with a controlling procedural response (such as their CARE-Index representations would suggest). Instead, they seem to respond to the painful affect of the situation with distancing, the response most consistent with their painful, unintegrated and often dismissed, imaged and episodic memory. In other words, under conditions of child distress, the behavior of abusing mothers appears to be affectively triggered through imaged and episodic representations of previous affectively similar experiences. Their current response to remembered painful affect of withdrawal and denial is reflected in the rejection of their children's need for contact and warmth.

This incongruity is consistent with the notion of dispositional representations from different memory systems that (1) regulate behavior under different circumstances and (2) are not integrated. The evidence from the AAI that a substantial proportion of mothers who abuse their children had dismissing attitudes toward attachment (i.e., incongruent semantic and episodic representations) confirms this finding.

The cases of adequate childrearing provide evidence regarding behavior that changes in response to situational characteristics and regarding integration of information from different memory systems. That is, adequate mothers were sensitive playmates who also provided tender consolation when children were distressed and who offered explanations of their parenting that were consistent with their observed behavior. Although adequate mothers reasoned about parenting at only a slightly higher level than abusing mothers, their behavior was more consistently supportive of children. That is, adequate mothers behaved at or *above* their level of parental reasoning, whereas abusing mothers behaved at or *below* their level of parental reasoning.

Because a single representation of parenting seemed to underlie adequate mothers' behavior in three varied conditions, it seems likely that their representations resulted from a complex integration of information from all memory systems. Indeed, the high proportion of adequate mothers classified as balanced confirms this interpretation.

The evidence regarding neglect suggests the impact of omission of semantic representations that could have enabled the parent to construct new and more supportive patterns of behavior rather than replicating the parent's own experience of parental failure to respond. Mothers who neglected their children continued to show behavioral inhibition even when their children were intensely distressed. They were unable to empathize with their children's distress. Frequently, such mothers either ignored their children's needs or expected their children to comfort them. (It should be noted, however, that the classification procedure used here reflected Main and Goldwyn's original indicators of the preoccupying pattern. With application of the dynamic-maturational expansion of the Main and Goldwyn system, this finding might have changed to a preponderance of compulsively isolated and/or depressed classifications. For empirical evidence, see Seefeldt, 1997.)

Relations Among the Memory Systems. Given the evidence presented earlier supporting the validity of the assessments, the direct relation among the memory system variables (without differentiation by child-rearing group) was investigated. With one exception, the relations were demonstrated even more clearly than we have described. Examination of the means and contrasts in Table 12.5 indicates that the Secure and A/C groups were indistinguishable with regard to semantic representations of parental behavior. Because these two groups represent the most and least competent parents, this requires explanation.

This problem has appeared before. When the CARE-Index was developed, it was extremely difficult to differentiate the interactive behavior (procedural representations) of adequate mothers from abusing mothers. Ultimately, subtle distortions in the organization of species-typical, infant-elicited behaviors were identified and described as a "pseudosensitive," false positive pattern typical of abusive mothers. Mothers of A/C children tend to display this pattern either in a pure form or mixed with unresponsiveness (Crittenden, 1985a, b, 1988a, b).

The A/C classification itself also presented this problem. Indeed, the classification was originally identified when a subgroup of children classified as secure (B) were found to be among the most seriously abused and/or neglected. Clearly, it made no sense that adequately reared and seriously maltreated children should both be securely attached when troubled children and mildly maltreated children were anxiously attached. Careful examination of the Strange Situation videotapes identified differences in the way that the maltreated children who were classified as secure organized their attachment behavior (Crittenden, 1985a, 1988b). This organization became the basis for the A/C classification.

In these two cases, it was argued both that the organization of behavior was different (thus, the underlying representations were different) and that the most distorted relationships, those most likely to fail, used behavior typical of secure dyads in a desperate attempt to maintain, in the context of relationship threatening discord, the parent–child relationship (Crittenden, 1988b).

In this study, some mothers, whose care of their children is dangerously inappropriate, described the basis of their parenting in terms that were as sophisticated and normative as those of normative mothers. Their observed behavior, as assessed using the CARE-Index and Strange Situation was, however, highly incongruent with these verbalized semantic representations. Of course, it could be that these mothers knowingly lied because they feared the consequences of stating their thoughts honestly.

It is also possible, however, that, for some very troubled women, semantic representations that were consciously available were not integrated with preconscious procedural and imaged representations and episodic representations. In other words, because their consciously held beliefs were derived from parental injunctions and social approval, these women may not have recognized the discrepancy between what they said and what they did. Believing that their reasons for parental actions were appropriate, they may truly not have understood why they were accused of abusing and neglecting their children.

Moreover, because abusive behavior is likely to occur under stress, it is probably associated with signifiers of danger. Therefore, its motivation in preconscious memory systems may not be recognized and, because of the affective arousal associated with it, processing may be aborted before either consciousness or cortical integration is achieved. If this is the case, each event of maltreatment could reinforce the neural pathways leading to a disposition to similar behavior in the future.

Evidence that unintegrated dispositional representations may explain these otherwise anomalous results can be found in the AAI classifications. The AAI is intended to assess integration of semantic and episodic representations.

Maltreating mothers rarely demonstrated such integration. Some, those classified as dismissing, articulated idealized semantic representations while describing highly discrepant episodes. Moreover, even though these descriptions were offered in the same interview, the women appeared unaware of the incongruity. Others, classified as preoccupied, offered confused and confusing explanations of their experience, again with apparent lack of awareness of their own confusion.

Thus, it seems plausible that for seriously troubled parents generalized verbal discussion of parenting practices may reveal little regarding actual behavior. If this is so, it suggests that intervention to teach such parents about parenting might effectively modify their semantic representations without actually modifying behavior that is regulated by procedural and episodic representations. (For a fuller discussion of processing in cases of child neglect, see Crittenden, 1993a.)

The Cultural Context and Intervention. As noted at the beginning of this chapter, this study drew from two disadvantaged subgroups in the United States. The two groups, however, had quite different historical experiences. One was isolated from other people and developed a pattern of enmeshed kinship relations that were often acrimonious over periods of generations. These families tended to be father-headed and marriage-based. The other had a history of forcibly sundered family ties and persecution by the racially different dominant population. These differences may be reflected in the patterns of childrearing observed in this study. Specifically, anxiously attached Appalachian children were more often classified as Type C in quality of attachment and anxiously attached African-American children as Type A. There was a tendency for Appalachian mothers to rely on episodic and imaged memory while omitting semantic memory – that is, to be classified as preoccupied on the AAI – and for African-American mothers to rely on semantic memory and omit episodic memory from processing (and thus be classified as dismissing). These patterns may reflect the historical patterns of close and acrimonious family relationships in an isolating environment for Appalachian families and of broken relationships in a hostile environment for African-American families. They may also reflect adaptive strategies of maintaining safety and protection under differing circumstances.

There were no effects for parenting intervention. Although this is disappointing, the results of this study may shed light on the problem. The mothers were all given the same parenting intervention, which consisted of information about child development and parenting strategies. The findings of this study, however, suggest that the mothers did not all process information in the same manner and that their difficulties with childrearing may have had varied cultural, interpersonal, and intrapsychic bases. This has two implications. First, an intervention that was appropriate for dismissing mothers might have augmented the problems of preoccupied mothers, and vice versa, thus averaging out any benefits of intervention. Second, addressing both the historical and current cultural context of the families might have permitted fine-tuning of the intervention to fit particular cultural experiences and beliefs. Furthermore, use of person-specific information regarding the use and content of the memory systems might have facilitated construction of interventions that would enable each mother to increase her conscious access to important information and to learn to use the information integratively to construct new approaches to parenting. This, rather than information about children and parenting, might have enabled the mothers to modify their mental and behavioral processes.

The findings of this study are provocative. Although they require replication and expansion, they are clear enough to justify further investigation into the function of memory systems and representations. By providing results that support theory regarding complex internal processing of information, they suggest the need to move beyond simple observation of behavior and questions regarding parental practices to the study of how information is perceived, integrated, and used by individuals.

CHAPTER THIRTEEN

Adaptation to Varied Environments

PATRICIA McKINSEY CRITTENDEN AND
ANGELIKA HARTL CLAUSSEN

Attachment theory addresses the protective function of certain dyadic relationships. In practice, however, quality of attachment is often treated as an individual variable. This chapter offers an alternative perspective in which attachment is viewed as one level in a hierarchy of systemic processes that extend from intra-individual systems (genetic, biochemical, physiological) to dyadic systems (communication, attachment relationships) to multiperson, macro-systems (family systems, social ecological systems). One function of organization at all of these levels is protection from danger.

Consonant with such a nested, multisystemic perspective, many researchers working outside of attachment theory have suggested the impact of biological influences on quality of attachment (Goldsmith & Alansky, 1987; Rothbart & Ahadi, 1994; Schore, 1994). Less attention has been paid to how macro-systemic factors might affect the self-protective strategies that evolve in populations influenced by these factors. It is entirely possible, however, that such strategies are responsive not only to parent and infant characteristics, but also to the safe and dangerous aspects of the environments in which adults raise children. Central to thinking about these influences is defining the critical aspects of danger.

This chapter first considers the nature of danger and of strategies for identifying and responding self-protectively to danger. This perspective is applied to contexts; that is, contexts are considered in terms of the most likely types of danger within them and the strategies most likely to be protective for those dangers. Next, the influence of context on dyadic pattern of attachment is considered, specifically the adaptive and maladaptive aspects of that influence. The approach is based in theory, with examples drawn from the chapters in this volume as well as the wider literature on attachment. Some of the examples reflect specific risks that range from minor threats, such as being a twin and placement in day care, to major threats, such as maternal depression, maltreatment, and institutionalization. The issue of cultural contexts, in which the historical danger may or may not be present in the child's experience at home, is discussed in chapter 19.

The effect of context on distributions is not meant to nullify the importance of individual differences tied to unique features of attachment figures and children. Rather, it is intended to support the notion that, in addition to dyadic effects, there are contextual effects (Hinde, 1992). It is widely recognized that pattern of attachment, that is, self-protective strategy, is multiply determined. The focus here is on the role of danger in the familial, community, and cultural context affecting children's organization of self-protective strategies.

DANGER

Most discussions of danger describe the phenomenon itself, for example, wild animals, sexually abusive adults, natural disasters. The approach taken here is more basic. What one needs to know about danger is *when* and *where* it may occur and how probable its occurrence is. In particular, it is useful to know when, in the sequence of one's own behavior, and where, relative to oneself, danger may occur. Information regarding timing can enable threatened individuals either to inhibit actions that elicit danger or increase its probability of occurrence or to display behaviors that serve a protective function by reducing the probability of danger. These two functions are characteristic of Type A behavior. Information regarding the location of danger can enable individuals to vary their alertness with regard to danger in ways that either foster a wide range of activities where there is low probability of danger or that arouse feelings of anxiety which focus attention where there is a relatively high probability of danger. Under these conditions, individuals can prepare to attack the source of danger, run from the danger, or seek help. These three actions reflect the three basic affective states (i.e., anger, fear, and desire for comfort) that constitute the mixed feelings associated with Type C attachment.

Two observations are of particular interest. First, most, if not all, dangers can be described in terms of timing, location, and probability of occurrence. Second, the strategies for dealing with temporally predictable danger differ substantially from those for dealing with contextually predictable danger.

For example, some parents are threatening when specified rules are violated; children can protect themselves by using a Type A strategy of doing what the rule specifies (compulsion) and failing to do what the rule forbids (inhibition). Other parents' aggression toward children is elicited, at least partially, by parents' internal feeling states. Because their behavior is less closely tied to children's behavior, such parents are experienced by children as unpredictable and inconsistent. Consequently, children's best self-protective strategy is to attend closely to the changes in parents' state (wary fearfulness), to threaten if the parent can be intimidated or made to feel guilty (anger), and to seek parental assistance frequently (desire for comfort). These are components of the Type C strategy.

CONTEXTS THAT INCREASE THE PROBABILITY OF CHILDREN USING A TYPE A STRATEGY

In Ainsworth's work, Type A was associated with maternal rejection of infant signals. In the research that has accumulated since then, Type A, in infancy, has generally been associated with more severe threat than has Type C. Nevertheless, most children classified as Type A do not show problems or live in dangerous environments. A new distinction may need to be made between low-subscript Type As (A1-2) and high-subscript, compulsive Type As (A3-6) – that is, those drawn from the dynamic-maturational expansion of attachment theory (Crittenden, 1995). Using this model (see Figures 1–3 in chapter 18), it would be expected that mothers of children classified as A-2 would keep their children safe and would respond appropriately to negative affect when it signals danger, for example, when the child is hurt and cries for help. But they would reject *unnecessary* negative affect. For example, in the Strange Situation, mothers know with absolute certainty that their children are safe. The children may not know this, and many feel unsafe. When they cry, the affect is unnecessary for safety; it signals only discomfort and the children's (inaccurate) perception of not being safe. Mothers of A1-2 infants prefer their infant not to cry under these conditions; they reject this display of unnecessary negative affect. Instead, they expect their infants to trust that they (the mothers) will be as protective and predictable as they have always been. Children of such mothers learn exactly that: they learn to ignore internal feeling states, especially when their mothers do not display anxious behavior, because these states do not accurately predict danger and because display of them accurately predicts maternal rejection. Such children become independent, positive-appearing children who use others as a guide to appropriate feelings and who experience rejection only in this limited domain of unnecessary negative affect.

The process for children using high-subscript patterns of attachment is hypothesized to be different. Their mothers are not always protective. Sometimes they fail to respond when a protective response is truly needed (in the extreme, this is child neglect); other times they respond with aggression toward the child (in the extreme, this is child abuse). These children learn something different. They learn to hide their (negative) feelings when their mother is available and to do what they can to increase their safety, but, when there is no protector, they do everything they can to get one, even an angry one. This produces extremes of behavior that, on the basis of understandings drawn from preschool-aged children's organization (Crittenden, 1992), would often be classified as a compulsive A pattern (i.e., A3, compulsive caregiving to an unavailable attachment figure and A4, compulsive compliance to an aggressive figure)[1].

Safe and Predictable Relationships in Contexts Where Independence Is Valued

The difference between A1-2 and A3-4 helps to explain the findings of Moilanen and her colleagues (see chapter 8 this volume). Finland is a northern country with long, often harsh winters. Furthermore, historically Finnish families were widely separated in an effort to survive economically in a forested land with short summers; self-reliance was essential. Malnutrition, illness, and death rates were relatively high (Klinge, 1994), even to the point of constraining the population genetically in ways that promoted survival on a meager diet (Groop & Tuomi, 1997). Today, Finland is a safe country in which the state protects children well: health care is exceptional; crowding, urban dangers, and poverty are almost nonexistent; and standards of behavior are well defined. Independence is safe and generally preferred to closeness. It gives great individual freedom, within a context of agreed-upon, self-regulated, safe interpersonal behavior. Not surprisingly, A1-2 appears to be the most frequent pattern among healthy Finnish toddlers (Moilanen et al., this volume). As is true everywhere else, this pattern is associated with inhibition of negative affect, but especially as infants mature into toddlers and young children, the known predictability of the safe context may elicit little negative affect. Furthermore, it is not surprising to find an industrious population that, relative to other cultures, emphasizes fun and happiness less and hard work and predictability more, and that has a higher than usual incidence of depression and suicide (Aro, Marttunen, & Lönnqvist, 1992; Diekstra, 1993). Put another way, the strategy that protects Finns from the invariant risk of winter itself creates certain kinds of psychological risk, in this case of disorders associated with inhibition of affect.

Child Abuse and Neglect

Child maltreatment addresses directly the issue of danger to children. For the basic premise of attachment theory to hold, endangered children should seek their attachment figures when threatened, and, based on the nature of the threat, they should organize strategies that reduce the probability of threat and increase the probability of protection. If children were to become disor-

---

[1] Main and Solomon (1986, 1996) have described similar behavior and labeled it disorganization. Given the self-protective function of attachment behavior, the notion of disorganization limits our understanding by (1) failing to identify the predictability, function, and organization of the patterns and (2) clustering together too many different patterns.

ganized in the context of danger, the attachment relationship would fail to fulfill its function *at the very time when the function was crucial to children's safety and survival.* This would call the theory into question. Maltreated children are almost exclusively classified as anxiously attached, although the exact effect depends on the age of the children and classificatory system used. If only the Ainsworth infant patterns are used, there is also a nontrivial proportion that is classified as Type B (Egeland & Sroufe, 1981; Schneider-Rosen & Cicchetti, 1984); this is an inexplicable outcome from the perspective of attachment theory. Using the Main and Solomon classificatory method with disorganization (Main & Solomon, 1990), the majority of maltreated children are classified as disorganized (Carlson, Cicchetti, Barnett, & Braunwald, 1989). Behaviorally, this classification is surely accurate; that is, maltreated children display the behaviors that Main and Solomon identify as indicative of disorganization. These data do not make clear whether the behaviors are incorporated into an organized strategy that reduces the threat to the child or whether the parental threat has left children unable to organize and, therefore, in greater danger. Other findings, however, indicate that, although signs presumed to indicate disorganization were found in all patterns of attachment, they were fewest in children classified as B1-4, A1-2, or C1-2 and greatest in those children showing a compulsive or obsessive strategy, that is, A3-4, C3-4, A/C, Insecure Other (Ziegenhain, Müller, & Rauh, 1996).

In the studies carried out by my colleagues and myself, type of maltreatment was considered to signify several different contexts.[2] These include the underresponsiveness of neglectful parents, the hostile intrusion and control of physically abusive parents, and their combination in abusive-and-neglectful parents. In previous work with the Ainsworth system plus A/C (but without the compulsive patterns), abuse and abuse-and-neglect (together) were associated with Type A/C (70%) and neglect with Type A (55%) (Crittenden, 1985). In the study reported here that used the Preschool Assessment of Attachment (Crittenden, 1995), and thus included the compulsive patterns, the results were similar but more clearly defined (Crittenden et al., chapter 12, this volume). Physical violence was associated equally with Types A and A/C, with three-quarters of abused and abused-and-neglected children falling in these classifications; among these, 92% showed a compulsive pattern (A3-4). Neglect, on the other hand, was more specifically associated with Type A (50%) and less with A/C (19%), with 40% showing a compulsive pattern. Beeghly and Cicchetti (1996) report that maltreated children use fewer internal state words, particularly negative state words, for self and others, which is consistent with Type A attachment. These results suggest that the strategies

---

[2] This approach is expanded to include sexual abuse, witnessing violence, and being the victim of community violence by Lynch and Cicchetti (1998), who also found differential developmental effects based on context.

shown by endangered children are very greatly affected by the context of danger to the point of substantially restricting the range of individual variation.

The questions become whether (1) for physically abused children, use of a compulsive compliant (A4) strategy of inhibition of negative affect and exhibition of compliant behavior reduces the probability of eliciting parental violence and (2) for neglected children, use of a compulsive caregiving (A3) strategy of inhibition of negative affect and display of false positive affect and caregiving to the parent increases the probability of receiving parental attention that could be protective if protection were needed. If these effects accrue, the strategies are almost certainly organized. In addition, there is the question of the costs of excessive reliance on these strategies. Lynch and Cicchetti's (1997) finding that resilient maltreated children, unlike nonmaltreated children, displayed high ego overcontrol and ego resilience suggests the presence of compulsive patterning and its association, in at least some cases, with adaptation. On the other hand, use of the compulsive Type A strategies with distortions of affect and an emphasis on hierarchically organized obedience would be expected to affect both intimate and peer relationships detrimentally. Rogosch, Cicchetti, and Aber (1995) provide evidence that maltreated children lack social competence with peers and often are aggressive toward them. Because peer relationships are not hierarchical, the anger that is inhibited in the presence of powerful people might be displayed with peers and less powerful people. The evidence that maltreated individuals have problems in close relationships in adulthood, for example, spousal and parental relationships, is quite extensive. (For a review, see Crittenden, 1996.)

Adoption after Institutionalization

Institutionalized children face the very real risk of not receiving sufficient and appropriate interpersonal attention and, sometimes, not even the basic care that they need to survive. Many develop strategies for enticing adults to attend to them; this reduces the risks associated with living in institutions. Concurrently, the very high levels of discomfort that they feel often lead to stress-related, stereotypic behavior and the long periods of inattention, sometimes augmented by malnutrition, can lead to developmental delay and physical lethargy. The effects are so severe that those who survive almost uniformly show very disturbed behavior. One measure of the power of this context to affect development is the tremendous reduction in the range of variation among institutionalized children, despite individual genetic differences in both infants and caregivers. For example, Crittenden et al. (1992) found that a third of a small sample of Greek institutionalized children were Type A and almost a half were Type A/C. Only one child was a normative Type C, suggesting that this strategy was not the dominant part of the effect. On the other hand, Lis found in a sample of Polish institutionalized children that all were anxiously attached, with 65% being extreme Type Cs with aggressive features (i.e., the equivalent of C3 in the Preschool Assessment of Attachment). Because Lis did not consider an A/C designation, it is not possible to know whether she had such children in her sample.

Differences in the institutions themselves might explain some of the differences. The Athenian setting was bright, modern, and almost familylike, with designated attachment figure/caregivers who cared for stable groups of only four infants, all day, everyday, until the children left the infant unit at age 2 years. That stability and predictability may have promoted the Type A organization. In Warsaw, the context was more constrained, with greater darkness, less access to the outdoors, and more children per caregiver. More importantly, the availability of attachment figures was far less predictable in person, time, duration, and function. Because basic care was provided by many people to all the children, children observed "their" caregiver caring for others. Moreover, because the attachment figure had to squeeze in a moment to play with the special child, this time had no predictability for either occurrence or duration and was always in competition with other uses for the time. The anxiety and aggression of the Polish institutionalized children could have functioned to increase the probability of the child's obtaining some attention, even if it was negative. In both cases, however, the context of institutionalization was so strong that it all but wiped out the Ainsworth patterns of attachment. In each case, however, the nature of the institution, in terms of the conditions of threat and of strategies that could reduce the threat, determined the nature of the skew in the distribution.

One question becomes how children from institutions adapt to placement in a (safe) adoptive home. Both Lis and Chisholm offer data, although again the findings differ. Lis found that of the 15 Polish children placed in adoptive homes, 14 were securely attached within the first two weeks. This seems astounding and is, in fact, more consistent with indiscriminant attachment than it is with the notion of security. Particular features of the behavior of the children classified as secure[3] were independence, ease with strangers, self-reliance, and cheerfulness. These descriptors are consistent with a Type A compulsive pattern of false brightness, inhibition of negative affect, and excessive self-reliance. Moreover, although there was a drop in four of seven measures of behavior disturbances (specifically those associated with negative displays), most of the children still displayed abnormalities a year after adoption. Given that all of the children had been anxiously attached and most often with extreme strategies, these results seem almost inexplicably positive unless reframed as compulsive A patterns. In either interpretation, however,

---

[3] This is a nice reminder of the importance of stating that children are "classified as" rather than actually "being" a particular type.

there is evidence for children's flexibility in being able to change strategy when the nature of danger in the context changed.

Chisholm's findings are less optimistic, but closer to expectation, with regard to children adopted in Canada from Romanian orphanages: one-third were securely attached (including a substantial proportion with atypical patterns), a quarter were classified as Type A with almost half of these being A3 (compulsive caregiving), a small proportion were Type C1-2, and one-fifth were classified as A/C or Insecure Other (Chisholm, 1998). Thus, the children showed a very wide range of response to their adoptive placement. Again, this suggests the responsiveness of children to change in the threatening aspects of context. In this volume, Chisholm describes the behavior of two such children, one classified as secure other and the other as compulsive caregiving. Both show false positive affect at least some of the time. Using these two as exemplars of the set of atypical children in the data set suggests that as many as 45% of the children may have displayed false positive behavior.

The difference in outcomes between the two data sets may reflect differences in the institutional settings or differences in classification methods. Fortunately, Chisholm's data are in videotaped form. When later investigators have new perspectives, these videotapes could be reviewed to seek evidence. Because Lis's data were written observations, if the observer did not see what we would now look for, we cannot know whether it was absent or simply unnoted.

CONTEXTS THAT INCREASE THE PROBABILITY OF CHILDREN USING A TYPE C STRATEGY

The Type C attachment strategy was associated in Ainsworth's original work with inconsistency of maternal response (Ainsworth, Blehar, Waters, & Wall, 1978). In the dynamic-maturation expansion of attachment theory, the critical component leading to Type C is unpredictable, intermittent positive reinforcement of children's negative affect, especially anger, fear, and desire for comfort (Crittenden, 1995). At 12 months, this should lead to relatively few Type C infants because, during the sensorimotor period, the Type C strategy cannot be organized around changing contingencies. By the preschool years, however, unpredictable positive reinforcement of negative affect should elicit the Type C strategy and, therefore, increase the proportion of children classified as Type C (Crittenden, 1992). This is supported by numerous studies, using either the Preschool Assessment of Attachment or the Cassidy-Marvin system (Rauh et al., chapter 14 in this volume; Speltz, Greenberg, & Deklyen, 1990; Stevenson-Hinde & Shouldice, 1992, 1995; Teti et al., 1995; Vondra, Shaw, Swearingen, Cohen, & Owens, in press). Some of the contexts that could produce especially high proportions of children classified as Type C are described later in this chapter.

Physiological Risk

Being a twin creates the obvious threat of having to share access to the parent with the co-twin. Although this is a familiar issue for siblings, it is heightened when both children are infants dependent on the mother for sustenance and biophysiological regulation. Being a twin is also associated with the added biological risk of a less fully mature organism (therefore, needing more attention than a full-term, healthy infant) and of a mother whose pregnancy and birth experience may have been more disruptive than that of a mother delivering only one infant. The question is whether this context of competition for essential resources and of fragility of both infant and mother (i.e., a context of having less and needing more) creates a particular sort of danger that elicits a particular sort of strategy used by twins to regulate maternal protective behavior. Chapter 8 by Moilanen et al. cites literature indicating that both mothers and infants in cases of twinning are expected to be more anxious with regard to attachment. Moilanen et al., however, found no differences in the distributions of Finnish twins and singletons, both of whom had a predominance of Type A. A lack of difference was also found for Canadian twins, but with a predominance of Type B for both twins and singletons (Goldberg, Perotta, Minde, & Corter, 1986). However, when risk factors were considered, vulnerable Finnish toddlers (most of whom were twins) were more likely to be classified as Type B or Type C than lower risk toddlers. Furthermore, the probability of being Type B (using the PAA) increased linearly with increasing numbers of risk factors.

Given the Finnish mothers' apparent preference for an independent child who shows relatively little negative affect, the bias in the distribution of both twins and singletons is not difficult to explain. Mothers' behavior would create predictable contingencies that would reinforce lowered displays of negative affect. This, in turn, would ease the burden of having twins, thus reducing the likelihood of the Type C pattern among Finnish twins.

The increase in Types B and C among risk children in Finland seems more difficult to explain. That is, why don't these distant mothers become *more* rejecting of their fragile children? The problem may lie in the presumption that mothers of Type A1-2 children are rejecting. As described earlier, they may be loving, protective mothers who foster independence in healthy children. When, however, their child is vulnerable – that is, when the negative affect accurately signals infant need for protection – they respond protectively. When the response is sensitively appropriate and the mother herself is calm and confident, her child may become Type B, but when the mother is too worried, too anxious, over- or underresponsive, her attention may carry an unpredictable quality that would increase the probability of Type C. This explanation goes beyond the data offered by Moilanen and her colleagues, but it offers a possibility of testing the hypothesis in future studies both in

Finland and other countries. The processes should be universal, even if the rates of their occurrence in different populations vary as a function of specifiable contextual factors.

Day Care

There are several reasons why day care could be a potential threat to children. When the schedule of attendance is irregular or complex (for the child's developmental comprehension of temporal patterning), when the choice of day-care service is changed frequently, or when children must share access to the alternate figure (the day-care provider) with too many other children, they may feel unprotected. Although these aspects of unpredictability and inconsistency do not affect all children in day care, when they do occur, they should lead to higher rates of Type C attachment, especially in toddlerhood.

Previous meta-analyses of the effects of day care have produced two sorts of findings. First, several studies have shown an increase in Type A attachment in infants (Belsky & Rovine, 1989; Clarke-Stewart, 1989; Lamb & Sternberg, 1990). In most cases, the studies used the Strange Situation at 12 months, although some studies used it as late as 15 or even 20 months of age. Second, in one case (NICHD Early Child Care Research Network, 1997), there was (1) no main effect for day care on the 15 month old's quality of attachment and (2) no increase in Type A classifications among toddlers attending day care.

With regard to the first issue, the authors of the NICHD study proposed that there is a cohort effect, with either parents or day-care providers improving children's accommodation in response to the concerns raised in the earlier studies. No evidence is offered to support or refute this perspective. An alternative explanation comes closer to one of the themes of this volume. The Ainsworth Strange Situation was designed for 11-month-old infants. It has been commonly used for 12-month-old infants, which seems unlikely to tap substantial developmental differences. It is less obvious that this is true for 15-month-old toddlers. Certainly, toddlers differ from 11-month-old infants in that they walk effectively and use language in far more sophisticated ways. These differences seem relevant to a procedure that assesses proximity seeking/exploration and infants' expectations. It may be that when classificatory criteria designed for 11-month-infants are applied to 15-month-old toddlers, they yield distribution shifts that favor the appearance of increased security. The Rauh et al. chapter in this volume provides evidence that at 21 months the original Ainsworth procedures produce an elevation in Type B, whereas both Ainsworth plus disorganization and the PAA produce lower proportions of Type Bs than expected in infancy. This creates the possibility that the effect of inflating Type B classifications may begin earlier than 21 months. If so, this could affect the distributions obtained in the NICHD study.

The second issue is whether, among toddlers and preschool-aged children, there would be an increase in Type C classifications among children placed in day care. The preliminary finding in the studies reported in this volume is that entry to day care may be associated with higher rates of Type C attachment using the PAA criteria (Bohlin & Hagekull; Rauh et al., chapters 5 and 14 in this volume). It is particularly noteworthy that these effects were not found at 12 months. This suggests that we may need to be more sensitive to subtle developmental changes than previously thought. Again, however, there are other effects as well, including issues of timing and behavior of the receiving day-care provider(s). Although the data are insufficient to confirm the Type C hypothesis, together with theory, they suggest a need to reconsider the issue of the effects of day care, using age-specific assessments, focusing on particular types of vulnerability, and testing for increases in Type C organization.

CONTEXTS THAT INCREASE THE PROBABILITY OF CHILDREN USING A TYPE A/C STRATEGY

Maternal Depression

Maternal depression is a threat because children's developmental context is relatively less protective, stimulating, and responsive to infant behavior than that of children with nondepressed mothers. Maternal depression is not, however, a unitary state; differences in type of depression might lead to various self-protective strategies. Extremely withdrawn, even neglectful, mothers might elicit a compulsive caregiving (A3) strategy from their children, whereas the aggressive C3 strategy, by heightening the intensity of the child's signal, should function to elicit and maintain attention from a weak and inattentive mother. The risk of the C3 strategy is that the child's anger could elicit the mother's anger; depressed mothers, however, may be unlikely to take such an instrumental approach. The A/C strategy is suited to variability in maternal behavior – for example, mothers who sometimes are unresponsive and at other times available but intrusive.

In the Teti et al. study, maternal unipolar depression was associated with higher rates of Types C (specifically C3), A/C, AD (anxious depression), and Insecure Other using the PAA at 21 months of child age. This is consistent with Cicchetti, Rogosch, and Toth (1998), who found more anxious attachment to depressed mothers than to nondepressed mothers. There are, however, different effects in other studies. Those studies that used the original Ainsworth system, the Main and Solomon disorganized category, or the Cassidy-Marvin system generally do not find effects for unipolar depression (see Teti, chapter 11, this volume). Bipolar depression has been associated both theoretically and empirically with the A/C pattern (Radke-Yarrow, Cummings, Kuczynski, & Chapman, 1985).

Institutionalization and Child Maltreatment

Although they are discussed earlier in this chapter, it should be noted that both institutionalization and child abuse are associated with high proportions of A/C organization.

ADAPTATION AND MALADAPTATION

Effects of Environments on Attachment Figures

Adaptation to attachment figures involves adaptation to conditions that are less enduring, across children's lives, than the macro-context of community and culture. Therefore, it is important that caregivers transmit critical features of this context to their children, even when (and possibly especially when) these characteristics are not part of the functioning of the attachment figure. For example, when the larger context is dangerous, although the mother herself is safe, it is essential that she prepare her child to use strategies suited to the external danger. Furthermore, the greater, more pervasive, and more deceptive the danger, the greater the child's need to learn these self-protective strategies soon and invariantly. In some cases, this may mean teaching children fear, distrust, inhibition, and/or compulsive behavior very early in life. When the context is stable, it benefits children to learn the strategies suited to it as soon as possible. On the other hand, when the context is variable, children need to learn to use more than one strategy flexibly. The anomalous situation is when the context is first stable in one way and then becomes stable in a completely different way. In this circumstance, the early impact of the context could have deleterious effects on children's ability to adapt.

Maladaptation

When the environment changes, what is learned early on may no longer be adaptive. The issue becomes whether the former strategy facilitates adaptation to the new conditions through acquisition of additional strategies. Two conditions are likely to limit the possibility of reorganization and thus expansion of individuals' repertoires of strategies to fit a wider range of environments. One condition is danger; the greater the danger the child has experienced, the less risk the child will be willing to accept in future contexts. In part, this is because danger elicits rapid precortical processing that, in turn, can result in unnecessary, self-protective responding. This precludes feedback regarding the actual dangerousness of the event, thereby generating erroneous, superstitious learning. Because the compulsive Type A (A3-6) and obsessive Type C (C3-8) patterns are those that result from exposure to greater danger, children using these patterns may find it more difficult to reorganize to more balanced patterns when the environment changes or when their own maturation makes an unchanged context less threatening.

For example, children exposed to maternal depression often develop self-comforting skills and learn to function in contexts that are relatively unresponsive to their unique needs and desires. This can be advantageous in the home and when the child is young. At the same time, however, such children may, in the future, feel abandoned in situations when other children simply feel free to do as they wish. Similarly, formerly institutionalized children may adapt to an environment of many nonintimate adults but find it more difficult to trust that permanent adults will remain accepting and available. There is risk that by remaining too vigilant, too open to strangers, and too demanding of attention, formerly institutionalized children in a permanent placement will both fail to explore the full range of possible self-development and disappoint attachment figures, who, becoming discouraged, may become less accepting of the children.

The other condition that is likely to limit reorganization is unpredictability of threat. The Type C patterns reflect adaptation to ambiguity of communication and uncertainty of response. Again, extreme contexts have greater and more detrimental effects. When ambiguous communications have sometimes signaled danger or when long periods of lack of response or positive reinforcement have been interrupted by the sudden intrusion of dangerous outcomes, it becomes less likely that the child will trust that conditions have changed, even when communication seems positive and responses are consistently positive.

Adaptation

In this chapter, adaptation has been considered from the perspectives of strategies that reduce the danger in individuals' developmental context and the ability of individuals to adapt their strategies to changed contexts. A particular issue has been to emphasize the accomplishment that construction of the compulsive Type A and obsessive Type C strategies requires and the suitability of these strategies to the critical developmental need for safety and survival. These strategies were included in an expanded Dynamic-Maturational model of quality of attachment. The new strategies were hypothesized to be associated with the experience of self-threatening conditions. The empirical question is whether the inclusion of these new subpatterns accounts for more variance in children's and adults' functioning than reliance on only the Ainsworth-based patterns.

Many of the studies cited in this chapter find an association of A3-4, C3-4, A/C, AD, and IO with threatening circumstances, but none tested the difference in the variance accounted for by the Ainsworth-based patterns as opposed to the Dynamic-Maturational patterns. Two studies published elsewhere have done so. Ziegenhain, Rauh, and Müller (1996) tested both the Type A versus Type C distinction and distinctions among severities of anxious attachment. They found significant differences in Type A as compared to Type C children on Bayley developmental quotient, social responsiveness, and gross motor activity. They also found differences when Types A and C were combined and degrees of anxiety were compared (i.e., secure versus anxious [A1-2, C1-2] versus very anxious [A3-4, C3-4, A/C, IO]), although this analysis accounted for less variance than the ABC analysis. Furthermore, 40% of the children classified as very anxious had signs of disorganization (as described by Main and Solomon) versus only 8 to 9% of children classified in the Ainsworth-based patterns. These results suggest that the Dynamic-Maturational patterns contained added information in terms of differences both between Type A and Type C and in severity of anxiety.

Teti and Gelfand (1997) tested a more constrained model that compared those anxious children classified as A/C, AD, and IO as compared to all other children (including A3-4 and C3-4). They found that the most anxious children were less emotionally positive and that their mothers were less emotionally and verbally responsive and had less social support as compared to all other children and mothers.

Although neither of these studies had enough subjects to test a full model of specific contrasts, the findings suggest the construct validity of the compulsive and obsessive Dynamic-Maturational patterns. Specifically, the distinction between Type A and Type C organization is supported (that is, information is lost when Types A and C are combined and analyzed as secure versus anxious). Furthermore, the distinctions among levels of severity are supported; that is, the Ainsworth patterns differ from the compulsive and obsessive patterns (A3-4 and C3-4), which differ from the more complexly organized A/C strategies and possibly less organized AD and IO patterns. Therefore, a two-dimensional model, based on source of information and degree of integration, may provide more comprehensive information about individual functioning than a more restricted model.

To conclude, it is possible that when mothers and children face threatening circumstances, organizations of attachment behavior may be constructed that maximize the probability of protection and survival of children in those contexts. The adaptations may, however, limit or distort behavioral and mental development in ways that become maladaptive at older ages or in less threatening circumstances. Specifically, for children who have experienced danger in self-threatening ways, changes in context may be difficult to discern and even more difficult to trust. As a consequence, the wariness that protected the children from past danger may persist, thus protecting them from enjoying the benefits of safer contexts.

CONCLUSION

This chapter has considered the effects of developmental context on children's organization of attachment behavior. A central notion has been to describe contexts in terms of (1) the risks to survival and development that they present and (2) the strategies that would be most protective in those contexts. Danger itself has been described in terms of when and where it might occur and the probability and severity of occurrence. Because these are central issues that underlie attachment strategies as well, a conceptual framework can be offered in which the need for protection from danger affects both evolved biological capacities and adaptation of these capacities to the specific environment in which each individual develops. By applying these notions to all levels of influence (from contextual to dyadic to individual), a single model can be used to understand a range of functioning. It should be noted, however, that children do not develop in single and uniform contexts. To the contrary, developmental contexts are characterized by change over time, nested effects of multiple and hierarchically different contexts, and the juxtaposition of hierarchically similar, but functionally different, contexts.

PART THREE

MATURATION

CHAPTER FOURTEEN

Stability and Change in Infant–Mother Attachment in the Second Year of Life

Relations to Parenting Quality and Varying Degrees of Day-Care Experience[1]

HELLGARD RAUH, UTE ZIEGENHAIN,

BERND MÜLLER, AND LEX WIJNROKS

INTRODUCTION

Quality of attachment, developed during the first 12 to 18 months of life, has been shown to be relatively stable into middle childhood and to predict a broad range of social, emotional, and cognitive behaviors in the preschool years (e.g., Main, Kaplan, & Cassidy, 1985; Sroufe, 1983; 1990; Thompson, 1993). Despite general stability, changes in attachment category have been observed as a function of major changes in life circumstances and/or the attachment figure's behavior (Jacobsen, Ziegenhain, Müller, Rottmann, Hofmann, & Edelstein, 1992; Thompson, Lamb, & Estes, 1982; Vaughn, Deane, & Waters, 1985). There is still much to be learned about conditions associated with continuity and change in attachment. Thompson (1993), for example, outlined three important research areas: (1) attachment as a developmental construct, (2) developmental changes in the relation between parenting quality and quality of attachment, and (3) contexts and conditions responsible for stability or change in attachment quality. These three areas are addressed in the present chapter using findings from the Berlin Longitudinal Study of Infants' Adaptation to Novel Situations (Rauh, Rottmann, & Ziegenhain, 1987; 1990). To begin, we discuss issues related to attachment classification at different stages of development and compare classification consistency across the systems devised by Ainsworth (Ainsworth, Blehar, Waters, & Wall, 1978), Main (Main & Solomon, 1990), and Crittenden (1993b). This is followed by an examination of two aspects potentially associ-

[1] *Acknowledgments:* This chapter is based on a longitudinal study on "Adaptation to Novel Situations in the First Year of Life" supported by grants from the German Science Foundation to the first author.

We would like to thank Pat Crittenden for her helpful suggestions and Jacqui Smith for reducing the text and putting it into proper English.

ated with changes in quality of attachment: maternal sensitivity at 3 and at 12 months, and day-care experience.

Attachment as a Developmental Construct

Infancy. Bowlby's concept of attachment as a behavioral system activated by the infant in potentially threatening situations (Bowlby, 1969) was operationalized by Ainsworth and Wittig (1969) in the paradigm of the Strange Situation. The scoring system devised by Ainsworth (Ainsworth et al., 1978) focuses on the sensorimotor and emotional-expressive strategies for promoting physical safety (i.e., securing the active presence of the caregiver) that are available to infants at the end of the first year of life. Three types of attachment strategies are distinguished. Type B quality of attachment represents the optimal biopsychological functioning of the attachment system. Type A and Type C classifications indicate viable, albeit less optimal, alternative strategies. Type B children openly express feelings of comfort or anxiety in their motoric regulation of proximity to the mother (or attachment figure). Type A infants seem to have learned that clear and immediate expression of need for proximity may result in rejection or distancing by the attachment figure. Although emotionally aroused and even stressed, they try to inhibit their expressions of anxiety (Main, 1981). Type C infants, in contrast, seem to have learned that their attachment figures reliably react only to strong, or even overemphasized, bids for closeness.

Most infants aged between 12 and 18 months can be classified according to these three main types. Some, however, are unscorable or exhibit behaviors that do not fit into the basic attachment categories. Main and Solomon (1990) listed such behaviors and interpreted them as signs of disorganization/disorientation (D behaviors). In most cases, infants with D symptoms also present a recognizable basic strategy (A, B, or C). It is assumed that these children are stuck in conflict between search for support and reassurance from the attachment figure and fear of the attachment figure (Main & Hesse, 1990). Main extended Ainsworth's classification system by grouping infants with D indexes in a separate class. This class consisted of "highly insecure" children who showed no clear organization in their attachment behaviors.

The scoring systems of Ainsworth and Main are hierarchically related. No infant identified as insecurely attached by Ainsworth's scorings would be classified as secure by Main's system. However, infants who were regrouped by Main's system into the D category could originate from all three of Ainsworth's basic groups. Consequently, use of the D category results in an increased number of infants classified as insecurely attached.

If Main's interpretation of D as indicative of insecurity and disorganization is correct, D infants originating from the B group should differ from the remaining Type B children in attachment-related behaviors and experiences.

Like anxiously attached infants, they would be expected to have more conflicting and less sensitive interactions with their mothers or more "unresolved" life events prior to the assessment of quality of attachment.

Post-infancy. Compared to infants, preschool-aged children are more able to represent their social worlds and to use psychological as well as motoric strategies. An avoidant infant, for instance, inhibits the display of attachment behavior by preventing him- or herself motorically from perceiving the stimuli that elicit attachment behavior (i.e., the sight of the mother). Preschool children who wish to inhibit their display of attachment behavior can still look at their mother, if necessary, without displaying desire for contact with her (i.e., they avoid her psychologically). Attachment, according to Crittenden (1992a, 1994) can be inferred from the function that a child's behavior serves in a particular situation. Crittenden's characterization of attachment quality for preschool-aged children (the Preschool Assessment of Attachment, or PAA, 1993) shares with Ainsworth and Main the major theoretical conceptions introduced by Bowlby (1969). The PAA, however, takes into account the child's growing cognitive, language, and social abilities as well as the essence of a goal-directed partnership.

Like the Ainsworth system, the scoring system developed by Crittenden (1993) for the preschool-aged children contains the three traditional attachment classifications that are now called secure-balanced (Type B), insecure-defended (Type A), and insecure-coercive (Type C). Crittenden's system also provides for a D category but restricts this classification to truly disorganized (nonstrategic) behavior. By reference to the basic psychological functions of A, B, or C patterns of attachment and by inclusion of symbolic behaviors in the scoring criteria, many behaviors that would be indicative of disorganization or disorientation according to Main's system can be reinterpreted as strategic and are so classifiable in Crittenden's system. Because children at the shift from the sensorimotor to the preoperational period ("terrible two") tend to acquire and to explore some coercive behavior, most insecure attachment patterns are expected to be reclassified as some kind of organized C pattern. Some D behaviors in Main's system, however, when seen in their functional context, appear to be behavioral fragments from secure or insecure categories. These behaviors may have strategic quality but may not be regulated or coordinated. A child presenting such mixed behaviors (or dual strategies) would be classified as defended/coercive (A/C) in Crittenden's system.

The relation between the Ainsworth, Main, and Crittenden classification systems is primarily one of psychological equivalence. There should be agreement in secure classifications: a child classified as B (securely attached) by Crittenden's more refined system should also be classified as securely attached in Ainsworth's or Main's systems. Similarly, infants identified as insecurely attached in Ainsworth's or Main's systems should also be classified as insecurely attached in Crittenden's system. Because the PAA system covers more types of behavior (particularly symbolic reactions and behaviors indicative of coping with an insecure attachment relationship), more children are expected to be classified as "insecurely attached" than in Ainsworth's or Main's systems.

Cross-classification. All three scoring systems require observations in the same classic Strange Situation paradigm. Direct comparisons of classifications are therefore possible. The outcome of one such comparison is reported later in this chapter. Using longitudinal data from the Berlin Study, we compare classifications obtained from the three systems during the transition from infancy to preschool.

Parenting Quality in Early Infancy and Quality of Attachment in the Second Year

Findings are inconsistent regarding the extent to which maternal sensitivity in infant–mother interactions predicts infant quality of attachment (Fagot & Kavanagh, 1993; Isabella, 1993; Pedersen & Moran, 1995; Rosen & Rothbaum, 1993; Seifer & Schiller, 1995; Thompson, 1993). Some of this inconsistency may be due to the inability of the traditional attachment scoring systems to take into account infants' developing representational abilities and increasingly more elaborated attachment strategies. Indeed, there may be a "developmental progression" in the potential of the three attachment scoring systems to differentiate infants with insensitive parenting experiences: namely, from Ainsworth to Main to Crittenden. So, for example, whereas at 12 months both Ainsworth's and Main's scoring systems can discriminate indications of prior experiences of maternal insensitivity, Main's system (which registers signs of disturbance in the infant beyond the traditional classification) provides a basis for further differentiation. At 21 months, however, the discriminating power of both of these systems is reduced, and that of Crittenden is enhanced.

Little research has been done on differentiating the parenting experiences of infants with insecure attachment qualities of either the A, C, or D types. According to Malatesta and co-workers (Malatesta, Culver, Tesman, & Shepard, 1989), the fear/anger organization during the Strange Situation of insecurely attached infants in the second year of life corresponded to their emotional expression in mother–infant play episodes during the first year. Infants' emotions, in turn, were moderately to highly concordant with maternal emotional expression during these assessments. We hypothesized that insecurely attached infants of the avoidant type A who show little emotional expression during the reunion episodes of the Strange Situation may have experienced insensitive mothers of predominantly depressed affect. Mothers with depressed affect would offer little emotional-expressive feedback for the socially referencing infant. In contrast, insecurely attached infants of the D or C type have likely experienced insensitive mothers with variable, discordant, affective expression interspersed with angry or aggressive bouts. General experience of maternal emotions during the mother–infant interaction in the first year is assumed to be a determinant of quality of attachment in addition to parameters of sensitivity.

Contexts and Conditions of Stability or Change: Infants' Day-Care Experience and Attachment

Do very early day-care experiences have hazardous consequences for the quality of infant–mother attachment? This question has generated heated controversy among social scientists and politicians (Belsky, 1988a, b; Lamb & Sternberg, 1989; Scarr & Eisenberg, 1993). Most studies to date have not sufficiently controlled for parental attitudes and parenting quality prior to day-care entry, age at day-care entry, mode of introduction into day care, and quality of day-care provision. Rottmann and Ziegenhain (1988; see also Rauh, 1990) observed 35 infants, who entered quality day care in Berlin at the age of 12 months. Like Lamb and Sternberg (1989), Rottmann and Ziegenhain found that day-care attendance by itself did not affect the quality of infant–mother attachment, as assessed immediately prior to day-care entry and at 18 months. Instead the mode of the infant's introduction into the new setting influenced the attachment relationship to the mother: Infants who changed their attachment relationship with the mother from secure to insecure (Main's scoring system) had all experienced an abrupt day-care entry at 12 months. These infants apparently attributed their feelings of anxiety or anger to the mother who had left them behind at the new setting. Their relationship to the care provider was not disturbed.

The Berlin Study described later in this chapter was designed to replicate and to extend these earlier findings. We assumed that, after controlling for maternal sensitivity prior to day-care entry, age at day-care entry and experience of quality day care per se should have no detrimental effect on infant–mother attachment. For the infant to blame separation distress on the mother, the infant would need to have reached an initial cognitive level of symbolic thought. We therefore hypothesized that the mode of introduction to day care (whether familiarization time is extremely short [abrupt] or prolonged [lenient]) would influence the attachment relationship to the mother only if infants were at least 12 months of age at the time of day-care entry. Abrupt familiarization with a day-care setting may decrease the probability of secure attachment of 12-month-olds (even those with prior sensitive parenting) and possibly contribute to a change of classification from secure at 12 months to insecure at 21 months.

In short, in this chapter three systems of classifying infant attachment from the classical Strange Situation will be compared and cross-validated in their synchronical relation as well as diachronically. Attachment classifications will be related to the infants' experiences with maternal sensitive interaction and emotional expression. Here we consider interactions during the stressful Strange Situation and in a familiar situation at home at 3 and 12 months. Quality of attachment and changes in quality will then be predicted from early mother–infant interaction prior to any day-care experience, age at day-care entry, and mode of familiarization with day care. We propose that coping with separation events, even when these involve high-quality day care, is a critical experience of paramount importance for young infants.

METHOD

Socioecological Background of the Empirical Study

The analyses and results presented here are part of a longitudinal study on "Infants' Adaptation to Novel Situations" initiated by Rauh, Rottmann, and Ziegenhain in West Berlin in 1987 (Rauh, Rottmann, & Ziegenhain, 1987, 1990). This project aimed at investigating infants' coping with day-care entry and day-care experience during the first year of life. A central goal was to relate adaptation in the newborn period and experiences at home to day-care coping, and to study the long-term effects of both infants' resilience and maternal sensitivity on attachment and interaction in the second year. Only parents who intended to place their infant in day care during the first year of life were included in the study. The study was not devised to evaluate the quality of day-care provision. Rather, day-care entry and experience served as a more or less standardized challenge setting in which to investigate the attachment behavior of young infants.

More than 20% of all children under 3 years of age in West Berlin (henceforth called Berlin) are put into day care (compared to only 1% in the western states of Germany). Most day-care centers are city run, institutionally combined with a nursery school, and provide quality care as well as educational programs. Children typically attend day care for four to six hours per day, five days per week.

Sample

Mothers were recruited between 1988 and 1990 from early registration lists for a day-care place and with the assistance of municipal day-care directors. Seventy-six of the 80 families approached in the last trimester of the prospective mothers' pregnancy and seen when their child was born continue their participation in the study. One family left the study when the child was about six months old because they moved from Berlin.

The final longitudinal sample consisted of 35 girls and 41 boys, born between 1989 and 1991, and their mothers. Fifty-five percent of the infants were firstborns. They were all full-term babies without major birth complications. Nine children were raised by a single mother. Mean maternal age at the birth of the child was 30.2 years (SD = 4.8). Average age of the fathers was 33.4 years (SD = 7.4). All fathers but one and all mothers but six had been in the workforce before the infant's birth. Nearly 40% of the mothers, but only 35.5% of the fathers, had matriculated (at least 13 years of education); 39.5% of the fathers but only 15.8% of the mothers had left school after less than 10 years of schooling. This difference in formal educational levels within couples is not atypical for Berlin. Sociodemographically, the sample was mainly middle to lower middle class, a typical level for the Berlin population of young German parents at that time.

Not all parents ultimately placed their infant in a day-care institution; they either did not succeed in finding a place, or they had decided to postpone the placement. Of the 75 infants followed into the second year, 59 entered day care before the age of 18 months; 35 of them before 12 months. Parental age or education did not influence the age of placement. Most infants (10 out of 11) with very early entrance age (3–5 months), however, were firstborns. There were no significant birth-order effects at later ages. At 12 months of age, more girls were placed, and at 18 months more boys. Whether this indicates a systematic adaptation of parental socialization decisions to sex-related irritability at this developmental level cannot be answered in this study. Few sex differences were found in the group of infants with "late" entry.

Procedure[2]

The children and their mothers were followed closely over the first two years of life. Researchers visited the families three times during the neonatal period. Maternal interactive behavior with the infant was videotaped at the infants' homes (Family Films) when the children were 3, 6, 9, 12, and 18 months of age. Three additional sessions were videotaped during the first month of day-care experience. Only the films at 3 months (i.e., before any kind of actual day-care experience) and at 12 months are used for the present analyses. The videotaping situation was half standardized. The mothers were instructed to fully undress, clean, and redress the baby. They were recorded

---

[2] We gratefully acknowledge the cooperation of Thomas Thiel who helped with all matters relating to videotaping and videoanalysis, and the assistance of several graduate students in gathering and analyzing the data. Our particular thanks are extended to the participating families who tolerated our intrusions into their lives.

from the moment they carried the baby to the diapering board. Following diapering, they were asked to interact "as usual" for the rest of the continuously videotaped 21 minutes. At 12 months (plus/minus 14 days around the first birthday and after the 12-month diapering interaction at home) and again at 21 months, mothers and infants were observed in the standard Strange Situation (Ainsworth et al., 1974) in the university video laboratory.

Instruments and Measures

Ainsworth Sensitivity Scale. Videotapes of the family interactions at 3 and at 12 months (diapering situation) were rated with the nine-point Sensitivity Scale of Ainsworth (Ainsworth, Bell, & Stayton, 1974; Grossmann, 1977). The four episodes of the 12-months Strange Situation (SST-12) with the mother present yielded a third global score of maternal sensitivity. Eighty percent complete agreement was obtained between two coders. For some analyses, the scale was dichotomized close to the median of the empirical distribution, with scores of 1–5 labeled "low sensitivity" and scores of 5.5–9 "high sensitivity."

Maternal Emotion Scales. Two bipolar five-point scales were developed to globally assess maternal emotions during the interaction with the infant (Ziegenhain, Dreisörner, Klopfer, & Rauh, 1992). The scales code maternal *Cheerfulness vs. Depression* and maternal *Emotional Balance vs. Hostile Irritation* as expressed in her posture, face, voice, and verbal comments. Agreement between two coders on a subsample of films was 90% and 100%, respectively.

Attachment. The Strange Situation videotapes were classified by certified and experienced coders[3] who had no knowledge of the study aims. The coders classified the tapes simultaneously according to Ainsworth and Main. Each infant was classified by different coders at 12 or at 21 months. Twenty-six tapes were classified independently by both coders; they agreed on the main attachment classes (A, B, C, and Unclassifiable, in the case of Ainsworth and A, B, C, D, and Unclassifiable in the case of Main) in 94% of the cases. Disagreements were resolved involving a third coder. An independent coder classified the 21-months Strange Situations according to Crittenden, and any scoring difficulties were resolved by consultation with Crittenden. By involving coders from both Europe and the United States, comparability across cultures was secured.

Mode of Day-Care Familiarization. Detailed reports were obtained from the mothers as well as from the day-care providers about their plans for day-care

[3] We would like to acknowledge the help of Teresa Jacobsen, Chicago, and Karin Grossmann, Regensburg.

familiarization. Mode of day-care familiarization was scored for only 54 infants; for diverse reasons, including a nursery school strike, data for five infants are not available. In this chapter we consider two dichotomous measures: *Duration of Daily Attendance* and *Maternal Company* during the first days. *Duration of Daily Attendance* was coded as a "lenient" introduction, when the infant stayed in the center only one to two hours in the first days, slowly increasing thereafter, but not longer than four hours/day toward the end of the fourth week. It was coded as "abrupt" when the infant stayed in the institution at least four hours from the first days. Twenty-three infants (43%) experienced an abrupt introduction to the day-care setting with respect to *Duration of Daily Attendance*. *Maternal Company* was coded as short ("abrupt") when the mother stayed with the child maximally two hours in the first three or four days and left him/her unaccompanied by her for at least one hour. It was coded as long ("lenient procedure") when the mother accompanied the child throughout the first week and left the child behind in the institution for no longer than one hour daily. Thirty-six infants (67%) experienced an abrupt introduction to day care with respect to *Maternal Company*.

Twenty infants (37%) experienced a very abrupt day-care familiarization period with long attendance and short maternal company. Three infants (5.5%) attended many hours from early on but with the prolonged presence of their mothers, and 16 infants (29.6%) had short attendance during the first days but were left unaccompanied by their mothers for relatively long periods. The remaining 15 infants (27.8%) experienced a lenient familiarization procedure in both criteria. The two criteria of familiarization correlate with $\varphi = .40$ ($\chi^2_{(1)} = 8.61$, $p < .001$).

RESULTS

First, the attachment classifications will be compared with respect to consistency over systems and stability over time. Then, attachment classifications will be validated against maternal sensitivity and emotional quality as assessed from mother–infant interactions at 3 and 12 months in the family and at 12 months in the Strange Situation (SST). Finally, the influence of day-care experience on quality of attachment will be presented.

Attachment Classifications

Comparisons Between Attachment Classification Systems. The distribution of attachment patterns in the Berlin sample obtained using Ainsworth's original classification system compares well with findings of other studies. At 12 months, nearly two-thirds (59.2%) of our infants were classified as securely attached. At 21 months, three quarters (74.7%) were securely attached (see

Table 14.1). The majority of the insecurely attached infants were of the avoidant Type A (25% and 10.5%, respectively).

As can be seen in Table 14.1, Main's system resulted in fewer classifications of secure attachment. However, all cases at 12 months and two out of five cases at 21 months who were unclassifiable in Ainsworth's system could now be resolved and put into the D class (disorganized/disoriented). Crittenden's system, applied here to infants at 21 months of age, enabled classification of three additional cases. Only 13 infants (17.3%) were identified as securely attached with this system, which is surprisingly low in comparison to the traditional systems of Ainsworth and Main.

At first glance it appears that the three systems relate poorly. Log-linear analyses, however, showed that Ainsworth's and Main's system corresponded significantly at 12 months ($LR_{(1)}$ = 37.46, $p < .0001$) and at 21 months ($LR_{(1)}$ = 27.37, $p < .0001$), as did Main's and Crittenden's systems at 21 months ($LR_{(1)}$ = 7.32, $p = .007$). Ainsworth's and Crittenden's systems did not correspond at 21 months.

There was a perfect inclusion relation between Ainsworth's and Main's systems. Infants who were classified as insecurely attached by Ainsworth's system were never classified as securely attached by Main's system; but about one-third of the infants (16 out of 45 at 12 months and 17 out of 56) who had been classified as securely attached according to Ainsworth were identified as in fact insecurely attached ("disorganized," D) when Main's system was applied. This high percentage of B-D children is unexpected from published research (van IJzendoorn, Goldberg, Kroonenberg, & Frenkel, 1992). There was also an inclusion relation between Main's and Crittenden's systems at 21

Table 14.1.   Distribution of Attachment Classifications at 12 and at 21 Months According to the Classification Systems of Ainsworth, Main, and Crittenden ($n = 76$ at 12 Months, $n = 75$ at 21 Months)

| Attachment Quality | Ainsworth | | Main | | Crittenden |
	12 Months (n)	21 Months (n)	12 Months (n)	21 Months (n)	21 Months (n)
B	45	56	29	39	13
A	19	8	12	2	23
C	7	6	5	2	30
D	—	—	30	29	1
A/C	—	—	—	—	2
IO	—	—	—	—	6
NC	5	5	0	3	0
Percent secure	59.2	74.7	38.2	52.0	17.3

NC = not classifiable; IO = insecure other.

months. Eleven of the 13 children classified as securely attached according to the PAA system had been identified equivalently by Main's (and Ainsworth's) system. Inspection of the classification records of the remaining two children showed that they were labeled as insecure of the A 1 type with Main's system and classified as secure of the B 1 type with Crittenden's system, a reclassification in theoretical accord with Crittenden's typology. In our further analyses, however, this pattern will be labeled as "inconsistent" with the proposed inclusion pattern.

Of the two basic types of insecure attachment, A and C, A was more frequently represented at age 12 months according to both Ainsworth's and Main's systems. Both types nearly disappeared at 21 months when Main's system was applied, while the percentage of infants classified as D ("disorganized/disoriented": 39.5% at 12 months and 38.7% at 21 months) remained unchanged and exceeded the usually expected 10% to 20%. With Crittenden's classification, the majority of the insecurely attached infants were diagnosed as being consistent in their psychological strategies, classified as insecure-defended (A: 30.7%) or as insecure-coercive (C: 40%). The correspondence across systems in these subclassifications was less systematic than was the identification as secure or insecure.

In short, across classification systems there is a nearly perfect inclusion relation, with Ainsworth's system probably oversampling secure attachment relationships and Crittenden's system insecure relationships.

Stability of Classification from 12 to 21 Months. Based on Ainsworth's system, most infants (83.7%) who had been classified as "secure" at 12 months received the same classification at 21 months as well, whereas stability within the insecure classification (27.3%) was low ($LR_{(1)} = 1.06$, *ns*, for overall stability; unclassifiable cases excluded). Main's system indicated stability over time ($LR_{(1)} = 3.50$, $p = .06$, unclassifiable cases excluded), due mainly to stable classifications within the B (66%) and the D (60%) types. Main's (but not Ainsworth's) classification at 12 months predicted Crittenden's classification at 21 months ($LR_{(1)} = 6.07$, $p = .014$, unclassifiable cases excluded); 51 out of 75 infants received the same classification as secure or insecure.

"Permissible" scoring patterns indicating stability of secure or insecure attachment and "nonpermissible" patterns indicating either a clear change in quality of attachment or inconsistency were created (Table 14.2) and tested using prediction analysis (von Eye & Brandtstädter, 1985). These patterns were constructed under the following premises: (1) that Main's system includes Ainsworth's classification but identifies more infants as insecurely attached than does Ainsworth's system, (2) that both Ainsworth's and Main's systems become less sensitive to signs of insecurity with increasing age and competence of the child, (3) that Crittenden's system identifies signs of insecurity at 21 months more sensitively than Main's system, perhaps even too

Table 14.2.   Stability of Insecure and Secure Classification over Time

		Main		Crittenden
		12 Months	21 Months	21 Months
Stably Insecure	$n = 25$	I	I	I
	$n = 17$	I	S	I
Insecure to Secure	$n = 1$	I	I	S
	$n = 3$	I	S	S
Secure to Insecure	$n = 9$	S	I	I
Stably Secure	$n = 11$	S	S	I
	$n = 8$	S	S	S
Inconsistent	$n = 1$	S	I	S
Pattern	$n = 1$	I	I	S

I = Insecure; S = Secure.

scrupulously, and (4) that stability of attachment relationship is expected to prevail. Nineteen infants were identified as stably secure, 42 as stably insecure, 3 as changing from an insecure to a secure relationship, 9 as changing from secure to insecure attachment, and 2 as inconsistent.

Under the hypothesis of stability of attachment classification from 12 to 21 months, 36% misclassifications could be avoided as compared to chance classification (*DEL* =.361, $z = 2.00$, $p = .022$).

It appears that during the developmental period studied, the combination of Main's and Crittenden's scoring systems enables the researcher to identify continuity in the quality of attachment relationships. Strict adherence to one system may fail to do so. For further support of this conclusion, the attachment classifications, separately for each system and in combination, were validated against their relationships to the infants' experiences with maternal sensitive interaction.

Maternal Sensitivity in the First Year of Life and Security of Attachment

Maternal Interaction Behaviors. Quality of mothering in the first year of life was assessed during two home observations at 3 to 12 months (diapering and free play, F-3 and F-12) and during the first Strange Situation Test at 12 months (SST-12), allowing for a longitudinal analysis within the family setting and a comparison across settings. At 12 months in the family setting, mothers received the lower scores on sensitivity and emotional behavior (balance and cheerfulness) as compared to the same situation when the infant was 3 months of age. The age changes were significant for maternal *Emotional Balance/Hostility* ($F_{(2,71)} = 30.54$, $p < .001$).

Maternal Sensitivity appeared to be moderately stable (F-3 to F-12 or SST: $r = .55$, $p < .001$ and $.50$, $p < .001$) as well as consistent over situations ($r = .51$, $p < .001$). *Emotional Balance* was slightly less stable ($r = .46$, $p < .0001$ and $.40$, $p < .0001$) but quite consistent over the situations at 12 months ($r = .53$, $p < .0001$). In contrast, *Cheerfulness* was little consistent over these situations (stability: $r = .42$, $p < .001$ and $.36$, $p < .01$; consistency $r = .24$, $p < .05$).

Although all three global scales of maternal behavior intercorrelate positively and significantly, the degree of intercorrelation varies from low to high depending on the age of the infant and the combination of scales (Table 14.3). The interrelation of the two emotion scales decreased from moderate to low with the age of the infant (i.e., the two maternal emotional reactions became more differentiated). The relations of *Sensitivity* to both of the emotional scales, however, remained moderately close, particularly to *Emotional Balance/Hostile Irritation*.

Maternal Interactive Behavior and Quality of Attachment as Assessed by the Three Classification Systems. In all observational situations, infants classified as securely attached (in any of the three systems and at either 12 or 21 months) had experienced mothers who, on average, had been more sensitive with the child, more emotionally balanced and friendly and more cheerful. Infants classified as insecurely attached had generally experienced mothers who had been somewhat insensitive as well irritated and hostile toward the infant and slightly depressed. Table 14.4 presents a summary of the results based on MANOVAs (over all three situations, unclassifiable cases excluded) and post hoc univariate and *t*-tests. With maternal sensitivity as the validation criterion, Main's classification at 12 months and both Main's and Crittenden's classifications at 21 months appear to be more valid than the attachment classification proposed by Ainsworth. The two maternal emotion scales, *Emotional Balance/Hostile Irritation* and *Sensitivity,* were similarly related to attachment. *Cheerfulness/Depression* seemed to be of less relevance for quality of attachment.

As Figure 14.1A demonstrates, the addition of the D category to the attachment classification in Main's extension of Ainsworth's system at 12

Table 14.3. Intercorrelation Between Sensitivity, Emotional Balance, and Cheerfulness ($n = 75$)

	Sensitivity		Emotional Balance
	x Emotional Balance	**x Cheerfulness**	**x Cheerfulness**
F–3 Months	.61***	.65***	.51***
F–12 Months	.71***	.49***	.31**
SST	.65***	.56***	.28*

*$p < .05$; **$p < .01$; ***$p < .001$.

Table 14.4.   Summary Table: Significant Differences in Experiences of Maternal
Interaction Behavior for Securely and Insecurely Attached Infants

Attachment Classifications by Months		Maternal Interactive Behavior Ratings		
		Sensitivity	Emotional Balance	Cheerfulness
Ainsworth	12	SST	—	—
Ainsworth	21	3	—	3
Main	12	3, 12, SST	3, 12, SST	3, 12, SST
Main	21	12, SST	12, SST	—
Crittenden	21	12, SST	12, SST	—

SST = Strange Situation; 3 = 3 months; 12 = 12 months.

months clearly differentiates infants with contrasting experiences of maternal sensitivity at 3 as well as 12 months at home and in the Strange Situation
(from which the classification of attachment was derived). Compared to all
insecure infants, infants re-scored D in Main's system from B in Ainsworth's
system (B-D, $n = 16$) had experienced the least sensitive mothers, particularly in both home situations. Only in the Strange Situations were these
mothers somewhat more sensitive. Differences between B-B and B-D infants
in experience of sensitive mothering were highly significant ($F_{(1,41)} = 16.54$,
$p < .0001$).

The attachment reclassifications from Ainsworth's to Main's system at 21
months led to similar improvements in differentiating infants with contrasting sensitivity experiences ($F_{(1,51)} = 5.83$, $p < .02$) (Figure 14.1B). With
Crittenden's system, only infants with highly and consistently sensitive mothering experience at 12 months at home and in the Strange Situation were
identified as securely attached. For this system, early experiences of maternal
sensitivity (at 3 months) appeared to be less relevant.

Figure 14.2(A to E) illustrate the differential sensitivity experiences of the
infants for all types of attachment classifications at 12 months and 21 months,
respectively. MANOVAs over all interaction assessments (F-3, F-12, and SST-
12) revealed main effects for attachment qualities on *Sensitivity* when attachment was classified according to Main at either 12 months ($F_{(3,70)} = 9.08$, $p <$
.000) or 21 months ($F_{(1,63)} = 8.56$, $p = .005$). There was no significant differential effect when the infants were classified according to Ainsworth, and only a
marginally significant effect for the Crittenden classification when the group
"Insecure Other" was eliminated from the analysis ($F_{(2,61)} = 3.02$, $p = .06$).
There were also significant main effects due to attachment qualities with
Main's classification at 12 and at 21 months on *Emotional Balance* ($F_{(3,70)} =$
5.29, $p = .002$ and $F_{(1,63)} = 6.90$, $p = .011$) and also with Crittenden's classification (only A, B, C; $F_{(2,61)} = 3.51$, $p = .036$). Finally, *Cheerfulness* was significantly

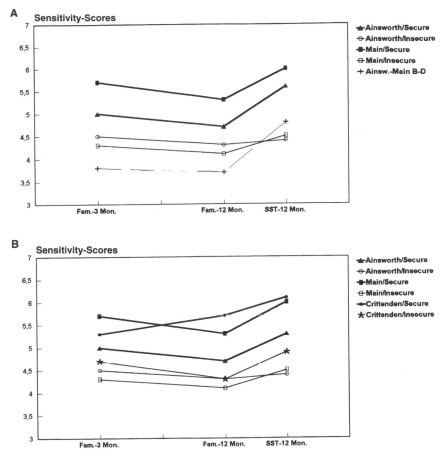

Figure 14.1. Level of Sensitivity Observed During Three Interaction Situations for Securely and Insecurely Attached Infants. (**A**) Classified According to Ainsworth's and Main's System at 12 Months; (**B**) Classified According to Ainsworth's, Main's and Crittenden's System at 21 Months. BD = infants classified as B by Ainsworth's and D by Main's System.

differentiated only for attachment types assessed at 12 months and scored according to Main ($F_{(3,70)}$ = 5.20, p = .003).

The interaction between situation and attachment type was significant at 12 months when attachment was classified according to Ainsworth ($F_{(2,67)}$ = 3.55, p = .034 with nonclassifiable cases excluded). B- and C mothers, unlike A mothers, improved in sensitivity from interaction at home to interaction in the Strange Situation. Clear differences were also apparent for A and C mothers with Main's classification. Whereas A mothers became less sensitive in the Strange Situation as compared to interaction at home, C mothers markedly improved their sensitivity.

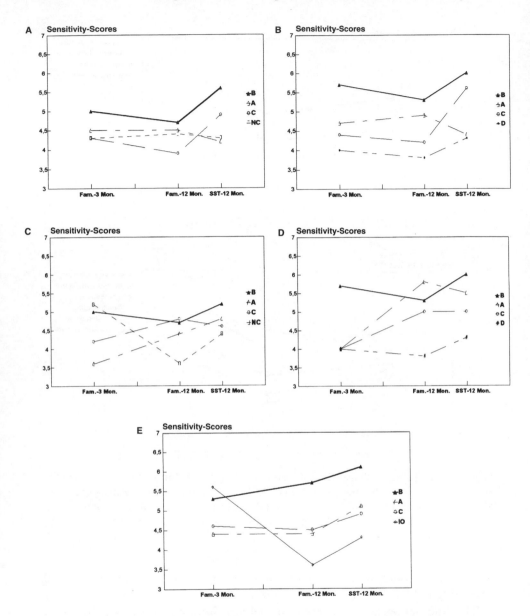

Figure 14.2. Level of Sensitivity Observed During Three Interaction Situations for B, A, C, D-Type, and Not-Classifiable (NC). Infants Classified According to: **(A)** Ainsworth's System at 12 Months; **(B)** Main's System at 12 Months; **(C)** Ainsworth's System at 21 Months; **(D)** Main's System at 21 Months; **(E)** Crittenden's System at 12 Months.

Interaction effects were also found between age of infant (3 to 12 months) and attachment quality, but only when attachment was assessed at 21 months (Fig. 3a and 3c). Nonclassifiable infants [Ainsworth's system, $F_{(3,69)} = 3.18$, $p < .03$] and Insecure Other infants [Crittenden's system, $F_{(3,66)} = 3.07$, $p = .034$] had mothers who were most sensitive when the infants were very young but became considerably less sensitive when the infants grew older. This tendency contrasted with the experience of infants with clear A, B, or C designations.

Discriminant analyses were performed for all attachment classification systems with all three maternal interactive-behavior ratings whenever significant relations could be expected (for selection of situations, see Table 14.4). A satisfactory discrimination of secure from insecure infants, based on maternal behavior, was only achieved for attachment classifications according to Main at 12 months (26% above chance classification). In general, the attachment group membership of insecurely attached infants was more successfully predicted by maternal behavior than was the case for securely attached infants. Mothers' behavior in the Strange Situation was the best discriminator (63.5 to 76% correctly classified), and maternal *Sensitivity* was the major contributing variable. Of all *Sensitivity* measures (F-3, F-12, SST-12), the combination of sensitivity at 3 months and in the Strange Situation correctly placed 70% of the infants as securely or insecurely attached (18% improvement over chance), but only when classified according to Main at 12 months.

In order to test further the hypothesis that level and consistency in sensitivity experience are important for attachment classification, sensitivity scores at all three assessments were dichotomized (low = 1-5 and high = 5.5-9), and mothers were grouped into three classes: those consistently high in sensitivity, low, or mixed. Infants with an experience of consistently high maternal sensitivity ($n = 7$) were exclusively classified as securely attached in Main's classification at 12 months. Infants with consistently low maternal sensitivity ($n = 28$) were (with only three exceptions) identified as insecurely attached (89%). The infants with mixed experiences ($n = 38$) were evenly distributed over both classes ($\chi^2_{(2)} = 21.60$, $p < .001$).

Finally, experiences with maternal sensitivity and emotions of infants identified as stably secure, stably insecure, changing from secure or insecure, or the reverse were analyzed (groupings as in Table 14.2). One-way analyses of variances were employed with post hoc tests using special contrasts (stably secure vs. secure to insecure, insecure to secure, and stably insecure infants, respectively). Significant differences in maternal *Sensitivity* were revealed for the stably secure and stably insecure groups for all observation situations. The same was true for maternal *Emotional Balance/Hostility* and *Cheerfulness/Depression* (Figures 14.3A–C). Infants who changed from secure to insecure attachment were midway between securely and insecurely attached infants in level of sensitivity experience. They were similar to insecurely attached infants in their exposure to maternal hostility and similar to

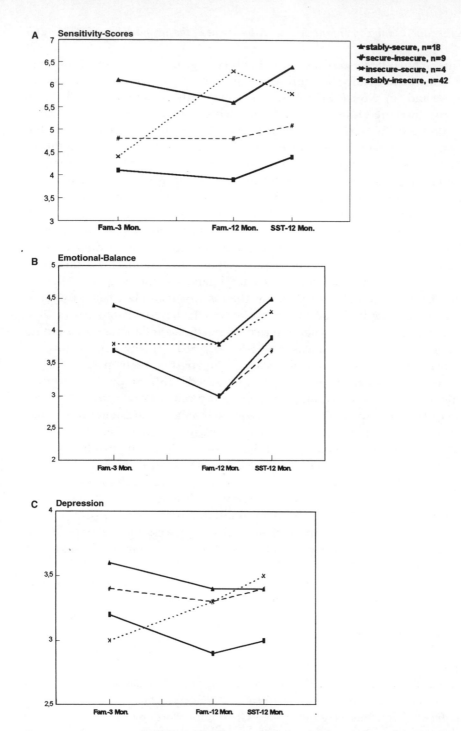

Figure 14.3. Level of Maternal Behavior at Three Observation Times for Stably-Secure, Stably-Insecure, Secure-to-Insecure, and Insecure-to-Secure Infants. **(A)** Sensitivity; **(B)** Emotional Balance/Hostile Irritation; **(C)** Cheerfulness/Depression.

securely attached infants in exposure to cheerfulness. Infants who changed from insecure attachment at 12 months to secure attachment at 21 months, however, had experienced a remarkable change in maternal behavior during their first 12 months of life. When they were 3 months old, their mothers were as low in *Sensitivity* and in *Emotional Balance* as were mothers of stably insecurely attached infants. Their mothers had also showed the most depressive symptoms at 3 months. When the infants were 12 months old, their mothers had become the most sensitive mothers and had become as friendly at home and in the Strange Situation as were mothers of consistently securely attached infants.

All these data confirm our proposals that experience of maternal sensitivity is related to the infants' quality of attachment. Marked changes in maternal sensitivity from early to late infancy seem to become reflected in infants' attachment strategies. Main's classification system was best able to mirror the infants' experiences with contrasting types of mothering. Crittenden's system enabled further discrimination, even though applied at the end of the second year of life.

Day-Care Experience and Attachment

The influence of day-care experience on quality of attachment was analyzed in two ways. First, attachment at 21 months was used as an outcome criterion for effects of day-care experience. Second, day-care experience was related to stability or changes in attachment relationships (using the classification groupings presented in Table 14.2 and Figures 14.3a-c). Comparisons were restricted to those infants who entered day care before 18 months of age. The focus of the comparisons was on differences between the group with early entry (before 12 months, $n = 34$) and late entry (after 12 months, $n = 20$). The infants who did not enter day care (who were excluded from these analyses) were similar in attachment distribution and maternal sensitivity to those with late entry. Maternal sensitivity assessed at 3 months (F-3) was chosen as an index of pre-day-care experiences for all children.

Day Care and Attachment at 21 Months.   Early- and late-entry infants did not differ in quality of attachment assessed prior to day-care entry. Mode of familiarization with day care (characterized as lenient or abrupt) also made no difference with respect to quality of attachment at 12 months of age.

In contrast, early versus late day-care entry was related to attachment assessed at 21 months for the Ainsworth ($\chi^2_{(1)} = 5.71$, $p = .02$) and Crittenden system ($\chi^2_{(1)} = 5.77$, $p = .04$, Fisher exact probability) but not for Main's system. Eleven of the 12 infants who started day care early were classified as insecurely attached according to Ainsworth. There were equal numbers of securely attached infants (according to this system) in both entry groups. In the case of the PAA system, 66% of the insecurely attached infants had entered day care early in contrast to only 25% of the securely attached infants. Mode of familiarization, but not duration of the infant's daily attendance, was related to the infants' security of attachment as classified according to Ainsworth ($\chi^2_{(2)}$ = 4.40, p = .04) or to Main ($\chi^2_{(2)}$ = 7.14, p = .009). Securely attached infants had mainly experienced a lenient mode of familiarization, and insecurely attached children an abrupt mode.

Log-linear analyses were performed with Main's attachment classification at 21 months in order to determine interaction effects between age at day-care entry, mode of familiarization (duration of infant's daily attendance), and maternal sensitivity prior to day-care experience. A significant high-order interaction was found (sensitivity by entry age by mode by attachment, $LR_{(11)}$ = 25.30, p = .008). The least complex model representing the empirical data was composed of two three-way interactions (sensitivity by age at entry by attachment and age at entry by mode by attachment, $LR_{(4)}$ = 4.33, p = .36). Because age at entry was part of both terms, the sample was split into infants with early and late entry and analyses were repeated. No interaction between sensitivity, mode, and attachment was found for infants with early entry into day care. In contrast, infants with late entry differed in security of attachment as a combined function of early maternal sensitivity and mode of familiarization with day care ($LR_{(4)}$ = 14.70, p = .005). Children who entered day care later were more likely to be insecurely attached at 21 months when they had experienced an abrupt mode of familiarization. Children who had entered day care late, but by a lenient mode of familiarization, were more likely to be securely attached. This relation was independent of maternal sensitivity prior to day-care experience. Mode of familiarization appeared to make a difference with regard to attachment only for infants enrolled into day care after 12 months of age.

Day Care and Stability of Attachment Relation. In a second sequence of log-linear analyses, the effects of age at day-care entry and mode of familiarization were computed for four groups of infants: those with stable secure or insecure attachment relationships, and those who changed in their quality of attachment (groups according to Table 14.2). The three-way interaction (age at entry by mode by attachment stability) turned out to be significant ($LR_{(10)}$ = 19.26, p = .037). The least complex model representing the empirical data comprised two terms, mode of familiarization and stability of attachment ($LR_{(8)}$ = 8.34, p = .40). Inclusion of maternal sensitivity prior to day-care experience led to a model with two second-order interaction effects, sensitivity by attachment stability and mode by attachment stability ($LR_{(4)}$ = 1.92, p = .75). All infants who changed from secure to insecure attachment had experienced an abrupt mode of familiarization with day care. Conversely, all infants who changed from insecure to secure attachment had experienced a lenient mode of familiarization. Furthermore, they changed from an insecure to a secure attachment relationship in spite of insensitive mothering experiences in early infancy. Nine out of eleven stably secure infants combined sensitive mothering experience with lenient familiarization. When entering day care late, these securely attached infants were always introduced in a lenient way. Even when they entered day care early, securely attached infants were typically adapted slowly. In contrast, stably insecure infants, had experienced insensitive mothering. Regardless of day-care entry age, abrupt or lenient familiarization did not influence their attachment relationships.

These results suggest that sensitive mothering experience is a major contributor to quality of attachment. Day-care experience, as such, did not seem to have a direct influence on this relationship. The kind of familiarization, however, did make a difference for some of the children but only in later infancy.

CONCLUSIONS

This study sought to answer three questions: (1) How do the three systems for classifying quality of attachment from the Ainsworth Strange Situation Test relate to one another? (2) To what extent is maternal sensitivity represented in these three systems? (3) Does day-care experience influence the infant's developing attachment relationship to his or her mother?

The three systems of classifying quality of attachment – the classical system by Ainsworth, its extension by Main, and the PAA developed by Crittenden for preschool children – yielded divergent numbers of infants identified as securely attached. Some caution should therefore be exercised in comparing classifications. With respect to the dichotomy secure/insecure, the three systems were consistent. All infants identified as insecurely attached by Ainsworth's system are classified in this same group also by Main's and by Crittenden's systems. Conversely, (nearly) all infants recognized as securely attached by Crittenden's system were classified equivalently by Main's and Ainsworth's systems. The two "misfitting" infants were identified as B-1 in Ainsworth's and Main's systems because they seemed to hesitate when the mother reentered the room. In Crittenden's system, such a slight initial hesitation would not preclude a B classification if the child, even at this physical distance, expressed emotional intimacy and relief. More infants are recognized as insecurely attached by Main's than by Ainsworth's system, solely because previously B infants can be reclassified as D. According to our findings, Main's classificatory system is sensitive to inconsistencies in the infant's attachment behaviors that escape notice in Ainsworth's system. Crittenden's system is more sensitive to signs of insecurity.

In our longitudinal observations, there was an impressive decrease with age in the number of infants identified as insecurely attached when categorized with the same classification system. To our knowledge, this age dependence of the attachment measure has not yet been recognized in the scientific literature. (Bretherton & Waters, 1985; Lamb & Sternberg, 1989; Rosen & Rothbaum, 1993; Isabella, 1993; van den Boom, 1995; van IJzendoorn, 1990). Most studies that report a high percentage of securely attached infants have tested children when they were older than 18 months. Lower percentages of securely attached infants are generally found at 12 months. Our distribution of secure and insecure infants agrees with the general literature when both age at assessment and system of classification are taken into account.

Two questions arise in relation to age changes (more "securely" attached infants with increasing age identified with the same system) and system changes (more "insecurely" attached infants from Ainsworth to Main to Crittenden): (1) Do systems become increasingly insensitive to signs of insecurity that indeed exist? (2) If so, which system is best suited for which age?

To examine these questions, we first tested the proposal that quality of attachment is usually a stable characteristic (continuity hypothesis). Changes in stability are thought to be due to major events in the child's life (Thomson, Lamb, & Estes, 1982). We found stability in Main's classification for 12 and 21 months and from Main at 12 months to Crittenden at 21 months. When ordering infants along the inclusion relation of systems at each age, particularly Main-12 to Main-21 and Crittenden-21, 36% more infants than by chance could be classified correctly on the basis of the continuity-stability hypothesis. Infants who clearly changed from a secure relationship at 12 months to an insecure relationship at 21 months and who belonged to the day-care attendance group had all experienced an abrupt introduction into day care. Their change had a substantial psychological basis.

Second, we tested the hypothesis that security of attachment is related to sensitivity of maternal interaction. If quality of attachment is a relatively stable characteristic resulting from early experiences in mother–infant interaction, then it should be represented in all classification systems. If classification systems become less sensitive with age, this decrease in discriminatory power should be represented in a decreasing differentiation of infants with sensitive or insensitive mothering experience. If this decrease in discriminatory power is primarily due to the instrument and not to the infant's changing personality architecture, the sharper instrument should reestablish this differentiation.

Indeed, all three systems differentiated infants with insensitive and sensitive mothering experience. At 12 months, Main's system was better than Ainsworth's, and at 21 months, both Main's and Crittenden's systems appeared to be better than Ainsworth's classification. When classifying infants over age and systems (Main-12, Main-21, and Crittenden-21), stably secure and stably insecure infants were clearly different in their mothering experiences at 3 and 12 months. Infants who changed from an insecure to a secure relationship to their mothers had experienced a marked positive change in maternal sensitivity and friendliness. That changes in maternal sensitivity can make a difference with regard to attachment (and other infant behaviors) has also been confirmed by van den Boom's Dutch intervention study with mothers of highly irritable infants (van den Boom, 1994, 1995).

These data strongly support theories about a sensitivity-attachment association. The controversy in the literature about this relation (Isabella, 1993; Malatesta et al., 1989; Pederson & Moran, 1995; Rosen & Rothbaum, 1993) may be due to inadequate measures of attachment for age of assessment, as well as to differences in the situational contexts and the ages at which sensitivity was observed. Rosen and Rothbaum (1993) assessed sensitivity immediately after the Strange Situation Test and when the children were 17 to 25 months of age. They found only a modest association between maternal or paternal sensitivity and attachment (Ainsworth's system). In contrast, Isabella (1993) observed a strong association between sensitivity and an inverse relation to rejection at 1, 4, and 9 months, with quality of attachment at 12 months. Maternal activity (in some respects similar to our *Cheerfulness* scale) was not predictive of later attachment. In Isabella's study, the early interaction observations (1 month) discriminated best. In our study, mother–infant interaction at 3 months was also a good predictor of attachment at 12 months, whereas interaction at 12 months (in the Strange Situation) was the best predictor for attachment at 21 months.

It appears that some developmental periods are better suited than others to assess predictive aspects of maternal behavior. In the early period, maternal sensitivity may represent the mother's overall attitude toward the child because the child does not yet contribute so much to this interaction. In addition, both the early period and novel or slightly stressful situations at later ages may be better suited for assessing maternal sensitivity than are familiar and routine situations. The Strange Situation at 12 months appeared to be well suited not only for assessing the infant's quality of attachment but also for diagnosing maternal sensitivity and emotional expression.

Taken together, our data support proposals that quality of attachment is a relatively stable characteristic of the infant in the second year of life and is related to experience of maternal sensitivity. Changes in quality of attachment appear to be related to major life events of the child and/or marked changes in maternal behavior.

We were less successful in identifying continuity in subclasses of insecure attachment over systems and time. If we compare Main-12 to Main-21 and Crittenden-21, the A to C relation changes: more infants were characterized as A than C at 12 months (Main's system) and more children as C than as A at 21 months (Crittenden's system). Main's system at 21 months differentiated mainly between secure and D infants. Infants presenting a C strategy at 12 months were mostly identified as C also in Crittenden's system at 21 months.

Several A children changed into Crittenden's C or the Insecure Other category. This could be a weak support for Crittenden's contention that at the end of the second year, for developmental reasons, a great number of children begin to explore C strategies. If so, this pattern should change in the following years.

At 12 months, A or C mothers (Main or Ainsworth classification) interacted differently in familiar and novel situations. While C mothers became more sensitive during the Strange Situation, A mothers became more insensitive with their infant. They seemed to be less able to deal with this situation. Interestingly, the behavior of A infants was much better controlled in the Strange Situation than was the case for C children who exhibited a lot of open stress behavior (Rauh, Dillmann, Müller, & Ziegenhain, 1995). Although A and C patterns could generally not be differentiated well on the basis of maternal sensitivity or emotions, differences were more convincing between mothers of securely attached infants and mothers of infants scored as D (Main's system). This was particularly true for infants rescored from B (Ainsworth) to D (Main). The largest differences in sensitivity were between mothers of B and D infants, even at three months. Mothers of later A or C infants were less insensitive and less hostile than mothers of D infants. Spangler and Grossmann (1993), as well as Hertsgaard, Gunnar, Erickson, and Nachimas (1995), reported that D infants reacted physiologically with heart-rate changes and increase in cortisone to the Strange Situation at 12 months in spite of overt stress reactions that were usually associated with lower physiological reactions in the other infants. According to their interpretation, these infants are highly insecure and revert to inadequate strategies (at high physiological costs) to cope with distress. We found few infants with D reactions at 12 months among those infants who changed from insecure to secure within Main's system. It seems that the D reactions of infants in the Strange Situation are intimately associated with maternal insensitivity and hostility. Analyses of the infants' role in the early mother–infant interaction during the diapering situation at home reported elsewhere (Rauh et al., 1995) showed that infants with A reactions according to either Main-12 or Crittenden-21 can already be differentiated at 3 months and are most clearly distinguished from future B-infants. It seems plausible that the development of a coherent A or C strategy by an infant is influenced by further variables such as the infant's temperament, whereas D appears to represent an actual intense conflict of the child dependent mainly on experience with maternal behavior.

Infants who were difficult to classify at the age of 12 months (Unclassifiable according to Ainsworth) had just experienced a major situational change in mothers' behavior from insensitive and hostile at home to sensitive and friendly in the Strange Situation. In contrast, infants difficult to classify at 21 months (Unclassifiable according to Main, or Insecure Other according to

Crittenden) had experienced a major long-term or longitudinal change in maternal sensitivity (3 to 12 months). The importance of such long-term changes for the infants' style and ability to cope with novel situations has also been mentioned by Isabella (1993).

Day-care experience has often been considered as detrimental to the development of a secure attachment relationships (Belsky, 1988ab). Similar to the study by Rottmann and Ziegenhain with another sample of Berlin infants (1988) and in accord with Roggman et al. (1994), we did not find that day care per se had a direct impact on the attachment relationship with the mother. Unlike most other studies, we compared groups of infants whose parents intended to make use of day-care provision but for several reasons placed their infant in day care either earlier than 12 months or later.

When attachment was assessed at 12 months in our study, one group of infants had already several months of day-care experience, whereas the other had not yet started. No difference in attachment and in the sensitivity-attachment relation was found between these groups. The same result emerged when the infants with the earliest day-care experiences (entry between 3 and 5 months) were compared to infants entering at 12 months, matched for socioeconomic status, sex, and birth order (Ziegenhain, Rauh, & Müller, 1996). The group of infants entering after 12 months of age and the group without day-care experience until two years also did not differ in their distribution of attachment at 12 months and the sensitivity-attachment relation (3 to 12 months). There was no indication that infants with repeated experiences of setting changes and separations from the parents differed in their behavior in the Strange Situation or in the meaning of their behavior as reflected in the sensitivity-attachment relation.

Another feature of the Berlin Study that differs from most other studies (Belsky, 1988ab; Roggman et al., 1994) was the fact that we recorded the infant's *mode of familiarization* with the day-care setting, a situation most akin to the separation situation in the Strange Situation. The duration of the mother's presence in the setting seemed to be of little influence. The duration of the infant's attendance in the setting in the first week, however, did make a difference, but only with regard to attachment quality at 21 months and for infants with late enrollment. All infants with day-care experience who changed from secure to insecure attachment had had an abrupt familiarization experience. All infants who changed from insecure to secure attachment had been leniently introduced to day care. In addition, they had experienced a change from insensitive to sensitive mothering. Again, these relations were confirmed with infants entering day care very early and immediately after 12 months (Ziegenhain et al., 1996).

These findings do not deny that day-care entry may be a stressful event for any young infant. But most likely the very young infants have not developed an at least rudimentary "working model" of their mother that enables them to attribute their experiences to the attachment figure. There are, however, quite strong indications that from about 1 year of age, infants tend to put the "blame" for their unpleasant, abrupt familiarization with day care on their emotional relationship with their mothers, and that these experiences can influence their future quality of attachment (Jacobsen et al., 1992; Rottmann & Ziegenhain, 1988; Rauh, 1990).

There are several limitations to our study. We concentrated on maternal influences on the infant with respect to quality of attachment. Moreover, we analyzed maternal behavior only at 3 and at 12 months. We clearly did not cover the full course and scope of the infant's experiences with his or her main caretakers. Our observations provide only limited information about changes in maternal behavior as a reflection of the developmental progress of the child, marital harmony, and family or occupational stresses. In some analyses, the numbers of infants in the subgroups were very small. The conclusions that we draw, however, are strongly supported by their replication in our previous study (Rottmann & Ziegenhain, 1988). In sum, the findings fully justify the time and effort invested in longitudinal assessment and open up avenues for further investigations.

CHAPTER FIFTEEN

Change and Continuity in Ambivalent Attachment Relationships from Infancy through Adolescence[1]

SYDNEY L. HANS, VICTOR J. BERNSTEIN, AND
BELINDA E. SIMS

At the heart of attachment theory is the notion of the secure base (Ainsworth, Blehar, Waters, & Wall, 1978; Bowlby, 1988). The secure base involves the balance between two interlocking behavioral systems: *the attachment system,* which functions to protect the child from harm, and *the exploratory system,* which functions to allow the child to learn and develop instrumental competence. When children experience stress or perceive that the mother is unavailable, they seek proximity to her. When children are confident of their safety and secure in the availability of the mother, they are able to comfortably explore and increasingly move beyond the immediate vicinity of the mother.

More than two decades ago, Mary Ainsworth identified a small group of infants who display such intense anxiety around attachment issues and direct so much of their behavior toward keeping the mother in proximity that they are unable to fully explore the world around them. Ainsworth (Ainsworth et al., 1978) observed 26 Baltimore 1-year-olds in the Strange Situation, a laboratory paradigm in which infants are separated from and reunited with their mothers. Four of these infants displayed great upset at separation but upon reunion were unable to make full use of their mothers for comfort – either expressing anger at their mothers or displaying extreme passivity. Ainsworth described these infants as anxious-ambivalent because of their apparent mixed feelings at reunion: obviously wanting their mothers to be close but actively resisting comforting contact and/or failing actively to seek contact. She referred to them as C infants, an arbitrary alphabetical designation to contrast them with two other attachment groups: the A, anxious-avoidant infants and the B, secure infants.

[1] *Acknowledgments:* The authors acknowledge Linda Henson, Karen Freel, Holly Furdyna, and Carrie Patterson who were involved in the collection of data from this sample and Geoff Goodman and Suzanne Cox who made the original attachment ratings. They wish to thank Alan Sroufe for providing us with training on Ainsworth's infant attachment rating system and to Patricia Crittenden for providing training on her Preschool Attachment Assessment and the encouragement and opportunity to prepare this manuscript.

Ainsworth collected data from home observations suggesting that mothers of C infants were inconsistently or minimally available to meet their infants' needs, though not rejecting or uncomfortable with physical closeness to their infants. Subsequent studies (see review by Cassidy & Berlin, 1994) generally confirmed the notion that mothers of C infants are somewhat unavailable to respond to children's signals (e.g., Crockenberg, 1981; Isabella, Belsky, & von Eye, 1989; Lewis & Feiring, 1989; Smith & Pederson, 1988; Vondra, Shaw, & Kevenides, 1995). Ainsworth argued that the behavior of the C infants in the Strange Situation reflects the infants' lack of confidence in their mothers' accessibility and responsiveness. Because C infants cannot be certain of their mothers' availability, they remain close to their mothers in order to monitor their mothers' actions and heighten their display of emotionality and dependence in order to draw the attention of their caregivers (Main & Solomon, 1986).

The ambivalent attachment pattern, while enabling infants to maximize the availability of their caregivers, is not without costs for the infants. By devoting so much effort to maintaining proximity and their mothers' attention, children are unable to comfortably explore and thus have no secure base. Data from several studies (reviewed by Cassidy & Berlin, 1994) suggest that ambivalently attached infants show uncertainty and fearfulness in new situations, inhibit exploration of the general environment, and inhibit exploration with toys.

Recently, a number of investigators have suggested that the ambivalent attachment strategy can be observed at stages in the life span after infancy. Main and Cassidy (1988) described a group of 6-year-olds who in interactions with their parents displayed exaggerated intimacy and dependency but who also showed ambivalence, including moderate avoidance and subtle signs of hostility. Cassidy and Marvin (1992) suggested that ambivalent 3- and 4-year-olds emphasize their dependence through initiation of intimate contact and sometimes big false smiles, but also express their anger through tantrums, petulance, and moderate avoidance. Crittenden (1992a, 1994) suggested that the relationships of preschool-age C children can be characterized as "coercive." Coercive children use angry behavior (including poutiness, whining, and openly displayed anger) in coordination with coy and winsome behavior (sweet looks, babyish voice, even frozen helplessness) to threaten or seduce attachment figures into meeting their needs. No data have been reported based on direct observations of the behavior of ambivalent dyads after the preschool years, although interview techniques have been used to study attachment issues in older children and adults (George, Kaplan, & Main, 1985; Main, Kaplan, & Cassidy, 1985).

C children are of particular interest both because of the inherent contradictions between strong proximity seeking and resistant behavior, but also because they so clearly illustrate the close relation and tension between the attachment and exploratory systems. Yet, ambivalent attachment remains the most poorly understood of Ainsworth's attachment types (Ainsworth, 1990; Cassidy & Berlin, 1994). In this chapter we will examine the behavior of C children and their mothers from infancy through adolescence. We will do so by reporting on two children observed regularly with their mothers from 12 months to 14 years of age who showed some stability in their employment of an ambivalent attachment strategy. While we acknowledge that children's attachment strategies can change with age as a result of changing life circumstances and developing cognitive and emotional competence (cf. Crittenden, 1995), we began this study with a bias that we would learn the most from studying dyads in which the C attachment strategy was a somewhat stable feature of the relationship. In our discussion, we will describe the core themes that are stable over time as well as consider parameters of change with development.

THE DYADS

Since 1978, we have followed longitudinally a sample of approximately 80 African-American inner-city children whose mothers were recruited during pregnancy. Numerous reports of data from this study have been made previously (e.g., Bernstein & Hans, 1994; Bernstein, Jeremy, & Marcus, 1986; Hans, 1989; Jeremy & Hans, 1985).

When the children were 1, 4, 8, 12, 18, 24, 30, 36, 48, and 60 months; and at 10 and 14 years, data were gathered on a variety of motor, cognitive, social, clinical, and family outcomes. Measures reported in this chapter include developmental assessments made on the Bayley Scales of Infant Development (Bayley, 1969) from 4 through 24 months of age, intelligence tests at 10 years (Wechsler, 1974), DSM-III-R (APA, 1987) diagnoses of the children made at 10 years based on answers given by children and their caregivers to a semi-structured clinical interview (DICA, Herjanic & Reich, 1982), and child behavior checklists (Achenbach, 1991abc) administered at the 14-year assessment to primary caregivers, teachers, and the adolescents themselves.

Most of the information included in this chapter comes from videotapes made of the children with their primary caregivers. At each session, the dyads were asked to participate in a variety of structured and unstructured activities in a laboratory living room. The activities varied with age of child but usually included playing with an age-appropriate toy, game, or puzzle; eating; and a free play session. At ages 12 and 18 months, a separation and reunion sequence was performed that corresponded to episodes 5 through 8 of the Ainsworth Strange Situation. Mother and infant were in the room alone with the mother sitting on the sofa; mother departed from the room, leaving the infant alone; a stranger entered to play with the infant; mother returned to the room. At age 10 years, the dyads also worked on problems together such as copying figures with an Etch-a-Sketch and completing a dot-to-dot puzzle while blindfolded with the other dyad member providing verbal instructions. At age 14 years, the dyads were asked to plan an activity and to discuss something about which they disagreed.

Two psychologists, trained by Alan Sroufe to rate the Strange Situation, rated all the separation – reunion sequences from 12 months. Both identified the same five infants as showing behavior typical of C infants. One infant was classified as an Ainsworth C2 infant, showing not only extreme passivity and helplessness at reunion, but also signs of disorganized attachment (Main & Solomon, 1986, 1990). Four infants were classified as Ainsworth C1 infants, showing extreme angry resistance at reunion. At 18 months of age, two of these C1 children again showed behavior typical of the ambivalent attachment pattern, one had dropped out of the study, and one was classified as securely attached. This chapter focuses in detail on the two children displaying consistent C1 attachment behavior at two ages.

The authors of this chapter watched all of the videotapes of the two dyads and transcribed segments of the videotapes that seemed relevant to Ainsworth's original descriptions of C dyads, such as those that involved proximity seeking, active resistance, fear, helplessness, or anger from the child or situations requiring the mother to respond to the child's needs. These materials were reviewed and discussed in an effort to identify features of the dyads that seemed core to the ambivalent attachment strategy. The section of this chapter that follows describes in detail the experience and behavior of the two dyads from 12 months to 14 years. These descriptions become the data for further discussion of the ambivalent attachment strategy.

"Gerome"

Gerome's mother, Rochelle, is a thin, tense, and reserved woman of above-average intelligence. During her senior year in high school Rochelle's first child, a daughter, was born two months prematurely. Rochelle graduated from high school and got steady employment as a school cafeteria worker. At age 21, she married her daughter's father and soon became pregnant again. During this pregnancy, Rochelle was worried and depressed. She took a leave of absence from her job out of concern that she might deliver prematurely again. Her husband supported the family through work as an electrician, but the marriage was complicated by his drug abuse.

Infancy. Gerome, who was the focus of our study, was born at term and in good health. Throughout infancy and toddlerhood, he was an active, responsive child who achieved developmental milestones on time. During the videotaped separation and reunion at 12 months, Gerome was a classic Ainsworth C1 infant. He showed upset when his mother left and continued to be upset in the presence of the stranger. At reunion, Rochelle greeted her son with an overbright, "Hi, Gerome, Hi!" Gerome reached up to his mother, who took him by the hand. He continued fussing. She asked, "What's the matter, you're not upset with me are you?" and took him to sit on her lap on the sofa. He repeatedly arched his back, cried, and squirmed to get down, quieting only when Rochelle gave him a bottle. After the separation portion of the session, Gerome did not fully settle down again during the taping.

At the 18-month videotaping session, Gerome again was classified as a C infant. When his mother left him to go to the bathroom, Gerome cried angrily and constantly, and could not be completely consoled on her return. Gerome and Rochelle never seemed able to coordinate their actions with one another in routines or play in a manner that did not involve conflict. Gerome's behavior was provocative, and Rochelle was patient but inflexible. During snack time, Gerome struggled with his mother on every point. When Gerome spilled his drink, Rochelle dutifully wiped up the spill. Gerome tried to grab the cloth, but his mother did not give it to him. When she was done with the cloth, instead of placing it out of his reach or sight, she continued to hold it in her hand in his line of reach. Gerome persistently grabbed for the cloth. He fussed, stomped his feet, and pushed the cup. In the only outburst of anger we ever saw from Rochelle, she slapped his hands. Gerome had the last word by shrieking and throwing the crackers. Later, when asked to play a game Gerome liked, Rochelle chose "horsey." He fussed at the suggestion and walked away from her. Instead of suggesting a different game, she picked him up and asked if he wanted to play horsey. He fussed, and she put him down. Gerome walked around the room, and his mother tried with no success to get him interested in her game. Finally, Rochelle gave up and sat on the sofa to watch him from a distance. Soon Gerome approached her with a smile and a laugh.

At 24 months there seemed to be a general tension between Gerome and his mother. Even though Gerome was positive and smiling during most of the session, he displayed bursts of intermittent anger, fussiness, and bossiness. His mother generally took his negative outbursts in stride, although she some-times looked hurt by them. They often seemed to be timed to get her atten-tion, and sometimes were defused by displays of more positive affect. For example, when the examiner asked Rochelle to initiate a game they liked to play, she chose marching around the room. Gerome initially joined in hap-pily, but when he wanted to take the lead he used an angry fuss to demand that she follow him. Gerome immediately switched back to smiling and laugh-ing openly, and she complied with his wishes. When his mother tried to inter-est him in a book, Gerome fussed and became angry. He hit the book and said, "No." His mother had a surprised look on her face and then said "No, No" to get him to stop the hitting. Gerome paused, then hit the book again, saying, "No." When he walked away, Rochelle went on trying to interest

Gerome in the book from a distance. He initially fussed at her but then started to repeat what she said in a mocking manner. Eventually, he approached her and snatched the book out of her hands.

Early Childhood. Rochelle's marriage deteriorated throughout the early years of Gerome's life. Her husband was physically violent toward her, worked only sporadically, and spent his earnings on drugs. A divorce was final when Gerome was $3\frac{1}{2}$ years old.

When we observed Gerome at age 4 years, he was subdued, lacking the affective brightness that had characterized him as an infant. His negativity, anger, and provocativeness frequently punctuated the interactions. For example, he whined after working on the puzzle. When his mother asked if he were tired, he shook his head and loudly shouted, "No." His mother said, "You're tired." He again replied, "No!" He refused to let his mother read to him, lying down on the floor, rolling cars over the book, and rolling cars to another part of the room. After spilling juice on himself and the table, he obligingly followed his mother's instructions to walk across the room for a tissue. However, when she told him to throw the tissue into the trash, Gerome handed it to her, saying, "Here, here." Rochelle pointed to the trash can and said, "Right there." Gerome said, "I can't see it," and dropped the tissue on his mother's lap. He sat down, took a sip of juice, and sloshed it around in his mouth. His mother told him to stop, Gerome continued, and his mother's tone sounded increasingly frustrated. After Gerome finished his juice, his mother asked if he knew what to do with the empty can. Gerome then said, "Throw it in the garbage – *you* throw it in the garbage." Throughout this session, Rochelle appeared patient and resigned.

At age 5, Gerome was calmer and less agitated, although as in previous sessions tension arose at transition points in the activities and following instruction from his mother. Working together on a puzzle, Rochelle said, "Put it back together." Gerome responded, "You do it, I can't do it." Rochelle suggested, "We can do it together," and Gerome replied, "You can do it by yourself, I can't do it." Gerome then crawled under the table. When he finally did try to put the puzzle together, he rejected all guidance from his mother. Throughout the session, Rochelle was tolerant and somewhat distant, but she persisted with the tasks that she was asked to do with Gerome.

School-age. Rochelle became an extraordinarily conscientious, single mother. She worked diligently at her job but made her children's education the center of her life. Beginning in nursery school, Gerome was enrolled in an academically rigorous parochial school more than an hour's drive from his home where he was the only African-American child.

Gerome had problems at this school from the beginning. The school arranged for him to receive speech therapy and after-school academic tutoring. When we spoke to Rochelle at the time of Gerome's tenth birthday, she was frustrated by his slow academic progress – both relative to other children in his school and relative to his sister. Rochelle was working closely with counselors at the school and carefully supervised his homework.

When our research staff saw Gerome at age 10, they found him a likable child. Testing suggested he was of average intelligence but that his verbal intelligence lagged considerably behind his performance intelligence. He described feeling well cared for and loved by his mother, but he indicated that she got on his nerves a lot.

When we observed Gerome at age 10 he often acted very silly. The interactions between him and his mother were boisterous and, while positive on the surface, suggested an underlying tension. Gerome switched back and forth from expressions of pleasure and positive affect to sarcasm and negative statements showing disapproval and frustration with her. Rochelle smiled and laughed during the interactions, although sometimes her laughter had a nervous edge to it. Most of Gerome's negative behavior seemed targeted at getting a response from his mother.

When Gerome was asked to fix a snack for his mother, he asked her what kind of pop she wanted. When she hesitated before replying, Gerome rolled his eyes and made an exasperated sound. His mother said she would share whatever kind of pop he wanted. Gerome said he did not want to share and then in a sarcastic tone asked his mother if she wanted juice instead. When Rochelle offered to help by asking Gerome, "What do you want *me* to do?" Gerome was silent. Rochelle asked, "Do you want me to put the peanut butter on the crackers for you?" Gerome replied, "Yes." His mother said, "No, *you're* supposed to do that." His mother smiled as she watched him work. Gerome asked his mother how many crackers he should spread peanut butter on for her. When she said three, Gerome said in exasperation, "That's it!" and threw the crackers on her plate.

When playing with a Ping-Pong basketball game, Rochelle first asked Gerome for instructions to the game. Gerome impatiently explained the rules to his mother. Rochelle seemed not to understand or trust Gerome's instructions and spent a great deal of time reading the instructions printed on the box. Gerome played by himself as his mother read. When she was done reading, Rochelle told Gerome that the shots he had already taken did not count because it was her turn. He responded sarcastically with "So what?" and threw the ball down. Switching to a more positive tone, he went back to playing the game with his mother. When Rochelle asked Gerome to conform with a particular rule, he insisted on playing his way, and she backed down.

Adolescence. When we saw Gerome at age 14, he was enrolled in a public high school in his home community – a working-class, predominantly African-American suburb. His sister had just graduated from college. Gerome played on the football team at school, and most of his interests seemed to focus on sports. Rochelle closely monitored Gerome's academic work and limited his social life. He was required to study each week night, whether or not he had homework. Family rules required Gerome to check in every two hours when away from home. He could only go to parties at his school, and his mother drove him to and from those. Rochelle indicated that Gerome chafed under such restrictions but that he did not openly rebel. As a freshman in high school, Gerome's grades were above average in math and science and below average in English and history. For Gerome, Rochelle indicated, "College is not a choice. He must go."

Gerome expressed to an interviewer his clear anger and bitterness against his mother's restrictiveness. He said that if he was not home when expected, his mother would go out into the streets looking for him and questioning his peers. This was a source of considerable embarrassment to him, but he seemed resigned to the fact that she was not going to change. He was beginning more often to sneak away and withhold information from her about his activities. He used the word "challenging" to describe her, elaborating that she always had to be right and have the last word about everything. His view was that she cared greatly about him but was difficult. Gerome had internalized his mother's values about education and expected to go to college and major in sciences.

On the Achenbach behavior checklists, Gerome, his mother, and his science teacher all reported that Gerome had trouble concentrating, argued a lot, and acted young for his age. His mother and teacher's responses placed him in the normal range in all behavior domains. Gerome himself reported a clinically significant number of somatic symptoms, including dizziness, fatigue, headaches, nausea, and stomach aches.

In observing Gerome with his mother at age 14, it was apparent that Gerome's bossiness and sarcasm with his mother had increased. When they were not engaged in a structured activity, they had little to talk about and shared little positive affect except nervous laughter. Gerome often oriented himself so that his side or back was toward her. They seemed uncomfortable with each other.

When asked to discuss where they might go on an outing, Gerome suggested McDonald's. Rochelle made a disapproving sound. With no sign of humor, Gerome then suggested Burger King (knowing full well that his mother would not find that suggestion any better). His mother said that it was not exactly what she had in mind. Gerome suggested that they go to the movies. His mother agreed to this, but then asked him what movie they should see. Gerome replied sarcastically, "I don't know, what's playing?"

When asked to discuss topics on which they disagreed, Gerome and his mother had uncomfortable discussions of why he could not get an earring or a beeper. Gerome argued that many teenage males had earrings. His mother said that it was not proper and had been associated with gangs. She then pulled back from her stance by saying that maybe he could have one when he went to college. In discussing why Gerome could not have a beeper, they went back and forth (not agreeing or compromising) until Gerome said, "Whatever!" and then, "I'm gonna get one anyway." His mother responded, "Not as long as you're living with me." Later during the snack, Gerome told his mother that her selection of raisins was disgusting. He then resurrected the beeper discussion, asking why he couldn't have one. His mother said, "She [the examiner] said that part was over." Gerome continued talking about it, unwilling to let go of the unpleasant topic. Gerome became quite frustrated by how long it took his mother to finish her raisins. "Do you have to eat them one at a time?" His mother asked him to eat some. He refused and she finished them.

Case Summary. Gerome was the youngest child born to Rochelle, a tense woman who, despite many difficulties in her own life, had devoted herself to providing for her children and securing them a good education. Rochelle seemed to experience little pleasure from life in general and from interaction with Gerome in particular. As an infant, Gerome fit the Ainsworth C1 attachment pattern during times of separation from his mother, displaying his upset and anger at her departure and at her return. As a young child he was often cheerful and energetic but expressed angry feelings openly and used them to manipulate his mother. Rochelle was quiet and attentive with her young son, but she often missed cues related to his desires and interests and failed to prevent or set limits on inappropriate emotional displays. At school-age, Gerome was still a likable child, but with his mother he was often silly and provocative. Rochelle showed some inclination to direct his behavior on structured tasks, such as during games, but she made little effort to control his emotional outbursts. At adolescence, Gerome became increasingly negative and passive in interactions with his mother. His body language and lack of communicativeness indicated on the surface that he wanted to avoid dealing with her, but in fact had the effect of drawing her attention more strongly to him. Although Gerome claimed to accept the high goals his mother had set for his education, his school performance was below his ability level. He experienced somatic symptoms suggestive of stress, and he obviously resented her micromanagement of his life.

"Kineta"

Kineta's mother Geneva is a well-groomed, pleasingly plump woman of average intelligence. She dropped out of high school as a junior and lived with her mother until age 22 when she married and started a family of her own. She is somewhat controlled and inhibited in her demeanor and reports phobias of heights, water, crowds, and bridges. Geneva and her husband already had two daughters and a son when Kineta was born. At that time Geneva acknowledged marital difficulties with her husband who was a heavy drinker.

Infancy. Geneva expressed great pleasure that Kineta was her most active and restless child. She said Kineta did not sleep well, cried frequently, and was calm only when being held. She said that Kineta whined when she was not close to her mother and "would like to be held all day if you would do it."

Throughout infancy and toddlerhood, Kineta's performance on standardized tests was in the normal range, although examiners administering the tests described her at various times as fussy, not interested in exploring test materials, inhibited and wary, extremely slow to warm up, and needing her mother to function at her maximal level.

When separated from her mother at 12 months, Kineta cried vigorously. At reunion, Kineta continued crying, weakly lifted one arm, and turned her face somewhat away from her mother. When picked up, Kineta stopped crying; but as her mother sat down on the sofa, Kineta began to fuss and lean out. Geneva asked, "What's the matter?" Kineta turned toward her mother but then pushed away; she leaned in but then fussed. She continued to fuss as her mother gently jiggled her until the three-minute reunion episode ended. Kineta's upset at separation and resistance at reunion placed her in the Ainsworth C1 attachment group.

At other moments during the 12-month interaction, Kineta was smiling and happy. Geneva did not spontaneously play with Kineta and often sat quietly watching Kineta play. When asked to play with her daughter, Geneva chose tickling and teasing games to which Kineta smiled reactively. When playing with a large selection of toys on the floor, Kineta often looked to her mother on the sofa or called out to her mother for attention. Geneva acknowledged Kineta's bids for attention but generally adopted a quiet, onlooking role.

At 18 months, Kineta's separation from and reunion with her mother in the laboratory again fit the ambivalent attachment type. At her mother's departure, Kineta stood soberly with a finger in her mouth but did not cry. After the stranger's entry, she was gradually able to return to play with little help from the stranger. However, when she heard her mother's voice, she immediately began to wail. As her mother approached, Kineta lifted her arms, screamed louder, and stomped her feet as she was picked up. She calmed down while in her mother's arms, but screamed and lifted her arms when her mother tried to put her down. On her mother's lap, Kineta squirmed and fussed. Geneva said, "You mad at me?", and tried to tease Kineta out of her upset by playing a game in which she pushed Kineta over backward. This game was somewhat rough and made Kineta more angry. After more than a few unsuccessful attempts to continue the game, Geneva stopped the efforts. Kineta remained on her mother's lap, fussing, screaming, and unresponsive to Geneva's efforts to calm her. Finally, Kineta slipped out of her mother's lap onto the floor in front of the sofa and regained her composure.

At the examiner's request, Geneva sat with Kineta on the floor to play with the toys. Geneva chose mostly to be an onlooker. She gave Kineta a bucket and shovel and told her to "stir it up." Kineta stirred the shovel and began to put blocks into the bucket. One block popped out of the bucket and across the room. Kineta assertively looked Geneva in the eye and pointed to the block. Geneva said, "You pick it up." Kineta looked down at her open hands in her lap as if to say, "with these little hands?" Geneva crawled to the other side of the room and retrieved the block.

At the end of the free-play session, Geneva was asked to get Kineta to clean up the toys. Geneva gently told Kineta to put the toys in the box. Kineta busied herself in play. Geneva again quietly directed Kineta to put the toys in the box, and Kineta placed a few. Geneva held a toy over the box as if to model how the task was done. Kineta batted the toy into the box. She methodically took several other toys out of the box and threw them across the room while Geneva watched passively. Once when Kineta threw a truck and hit her mother in the arm, Geneva only smiled. Eventually, Geneva put the toys in the box herself.

At other times during the 18-month session, the interaction between Geneva and Kineta seemed more comfortable and intimate. During the snack, Kineta lounged quietly on her mother's lap eating a cracker as her mother read a magazine. Several times she spontaneously looked up into her mother's face, and Geneva often gently stroked or patted Kineta, even though her attention was on the magazine.

At 24 months, Kineta was passive and sulky throughout most of the video-taping, not smiling once in 45 minutes. Her passivity, coupled with resistance, was dramatic when Geneva was asked to read a book. Geneva sat on the sofa with Kineta on her lap and opened the book. Kineta stared at the book, with her arms limp at her sides, her face expressionless. Geneva turned a few pages, leaning over to check Kineta's facial expression several times. Geneva said, "Turn it." Kineta made no response. Geneva took Kineta's hand in her own and touched it to the book, pointing to different pictures. When Geneva let go of Kineta's hand, it fell back limply to her side. Geneva pointed to pictures in the book. Kineta sat frozen with her arms still at her side, leaning back into her mother. Geneva continued turning pages. Kineta stared blankly at the book. Geneva said, "What's that?" Kineta stiffened and fell over sideways off Geneva's lap and onto the sofa, like a rag doll. Geneva said, "Come on, look, huh?" with a pleading tone. She put the book on the coffee table in front of her and placed Kineta, standing, on the floor facing the table. Kineta whimpered, lifted her arms up and away from the book, and leaned back into her mother. Geneva said, "You don't want to?" and picked up Kineta. Kineta was again limp and passive on her mother's lap. Geneva continued to point and turn pages. Kineta stared off into space away from the book. Geneva turned toward the examiner and said, "I don't think she's ready yet."

Early Childhood. At 30 months, all of the energy in the dyad was coming from Kineta, who kept up a constant flow of jabber and directives. During a free-play session, Geneva sat next to Kineta on the floor and watched her play. Kineta frequently tried to engage her mother, asking the names of objects and for help with dressing the dolls. When Kineta gave commands, her mother generally complied. Once Kineta suddenly pushed a truck across the room where it landed under the coffee table. She said, "Get it, Mom." Geneva said, "You get it." Kineta responded, "No," and turned her back to her mother. Geneva stood up, walked to the coffee table, bent down to get the truck, and returned the truck to the play area without any further comment.

When Geneva was asked to get Kineta to clean up the toys, Kineta's resistance and Geneva's passivity prolonged what should have been a quick process into an extended give and take. Kineta and her mother were both completely off task, playing with the dolls and putting them into bed. Eventually, without any discussion, Geneva stood to take the phone to the toy box. Kineta saw what her mother was doing and protested. Geneva put the phone down and Geneva stood silently in the middle of the room with Kineta playing at her feet. Finally, the examiner came into the room to complete the cleanup. Throughout the 30-month session, Kineta almost always got her immediate desires met either by being bossy or resistant, but her bossiness and resistance were usually tempered by a sweet tone of voice. Geneva generally gave into Kineta rather than display anger.

School-age. When Kineta was 10, her family was struggling. Although both parents worked outside the home, they had many unpaid debts. Kineta's oldest sister had run away from home, and her older brother had a drug problem and had been hospitalized with severe depression. Another older sister was pregnant at age 14. Her father was drinking heavily, and his punishment of the older children was becoming abusive. Geneva, though open to talking about these problems, sounded passive and victimized. She chose not to help her husband face his drinking problem because she felt her efforts would make him drink all the more. Even though her three adolescent children all had serious problems, she did not seem particularly inclined to consider the causes of these problems, their implications for Kineta, or her own role and responsibility in the outcome of the children.

Geneva described Kineta at age 10 as quiet, reserved, shy, and agreeable. She indicated that she was proud of Kineta because "She's a lady; she's really feminine, she cares about the way she dress, what she wears, jewelry and her personality." Geneva described motherhood as greatly satisfying. "We all grew up together. Everybody says we act like sisters." Despite Geneva's obvious pride in Kineta, our examiners found her an unappealing child. She was aloof, disengaged, and even somewhat disrespectful with staff members. She was of below-average intelligence. She described numerous fears and anxieties and met diagnostic criteria for overanxious disorder.

Throughout the videotaping at age 10, Kineta displayed sullenness alternating with smiles and giggles. Most of the sullenness was directed at the examiner, the giggles at her mother. Kineta was prone to frequently saying, "I don't get it!" or "Do I have to?" and shrugging her shoulders or flipping her arms and head in a haughty, disgusted manner. When listening to instructions from the examiner, she usually stood with her hands planted firmly and defiantly on her hips. She frequently "played dumb" with the examiner, pretending not to understand simple questions. When frustrated, she degenerated into immature behavior. When playing a game with her mother she did not seem especially competitive, but when she lost, she became silly, disengaged, and inattentive. When her mother tried to explain a difficult task to her, Kineta exclaimed "Oooooh" with an exaggerated mocking tone, followed by giggles.

Even at age 10, Kineta maintained considerable physical intimacy with her mother. She would sit next to her mother and lean against her body. Geneva often put her arm around Kineta's shoulder. They both touched each other's hands to punctuate their conversations.

Kineta was an expert at passively drawing attention to herself. The most remarkable instance of this was when Geneva was asked to complete a brief questionnaire and Kineta was asked to draw a picture with marker pens. Kineta approached this task reluctantly at first but showed increasing interest as she discovered that by prolonging the task she could attract her mother's attention and provoke the examiner's annoyance. To begin, she contemplated the markers, made an exaggerated toss of the head, and looked over her shoulder to see if her mother was watching. She asked herself out loud, "What could I draw?", and looked up at the ceiling as if for inspiration. She checked her mother again. She slowly and theatrically removed the caps from the markers, yawning loudly to attract attention to her boredom. She told her mother that she wanted to go home. Geneva said, "You're supposed to color, aren't you?" Kineta shrieked, "I am!" as if offended and began drawing. When her mother was done with the questionnaire, instead of hurrying to finish up and go home, Kineta continued drawing. Geneva tapped her pencil impatiently on her clipboard and reread the questionnaire. Kineta was seemingly engrossed in her drawing, frequently switching markers, feverishly capping and uncapping pens. Geneva stood next to Kineta at the table watching. Kineta decided she had put the marker caps on wrong. She dramatically removed all the caps and replaced them properly. Geneva stepped back and sat down on the sofa again, resigned to further waiting. After a while, she asked, "Are you done?" Kineta responded, "Well [long pause] I need just a moment. I have to do a few more things." She went back to taking caps off pens and drawing. Her mother quietly said, "Okay," and looked down at her hands in her lap. Kineta began drawing on the back of the paper, continuing her flurry of switching pens and caps. Her mother asked, "What are you doing?" Kineta said, "You'll see." Geneva stood and watched Kineta remove the caps and make a single mark with each pen. Geneva sat down again to wait. After a while, Geneva stood and looked. "What is that?", she asked. Kineta said, "You know what that is, right?" After a long pause she said angrily, "The sky!" and rolled her eyes in disgust. Suddenly Kineta emitted a shrieky and disarming giggle. Her mother smiled, kept looking on, and then sat down again and picked at her finger nails. In the end, the examiner broke off the drawing task.

Adolescence. When we saw Kineta at age 14, Geneva continued working, but her husband was unemployed and not looking for a job. His drinking was a source of great problems between them. She was considering a divorce but feared she would have to pay alimony to him. She sometimes gave him money for liquor, hoping he would leave the house. She continued to experience difficulties raising Kineta's siblings.

At age 14, Kineta was a large girl who spent much effort styling her hair and caring for her nails. Geneva said Kineta was the child who caused her the fewest problems. She described Kineta as friendly, cheerful, and agreeable, but argumentative. Our staff perceived her as vacuous and sullen. Kineta said she was bored by just about everything and reported sleeping most weekend days. Kineta reported feeling very close to her mother and in particular stated that her mother was "nice and fun" and that they disagreed about few things other than whether she could go over to boys' houses after school.

On the Achenbach behavior checklists, Kineta, her mother, and her health education teacher all reported that Kineta had stomach cramps, was argumentative, was overweight, and was doing poorly in school. Her own and her mother's responses placed Kineta in the normal range in all behavior domains. Her teacher's responses placed her in a clinically significant area in terms of somatic complaints.

We videotaped Kineta and her mother sitting at a small table. After the examiner had given them instructions and left the room, Kineta rolled her eyes and sighed to her mother. Immediately after this display of indignation, they giggled together. Throughout the taping Kineta and Geneva were notable for their shared silliness, finding much to giggle about and often touching hands. Their interaction had the feel of young girls enjoying one another's company, talking about clothes and boys. Kineta sometimes became somewhat assertive with her mother, whining "Listen" and "Mom!", but typically concluded displays of exasperation with gales of giggles. Kineta dominated the interactions. She was very theatrical, acting out little scenes as she discussed things that had happened to her. In the disagreement task, Geneva and Kineta talked about her curfew and about not being able to go to a boy's house after school. Kineta persistently explained to her mother why she thought she should have more freedom, and although Kineta's arguments were not particularly convincing, Geneva did little to counter them other than to say, "No." In the end, Geneva backed off considerably from her initial stance by indicating, "I'll have to think about it."

Case Summary. Kineta was the youngest of four children. Their mother, Geneva, was a pleasant, but very passive, woman who took satisfaction from her closeness with her daughter. At all ages, Kineta was the energy source in their relationship. As an infant, Kineta was a C1 infant who displayed upset at separation from her mother but showed mixed feelings of anger and desire at her mother's return. As a young child, Kineta effectively engaged and manipulated her mother through both fussiness and displays of positive affect. By and large, Geneva was an onlooker to Kineta's play activities, rarely engaging her in interaction or responding to Kineta's invitations. When Geneva did try to engage her daughter in activities or to offer her comfort, her behavior was inept. As an older child Kineta reported experiencing extreme levels of fear and anxiety. In her interactions with her mother, she was often energized and effervescent but just as often provocative and moody when she was bored or displeased. Geneva was tolerant of her daughter's unpleasant behavior and seemed to take quiet pleasure in her more positive and spirited actions. By adolescence, Kineta was often sullen, but at other times she showed genuine positive emotional connectedness with her mother that seemed to reflect an almost peer-like relationship.

DISCUSSION

In the comments that follow, we will discuss how the interactions between ambivalently attached children and their mothers were organized over time, focusing on points of constancy as well as age-related change. We will do so by first addressing the insecure nature of the children's attachment relationships, then describing the children's ambivalent attachment strategies and the behavior of their mothers, and finally discussing some of the emotional and developmental costs of the ambivalent attachment strategy for children. For the sake of clarity, we have described children's and mothers' behavior separately, although we hope the information presented will illustrate that attachment behavior should best be conceptualized as a dyadic system – in this case a dissatisfying dyadic dance.

Insecure Attachment Relationships

Bowlby viewed life at all ages as a "series of excursions, long or short, from the secure base provided by our attachment figure(s)" (Bowlby, 1988, p. 62). For the two C children described in this chapter, it appeared that these excursions were often brief and infrequent and that the base was not especially secure.

Beginning at the end of the first year of life, human infants seek comfort and reassurance from their caregiver during times of pain, illness, fatigue, the presence of unfamiliar things, or the seeming unavailability of that caregiver. They engage in a variety of attachment behaviors – crying, reaching, calling out, approaching, cuddling, and clinging – to secure the presence of the caregiver. For most infants, once physical proximity to the caregiver has been achieved, attachment behavior ceases and the child is able to comfortably engage in other kinds of behavior such as exploration. As children grow older, comfort is derived less from physical proximity and more from psychological availability (Bowlby, cited in Ainsworth, 1990).

For the children described in this chapter, a comfortable state never seemed to be achieved, and the quest for the attention of the mother was ongoing. Compared to other children in the same study, the two C children invested a remarkable amount of effort at all ages in attracting and keeping their mothers' attention. In fact, in the laboratory setting we rarely observed psychological disengagement between the C children and their mothers. Even after particular interactions had played out their natural courses, we often saw (and felt uncomfortable by) efforts to sustain them. Kineta kept the examiner and her mother engaged and in agony by prolonging the cleanup at 30 months and her drawing activity at 10 years. At age 14, Gerome never would drop the topic of getting a beeper. Even when a child seemed to be ignoring the mother, such as when 10-year-old Kineta busily removed and replaced the caps from her marker pens, the behavior was designed to draw the mother's attention. This organization of behavior to achieve near-continuous involvement between child and mother was notable because of the already close physical proximity of the dyads in the room and the low level of threat most of the situations posed to the children. The C children seemed unsure of their mothers' availability despite her physical presence and invested much effort in drawing their mothers' attention even in the absence of threatening events. Although the children – especially at older ages – were successful at achieving their mothers' nearly continuous involvement, that involvement was often tense, suggestive of ongoing anxiety and raising questions about the mother's effectiveness in giving the child a sense of security.

Children's Use of Affect to Increase Mothers' Involvement and Availability

Main (1981) described the strategy of the C infant as exhibiting a heightened display of emotionality and dependence in order to draw the parent's attention. Ainsworth (Ainsworth et al., 1978) described two distinct ways of executing this strategy in the Strange Situation, both employing potent displays of raw affect – fear, anger, and/or desire – to gain the mother's attention and responsiveness. C1 children display a desire for proximity in combination with anger.

Our longitudinal observations suggest that after infancy the attachment strategy of the C child continues to be achieving high levels of maternal availability through use of exaggerated, and for the most part uncomfortable, emotional displays. Our observations, however, also suggest that important changes in attachment strategy do occur after infancy. First, children begin to distort their displays of affect in service of manipulating the parent. Second, individual children begin to coordinate and combine the two affective components of the ambivalent strategy – anger and fear/helplessness – that during infancy had generally been displayed by two different groups of children. Third, the focus of the affective emphasis of the ambivalent strategy changed from display of the child's uncomfortable affect to creation of uncomfortable affect in the parent.

We first observed children falsifying their affective displays during the middle of the second year. Children expressed the same fear, anger, and desire they showed during infancy, but in a manner that appeared false and that enabled them more reliably and efficiently to manipulate their mothers' attention. In particular, they would abruptly shut off and initiate emotional displays to allow their mothers only to perceive particular affective messages. When reunited with her mother after separation at 18 months, a calm Kineta abruptly began to wail. Gerome's early bursts of negative affect often seemed to come from nowhere in strong reaction to his mother's actions, and his negative displays suddenly ended when he got his way. At 18 moths when Kineta's toy popped across the room, she adopted a clearly feigned helpless stance to avoid picking it up. Such displays of strong feelings no longer, on close scrutiny, appeared genuine. Emotional displays were becoming tools used to achieve the goal of involving the mother.

During the third year, the children began to control their display of affect by alternating in an organized manner between angry and helpless displays. Crittenden (1992a, 1994) has discussed how the anger expressed by C children places them at risk for angry retaliation from the caregiver and that beginning in the preschool years C children, like animals of other species, will disarm their angry displays with coy behavior such as shy glances, open-mouthed grins, protruding tummies, and exposed necks (see Marvin & Mossler, 1976, for more discussion of coy behavior). These displays signal to the mother that the child is vulnerable, nonaggressive, and in need of nurturance. When 2-year-old Gerome wanted his mother to march behind him, he followed his fussing with an appealing smile that worked to win her over. When Kineta was a teenager and her complaining became increasingly obnoxious, she would lean toward her mother, intimately touch her mother's hands, and giggle so as to diffuse some of the tension before she proceeded with more complaining. Crittenden (1992a, 1994) has clearly described the coercive power of the alternation and coordination of threatening (angry) and disarming (helpless) behavior to gain the availability of a parent without incurring risk. Such a strategy can only work after the infancy age period since sophisticated self-regulatory and social skills are required in order to inhibit the display of genuine feelings, to substitute the display of other feelings, and to read the mother's affect for cues about when appeasement may be necessary.

Preschool C children also began to manipulate their mothers' attention with displays of behavior in which their anger is disguised – although just barely – by a veneer of childishness. Their anger is expressed indirectly through behavior that is provocative but not overtly threatening. Gerome was provocative when sloshing his juice around and around in his mouth at age 4 years. Kineta was provocative when wildly tossing toys into the box while cleaning up at 30 months. Although provocative behavior strongly draws the mother's attention and although it is annoying to the mother, she restrains her anger because it is not clear whether the child is intentionally being naughty or simply expressing age-appropriate exuberance. Thus, the provocative behavior of the preschooler is a blend of angry and feigned immature behavior: a joining of behavior from the strategies used by Ainsworth's two types of C infants. Although provocative behavior on the surface appears immature, it is actually a sophisticated strategy that requires children to possess accurate models of what kinds of action are likely to annoy their parent and thereby attract the parent's attention and what types of actions are likely to turn parental annoyance into anger. To make these judgments, children must have knowledge of social conventions in general and expectations about what kinds of actions will be tolerated by their own mothers in particular.

During middle childhood and adolescence, children's efforts to annoy their parents were increasingly passive (perhaps one could say passive aggressive) and reflective of a sophisticated understanding of social transgressions. The children at this age understood that the seriousness of a transgression is determined by the perpetrator's degree of active effort and intention, and they had discovered ways of "innocently" expressing their anger. By acting passively rude, they could claim not to have done anything. By acting bossy, they were only obediently following the examiner's instructions or trying to help the mother be more comfortable. By bickering or engaging in annoying and convoluted arguments, they were only expressing their honest opinions. By feigning helplessness, which serves to anger parents of older children, they were also expressing their need for ongoing nurturance. Despite the subtlety of these new provocative ploys, many of which blended angry and passive/helpless actions, older children still sometimes needed to disarm their mothers' building anger. Instead of the coy behavior observed in preschoolers, the older children engaged in giggles, clowning, or physical touches to remind their parents of their charm and immaturity. Thus, with age, the angry C1 strategy commingles with the passive C2 strategy.

A final developmental trend to note in the C strategy comes in the shift of focus from the child's affect to the mother's. Although the goal of the C child is always to increase the attention, availability, and involvement of the mother, it is only with development that the child discovers that the way to do so is not simply through expression of his or her own feelings, but rather through creation of uncomfortable feelings in the mother. Instead of only expressing anger, with age the child increasingly tries to engage the mother by provoking her anger. Instead of only expressing helplessness, the child increasingly tries to create feelings of helplessness in the mother. The combination of the child expressing uncomfortable affect and creating uncomfortable affect in the mother eventually leads to a relationship in which tension becomes the normal state and the glue that draws and holds the dyad together.

Mothers' Inconsistent and Ineffective Parenting

C children's attachment strategies suggest that they hold a working model in which they are uncertain about their caregivers' availability to respond. Ainsworth suggested that such a working model derives from the experience of insensitive (though not rejecting) mothering (Ainsworth et al., 1978) and mothers' inconsistent responding to infant signals (Ainsworth, 1984). Learning theory would suggest that inconsistent parental responsiveness to attachment behavior provides the child with an intermittent reinforcement schedule that decreases the likelihood that attachment behavior will be extinguished (Cassidy & Berlin, 1994). While theoretically the concept of inconsistent mothering is appealing, it is difficult to operationalize and has not yet been held to close empirical scrutiny (see Cassidy & Berlin, 1994). Data from observations of C-group mothers have tended to report low-average responsivity levels that might or might not be reflections of inconsistency.

One pattern of maternal inconsistency would be a mother who is only intermittently engaged in monitoring her child but who, when she does notice the child's signals, responds appropriately. Such a parent might be one who is preoccupied with personal concerns that allow her only to intermittently attend to and notice her child's needs. In our observations, we saw no evidence that the mothers were only intermittently available to see their children's needs. In fact, they were generally quite aware of their children's activities, although this could have been a function of the laboratory observation setting.

We prefer to characterize the two mothers' response style as inconsistent in effectively meeting the child's needs. This inconsistency, however, was not intermittent in the sense of being random and unpredictable (from the perspective of the researchers). Mothers generally responded to affective signals from the child but were often oblivious to more subtle cues about the children's likes and interests. Mothers responded to clear emotional signals with engagement, but when children simply wanted their mothers to play or work in a particular way, the mothers failed to understand either the invitation to join their children, or the child's plan for the activity, or they imposed their own agenda on the activity. Rochelle rarely noticed Gerome's lack of interest in activities until he voiced strong complaints. Geneva, when asked to play with Kineta, resorted to tickling and teasing games that were overstimulating to the child. By responding preferentially to the children's angry or helpless behaviors, but not to cues related to their interests or ideas, the mothers were reinforcing the child's display of strong affect and also communicating the relative unimportance of their ideas and actions. The mothers' lack of consistent responding did not seem to result from a lack of concern or affection for their children or a failure to attend to their children, but from a failure to *understand* the meaning of subtle signals in terms of the children's needs and to understand their own role in meeting their children's needs. Others have suggested that such behavior results from a mother's preoccupation with her own attachment history (Cassidy & Berlin, 1994; Main & Goldwyn, in press).

The passivity and ineffectiveness of the mothers we observed was perhaps the most striking aspect of their behavior over time. Mothers reacted to their infants' intense upset but did little to reduce it or prevent it. Mothers tolerated and indulged the oppositional behavior of their toddlers and preschoolers. Mothers of older children passively accepted provocative behavior and even overt hostility from the child. They responded with tolerance, sometimes tinged by helpless frustration or exasperation. They responded as if they did not understand their power to shape the child's behavior. It was clear that the C-group mothers in the sample perceived themselves as somewhat ineffective. This was expressed through their sighs and helpless body language but occasionally also through their verbal communication with the researchers about the child.

Central to the C mothers' ineffectiveness with their children was their tendency to become emotionally aroused themselves by their children's affective displays. When the C children were helpless or angry, their mothers often responded with helplessness or anger. When the children giggled, so did their mothers. Mothers often were drawn into the negative and immature features of the strategy – bickering incessantly with the children. The mothers resonated to their children's affective states rather than responding with structure. By resonating with the children's affect, mothers failed to provide a calm, stable affective platform from which the children could regulate their own strong and often out-of-control behavior. This resonance reflected a certain passivity in the mothers, best shown in our sample by Kineta's mother who often helplessly and anxiously looked on as her children expressed negative feelings.

Possible Risk and Protective Factors Associated with the C Attachment Strategy

Inherent in the evolutionary and organizational perspective of attachment theory is the notion that the C strategy is in some respects adaptive for the child's survival. It is a strategy designed to gain for the child the availability and protection of a mother who otherwise might not respond sufficiently to the child's needs. Yet the C strategy also carries psychological costs to the child. Several of these will be discussed below.

First, the dissatisfying dyadic dance of the C children and mothers is incompatible with individual instrumental competence. Just as the attachment and exploratory systems cannot be activated at the same time during infancy, attachment behavior is incompatible with other instrumental behavior as well. Most interactions, particularly those structured in the laboratory, have an external agenda that goes beyond interpersonal goals – putting a puzzle together, planning an outing, eating a snack. In C dyads, the overt agenda of the moment rarely is completed or mastered in an efficient manner. When the mother makes an effort to direct the child, she rarely gets the child to do what she wants. When she makes an effort to teach, she is unable to structure the situation so that the child has the experience of mastery. When the child asks for comfort, he or she gets the mother's attention but is not comforted at the end. When disagreements are broached, they are never completely resolved. When the child is faced with a new set of toys, he or she does not fully exploit their possibilities. When there is a job to be done, it takes a very long time. So much attention is directed toward the relationship and toward affective expression that there is no room for a focus on any other goal. The effect is two people who are very involved but spinning their wheels around instrumental tasks. Display of instrumental competence in both the child and mother is forgone in service of the relationship. Taken to an extreme, such a focus on relationships and the accompanying inability to actively embrace and accomplish tasks of a less interpersonal nature could be an impediment to achievement in academic and vocational settings. Both children we observed were academic underachievers. One factor in their underachievement may have been their general anxiety and need to allocate their psychic energy to affective expression and relationship issues.

Second, the intense emotional involvement in the C dyad may ultimately become an entanglement and enmeshment of the two individuals. The goal of the C child's behavior is achievement of physical and psychological involvement with the parent, and enactment of the C strategy requires a high level of skill at perceiving and understanding the mother's feeling states. It would

seem easy for children enacting the C strategy to lose a sense of the boundaries between themselves and their mothers. Kineta and her mother had such
a level of intimacy by her adolescence that they seemed to anticipate each
other's every move. There was no physical or emotional separation. They constantly laid hands on one another and shared gales of giggles that seemed
unexplainable to the outside observer and seemed to foreshadow perpetual
immaturity and emotional dependency for Kineta. Gerome, by adolescence,
seemed to escape this over-closeness, perhaps out of an awakening sense of
gender norms. Such a closeness, particularly by adolescence, could be an
impediment to formation of autonomous thinking, identity, self-confidence,
and relationships with peers.

Third, the insecurity experienced by the child in the C ambivalent attachment relationship may extend to a more pervasive, and possibly handicap-
ping, experience of anxiety in many contexts. Kineta had a clear history of
extreme levels of anxiety that had affected her functioning in school and
other settings. At adolescence, both children experienced a significant number of somatic signs that could be indicators of underlying anxiety.
Generalized symptoms of anxiety may well derive from the on-going attachment relationship within which the child must work to elicit nurturing from
the mother. Through the display of intense affect, the child achieves immediate gratification (Crittenden, 1995a) – the mother's attention – but this is
only briefly satisfying because the underlying uncertainty and anxiety about
her availability in the future quickly reappear and may intensify upon moving
into settings such as school that require physical distance from the mother.

Fourth, the emotion-laden and sometimes aversive behavior patterns of C
children may place them at risk for conflictual relationships with other people, especially those who care for them. At younger ages such behavior may
be viewed as oppositional, at older ages as passive-aggressive. Yet despite their
clearly oppositional behavior, it is noteworthy that neither of the children in
the sample by the age of 14 was engaging in antisocial behavior such as
aggression to people, destruction of property, theft, or serious violation of
rules that would be indicative of conduct disorder.

We want to end by noting that the two children described in this chapter
were selected from a sample of very high-risk families living in impoverished
and often dangerous inner-city neighborhoods. By adolescence many of the
children in the sample were evidencing severe behavior problems. We
observed young people who had attempted suicide, engaged in cruel and violent acts, failed in their school work, run away from home, participated in
gangs, used and sold drugs. Neither of the children with ambivalent attachment strategies exhibited such extremely psychopathological behavior. Some
of the other parents in the sample could be characterized as rejecting or
neglecting. Some had completely abandoned their children. The two mothers described in this chapter have done a better than average job of providing

for their children under challenging circumstances. We suspect that the children's intensely involved relationships with their mothers, though ambivalent, may have provided them with a measure of protection from the problems experienced by so many of their peers. The psychological energy of these children was so focused on maintaining their involvement with their parents that, at least by the age of 14, they had not established connections to the kinds of deviant peer groups that had influenced many of their peers. We nevertheless have concerns for the near future of both children as they enter the period of late adolescence where developmental challenges include establishing autonomy from family, developing meaningful relationships with members of the opposite sex, and preparing for achievement in a life of work. Moving on and moving out are likely to be especially challenging to young people with anxious ambivalent attachment histories.

CHAPTER SIXTEEN

Attachment Models, Peer Interaction Behavior, and Feelings about the Self

Indications of Maladjustment in Dismissing/Preoccupied (Ds/E) Adolescents[1]

KATHERINE A. BLACK, ELIZABETH JAEGER,
KATHLEEN McCARTNEY, AND
PATRICIA McKINSEY CRITTENDEN

INTRODUCTION

Several researchers have documented an association between children's attachment to parents and their peer interactions. These findings are consistent with attachment theory, which posits that attachment models created in infancy affect behavior in subsequent relationships. Very few studies, however, have examined attachment and peer relations among adolescents. In the following chapter, we show that attachment, as measured by the Adult Attachment Interview (AAI) (George, Kaplan, & Main, 1985), predicts adolescent girls' behavior with their best friends as well as their feelings about themselves. We focus on the dismissing/preoccupied (Ds/E) adolescents, as they appear to be the most maladjusted. Finally, we discuss the developmental issues relevant to using the AAI with young adolescents, for these may impact the interpretation of our findings as well as the direction of future research.

Internal Representational Models

Based on interactions with early caregivers, children internalize representations of their attachment figures as well as of themselves in relation to those attachment figures (Bowlby, 1973, 1982, 1988). These internal representational models contain information about how children expect their care-

[1] *Acknowledgments:* We are grateful for support for this project, which was provided by grants to the second author (U10-HD25455) and to the third author (U10-HD25451) from NICHD. We would like to thank Frances Chickering, Eric Dearing, Tonya Benton, and Jennifer Ruh for their comments on earlier drafts of this manuscript. We would also like to thank Jennifer Ruh for coding the videotapes. Finally, we would like to thank the young women who participated in our study. Requests for reprints should be addressed to Katherine A. Black, Department of Psychology, University of Hartford, 200 Bloomfield Avenue, West Hartford, CT 06117.

givers to respond and about how acceptable or unacceptable children think
they are to their caregivers. Individual differences in the content of internal
representational models result from differences in the availability and responsivity of early caregivers. For example, if caregivers are available and responsive, children internalize models of their caregivers as trustworthy and of
themselves as worthy. On the other hand, if caregivers are rejecting, intrusive,
or intermittently responsive, children internalize models of their caregivers as
untrustworthy and of themselves as unworthy. On the basis of these models,
children forecast how available and responsive their caregivers are likely to
be, and they make plans regarding how to behave, particularly in novel situations where they expect they may need their caregivers. Eventually, internal
representational models are generalized to others and to feelings about the
self outside of relationships with early caregivers. In turn, they serve to guide
individuals' behavior in subsequent relationships throughout the life span,
including those with peers (Bretherton, 1985).

By adulthood, the assessment of internal representational models is typically evidenced in how individuals organize, process, and communicate about
attachment information, rather than in the behavioral patterns observed in
infancy. Kobak and Cole (1994) argue, however, that with the onset of formal
operations, the cognitive competence underlying adult expressions of security is available during adolescence. Specifically, adolescents possess the skills
to describe abstract aspects of themselves and their relationships, to contrast
these with alternative models, and to distance themselves enough from immediate experience to generalize appropriately about those experiences.
Moreover, they argue that changes in adolescents' abilities to reason allow
them to operate on (or monitor) these abstract, differentiated models in
more sophisticated ways. Furthermore, adolescents can consider several
aspects of models simultaneously as well as evaluate the validity of abstract
propositions regarding the self and attachment figures. These skills enable
adolescents to detect and correct inconsistencies in their models of themselves and others.

Just as individual differences in the behavioral patterns of attachment are
observed in infancy, so adolescents differ in their ability to monitor and evaluate their models of self and parents. During the AAI some individuals are able
to access both generalized and episode-specific information, describe and
evaluate their experiences without distortion, and present an internally consistent and plausible picture of their attachment relationships and the effects
of these relationships on themselves. These individuals also sometimes
engage in metacognitive monitoring whereby they actively attempt to resolve
any discrepancies that arise in their narrative during the interview. Those who
are able to present such coherent narratives during the AAI are described as
"free to evaluate" or as having an "autonomous" state of mind with regard to
attachment.

Nonautonomous individuals, on the other hand, distort attachment-related information. For example, dismissing individuals use strategies that divert their attention from attachment cues. During the AAI, they avoid recalling episode-specific information about their attachment experiences, which keeps their feelings at a distance. Preoccupied individuals use strategies that continually focus their attention on the details of attachment relationships without allowing them to draw sound generalizations about these relationships. Thus, they may display intense feelings (i.e., anger or passivity) when discussing their attachment relationships. According to Main (1991), the distortions created by nonautonomous strategies take up the epistemic space necessary to monitor attachment models for inconsistencies and errors. According to Crittenden (1997), the distortions function to reduce ambiguity, and therefore speed processing time in working memory. This leads to more rapid self-protective responses, but as Kobak and Cole (1994) point out, it also leads to difficulties in identifying and successfully resolving interpersonal problems. As such, nonautonomous adolescents would be expected to have more difficulty talking about their problems with peers than autonomous adolescents.

Attachment, Patterns of Communication, and Peer Interactions

Of particular relevance to the present study is the association between attachment to parents and the ways in which children communicate about their feelings (Bretherton, 1987; Cassidy, 1994). Secure children share their emotions freely and directly with their parents because they know that they will be responded to sensitively. For example, during the reunion episodes of the Strange Situation, secure infants actively seek proximity or contact with their mothers and are soothed by their presence. Once comforted by their mothers, they return easily to play (Ainsworth, Blehar, Waters, & Wall, 1978). Avoidant infants, on the other hand, minimize the expression of negative emotion because this strategy reduces the risk of rejection from the attachment figure. Spangler and Grossmann (1993) reported that although avoidant infants were as physiologically aroused upon separation from their mothers during the Strange Situation as secure infants, they showed fewer negative vocalizations. Finally, anxious-ambivalent infants heighten their emotional negativity to keep their caregivers in proximity. As such, during the Strange Situation, anxious-ambivalent infants are often extremely distressed (Ainsworth, Blehar, Waters, & Wall, 1978).

Given that attachment is associated with how children communicate about their feelings to parents, it should also be associated with the quality of children's relationships with peers. In general, children who were securely attached as infants to their parents are more socially competent and more well-liked by their peers than are insecurely attached children (Belsky &

Youngblade, 1992; Cohn, 1990; Elicker, Englund, & Sroufe, 1992; Fagot & Kavanagh, 1990; Turner, 1991). Theoretically, we would expect this association to continue during adolescence. Indeed, Kobak and Sceery (1988) reported that first-year college students classified as autonomous with the AAI were rated as more ego-resilient, less anxious, and less hostile by their peers than those classified as nonautonomous.

Friendships during adolescence are more intimate than those during childhood, which has been partially attributed to increased independence from parents (Berndt, 1982). According to Weiss (1982), adolescents sometimes direct attachment behavior toward their peers. Therefore, the effects of attachment models on communication patterns may be most pronounced when adolescents are interacting with intimate friends, namely *best* friends. Using a paper and pencil measure of the perceived quality of relationships with parents, Black and McCartney (1997) categorized female adolescents as high versus low in security and found that high-security adolescents had more positive interactions with their best friends during videotaped tasks than low-security adolescents. The present study extends these findings by examining the association between attachment models, as measured by the AAI, and observations of adolescent females' communication patterns with their best friends.

Attachment and the Self

Because attachment theory predicts that children develop parallel internal representational models of themselves to their models of others (Bowlby, 1973, 1980, 1982, 1988; Bretherton, 1985), it is reasonable to predict associations between attachment to parents and feelings about the self. Indeed, investigators have found associations between secure attachment to parents and higher self-esteem in children (Cassidy, 1988) as well as between perceived security with parents and higher self-esteem in adolescents (Armsden & Greenberg, 1987; Black & McCartney, 1997; Raja, McGee, & Stanton, 1992; Rice, 1990). In addition, researchers have suggested that an individual's locus of control may have familial origins (see Crandall & Crandall, 1983; Lefcourt, 1982). Katkovsky, Crandall, and Good (1967) found that mothers of children with an internal locus of control were rated by observers as more nurturing, protective, affectionate, and approving than mothers of children with an external locus of control. In the same study, parental rejection, either by mothers or by fathers, was significantly associated with an external locus of control in girls. Black and McCartney (1997) reported that adolescent females categorized as high in perceived security had higher internal and lower unknown and powerful others control scores than those categorized as low in perceived security. The present study examined the association between AAI classifications and two measures of the self, namely, self-esteem and locus of control.

Ds/E Category

During the AAI, some individuals exhibit both dismissing and preoccupied strategies. Using guidelines established by Main and Goldwyn (in press), these individuals are typically assigned to the Cannot Classify (CC) category. However, because "dismissing/preoccupied" or "Ds/E" better identifies the attachment strategies utilized by these individuals, these labels will be used in this chapter instead of "Cannot Classify."

The Ds/E pattern is parallel to one observed in infancy. During the Strange Situation, some infants display both avoidant and anxious-ambivalent patterns of attachment. These children, labeled A/C, experience more risk factors than other children and have parents with more interpersonal problems than other children (Crittenden, 1985a, 1985b; Crittenden, Partridge, & Claussen, 1991; Radke-Yarrow, Cummings, Kuczynski, & Chapman, 1985). Specifically, the developmental history for children classified as A/C is typically one of alternating threatening experiences (e.g., abuse and neglect).

Like A/C children, Ds/E adults often have the most disturbing attachment histories and are at the greatest risk for later psychopathology. Allen, Hauser, and Borman-Spurrell (1996) administered the AAI to a sample of 25-year-olds, half of whom had been psychiatrically hospitalized during adolescence and half had not. After controlling for previous hospitalization, gender, and socioeconomic status, they found that Ds/E individuals reported higher levels of criminal behavior than autonomous or preoccupied individuals, more psychological distress than unresolved or autonomous individuals, and lower levels of self-worth than individuals in any of the other attachment groups. Within clinical adult samples, there is generally an overrepresentation of Ds/E individuals. Van IJzendoorn and Bakermans-Kranenburg (1996) reported that approximately 40% of the individuals in clinical adult samples are classified as Ds/E or Unresolved (with regard to loss or trauma), whereas only 19% of women and 17% of men in nonclinical samples are assigned to these categories. Generally, the Ds/E category is associated with histories of psychiatric disorders, marital and criminal violence, and experiences of sexual abuse (Hesse, 1996).

Hypotheses

In keeping with previous research, we tested the hypothesis that adolescents classified as autonomous would exhibit more positive communication patterns with their best friends than adolescents classified as nonautonomous. Our operational definition of a positive interaction was low conflict and withdrawal scores, and high communication skills, support-validation, and problem-solving scores. Given that children develop complementary models of the self, it was also hypothesized that adolescents classified as autonomous would be more well-adjusted than adolescents classified as nonautonomous. Our operational definition of adjustment was high self-esteem and internal locus of control scores and low unknown and powerful others control scores. Given the association between the Ds/E category and maladjustment in adults, we further hypothesized that Ds/E adolescents would have more negative interactions with their best friends and would be less well-adjusted than adolescents classified as autonomous.

METHOD

Participants

The adolescent girls discussed here were part of a larger study concerning interaction behavior among best friend dyads (see Black & McCartney, 1997). Although relationships with parents are important to male and female adolescents (Bowlby, 1982), the influence of attachment to parents on adolescent friendships may be different for girls and boys. For instance, research has indicated that female friendships involve more intimacy than do male friendships (Fischer, 1981; Hunter & Youniss, 1982; Sharabany, Gershoni, & Hofman, 1981). As such, self-disclosure is more common, and conflict is distressful (Maccoby & Jacklin, 1987). Because the effects of attachment may be more observable in female–female interactions, this sample was restricted to girls.

Thirty-six girls (hereafter referred to as *focal adolescents*) were recruited to participate in the study. They, in turn, recruited their best friends. Most of the girls were from white, middle-class families. Focal adolescents ranged in age from 16 to 18 ($M = 17.1$) years. All of them were juniors or seniors in high school. Their parents were well-educated; 47% ($n = 17$) of mothers and 50% ($n = 18$) of fathers had college degrees. Sixty-four percent of the participants ($n = 23$) had parents who were married, 31% ($n = 11$) of them had divorced parents, and the remainder ($n = 2$) had parents who were separated.

Procedure

Adolescent girls were recruited through two local high schools. Parents gave their consent for the girls to participate in the study. Free movie tickets were offered to each adolescent and her best friend for their participation in the study.

All assessments took place in the lab. The girls were seated in chairs at a 90-degree angle to each other. A video camera was behind a one-way mirror and could not be seen by the participants. Three conversation tasks were presented by a tape recorder. The first task, which lasted three minutes, was designed to put the adolescents at ease. They were asked to pretend that they had won $1,000 in a raffle and to discuss what they would do with the money. In the second task, one adolescent (randomly determined) was asked to think about the last time she was upset about something that remained unresolved. She was instructed to describe to her friend why she was upset, to discuss the situation with her, and to come to a solution to the problem. After five minutes, the tape instructed the dyad to stop their discussion. In the third task, the instructions from the second task were repeated but directed to the other adolescent. Again, after five minutes, the tape instructed the dyad to stop their discussion. After the interaction tasks, one adolescent was interviewed concerning her relationships with her parents while her best friend completed questionnaires in another room. When the interview was completed, the participants switched places so that each would have a chance to complete the questionnaires as well as to be interviewed.

Measures

Attachment. The interview administered was a modified version of the Adult Attachment Interview (AAI) (George, Kaplan, & Main, 1985). Participants were asked to describe their childhood relationships with their mothers and their fathers, to provide evidence in the form of specific memories to support these descriptions, and to evaluate the effects of these early experiences on their current personality. Because of the age of the girls, however, the occurrence of early losses was documented but not extensively probed, and questions regarding parental abuse and threatening behavior were eliminated. All interviews were audiotaped and later transcribed verbatim.

Each transcript was analyzed in several steps (Main & Goldwyn, in press). First, from the childhood experiences provided during the interview, the participant's relationships with both parents were rated on five nine-point scales: loving, rejecting, involving/role-reversing, neglecting, and pressure to achieve. Second, the participant's present state of mind with respect to attachment was assessed using six nine-point scales: idealization of the parent, involved/involving anger, derogation of attachment, insistence on inability to recall childhood, metacognitive monitoring, and passivity of discourse/thought relevant to attachment. Third, discourse concerning experiences of loss or trauma was rated for indexes of disorganized or unresolved thought processes. Although such instances were not probed for specifically, several of the girls discussed these types of experiences sufficiently to assign ratings. Fourth, overall ratings for coherency of discourse and mind were assigned. In the final step, each participant's transcript was assigned a classification (i.e., Dismissing, Autonomous, Preoccupied, Unresolved, or Dismissing/Preoccupied) on the basis of its overall fit to the characteristics of the major attachment categories defined by Main and Goldwyn (in press).

In general, individuals classified as dismissing (Ds) attempt to limit or cut off the influence of attachment relationships in their lives. This is accomplished by idealizing or by devaluing their relationships with significant others. Although they may relate negative experiences with attachment figures, they consider themselves unaffected by such incidents. Individuals classified as autonomous (F), on the other hand, value attachment relationships and attachment-related experiences. Some autonomous individuals describe their parents as being loving and supportive throughout childhood. Others who report more negative experiences occurring in childhood seem to have come to terms with the past and seem relatively objective concerning any particular incidents. Autonomous individuals also recognize the part they play in relationship difficulties. Individuals classified as preoccupied (E) are enmeshed or entangled in particular attachment relationships. These individuals seem to perseverate on the past and are unable to come to terms with their feelings concerning particular experiences. Those given an Unresolved (U) classification show some disorganization/disorientation in thinking or discourse regarding experiences of loss or trauma. This classification is assigned in conjunction with a best-fitting alternative adult category (e.g., Unresolved/Dismissing). Finally, some adults exhibit both dismissing and preoccupied strategies, and are assigned to the dismissing/preoccupied (Ds/E) category.

We also sought evidence of distortions beyond those described by Main and Goldwyn (see Crittenden, 1997a). In Crittenden's expanded model, the dismissing classification has been further delineated into inhibited (A1-2), compulsive caregiving (A3), compulsive compliant (A4), and isolated/promiscuous (A5-6) categories, all of which are characterized by falsification of affect. The preoccupied classification has been differentiated into threatening/disarming (C1-2), aggressive/helpless (C3-4), punitive/seductive (C5-6), and menacing/paranoid categories (C7-8), all of which are characterized by falsification of cognition. These expanded patterns can be displayed alone or within the Ds/E combination. In these adolescent transcripts, we found evidence for the compulsive caregiving and compulsive compliant subpatterns as well as for the punitive/seductive subpattern. Specifically, transcripts were assigned to the compulsive caregiving category when dismissing discourse was combined with role-reversing content. In other words, the adolescent spoke from the perspective of the attachment figure and exonerated the parent for recalled lack of appropriate caregiving. Compulsive compliance was assigned to transcripts when dismissing discourse was combined with content of harsh punishment described from the parent's perspective and with inappropriate exoneration of the parents. In addition, Ds[A4] speakers showed compliance with the interviewer. Transcripts assigned to the punitive/seductive classification had deceptively illogical reasoning, outbursts of intense anger, and/or attempts to "seduce" the interviewer into rescuing the speaker. In each of these cases, the other aspects of the discourse met Main and Goldwyn's (in press) criteria for the dismissing, preoccupied, or dismissing/preoccupied classifications.

The final expansion beyond Main and Goldwyn that we found involved reorganization (R). In some transcripts, there was evidence of both a prior attachment organization and an emerging strategy. In other words, some adolescents seemed to be actively reorganizing their models without yet having achieved the new integration. In contrast to the dismissing/preoccupied category where two insecure theoretically divergent patterns are exhibited, those assigned an R either exhibited two secure patterns or one secure and one insecure pattern. In addition, with the dismissing/preoccupied category, there is strong evidence for two patterns, whereas with the R classification, there was more evidence for one pattern than the other. As such, R cases were given a final classification matching the pattern for which there was more evidence.

The AAI has been validated in several studies with adolescents, although all of the samples consisted of adolescents at-risk or of college students. For instance, Ward and Carlson (1995) found concordance between adolescent mothers' AAI classifications and their infants' Strange Situation classifications. Autonomous adolescent mothers were also found to be more sensitive with their infants at 3 and 9 months than nonautonomous mothers. Rosenstein and Horowitz (1996) found concordance in AAI classifications between psychiatrically hospitalized adolescents and their mothers. Finally, in the same clinical adolescent sample, a positive association was found between the dismissing attachment style and externalizing symptoms (Reimer, Overton, Steidl, Rosenstein, & Horowitz, 1996). In a normative sample of college students, autonomous adolescents displayed less dysfunctional anger and less avoidance during a problem-solving task with their mothers than nonautonomous adolescents (Kobak, Cole, Ferenz-Gillies, Fleming, & Gamble, 1993). Similarly, Cole-Detke and Kobak (1996) reported that the use of preoccupied strategies among female college students was associated with depression, and the use of dismissing strategies was associated with eating disorders.

In the present study, two coders (i.e., the second and fourth authors, both of whom were trained by Mary Main) agreed to assign the best-fitting Main and Goldwyn classification to each transcript. In addition, they noted when there was evidence of reorganization. Finally, the fourth author assigned additional classifications from the Crittenden (1997a) expanded model when aspects of the transcripts were not fully captured by the Main and Goldwyn system. Both coders worked through 5 initial transcripts and reached consensus on their classifications. They then jointly coded 22 of the 36 transcripts. Interrater reliability with regard to the Main and Goldwyn classifications was good, with 82% (18/22) agreement (Cohen's kappa = .77). The second author coded 4 and the fourth author coded 5 of the remaining 9 transcripts. It was agreed that one transcript did not contain enough information to be coded. It was dropped from all analyses reported in this chapter.

The first author coded the transcripts for whether or not the adolescent experienced any potential risk factors, such as abuse,[2] parental separation/divorce, or trauma. Trauma was defined broadly as any potential risk factor other than abuse or parental separation/divorce, including parental alcoholism, childhood illness, loss of parent or significant other, and repeated separations from parents. The coder also indicated whether or not the adolescent had ever been in therapy.

Self-esteem. Participants completed the Self-Perception Profile for Adolescents (Harter, 1988), which was designed to measure feelings concerning scholastic competence, social acceptance, athletic ability, physical appearance, job competence, romantic appeal, behavioral conduct, close friendships, and global self-worth. Forty-five items (five items for each subscale) were rated on a four-point Likert scale. Harter (1988) reported that Cronbach's alphas for the subscales ranged from .74 to .89. Some subscales, particularly those that focus on the cognitive and social domains, have been validated in samples of ninth graders (Harter, 1982). For instance, the correlation between feelings of scholastic competence and teacher ratings of cognitive competence was .73. The correlation between feelings of social acceptance and sociometric standings in the classroom was .59. Because overall self-esteem was of more interest in the present study than its specific components, we averaged the nine subscale scores.

Locus of Control. Participants also completed the Multidimensional Measure of Children's Perceptions of Control (Connell, 1985), which was designed to measure locus of control in four domains (cognitive, social, physical, and general). Participants responded to 48 items concerning reasons for success and failure in the four contexts. Items are rated on a four-point Likert scale, which yielded scores for the degree to which participants feel that their successes and failures are due to internal, unknown, or powerful others control. Cronbach's alpha values for the internal, unknown, and powerful others control subscales ranged from .39 to .61, .52 to .67, and .48 to .64, respectively (Connell, 1985). In addition, third- through ninth-grade children with higher unknown control scores in

---

[2] Although questions concerning experiences of abuse were not asked, some adolescents spontaneously provided such information.

the cognitive domain had lower scores on standardized achievement tests as well as lower perceived cognitive competence. Children with high powerful others control scores in the social domain had lower teacher, peer, and self ratings of social competence. In the present study, locus of control across the cognitive, social, physical, and general domains was of more interest than locus of control within specific domains. Therefore, the three subscales, internal, unknown, and powerful others control, were averaged scores across the four domains.

Peer Interaction Behavior. The videotaped interactions were coded using a modified version of the Interactional Dimensions Coding System (Julien, Markman, Lindahl, Johnson, & Van Widenfelt, 1987). This system contains qualitative scales for conflict, withdrawal, communication skills, support-validation, and problem solving. Conflict is the degree of tension, hostility, and negative affect displayed by the adolescent. Behaviors indicative of conflict include putting down the friend, using sarcasm, disagreeing more often than agreeing with the friend, and being defensive. Withdrawal involves avoidance of the interaction or problem discussion. Behaviors coded include avoiding eye contact with the friend, displaying low levels of self-disclosure, and diverting the problem discussion. The communication skills scale focuses on appropriate and positive expressive skills, as evidenced by expressing emotions and opinions in a clear manner, displaying high self-disclosure, and asking the friend for more information. Support-validation focuses on both the adolescents' listening and speaking skills, which convey supportiveness and understanding to the friend. Behaviors include assenting while the friend is speaking, expressing warmth or concern toward the friend, agreeing with or acknowledging what the friend is saying, and encouraging or flattering the friend. Problem solving is the ability to define the problem and design a solution. This ability involves proposing specific plans to solve the problem and making a commitment to take action. Focal adolescents were assigned scores (ranging from 1 to 5) on each qualitative scale, once for their behavior during their own task and once for their behavior during their friend's task.

The first author trained a research assistant to use the coding system, using the first 10 videotaped interactions from the current study. Raters were blind to participants' attachment classifications as well as their self-esteem and locus of control scores. Consensus was reached on the first 10 tapes, and these scores were used in later data analyses. Reliability was then assessed on 10 new videotaped interactions for each of the 5 qualitative ratings. Correlations between each coder's ratings for each construct were as follows: conflict ($r = .86$), withdrawal ($r = .76$), communication skills ($r = .57$), support-validation ($r = .65$), and problem solving ($r = .72$). After reliability was assessed, the research assistant coded the remaining 16 tapes.

RESULTS

Attachment Classifications

Table 16.1 shows the distribution of Main and Goldwyn (in press) and Crittenden (1997a) classifications combined. Notice that five of the transcripts (i.e., two in the dismissing category, one in the preoccupied, and two in the dismissing/preoccupied category) also had subclassifications from Crittenden's expanded system. It should also be noted that seven cases were assigned an R for reorganization. Two of these adolescents displayed two secure patterns (i.e., F2 and F4). The other five adolescents appeared to be moving from dismissing or preoccupied strategies to secure ones. For two of these five cases, there was enough evidence of coherence, by adult standards, to assign them to the newer, more secure classification; the other three cases were assigned to insecure categories.

When the subcategories in Table 16.1 are collapsed, 34% ($n = 12$) of the 35 adolescents were classified as autonomous (F), 31% ($n = 11$) were classified as dismissing (Ds), 17% ($n = 6$) were preoccupied (E), and 17% ($n = 6$) were assigned to the Ds/E category. Three transcripts were given a primary classification of Unresolved; the secondary classifications for these three cases were preoccupied, dismissing, and Ds/E, respectively. Because questions addressing loss and trauma were not extensively probed during the interview, unresolved classifications could not be assigned with confidence. Therefore, these three transcripts were assigned to groups matching their secondary classifications, which are reflected in the percentages provided above. It is also important to note that the percentages of adolescents assigned to the dismissing and autonomous categories are similar to those reported by another study of young adolescents (see Ward & Carlson, 1995).

Descriptive Statistics

Table 16.2 shows the means, standard deviations, and ranges of the peer interaction behaviors as well as the self variables for the entire sample. Self-esteem, the three locus of control variables, and all but one of the peer interaction behaviors were normally distributed. Conflict during own and friend's tasks was positively skewed.

Table 16.1.   Distribution of Main and Goldwyn (in press) and Crittenden (1997) Classifications

	Ds[A5-6]	Ds[A3-4]	Ds1-3	F1-5	E1-2	E[C3-4]	E[C5-6]	E[C7-8]	Ds/E	Ds[A]/E[C]
n	0	2	9	12	5	0	1	0	4	2

Table 16.2.   Means, Standard Deviations, and Ranges of the Peer Interaction Behaviors and the Self Variables

	Mean	SD	Range
Peer Interaction Behavior			
During Own Task			
Conflict	1.46	1.09	1.00–5.00
Withdrawal	2.34	1.19	1.00–5.00
Communication skills	3.37	.97	2.00–5.00
Support-validation	2.26	.61	1.00–3.00
Problem solving	1.66	.73	1.00–3.00
Peer Interaction Behavior			
During Friend's Task			
Conflict	1.40	1.01	1.00–5.00
Withdrawal	1.69	.76	1.00–3.00
Communication skills	2.86	.77	1.00–4.00
Support-validation	3.11	1.02	1.00–5.00
Problem solving	1.63	.91	1.00–4.00
Self-esteem	15.01	1.97	11.11–18.13
Locus of Control			
Internal	12.60	1.24	9.67–15.25
Unknown	8.05	1.83	4.00–13.50
Powerful others	8.02	1.92	4.00–12.25

Demographic Variables

There were no differences between autonomous and nonautonomous (Ds, E, and Ds/E) adolescents on age, number of siblings, birth order, or socioeconomic status. The lack of association between age and attachment is consistent with Ward and Carlson's (1995) findings.

Peer Interaction Behavior

Given the sample size and the number of dependent variables, there was not sufficient power to analyze the data with multivariate models (e.g., with an overall effect of .64, our power in a MANOVA with five dependent variables would be 32% (Stevens, 1980)). For this reason, these data were analyzed with univariate models, specifically with one-tailed contrasts within ANOVA models. The first contrast within each univariate model compared adolescents classified as autonomous with those classified as nonautonomous (Ds, E, and Ds/E), and the second contrast tested the difference between autonomous adolescents and Ds/E adolescents on the peer interaction behaviors during own and friend's tasks. Table 16.3 shows the means, significance tests, and effect sizes for both of these contrasts. Adolescents classified as autonomous tended to have lower withdrawal scores during their own task than adoles-

Table 16.3. Means of Four Attachment Groups on Peer Interaction Behavior during Own and Friend's Tasks

	Dismissing (n = 11)	Autonomous (n = 12)	Preoccupied (n = 6)	Ds/E (n = 6)	Autonomous versus Nonautonomous		Autonomous versus Ds/E	
					$t_{(31)}$	d	$t_{(31)}$	d
Own Task								
Conflict	1.73	1.17	1.50	1.50	ns	.36	ns	.22
Withdrawal	2.27	2.00	2.00	3.50	1.48†	.53	2.72**	.98
Communication skills	3.64	3.58	3.00	2.83	ns	.45	1.57†	.56
Support-validation	2.27	2.42	2.17	2.00	ns	.43	1.34†	.48
Problem solving	1.64	1.50	2.33	1.33	ns	.39	ns	.18
Friend's Task								
Conflict	1.36	1.25	1.50	1.67	ns	.25	ns	.29
Withdrawal	1.91	1.58	1.67	1.50	ns	.14	ns	.08
Communication skills	3.00	2.67	2.83	3.00	ns	.35	ns	.30
Support-validation	3.00	3.17	3.00	3.33	ns	.05	ns	.11
Problem solving	1.36	1.50	2.33	1.67	ns	.32	ns	.14

† $p < .10$; ** $p < .01$.

cents classified as nonautonomous. Although the tests for communication skills and support-validation during own task were not significant, the means were in the predicted direction and the effect sizes were moderate. Ds/E individuals exhibited significantly more withdrawal during their own task than autonomous adolescents. In addition, Ds/E adolescents tended to have lower communication skills and support-validation scores during their own task than autonomous adolescents. There were no differences between autonomous and nonautonomous or between autonomous and Ds/E adolescents on peer interaction behavior during the friend's task.

Self Variables

Again, a series of one-tailed planned comparisons were conducted within ANOVA models. Autonomous adolescents were compared with nonautonomous adolescents and with Ds/E adolescents on self-esteem and the three types of locus of control. Table 16.4 shows the means, significance tests, and effect sizes for both of these contrasts. There were no significant differences between autonomous and nonautonomous adolescents on any of the self variables, although the means for self-esteem and powerful others control were in the predicted direction and the corresponding effect sizes were moderate. Ds/E adolescents had significantly more feelings of powerful others control than autonomous adolescents. In addition, Ds/E adolescents tended to have lower self-esteem than nonautonomous adolescents. The test for unknown control was not statistically significant, but the means were in the predicted direction and the effect size was moderate.

Across both the peer interaction and self analyses, 6 (or 21%) of the 28 tests were trends (i.e., $p < .10$) or were significant. This result is twice that which would be expected by chance alone. In addition, the effect sizes were moderate for all of the trends and were large for all of the significant results.

Risk Factors

Transcripts were also coded for whether or not the adolescents experienced abuse, parental separation/divorce, trauma, as well as whether or not they had ever been in therapy. Table 16.5 shows the percentages of adolescents classified as dismissing, autonomous, preoccupied, and Ds/E who experienced these "events," as well as the significance tests and effect size estimates comparing autonomous with nonautonomous adolescents and with Ds/E adolescents. Autonomous adolescents were less likely than nonautonomous adolescents to have experienced abuse or trauma. In addition, they were less likely to have been in therapy at some point in their lives. Ds/E adolescents were more likely than autonomous adolescents to have experienced abuse, parental separation/divorce, and trauma. The finding for abuse is consistent

Table 16.4. Means of the Four Attachment Groups on the Self Variables

	Dismissing ($n = 11$)	Autonomous ($n = 12$)	Preoccupied ($n = 6$)	Ds/E ($n = 6$)	Autonomous versus Nonautonomous		Autonomous versus Ds/E	
					$t_{(31)}$	d	$t_{(31)}$	d
Self-esteem	14.61	15.54	15.59	14.08	ns	.40	1.49†	.54
Locus of Control								
Internal	12.63	12.52	13.38	11.92	ns	.10	ns	.36
Unknown	7.66	7.97	7.97	9.00	ns[a]	.24	ns[b]	.59
Powerful others	7.72	7.56	7.94	9.58	ns	.46	2.18*	.78

[a] Degrees of freedom (11) based on separate variance estimates.
[b] Degrees of freedom (5.3) based on separate variance estimates.

† $p < .10$.
* $p < .05$

Table 16.5. Percentages of Adolescents in the Four Attachment Groups Who Experienced Abuse, Parental Separation/Divorce, Trauma, and Therapy

	Dismissing (n = 11)	Autonomous (n = 12)	Preoccupied (n = 6)	Ds/E (n = 6)	Autonomous versus Nonautonomous		Autonomous versus Ds/E	
					$x^2(1)$	ϕ	$x^2(1)$	ϕ
Abuse	0	0	33	67	3.78†	.33	10.29**	.76
Parental separation/divorce	64	17	67	67	ns	.27	4.50*	.50
Trauma	27	8	67	67	5.46*	.40	6.78***	.61
Therapy	0	0	17	67	3.04†	.30	10.29**	.76

† $p < .10$; * $p < .05$; ** $p < .01$; *** $p < .001$.

with studies that documented an association between the A/C category and maltreatment in children (Crittenden, 1985a, 1985b) as well as with a study that found an association between the Ds/E category and experiences of sexual abuse in women (Stalker & Davies, 1995). Interestingly, all of the Ds/E adolescents (compared to 17% of the autonomous adolescents) experienced at least one of the risk factors listed above. These experiences lead the Ds/E adolescents to seek treatment, as evidenced by the fact that they were more likely than autonomous adolescents to have been in therapy at some point in their lives.

DISCUSSION

Summary of Findings

The findings from this study demonstrate that attachment, as measured by the AAI, predicted adolescent females' peer interaction behavior with their best friends, albeit only when they discussed their own problems. Specifically, autonomous adolescents tended to have lower withdrawal scores than nonautonomous adolescents during their own task. This finding is consistent with the idea that autonomous individuals are able to express negative emotions more freely and directly than nonautonomous individuals (Cassidy, 1994). Ds/E adolescents could also be differentiated from autonomous adolescents based on their behavior during their own task. In particular, Ds/E adolescents had significantly higher withdrawal scores. Moreover, there were trends for Ds/E adolescents to have lower communication skills and support-validation scores than autonomous adolescents. Taken together, these findings suggest that Ds/E adolescents had difficulty discussing their problems. Although most of them appeared angry or upset about their identified problems (e.g., argument with parents), they could not discuss their feelings about these problems. Their high withdrawal scores reflect observations that, instead, they fidgeted, avoided eye contact with their friend, changed the subject to something less threatening, or completely stopped talking. Their low support-validation scores also suggest that they were deficient in basic social interaction skills, such as nodding or assenting while their friends were speaking, acknowledging or agreeing with what their friends said, and encouraging or flattering their friends.

Adolescents' attachment was not predictive of behavior during their friend's task. Because discussing their own problems was most likely to be more anxiety-provoking than listening to friends' problems, it may be that the attachment system was activated during adolescents' own tasks but not during their friends' task. During the interactions, participants rarely discussed problems pertaining to their relationships with their best friends. If they had, both tasks would be mutually anxiety-provoking situations and thus, both would activate the attachment system. In this case, we would predict that attachment would be associated with behavior in the adolescents' own tasks as well as their friends' tasks. It is also possible that adolescents do not yet function as attachment figures for their peers. The effects of attachment on "listening" behavior may be more apparent when individuals begin to function as attachment figures for others, as is the case for parents with children or between romantic partners.

A second finding in this study was that AAI classifications predicted feelings about the self. Specifically, Ds/E adolescents had significantly higher powerful others control scores than autonomous adolescents, and there was a trend for Ds/E adolescents to report having higher self-esteem than autonomous adolescents. These findings are consistent with attachment theory, which hypothesizes that children who have had insensitive and unresponsive caregivers internalize models of themselves as unworthy. It is not surprising that Ds/E adolescents were feeling powerless, given that they were more likely than autonomous adolescents to have experienced abuse, parental separation/divorce, and trauma as children.

Differences Between Adolescent and Adult AAI Transcripts

What do the findings suggest about the future adaptation of these adolescents? In trying to answer this question, we could not escape considering their developmental circumstances and whether these might affect the validity or interpretation of the AAI classifications. Adolescent transcripts were similar to those of adults in many ways: (1) all of the questions asked during the interview were answered, (2) the entire range of discourse markers used in the adult system were present, and (3) for the majority of adolescents, a singular state of mind with regard to attachment could be detected. However, there were important differences, with respect to the content, discourse, and classifications, between adolescents' transcripts and those typically produced by adults. What follows is a qualitative, rather than quantitative, analysis of those differences.

Content. Three major differences in content were apparent. First, these adolescents tended to focus on their present relationships with parents. Even when asked to describe early childhood relationships, at least half of the girls also mentioned something about the current state of the relationship. Moreover, when giving memories to support the adjectives they provided, most of the girls described recent episodes with mothers and with fathers. Most adults, on the other hand, describe childhood incidents to support their adjectives. The second difference was that the adjectives chosen to describe relationships with parents were often relatively homogeneous in that they were either all positive or all negative (e.g., "tense, obnoxious, forceful, domineering"). Adult descriptions tend to be richer and more varied (e.g., loving, strong, strained). The final difference in content was that when adolescents were asked to speculate about the effects of their early experiences with parents on themselves, their responses were often very general (e.g., "I'm stable") or relatively impersonal (e.g., "I'm more responsible"). In fact, fewer than half of them connected their early experiences to how they felt about themselves or to their behavior in other important relationships. More adults are able to speculate about how their relationships with parents have affected their personality or behavior.

Discourse. The next set of differences between adolescent and adult transcripts concerned the discourse markers indicative of three "state of mind" scales, namely, passivity of thought, involving anger, and insistence on lack of recall. Although population norms are not available for these scales, scores assigned in this adolescent sample seemed to be lower than those typically assigned in adult samples. For example, indexes of passive thought were present in these transcripts, but no transcript received extreme scores (6 or above on a nine-point scale). In addition, no transcript contained marked examples of passive discourse throughout. In several examples the speech fit the general description of passive discourse in that it was vague and confused, but the strongest discourse marker observed was unfinished sentences, which is usually regarded as a rather weak example. "Involving anger" was another scale on which adolescents received, at most, only moderate scores. Although some of them spoke angrily and at length about their relationships with parents and seemed very preoccupied with their current interactions with them, they showed relatively minor violations of discourse. In adults, anger is more often reflected in serious discourse violations and is indicative of preoccupation with the past. Finally, scores assigned for the "insistence on lack of recall" scale also tended to be much lower than those typically seen in adult transcripts. Like adults, some of these adolescents would initially claim a lack of memory; however, among adolescents, this initial lack of memory was more often belied by vivid memories.

Classifications. The first difference concerning classifications was that the distribution in this adolescent sample differed from that found in normal adult samples. Similar to another study of young adolescents (Ward & Carlson, 1995), we found a larger proportion of adolescents assigned to the dismissing classification and a smaller proportion assigned to the autonomous category than is typically found in adult samples (van IJzendoorn & Bakermans-Kranenburg, 1996). Unfortunately, it is difficult to evaluate how typical our proportion of cases assigned Ds/E (17%) is compared with other adolescent and adult samples. This is because in other studies, cases assigned to the unresolved and Ds/E categories are usually combined and reported as one category. For example, van IJzendoorn and Bakermans-Kranenburg (1996) reported that 20% of older adolescents and 18% of adults are classified as unresolved or Ds/E. In the Ward and Carlson (1995) sample of adolescents, 26% were assigned to the unresolved category, with no indication of the proportion assigned to the Ds/E category.

The second difference regarding classifications was that some adolescents' responses seemed to indicate that their states of mind were undergoing reorganization. There was evidence in the discourse of both a prior attachment organization and an emerging strategy. For example, three adolescents appeared to be moving from dismissing strategies to secure ones. These adolescents were dismissing of effects of early attachment experiences on themselves, but their valuing of attachment was also evident. Although similar to adults classified as F2, these adolescents seemed more restricted and had a less mature perspective than adults who qualify for this classification. It may be that these adolescents were attempting to integrate disparate attachment models from childhood, which would explain why we saw evidence of both prior and emerging attachment strategies. In adults, we assume this process has been completed.

Finally, several attachment categories can be found among high-risk samples of adults that we did not see in this sample. Crittenden (1997a) proposes that, with development, there should be increasing differentiation in patterns of attachment, particularly for endangered individuals. Those individuals who have experienced the most danger, especially the most unpredictable and deceptive danger, are in the most need of protective strategies. With the availability of increasingly complex mental strategies, as well as exposure to new dangers, we should expect to see patterns of attachment in adolescence and adulthood that were not apparent during childhood. Although this was a normative sample, a little more than half of the adolescents had experienced abuse, parental separation/divorce, or trauma. Three adolescents (two in the dismissing category and one in the Ds/E category) fit one of the compulsive subgroup patterns and two (one in the preoccupied category and one in the Ds/E category) fit the punitive/seductive pattern; thus, 14% of the sample fit into Crittenden's expanded model. However, we did not see several of the more pathological categories Crittenden has observed in endangered adults; those that she proposes do not organize until adulthood (i.e., A5-6, C7-8).

Proposed Reasons for the Differences Between Adolescent and Adult AAI Transcripts

To summarize, there were several differences between adolescent and adult AAI transcripts: (1) the focus on the present relationships with parents, (2) the homogeneity of adjectives, (3) the generality of some responses, (4) the frequency and intensity of discourse markers indicative of three state of mind scales, (5) the distribution of classifications, (6) the presence of prior and emerging attachment strategies, and (7) the absence of some attachment patterns exhibited by endangered adults. We propose that these differences can be attributed to one or both of the following: (1) the onset of formal operations, and thus the acquisition of metacognitive skills, had just recently occurred for these adolescents, and (2) these adolescents were still actively involved in their attachment relationships with parents. The differences that can be attributed to each reason are discussed below.

New Metacognitive Skills. The advent of formal operations in adolescence makes possible the meta-monitoring of thought, a necessary skill for adult expressions of security (Kobak & Cole, 1994). Although this may be true, it is also the case that metacognitive skills are new for adolescents. This may explain the differences we observed in the content, discourse, and classifications of adolescent transcripts.

With regard to content, we should recall that adolescents' adjective choices were more homogeneous and their responses were more general and impersonal than those provided by adults. In other words, adolescents' responses were not as rich, varied, or insightful. Given the recent onset of formal operations, it may be that adolescents have not yet had the time to reflect on past experiences.

The fact that metacognitive skills are new in adolescence may also explain differences in discourse. It is possible that young adolescents have not yet fully developed the range of distortions of attachment information seen in adults because the intellectual skills underlying such distortions are only beginning to emerge. If this is true, the discourse markers used to reliably predict such distortions in adults may be less reliable predictors of mental processes in adolescents. For instance, a passive state of mind may be formed in adolescence, but indicators of this passivity are not described in the adult system. In addition, adolescents may have had lower insistence on lack of recall scores because memories contradictory to positive semantic generalizations about parents may not be fully recognized and thus do not need to be forgotten. Alternatively, the interview may not elicit the distortions made by adolescents. Redirecting the questions to address the present issues in adolescents' relationships and the separation issues of the near future may better activate the attachment system during adolescence and thus make their distortions more evident. It is important to note that, in our study, we used a modified version of the Adult Attachment Interview. Omitting key questions, such as those regarding early losses and parental abuse, may have inadvertently contributed to some of the differences we documented above.

Finally, the fact that metacognitive skills are just beginning to emerge may explain the differences in classifications. For instance, more adolescents in this sample were assigned to the dismissing category than is typical in adult samples. More than half of the dismissing adolescents were given the subclassification of Ds3. A hallmark of this subgroup is the denial of any effects of untoward parenting on the self. The AAI coding system, designed for adults, may misclassify some adolescents as dismissing because they are not yet able to fully comprehend and report the effects of their experiences on the self. The fact that metacognitive skills are new could also explain why some adolescents' attachment models were in the process of reorganization as well as why some strategies observed among adults were not seen in this sample. Young adolescents have not possessed the necessary mental skills long enough to fully integrate disparate attachment models or to develop more distorted attachment strategies.

Socio-emotional "Context" of Adolescence. The transcripts confirm that adolescents are still actively involved in attachment relationships with parents. As such, they may lack the physical and psychological distance from parents as well as the temporal distance from childhood necessary to fully evaluate their attachment relationships. We believe this "context" contributed to differences in content and discourse between adolescents' transcripts and those typically produced by adults. For example, the fact that adolescents are still attached children would explain the focus on their present relationships with parents. During the interview, adolescents evaluated their parents on the basis of their current satisfaction with parental fulfillment of their attachment needs. It is important to note here, however, that most adolescents have not yet begun to function as hierarchical attachment figures (with children), and they are just beginning to serve as reciprocal attachment figures (with peers and partners). Thus, they may lack an important comparison to judge the quality of care they received.

The socio-emotional context status of adolescence may also play a role in how these adolescents chose to describe their relationships with parents. According to Erikson (1968), adolescents are confronted with the task of constructing an identity. Blos (1962, 1979) argues that differentiation of the self from parents is critical to identity development. During this individuation process, it is common for adolescents to see others in "black or white." These reality distortions, which first surface in infancy, reappear during adolescence, as individuals attempt to impose their own order on the environment. This could explain why most of the adolescents in this sample chose either all positive or all negative adjectives to describe their relationships with parents. In addition, Bowlby (1973) suggested that because children are dependent on their parents for protection and care, it is too threatening to admit parental failings. This may also explain why some adolescents chose all positive adjectives to describe their relationships with parents.

Some of the differences in discourse, and thus in the "state of mind" ratings, may also have been the result of the adolescents' ongoing embeddedness in attachment relationships. For example, it may be that adolescents who exhibit mild indicators of passive thought are preoccupied with achieving comfort from their parents, but have not yet developed a fully passive state of mind. Passive thought, as judged by adult standards of discourse, may only become apparent after conscious hopes of achieving this comfort are dashed by the inevitable separation of adulthood. In addition, immersion in childhood may prevent enough distance to "forget," which explains adolescents' low insistence on lack of recall scores. Finally, instead of being indicative of angry enmeshment, the current anger expressed by these adolescents may reflect real decrements in the synchrony and perceived supportiveness of relationships with parents. An inherent assumption in the state of mind scales is that the type of "involved" relationship with parents typical in adolescence is no longer appropriate in adulthood. Thus, evaluating whether or not moderate indexes of preoccupation with relationships, in either the passive or angry form, are inappropriate is difficult during adolescence.

Conclusions and Future Directions

Our original question concerned what we might predict about the future adaptation of these adolescents. Like other researchers (see Allen, Hauser, & Borman-Spurrell, 1996; Hesse, 1996), we documented the associations between the Ds/E category and negative attachment histories as well as maladjustment. Moreover, for the first time, this study provided evidence that Ds/E adolescents are at risk in the peer environment. Without intervention, some of them will likely continue to be maladjusted and to engage in maladaptive behavior with friends and, later, with romantic partners. Studies that examine the clinical sequelae of the Ds/E status may identify such interventions, both natural (e.g., healthy friendships and healthy romantic relationships) and experimental (e.g., different forms of therapy).

We are less confident speculating about the future of adolescents assigned to the autonomous, dismissing, or preoccupied categories. We were unable to demonstrate that dismissing and preoccupied adolescents were less competent than autonomous adolescents. The failure to document such differences may be due to limited power. Alternatively, it may suggest that adult methods are not sensitive enough to capture normative patterns of variation in adolescents' states of mind. Thus, differences between extremes (autonomous versus Ds/E) may be reliably detectable during adolescence, but those between security and milder forms of insecurity may not be.

Even if we assume adult methods can accurately capture all patterns of security and insecurity in adolescents, another issue to consider in predicting the future adaptation of these girls is whether or not we would predict stability in attachment models. Given the changes occurring in mental development and in life circumstances, there is little reason to predict great stability from midadolescence to adulthood. These changes may provide opportunities for some nonautonomous adolescents to develop more autonomous mental models of the self and attachment figures. It is similarly possible that as the mental abilities necessary to develop more sophisticated distortions mature, some seemingly autonomous adolescents may become nonautonomous. In addition, the stresses associated with the transition to adulthood (e.g., leaving home, marriage, parenting) may challenge the adaptive capacities of adolescents who had a secure childhood largely free of adversity. In sum, except for the most at-risk adolescents, how much midadolescent attachment status tells us about future adaptation awaits further research.

In particular, longitudinal research could determine what factors promote stability and change in AAI classifications from adolescence to adulthood. Such studies could also examine the power of AAI classifications assigned in adolescence to predict adjustment and interaction behavior in adults. The current study investigated the association between adolescent attachment and peer interactions in girls only. It is critical to determine the extent to which these findings generalize to boys. Future studies should also continue to investigate how and why adolescent AAI transcripts differ from those produced by adults. These studies can further identify the normative processes involved in the development of attachment models during adolescence.

CHAPTER SEVENTEEN

Attachment Representation in Adolescence and Adulthood

Exploring Some Intergenerational and Intercultural Issues

ISABEL SOARES, ELISABETH FREMMER-BOMBIK,

KLAUS E. GROSSMANN, AND M. CAROLINA SILVA

Bowlby's concept of internal working models has received special attention from attachment researchers, especially after the pioneering work of Main, Kaplan, and Cassidy (1985). According to Bowlby's ideas (1969/1982, 1973, 1980), these authors pointed out that individual differences in attachment relationships can be conceptualized as individual differences in internal working models. In this sense, they proposed to investigate these individual differences related not only to patterns of nonverbal behavior, but also to patterns of language and thought. This new focus on representation and language offers new possibilities for the study of attachment not only in infancy or childhood, but also in later life. The assessment of attachment representation in adolescence and adulthood has been provided by the Adult Attachment Interview or AAI (George, Kaplan, & Main, 1985), which was designed to assess individuals' ability to integrate their specific memories into a more general understanding of their experiences and relationships with parents.

This conceptual and methodological "move to the level of representation" (Main et al., 1985) can contribute by clarifying and giving supportive evidence to the notion of intergenerational transmission of attachment. Bowlby suggested that internal working models of the self and the parents develop in childhood and play a major part in the intergenerational transmission of attachment patterns "through the medium of family microculture" (Bowlby, 1973, p. 323). The central issue for research is to know whether the quality of the attachment relationship between the parent and his or her child is related to the quality of the attachment relationship between the parent and their parents. To address this issue, longitudinal studies were carried out to deter-

[1] *Acknowledgments:* The authors would like to thank the colleagues from the Porto Attachment Research Group, António Fonseca, Cristina Almeida, Graça Machado, Lúcia Neves and Margarida Rangel Henriques, for their excellent collaboration in this work. A special thanks is addressed to Dr. Karin Grossmann (University of Regensburg) for her very helpful suggestions and comments.

mine the match between Adult Attachment Interview classifications and infant Strange Situation attachment classifications.

The development of the adult attachment scoring and classification system by Main and Goldwyn (1993) yielded the identification of four major patterns of organization from the interview transcripts. Secure/Autonomous adults (F) tend to value attachment relationships and to regard them as influential on development and personality. They are able to describe them coherently, whether or not their attachment experiences and relationships were positive or negative (e.g., loss, maltreatment, rejection). They lack idealization of their parents and do not feel angry about their past experiences. Dismissing adults (Ds) attempt to devalue the influence of attachment relationships and experiences in thought, in feeling, or in their own development, and they tend to idealize parents without being able to illustrate with specific episodes of secure interactions. Preoccupied or enmeshed individuals (E) are not able to describe their attachment history in a coherent way; they are confused, unobjective, and emotionally entangled with family relations and/or past experiences; and their sense of personal identity and autonomy seems confused, undifferentiated, or weak. Through their discussion of loss or of frightening/abusive experiences (e.g., physical and sexual abuse), the disoriented/disorganized adults (U/d) show evidence for the continuing presence of unresolved/disorganized ideation or behavioral reactions or of disorientation from the discourse context.

The hypothesis that infants and parents would use similar strategies to deal with attachment figures in stressful situations has been receiving empirical support. The Adult Attachment Interview has been most extensively validated with parents of infants in terms of matching to the child's Strange Situation classification. According to Main and Goldwyn (in press), the basic finding summarizing Adult Attachment Interview studies conducted to the present is that parents assigned to the four major adult attachment classifications are normally expected to have infants whose behavioral response to them in the Ainsworth Strange Situation is classified as follows: secure infants (B) would have secure/autonomous parents (F); avoidant children (A), dismissing parents (Ds); resistant children (C), preoccupied parents (E); and disorganized infants (D), disoriented parents (U/d). Strong correlations between the parental attachment organization as assessed in the Adult Attachment Interview and the organization of the infant's attachment toward the parent as assessed in the Ainsworth Strange Situation were originally reported by Main et al. (1985) in a sample of white upper-class mothers and fathers. Significant correspondences between Strange Situation classifications and maternal working models were also found in U.S. middle-class mothers (Ainsworth & Eichberg, 1991) and in adolescent mothers as well (Levine, Tuber, Slade, & Ward, 1991; Ward & Carlson, 1995).

The first study on the relation between adult and infant attachment outside of the United States has been carried out in the context of the Bielefeld and Regensburg longitudinal studies (Grossmann, Fremmer-Bombik, Rudolph, & Grossmann, 1988). Using a different coding system to classify the attachment interviews, called the Regensburg method for analyzing the adult attachment interviews (which will be described later in this chapter), the German researchers found an impressive relation between parents and infants' attachment in two different longitudinal projects. Other European studies conducted in Leiden, Netherlands (van IJzendoorn, Kranenburg, Zwart-Woudstra, Busschbach, & Lambermon, 1991) and in London, England (Fonagy, Steele, & Steele, 1991) also showed correspondences between the mother's classification and the infant's attachment organization. While strong retrospective and concurrent associations between maternal and infant patterns of attachment have been noted, the Fonagy et al. study was the first to report a prospective investigation of such associations and to show that maternal representations of attachment, during pregnancy, predict subsequent infant–mother attachment patterns.

Although the conceptualization of attachment as representation offers new possibilities for developmental analysis of attachment, as well as for the exploration of the quality of attachment from a life-span perspective, the review of the literature shows that only few assessments of adolescents have been conducted in light of attachment theory. However, from different conceptual frameworks adolescence is recognized as a particularly fruitful period for the study of attachment (Bluestein, Schultheiss, & Prezioso, 1993; Greenberg, Siegel, & Leitch, 1983; Grotevant & Cooper, 1985; Hill & Holmbeck, 1986; Lapsley, Rice, & Fitzgerald, 1990; Quintana & Kerr, 1993). Within the framework of Bowlby's theory, the work of Kobak may be seen as a particularly convincing example (Dozier & Kobak, 1992; Kobak & Sceery, 1988; Kobak, Sudler, & Gamble, 1991).

The first study to be reported here was designed to assess attachment representation in adolescents and their mothers, and it permitted analysis not only of age differences but also of intergenerational (dis)continuities in terms of attachment classifications and supportiveness of attachment figures. The Adult Attachment Interview was used to assess attachment representation, and analysis and classification of the interview transcripts were based on the Regensburg method. The first author received intensive training in this method in the University of Regensburg, which made possible the elaboration of a Portuguese version of the Regensburg method (Soares, 1992). This work facilitated further refinements of the Regensburg method and exploration of the similarities and differences among German mothers from Regensburg and Bielefeld, located in south and north Germany, respectively, and Portuguese mothers from Porto, a town in the north of Portugal. The second study reported here attempted to find similarities and differences among these three culturally different samples in terms of maternal attachment representation patterns and supportiveness of their attachment figures.

STUDY 1

This study was designed to address two main questions: (1) Are adolescents different from adults in terms of quality of attachment representation and specific attachment-related criteria? (2) Do adolescents and their mothers show concordance in terms of their attachment representation patterns?

Method

Sample. The subjects were 60 adolescents and their mothers from Porto, a northern town of Portugal.[2] The adolescents were recruited from all the tenth and eleventh grade students at a public secondary school on the basis of the following criteria: age (16 or 17 years old); absence of school failure; family status (two-parent household family and at least one sibling); parents' occupational status (both with a job); and educational level (at least the ninth grade for both parents). Within this group, adolescents were assigned to the sample based on an orthogonal factorial design with two factors: gender (male/female) and age (16/17 years old). Each of the four cells contains 15 subjects.

Procedure. The adolescents were first contacted at the school psychologist's office by the first author. A letter was addressed to the mothers of those adolescents who agreed to participate in the study. Two days later, they were contacted by phone, and, in the event of a positive response, an appointment for the assessment was set up within a one-month period. The adolescents and their mothers were interviewed individually, on the same day, at the family's home or at the school psychologist's office, according to the subjects' choice.

Measure. For assessing the subject's attachment representation a Portuguese version of the Adult Attachment Interview (AAI) (George, Kaplan, & Main, 1985) was used. AAI probes for descriptions of close relationships, specific supportive memories, assessments of relationships in childhood, and current

---

[2] The most recent national inquiry based on a representative sample of Portuguese youngsters aged 15 to 29 years (Pais, 1989) showed that this population is concentrated in urban and littoral towns. The majority lives with both parents: about 74% of the fathers are employed, and 63% of the mothers work at home. It was estimated that 43% of the youngsters are students and 60% have a higher school level than their parents. This finding reflects the recent expansion of the compulsory full-time education period and the democratization of the Portuguese educational system.

evaluations of these childhood experiences and relationships. The interviews were conducted by four psychologists who received training with the AAI in a preliminary study with an independent sample. Each psychologist interviewed 30 subjects, 15 mothers, and 15 children from other mothers. Each interview was audiorecorded and transcribed in order to be further analyzed and classified. The 120 interview transcripts of 60 mothers and their 60 adolescent children were randomly assigned to six raters, who had already received training in the preliminary study. The raters were aware of the study objective but blind to the identity of the subjects.

Method of Analysis. Analysis of the attachment interview transcripts was based on a Portuguese version of the Regensburg method for analyzing the AAI. The Portuguese version is based on the Regensburg method's manual that was translated from English into Portuguese. The first author received training at the University of Regensburg from Fremmer-Bombik, thereby ensuring that the Portuguese manual followed the same guidelines and specific rules of the original version.

The Regensburg method requires specific procedures, including several stages of qualitative and quantitative analyses in order to identify the patterns of attachment representation (for details, see Fremmer-Bombik, Rudolph, Veit, Schwarz, & Schwarzmeier, 1989). These patterns are identified on the basis of four dichotomous parameters that are considered to reflect the subject's attachment representation: presentation of each attachment figure (supportive vs. unsupportive), attachment relevant information (high vs. low), reflections and involvement on their own attachment experiences (high vs. low), and defensiveness against the interview (high vs. low). These four parameters are operationalized in terms of quantifiably attachment-related criteria, as, for instance, expressions of feelings, memories, attachment relevant statements, defensive strategies as idealizations, or evasions from the interview topic (Grossmann et al., 1988). Based on this set of attachment-related criteria, four distinctive patterns may be identified: secure-positive, secure-reflective, insecure-incoherent, and insecure-repressive (see Table 17.1).[3]

Interrater Reliability. The interrater reliability was assessed on the basis of 40% of the mothers' interview transcripts and 40% of the children's. Twenty-four adolescents' interviews and 24 mothers' interviews were randomly assigned to a second independent rater (excluding necessarily the respective interviewer). Following this design, an analysis of the variance random effects model was used to estimate the three variance components, due to the subjects' error-free scores, due to raters, and due to random errors, for each of

---

[3] See Grossmann et al. (1988) for details concerning the correspondence between the patterns of infant–mother attachment in the Strange Situation and these four patterns.

Table 17.1. Attachment Representation Patterns and Criteria

Secure-Positive	At least one supportive attachment figure
	Attachment relevant information
	Episodic memories and feelings
	Evidence for evaluations within a realistic view of attachment figures
	Feelings and reflections about attachment experiences
	Low defensiveness
Secure-Reflective	No supportive attachment figure
	Very rich memories
	Open communication about attachment adopting a balanced and reflective attitude
	Ability to cope with negative episodes and feelings
	No defensiveness against the interview
Insecure-Incoherent	One supportive attachment figure presented but few reflections about attachment
	Memories not questioned, contradictions not analyzed
	Low reflectiveness and high defensiveness that belie the positive picture of childhood
	High defensiveness
Insecure-Repressive	No supportive attachment figures
	Few attachment-relevant statements
	Difficulties recalling the past or even the present
	Positive picture of their attachment presented without any supportive evidence or negative experiences referred but few feelings
	Low reflectiveness and high defensiveness

the 22 attachment criteria defined in the Regensburg method (for details, see Fremmer-Bombik et al., 1989). The estimated reliability coefficients were then calculated as the ratio between the first component (due to subjects' error-free scores) and the sum of all three variance components (Fleiss, 1986). From the 22 reliability coefficients computed, 16 (72.7%) ranged from 0.92 to 0.99, 4 (18.2%) ranged from 0.86 to 0.89, and 2 of them were below these values, 0.78 and 0.66. Overall, these results show that the reliability of these criteria was good, since most of the variability present in the measurements was due to subjects' and not to the raters' differences.

Results

Data are reported first for parents (as adults) and their children (as adolescents) separately. In the second section, the analysis centers on the mother–child pairs.

Adults' and Adolescents' Attachment Representations. Most of the adults (70.0%) and most of the adolescents (78.3%) presented a secure attachment representation. Within a secure representation, 61.7% of the adults and 78.3% of the adolescents showed a positive pattern, but the reflective pattern was not found in the adolescents' sample in contrast with 8.3% of the adults. In terms of insecure representation, 16.7% of the adults and 10.0% of the adolescents presented the incoherent pattern, and the remaining 13.3% of the adults and 11.6% of the adolescents showed the repressive pattern. No gender differences were found among the adolescents' attachment patterns.

To examine in detail the relation between the criteria and the patterns, a discriminant analysis (DISCRIM) was performed on criteria scores using patterns as grouping variable.

For the adults, three discriminant functions were calculated with a combined $c^2 = 121.4$, $df = 60$, $p < .001$. After removal of the first function, the second function still accounted for a significant variance $c^2 = 59.0$, $df = 38$, $p < .05$. These two functions accounted for 60% and 28%, respectively, of the between-group variability. The third function did not contribute significantly toward further explaining the between-group variability. As shown in Figure 17.1, the first discriminant function separated maximally the positive pattern from the reflective pattern. The second function discriminated the repressive pattern from the others.

In regard to the adolescents, two discriminant functions were calculated with a combined $c^2 = 80.0$, $df = 40$, $p < .001$. The first function accounted for 79.2% of the between-group variability, but the second function did not contribute significantly to the variability. As shown in Figure 17.2, the first discriminant function separated the positive pattern from the incoherent and repressive patterns.

Using the discriminant weights, we correctly classified 90% of the adult sample (94.6% in the positive pattern, 100% in the reflective pattern, 70.0% in the incoherent pattern, and 87.5% in the repressive pattern) and 93.3% of the adolescent sample (93.6% in the positive pattern, 83.3% in the incoherent pattern, and 100% in the repressive pattern).

Tables 17.2 and 17.3 show the criteria that contributed significantly to the discrimination of the patterns for adults and for adolescents, respectively. For the adult sample, these criteria are as follows: expression of *Memories* along the interview; a defensive strategy called *Block;* attachment-relevant statements referring to both parents *(At-Rel Pa);* presentation of an attachment figure as supportive *(Sup-at-fig);* and presentation of the attachment figures as unsupportive *(Unsup-at-fig).* For the adolescents the main criteria are the following: attachment-relevant statements along the interview *(At-Rel Stat),* expression of *Reflections;* expressions of *Feelings;* all kinds of *Defenses* which integrate blocks, evasions, devalues, idealizations, and anger; and stories related to the past *(Past stories)* and the criteria related to *Block,* to the sup-

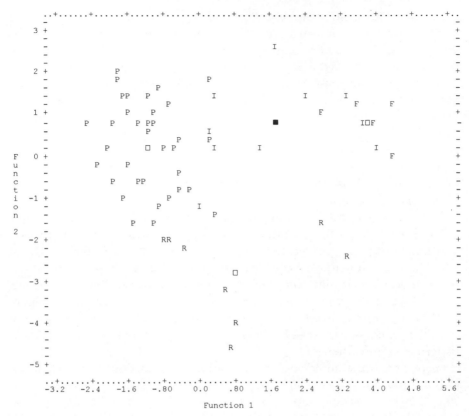

Figure 17.1.   Scattergram of Cases on the Two Discriminant Functions Derived from the Adults' Criteria. □ Centroid of Positive group (P); □ Centroid of Reflective group (F); □ Centroid of Repressive group (R); ■ Centroid of Incoherent group (I).

portive attachment figure *(Sup-at-fig)*, and to the unsupportive attachment figure *(Unsup-at-fig)*.

For the adults (Table 17.2), as can be seen by the correlations of the discriminant functions with the criteria, the first function (reflective pattern vs. positive pattern) is highly correlated with each type of attachment figure *(Sup-at-fig* and *Unsup-at-fig)*: all the adults in the reflective pattern had unsupportive attachment figures, and all the adults in the positive pattern had supportive attachment figures. The second function (repressive pattern vs. the others) is more highly correlated with *Block* and *Memories:* the adults in the repressive pattern presented on average more *Block* and less *Memories* than the remaining adults.

For the adolescents (Table 17.3), the first function (positive pattern vs. the others) is highly correlated with the criteria related to the supportive attachment figure *(Sup-at-fig)* and with *Reflections:* all adolescents in the positive pat-

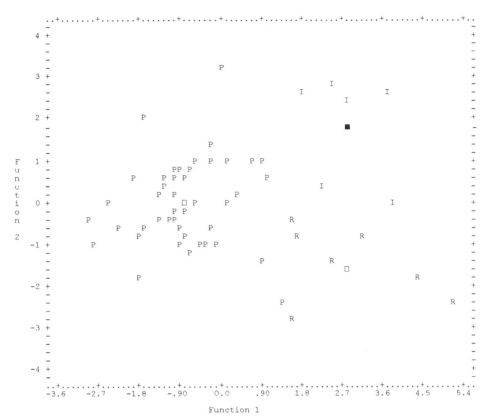

Figure 17.2. Scattergram of Cases on the Two Discriminant Functions Derived from the Adolescents' Criteria. □ Centroid of Positive group (P); □ Centroid of Repressive group (R); ■ Centroid of Incoherent group (I).

tern had supportive attachment figures and more reflections than the remaining adolescents.

Mother–Child Attachment Representations. Table 17.4 shows the joint distribution of adolescents and their mothers, with regard to the secure/insecure dichotomy. Looking at the matching/mismatching between the 60 mothers' and their adolescent children's classifications, 43 child–mother pairs (71.7%) were judged to fall within the corresponding categories—36 dyads were judged as secure and 7 as insecure. The mismatches were found mainly among insecure mothers, 11 out of 18 with a secure child, and only 6 out of 36 secure mothers with an insecure child. For testing the hypothesis that the mother and child attachment representations were independent, the kappa statistic and the respective standard error were used (Fleiss, 1981). The value for this statistic (kappa = .27, *p* < .05) revealed a concordance between

Table 17.2. Results of the DISCRIM for the Adult's Sample: Means and Univariate F-values for Each Significant Criterion and Correlations Between the Criteria and Discriminant Functions

	Patterns					Univariate $F(3,56)$	Correlations with Discriminant Functions		
Criteria	Incoherent	Repressive	Positive	Reflexive			F1	F2	F3
Memories	0.020	0.016	0.044	0.036		3.48*	0.17	−0.20	0.32
Block	0.002	0.005	0.002	0.000		3.50*	0.05	0.35	−0.21
At-Rel Pa	0.444	0.978	0.588	1.362		2.91*	−0.14	0.14	0.38
Sup-at-fig	0.500	0.750	1.000	0.000		26.13**	0.70	0.12	−0.15
Unsup-at-fig	0.400	0.250	0.000	1.000		24.33**	−0.67	−0.08	0.31

** $p<.01$; * $p<.05$, otherwise not significant.

Table 17.3. Results of the DISCRIM for the Adolescents' Sample: Means and Univariate F-values for Each Significant Criterion and Correlations Between the Criteria and Discriminant Functions

| Criteria | Patterns | | | | Correlations with Discriminant Functions | |
	Incoherent	Repressive	Positive	Univariate $F(2,57)$	F1	F2
At-Rel Stat	0.119	0.098	0.147	4.09*	0.24	0.13
Reflections	0.166	0.125	0.227	8.27*	0.34	0.18
Memories	0.006	0.012	0.019	4.30*	0.24	−0.16
Feelings	0.010	0.004	0.016	4.53*	0.24	0.18
Defenses	0.009	0.022	0.013	3.34*	−0.10	−0.39
Block	0.003	0.017	0.004	12.05**	−0.27	−0.64
Past stories	3.333	0.571	1.787	3.93*	−0.01	0.47
Sup-at-fig	0.666	0.571	1.000	14.63**	0.46	0.12
Unsup-at-fig	0.166	0.142	0.000	4.09*	−0.25	0.05

** $p < .01$; * $p < .05$, otherwise not significant.

Table 17.4.   Marginal and Joint Distribution of Attachment Representations of Mothers and Children (%)

Mother–Child	Secure	Insecure	All
Secure	36 (60.0)	11 (18.3)	47 (78.0)
Insecure	6 (10.0)	7 (11.7)	13 (22.0)
All	42 (70.0)	18 (30.0)	60 (100.0)

mother and child classification. A stratified analysis in terms of gender indicated a significant concordance for daughters (76.7%, kappa = .38, $p < .05$) but not for sons (66.7%, kappa = .17, $p > .1$).

Regarding the four attachment patterns (positive and reflective patterns within a secure representation and incoherent and repressive patterns within an insecure representation), no concordance was found. The reflective pattern was not found in our adolescent sample.

Discussion

The adults' and adolescents' distributions across the patterns were similar, except for the reflective pattern, which was not found in the adolescent sample. More studies using this method are necessary to clarify this result. The DISCRIM suggests that the Regensburg method may be an adequate method to classify the AAI. This is particularly important because this is the first study to use this method with a non-German sample.

With regard to the criteria used by the Regensburg method, there are similarities and differences between the adults' and the adolescents' samples. Overall, the two criteria related to the supportiveness of the attachment figures (*Sup-at-fig* and *Unsup-at-fig*) seem to offer a significant contribution for discriminating the patterns, particularly in the adult sample. Moreover, the criterion of *Block* was significant for discriminating the adults' patterns, while the criterion of *Reflections* was significant for discrimination of patterns in the adolescent sample.

Globally, adolescents present more variability than adults in terms of the number of criteria that contribute significantly to discriminate the patterns.

With regard to the results in terms of the mother–child pairs, this is probably the first study to compare mothers' and adolescents' AAI classifications. Therefore, our results can only be compared with those from studies in which mothers' classifications are compared with infants' or children's classifications. Our finding of 72% matching is somewhat below the 78% obtained in the Regensburg study (Grossmann et al., 1988). Using the AAI Classification System, Main and Goldwyn (in press) found a match of 73% between the three pattern-classifications (Ds/F/E) of the parent and the A/B/C classification of the infant in relation to that parent. Similarly, Green-Eichberg and Ainsworth (1991) reported a concordance of 74%.

The concordances reported represent only indirect confirmation of Bowlby's hypothesis about intergenerational continuity, because they link adolescent attachment classification to the mother's concurrent model of early attachment relationships rather than to past representational models. Furthermore, two limitations on the meaning of the classification of attachment representation must be recognized. We may think that classification as presented here reflects the current organization of the individual's interactions with parents. However, our study did not examine this hypothesis. If so, we should have investigated the relation between attachment classification and current relationships with parents, and, in addition, some present assessment of parent–child interaction would have been necessary. To assess the stability of the parent–child relationship and attachment organization, we would need a longitudinal study.

Forty-three mother–child pairs offered support to the notion of "continuity across generations." However, as Crittenden, Partridge, and Claussen (1991) assert, following Bowlby's ideas about the possibility of change under certain kinds of conditions, it seems unreasonable to expect near perfect matches between the model of the parent's attachment to their own parents and the child's model. According to Sroufe and Jacobvitz (1989), such an outcome could only be expected for the most stable of populations.

Concerning the 17 mismatched mother–adolescent pairs found in our study, two different conjectures can be made.

First, for secure adolescents from insecure mothers, a possible answer or clarification could come from their fathers' or other attachment figures' assessments. These figures may be a secure base for these adolescents. Based on qualitative analysis of these interviews, we received some support for this idea, although the insecure relationship with the mother, father, or even grandmother seems to represent meaningful emotional support for some adolescents. However, as Bretherton points out (1985) in regard to these nonconcordant relationships, it is not yet clear how different models can be integrated into a single inner model and in what situations different or integrated models may operate. Besides, we may consider the potential conflict it can provoke within the system of familial relationships and as Ainsworth questions about "how these possible disparities are managed" and "how they are combined together into one complex, but integrated model" (1990, p. 475).

Second, the insecure adolescents with secure mothers clearly are a challenge for the theory. A qualitative analysis of these six interviews revealed, for instance, that one of these adolescents was still emotionally disturbed by her long separation from her parents at 7 years of age, so much so that she considered her life to have been "cut" into two periods—life before the separation and life after the separation. This early separation from parents may be considered an attachment stressor that Bowlby (1973) believed could jeopardize an attachment relationship. Obviously, however, further studies are required to support these speculative comments and to understand this particular mismatch.

The finding of no reflective pattern in the adolescents is also noteworthy. As noted before, the reflective pattern means that the subject, despite the most adverse attachment experiences, "has developed a post-hoc understanding of them which was deep enough to achieve the necessary mental integration of his/her emotions" (Grossmann & Grossmann, in preparation). In our study, five mothers presented a reflective pattern. These mothers may be considered to be an example of positive change in attachment status: They view themselves as insecure young children, and they attribute the change to the opportunities they had in late adolescence and adulthood to develop new and constructive relationships outside the parental system. They seem to have been successful in revising their earlier models of parents and self. In a certain way, these assumptions were reinforced by the finding that their children were judged as secure, presenting a positive pattern of attachment representation. This finding can be an indirect support to Grossmann and Grossmann's belief that the reflective mothers "developed an openness for reality and for their own children's expressions of their emotional needs" (in preparation).

The reflective pattern seems to express a process of change of the early internal models. Why wasn't it found in our adolescents? According to the Regensburg method, the reflective pattern is characterized by an absence of supportive attachment figures. Only five adolescents (8%) did not present any supportive attachment figure, in contrast with the mothers' sample where no supportive figures were found for 12 mothers (20%). In spite of their unsupportive attachment figures, 5 of these 12 mothers were classified as secure, whereas all the adolescents with unsupportive attachment figures were considered insecure. This result shows that, more often than the adults, the adolescents tend to present a positive picture of their attachment figures. This difference may reflect a developmental process whereby one's perspectives become harsher and demanding with age, or when the actual physical and psychological proximity of the attachment figures is great, the tendency is to identify someone as fulfilling this role. Similarly, this might suggest reasons for a higher percentage of secure adolescents than mothers.

None of these five adolescents was able to reflect on negative experiences in order to present a coherent and integrated model. Based on the interviews of our reflective mothers, we think that these adolescents are still too young and still too much "involved" within the family system—either for being enmeshed or for being cut off from parental attachment relationships. Perhaps the favorable conditions needed to reevaluate their internal working models have not yet emerged, namely, moving outside of the parental relationship, forming intimate relationships with peers as well as being able to evaluate the existing relationship within the context of a range of possible relationships (Main et al., 1985). If these speculations are accurate, we can foresee that at least some of them may have constructive encounters in future life, and, if so, the revision of their insecure models may occur. Only a longitudinal study of these adolescents can bring some supportive evidence for these assumptions.

A preliminary data analysis of the Bielefeld sample's children at 16 years of age revealed a high correspondence between their AAI classifications and their mothers' AAI classifications (Zimmermann, in preparation). A cross-cultural comparison between the results from these Bielefeld adolescents and the results from our Portuguese adolescents may be an interesting study for the near future.

STUDY 2

This study attempted to explore the similarities and differences among Regensburg, Bielefeld, and Porto mothers in terms of the attachment representation patterns as well as the supportiveness of the attachment figures assessed by the Regensburg method for analyzing the Adult Attachment Interview. This method was first elaborated within the Regensburg and Bielefeld longitudinal studies, and it was adopted in Study 1.

Method

Sample. The Portuguese subjects for this study were the 60 mothers from Porto who took part in Study 1. The German mothers were recruited from the Regensburg and the Bielefeld longitudinal samples: 45 mothers from Regensburg and 44 mothers from Bielefeld participated in this study. (For detailed descriptions of these two longitudinal samples, see Grossmann, Grossmann, Spangler, Suess, & Unzner, 1985 and Wartner, Grossmann, Fremmer-Bombik & Suess, 1994).

Measure and Method of Analysis. The Adult Attachment Interview (George et al., 1985) was used in the three samples to assess mothers' attachment representation. Each subject's interview transcript was classified based on the Regensburg method of analyzing the AAI (Fremmer-Bombik et al., 1989) already described in Study 1. The Portuguese and the German researchers underwent extended and intensive training to enable them to use the same rules for classifying the interview transcripts. Based on the rules of the Regensburg method, the authors used the same algorithms to identify the patterns and to classify the attachment figures. For this reason, it is possible to analyze the data and to compare the results in terms of the patterns and supportiveness of the attachment figure, but not at the criteria level because this is based on the means of each sample. The supportiveness of the attachment figures is related to the way the subject describes the attachment figures during the interview, that is, as supportive or as unsupportive or even not possible to classify (unclassifiable).

Results

The distribution of Porto, Regensburg, and Bielefeld subjects in terms of secure versus insecure attachment representations is presented in Figure 17.3. There are no significant differences among the three sample distributions. For all three samples combined, it was found that 65.8% of the subjects presented a secure attachment representation, and 34.2% showed an insecure attachment representation.

Significant differences existed between Portuguese and German mothers ($c^2 = 13.9$, $df = 3$, $p < .01$), with respect to the incoherent pattern—in Porto 16.7% vs. 4.5% in Germany—and to the repressive pattern—13.3% in Porto vs. 32.6% in Germany. Looking at the distributions of the three samples by the patterns (Figure 17.4), we again found significant differences ($c^2 = 20.8$, $df = 6$, $p < .01$), which are related to an increased proportion of reflective mothers in Regensburg as well as of incoherent mothers in Porto, contrasting with a decreased proportion of repressive mothers in Porto. No significant differences exist between the distribution of the Regensburg and Bielefeld mothers.

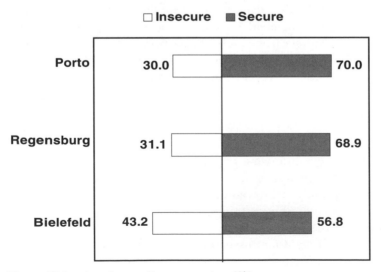

Figure 17.3. Attachment Representation (%).

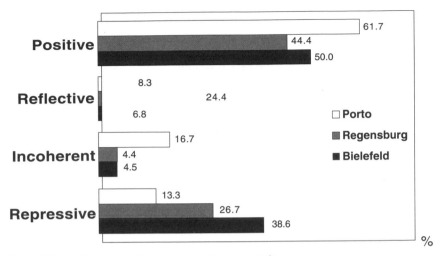

Figure 17.4. Patterns of Attachment Representation.

Portuguese and German mothers also differed significantly in terms of the type of attachment figure they presented (c^2 = 14.6, df = 4, p <.01): more Portuguese mothers presented a supportive attachment figure (80%) than German mothers (51.7%), in contrast to the proportion of mothers with only unsupportive attachment figures (18.3% in Porto vs. 39.3% in Germany). Although no significant differences were found between Regensburg and Bielefeld mothers, major differences were found between Porto and Regensburg mothers (Figure 17.5): 80% of Porto mothers in contrast with 48.9% of Regensburg mothers presented a supportive attachment figure, while only 18.3% of Porto mothers presented unsupportive attachment figures in contrast with 44.4% of Regensburg mothers.

Discussion

We found similar distributions of attachment representations (secure vs. insecure) in Portuguese and German samples (Figure 17.3), but different distributions of the four patterns of attachment representation (Figure 17.4) and of presentation of the attachment figure (Figure 17.5).

There were more secure-reflective mothers in Germany and more insecure-incoherent mothers in Porto, which shows that more German mothers had to reflect on nonsupportive attachment experiences than Porto mothers. For Porto mothers it seemed more difficult to speak about nonsupportive experiences, which may explain why we found more of them in the incoherent pattern. The major incidence of the reflective pattern in Regensburg mothers suggests that, although they may have experienced more adverse

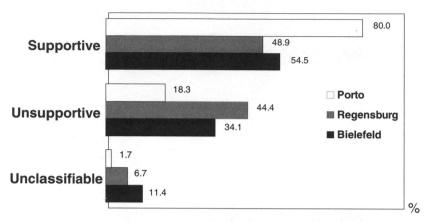

Figure 17.5.   Supportiveness of the Attachment Figure.

attachment experiences, they were able to reevaluate themselves and to develop a new and more autonomous working model. The finding of more repressive mothers in Bielefeld than in the other two samples seems to be in accord with 99% avoidant babies to their mothers found in Bielefeld (Grossmann, Fremmer-Bombik, Friedl, Grossmann, Spangler, & Suess, 1989).

The results found and the interpretations offered should be interpreted with caution since this study explores data from different social-cultural contexts.

Although the Regensburg method was reliably applied in both cultures, cross-language reliability was not controlled for. However, it is tempting to analyze narratives of present attachment representation not only from an individual perspective, but also from a cultural (or epochal) point of view. Universal versus culture-specific or individual aspects of attachment development can ultimately be disentangled only in comparisons across epochs and cultures (Grossmann & Grossmann, 1990).

CHAPTER EIGHTEEN

A Dynamic-Maturational Approach to Continuity and Change in Pattern of Attachment

PATRICIA McKINSEY CRITTENDEN

Much of the work in attachment beyond infancy has been based on two assumptions: (1) that the array of infant patterns of attachment represents the array of patterns found at later ages, with only age-appropriate changes in how they are displayed, and (2) that there is continuity of pattern across individuals' life spans. An alternative approach is that of expecting a dynamic interaction of maturation, with experience leading to both change and continuity in pattern of attachment. In this model, three kinds of change are possible: (a) change from one pattern to another, (b) change in the array of possible strategies, and (c) change from simple substrategies to more complex and sophisticated substrategies within a dominant pattern. These kinds of change can be described as lawful (i.e., they are not random, and the conditions underlying them can be specified), but with varying degrees of predictability. For populations, the predictability may be quite high, whereas, for individuals, it may be considerably lower. Because they are marked by substantial neurological change, two periods of maturational shift are emphasized as leading to predictable change: infancy to preschool-age and school-age to adolescence. This chapter addresses the two issues of a finite array of patterns established in infancy versus a developmentally expanding array and continuity of individuals' patterns versus variable developmental pathways.

WHY MIGHT THE INFANT PATTERNS BE INSUFFICIENT TO DESCRIBE PATTERNING AT LATER AGES?

The infant patterns of attachment described by Ainsworth and her colleagues (Ainsworth, Blehar, Waters, & Wall, 1978) have generally been used as the basis for thinking about pattern of attachment at all later ages (see Figure 18.1). Nevertheless, there is a basis for questioning whether human behavior after infancy can be adequately described if the description is constrained to a model based on infancy. Two reasons are discussed: the immaturity of the infant organism and the limited contexts in which infants function.

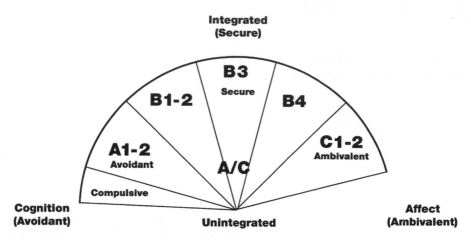

Figure 18.1. A dynamic-maturational model of attachment: infant patterns.

Neurological and Mental Immaturity

The immaturity of infants at 12 months of age is critical to thinking about whether their patterns of thought and behavior could reflect the full range of patterns found in older humans. Specifically, infant brain development, especially cortical development, is far from complete. This has implications for both infants' processing of information and their organization of behavior. Infants' inability to use language limits considerably how they gain, retain, and use information as well as how communication with others can be used strategically to promote safety and comfort. Another limitation is infants' inability to selectively inhibit behavior in the presence of eliciting conditions. That is, in order to inhibit attachment behavior, infants must avoid perception of the elicitors of the behavior—hence, the term *avoidant* for the infant Type A pattern of attachment. Infants are also unable to deceive; for example, they cannot feel angry and look happy or sneak a forbidden object while pretending to do something else. Because older humans can and do inhibit behavior and falsify their display of behavior, they can organize self-protective strategies that infants cannot. Infants also find it difficult to respond adaptively to changing contingencies, interactive contingencies, and multiply caused events. Because older humans can manage these complexities, they can construct and implement more complex strategies than infants. Finally, the cortical development of older humans permits more complete integration of information, thus yielding the possibility of new mental and behavioral strategies.

Given the extent of these differences between infants and older people, the question becomes whether there is anything about the infant patterns that *is* reflected at later ages. In both empirical and theoretical work, it seems that the Ainsworth ABC trichotomy can be reduced to two sorts of information and their integration (Crittenden, 1995). The Type A pattern can be thought of as a "cognitive" pattern that is organized on the basis of previously experienced, predictable, temporal contingencies. In other words, it is an implicit attribution of causal relations between temporally ordered events. In a dynamic-maturational approach to attachment theory, this sort of information is labeled "cognitive" information. The Type C pattern can be thought of as an affective pattern, one in which feelings organize and motivate behavior; that is, the Type C strategy is organized on the basis of "affective" information. Type B then becomes an occasion-specific, balanced use of both sorts of information. What the dynamic-maturational expansion of the Ainsworth system has in common with the infant patterns is the difference between Types A and C with regard to the relative influence of cognition or affect on thought processes and behavior. What differs is the array and assortment of transformations of cognitive and affective information that can be used to organize behavior.

Infants display their motivations transparently; older individuals do not. By the middle of the second year of life, children become able to *omit* some information from processing, as, for example, Type A[1] children do with regard to display of negative feelings and Type C with attention to verbally stated contingencies. Later, children become able to *distort* information. Type C children exaggerate (i.e., distort) the display of affect in ways that change the probabilities on attachment figures' behavior. School-age children distort cognitive information when they exaggerate true cognitive (temporal or causal) relations to extend predictability and certainty beyond reality, for example, "I'm *always* happy and *never* angry with my parents." This is often incorporated into the Type A strategy. Preschool-age children can also *falsify* information, especially affect, usually by inhibiting the display of negative affect while concurrently substituting a display of positive affect (a function typical of some Type A children). By the school years, children falsify cognitive information by inhibiting evidence of their true intentions and displaying inaccurate and misleading cognitive information. For example, they can appear to intend to play while, nevertheless, planning how to snitch forbidden cookies from the kitchen. Cognitive falsification becomes part of some Type C subclassifications. These transformations of information create the possibility for a whole range of new strategies for self-protection that, in the dynamic-maturational model proposed here, become the basis for new subpatterns within the basic ABC framework established by Ainsworth.

---

[1] Most children learn all of these transformational processes. The notation of Types A and C is meant to identify functions that become integral to the organization of that strategy.

Limited Contexts for Learning and Acting

The social ecology of infancy is very constrained. Infants live at home with a few caregiving adults and, possibly, spend some part of their time in the care of familiar other people, for example, grandparents and day-care providers. Furthermore, within these restricted environments, their mobility is very limited. Infants affect their relationships with important people, but they can do very little to select the contexts in which they will develop. Instead, attachment figures largely control the range of influences that affect infants. One critical aspect of these constraints is the limited sources of danger to which infants are exposed. Parents can be a source of danger or they can fail (or be unable) to protect their infants from a source of danger, but infants cannot expose themselves to danger.

This changes dramatically with the onset of locomotion in toddlerhood. By roughly 15 months of age, most toddlers have clear desires that they are prepared to act on, with or without their attachment figures' support and protection. The world of toddlers contains (1) newly accessible dangers, for example, cars, hot stoves; (2) new contexts, for example, neighbors' yards, preschool; and (3) a wider range of familiar interactants around whom toddlers organize their behavior, for example, siblings, peers, relatives. By the school years, the range of influences on children is increasingly beyond the direct influence of parents. That is, children seek and establish their own peer groups, are placed in schools and classrooms that expose them to new sorts of people who use new strategies, and function in extrafamilial organizations that influence their construction of interpersonal strategies. The onset of puberty is a maturation shift of profound consequence for the function and organization of attachment strategies. Adolescence continues both the pattern of expansion of contexts and children's influence on selecting their own developmental contexts.

Until individuals have experienced this widening array of contexts, it is not possible for them to develop the sophisticated strategies that will be necessary for managing and being safe in complex circumstances. Moreover, although the infant strategies can be seen indistinctly in the behavior of older humans, with increasing age, so much detail is omitted that some theorists and researchers, looking at the sparsity of the infant attachment patterns and the wide variegation of behavior at later ages, have asserted that attachment is a stage-salient issue only in infancy (Erikson, 1950). This perspective does not preclude infant pattern of attachment from having long-term effects across the life span, and there is ample evidence and wide agreement that it does (Farrell-Erickson & Egeland, 1994; Jacobsen & Hofmann, 1997; Rutter & Maughan, 1997; Wartner, Grossmann, Fremmer-Bombik, & Suess, 1994; Waters, Merrick, Treboux, Crowell, & Albersheim, in press; Weinfield, Sroufe, & Egeland, in press). Nevertheless, this perspective is somewhat different from considering that (1) attachment remains a stage-salient function at all ages and (2) the organization of strategies for self-protection is a life-long developmental process that interacts with maturation to permit increasing complexity of organization after infancy. Although the conclusion that attachment is solely an infant issue may be erroneous, the premise seems accurate: the infant patterns provide too limited a range of strategic interpersonal behavior to constitute a sufficient basis for describing self-protective behavior across the entire life span. It seems essential that we elaborate attachment theory, in ways that are compatible with biological maturation and ecological complexity, to reflect the complexity and variation of adult behavior.

Empirical Data Relevant to the Effects of Maturation

There are now many longitudinal sets of data that begin with pattern of attachment in infancy and look for evidence of effects later in life. Three general findings are worth noting here. First, researchers have demonstrated that differences in pattern of attachment in infancy are predictive of differences in social-emotional functioning at later ages (e.g., Belsky, & Youngblade, 1992; Freitag, Belsky, Grossmann, & Grossmann, 1996; Lyons-Ruth, Easterbrooks, & Cibelli, 1997; Ogawa, Sroufe, Weinfield, Carlson, & Egeland, 1997; Suess, Grossmann, & Sroufe, 1992; Urban, Carlson, Egeland, & Sroufe, 1991). Second, the extent of this effect decreases as the time since infancy increases (Carlson, Jacobvitz, & Sroufe, 1995; Erickson, Sroufe, & Egeland, 1985; Freitag et al., 1996; Vaughn, Egeland, Sroufe, & Waters, 1979; Warren, Huston, Egeland, & Sroufe, 1997). There is nothing surprising in these two effects, and they can be demonstrated for other kinds of variables as well. It is noteworthy that neither effect takes maturation into consideration. The second effect, however, leaves open the question of whether refinement in the way we conceptualize attachment at later ages and in the complexity of the models that we use to define continuity might not account for greater portions of the variance in developmental pathways.

The third observation is that, when infancy-based assessments of attachment are applied to older people, the proportion of disorganized and "cannot classify" designations tends to increase with age (Egeland & Sroufe, 1981a; Lyons-Ruth, Repacholi, McLeod, & Silva, 1991; Vondra, Shaw, Swearingen, Cohen, & Owens, in press). This is very difficult to explain. Why should maturation increase the number of inexplicable, maladaptive, or disorganized strategies? Maturation ought to have the opposite effect – that of improving organization and fit of organization to context. The point is that, if we reconceptualize patterning to permit a maturation-based increase in the number and type of subpatterns, we should find the opposite effect from that which is now apparent. When a dynamic model based on maturation is applied, we should find more, and more adaptive, organization at every age, until possibly old age. Although the data are not yet available to test this hypothesis, the theory is articulated, and there are assessments based on this dynamic-maturation approach to attachment theory at all ages except the school years (this is under development). Thus, the hypothesis is testable. Moreover, often it can be tested using existing data sets that require only recoding of archival data.

WHY MIGHT THERE BE DISCONTINUITY IN INDIVIDUALS' FUNCTIONING AND IN TRANSMISSION OF PATTERNS ACROSS GENERATIONS?

Periods of Developmental Discontinuity

Attachment theory has always carried the notion of change in pattern of attachment across individual lives. Bowlby included it implicitly in his notion of developmental pathways, and numerous researchers have referred to the idea that major life events (e.g., loss, divorce, marriage), can precipitate change in interpersonal strategies and representations of relationships. Furthermore, attachment theorists consider psychotherapy to be one way to effect change in attachment relationships. The difference in conceptualization offered here is that maturation itself is presumed to interact with individual functioning in ways that can lead to change in pattern of attachment, that is, mental strategies for managing information and behavioral strategies for keeping the self safe and managing relationships. Two sorts of process might be expected. First, newly maturing competencies could lead to the modification of old strategies to create new substrategies. Second, maturing integrative processes might function more fully, leading to more balanced and flexible strategies.

If maturation generates possibilities for change in strategies, it should follow that the greater the maturational change, the greater the proportion of children whose patterns of attachment would change. If so, periods of rapid maturational change should be associated with (1) individual change in pattern of attachment and possibly (2) changes in the distribution of the patterns of attachment in the population. Based on neurological evidence, a dynamic-maturational perspective predicts two periods of relative discontinuity in strategy – one in the transition from infancy to the preschool years (i.e., around the end of the second year of life), and the other at puberty. Although it is not a focus of the studies in this volume, a third period of discontinuity is predicted for very old age when neurological deterioration combined with greater vulnerability from loss of physical competence, spousal support, and economic resources may lead to increase in the use of Type A patterns of isolation or Type C strategies that elicit both caretaking and comfort.

Preschool Years. A number of new competencies affect children's functioning beginning near the end of the second year of life, that is, during the preoperational shift. These include effective locomotor skills, the ability to regulate display of affect (including use of false positive affect, exaggerated affect, and coyly disarming behavior), use of language, and intuitive awareness of changing contingencies among events. In addition, preschool-aged children begin to function in out-of-home contexts with nonfamilial interactants. The sum of these changes exposes children to new threats while concurrently creating the possibility for more sophisticated self-protective strategies. In particular, as described in Crittenden (1992) and applied in the present volume by Chisholm, Crittenden et al., Hans et al., Moilanen et al., Rauh et al., and Teti, many preschool children organize danger-deflecting and attention-getting strategies. Specifically, those Type A children who are threatened by the absence of parental attention sometimes organize a danger-deflecting strategy of compulsive caregiving (A3), whereas children threatened by anger and violence from caregivers sometimes organize a different danger-deflecting strategy of compulsive compliance (A4) (see Figure 18.2). Organization of the mixed feelings of the Type C pattern of infancy transforms ambivalence into several coercive substrategies. These strategies distort the display of affect by exaggerating part of the child's mixed feelings while inhibiting the display of other feelings, and then alternating the displayed and inhibited feelings on the basis of the changing contingencies of parental behavior. The outcome is a mild version of coercion (C1-2) that is used by many 2-year-olds and a more intense form of the strategy (C3-4) used by children who feel threatened by the unpredictability of parental behavior (see Figure 18.2).

The various aspects of maturation do not occur at one moment in complete form. To the contrary, they first appear in amorphous form and are slowly refined. They also appear at different times, with locomotion preceding language, inhibited negative affect preceding displayed false positive affect that, in turn, precedes split, exaggerated, and alternated coy and angry displays. Consequently, it would be expected that the infant strategies would be transformed progressively, and possibly unevenly, into more sophisticated preschool strategies. Both the evidence regarding the timing of these changes and observations of children's behavior suggest that various aspects of the preschool strategies develop slowly over a period of about a year from roughly 15 to 30 months. The primary effect of the changes is expected to be an increase in the proportion of children using the Type C strategy, with a peak expected around 24 months when children communicate with affect well and with language poorly.

Adolescence. The major neurological changes associated with puberty initiate a period of rapid change that affects adolescents physically, intellectually, emotionally, and psychosocially (Benes, Turtle, Khan, & Farol, 1994; Kostovic,

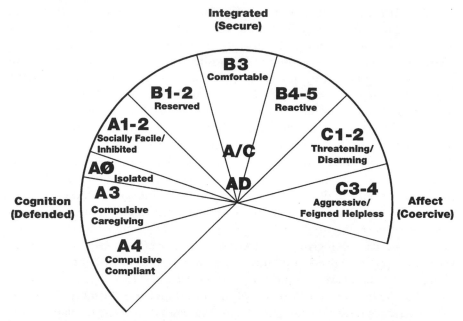

Figure 18.2.   A dynamic-maturational model of attachment: preschool patterns.

Judas, Petanjek, & Simic, 1995; Pujol et al., 1993). However, in spite of clear
awareness that this is a period of profound importance, the neurological
study of it is scanty, with the study of psychological functioning being more
fully developed.

Intellectually, adolescents become able to think about themselves and others in newly complex ways, and, psychosocially, the focus of their interpersonal behavior shifts to a central interest in the other gender. That is,
strategies for attracting a sexual partner must be integrated with existing
strategies for managing attachment relationships (Crittenden, 1997a, c).
Sexuality, together with adolescents' increasing competence with self-care
and their preparation for establishing homes independent of their parents,
creates a new set of circumstances that challenge adolescents. Specifically,
adolescents face the tasks of selecting trustworthy and suitable partners, managing intimacy (while avoiding both isolation from and enmeshment in relationships), regulating sexuality (while avoiding disease and parenthood), and
achieving independence from parental attachment figures. Compared to the
threats facing preschoolers, the threats facing adolescents are largely psychosocial, and the solutions that will resolve them are indeterminate.
Managing them successfully requires far more mental integration than
preschoolers' mastery of a physically threatening environment and hierarchical relationships.

Specifically, suitable information must be gathered, interpreted, and integrated. Thus, one central issue for all adolescents is recognizing others' transformations of information: the omission, distortion, falsification, and misconstruing of information communicated by others (Crittenden, 1997a). In other words, adolescents must learn to differentiate appearance from reality. This requires both savvy intuition and the ability to examine these intuitions consciously to discern true from transformed information and to organize adaptive responses. In many cases, the responses will be more elegant strategies that themselves use transformed information. In addition, adolescents need an increased repertoire of strategies to cope safely with the extrafamilial environment. Put another way, infants and preschool-aged children adapt with increasing *specificity* to their familial context. School-aged children and especially adolescents function in an increasing variety of contexts for which they need a wide range of strategies. Consequently, they adapt by increasing their *variability* of strategy such that they become able to use as many of the strategies as possible, including treacherous strategies.

Four implications of this perspective on adolescence are proposed. First, new substrategies would be expected to be organized. Several of these substrategies have been described elsewhere (Crittenden, 1995) and include compulsive promiscuity (isolated, A5), compulsive self-reliance (A6), obsession with revenge (punitive, C5), and obsession with rescue (seductive, C6) (see Figure 18.3). Second, in the process of expanding strategic competencies and in recognition of the reduced threat from parents, many adolescents would be expected to reverse strategies or reorganize their strategies. That is, there should be a number of A <->C reversals and many adolescents in the process of reorganization, that is, R (A or C->B). The need to reorganize should affect all adolescents, including those using strategies associated with relative safety (i.e., A1-2, B1-5, C1-2); these adolescents need to come to terms with the range of duplicitous strategies that other people use. Third, more A/C combinations would be expected than at younger ages as some adolescents add to their repertoire of strategies without actually integrating the strategies. Finally, in view of the evidence that neurological development extends at least into early adulthood (Benes et al., 1994; Pujol et al., 1993), full integration, particularly of objective and emotional information, would not be expected among adolescents. Neither would full comprehension and integrated use of all transformations of information be expected. Thus, some forms of psychopathology would develop first in adolescence (e.g., schizophrenia), whereas others might require further maturation (e.g., psychopathy).

Transgenerational Transmission. The evidence in support of transgenerational transmission of patterns of attachment has two primary limitations: (1) the highest levels of continuity are associated with Type B attachment, upper-middle-class status, and stability of family circumstances and (2) the larger

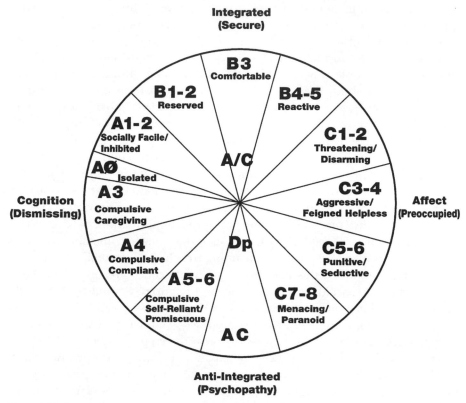

Figure 18.3.   A dynamic-maturational model of attachment: adult patterns.

proportion of variance is not accounted for by the continuity hypothesis. As proposed here, a better hypothesis is that when lack of self-threatening danger is constant, patterns of attachment are likely to be constant, whereas when there is substantial danger, parents' self-protective strategies will often create threat to their children who will organize around that threat. Often that organization will be the reverse of the parents' patterns. Thus, a feigned helpless parent (C4) will often induce a compulsive caregiving (A3) strategy in one or more of the children, or a compulsive compliant (A4) parent will induce aggression in the children (C3). This meshing of opposite strategies is likely to create both superficial harmony and psychological disharmony. This, in itself, is likely to maintain the imbalanced generational swinging between patterns. The issue is more easily understood if one thinks less about "transmitting" patterns in some nebulous, unspecified manner and instead considers what sort of environment (in terms of contingencies and dangers) a parent's pattern is likely to create for children. Because children organize on the basis of experienced contingencies, especially contingencies related to danger, evaluating these in children's developmental context should improve prediction.

Empirical Evidence. This volume provides some preliminary support for the theoretical propositions of (a) discontinuity across the preschool and adolescent periods of maturation, (b) maturation-based change in distributions, (c) individual change in developmental pathways, and (d) transgenerational change in strategy. Several authors have found the correlates of children's behavior to change from infancy to preschool-age and from school age to adolescence (Belsky, Hsieh, & Crnic, 1998; Chess, & Thomas, 1984; Hinshaw, Lahey, & Hart, 1993). The most uniform finding is an increase in the proportion of children classified as Type C from the smallest proportion in infancy to the most frequent classification in the preschool years (chapters 5, 6, 8, 12, & 14, this volume; Teti, Gelfand, Messinger, & Isabella, 1995; see Table 19.2). Similar findings are reported by Fagot and Pears (1996) and Vondra et al. (in press). In addition, there is a corresponding reduction in the proportion of preschool-aged children classified as Type B, as compared to infancy. Furthermore, in those preschool-aged samples that contained endangered children, there were increased proportions of compulsive (A3-4), obsessive (C3-4), compulsive/obsessive combinations (A/C), anxious depressed (AD), and insecure other (IO) classifications (Chisholm, 1998; Crittenden et al., chapter 12 in this volume; Fagot & Pears, 1996; Teti et al., 1995; Vondra et al., in press).

With regard to adolescents, the study by Black and her colleagues (chapter 16, this volume) finds preliminary support for the hypothesis of distributional changes in adolescence that emphasize reorganization, reversals between Types A and C, and A/C combinations. That is, the proportion of Type B adolescents is relatively low, the number of reorganizing classifications and reversals or combinations quite high, and the less balanced classifications are associated with a history of self-threatening experiences or danger. The study by Soares and her colleagues, however, has different findings. In this study, the range of classifications is reduced from infancy, with Types A and C being indistinguishable. Whether this reflects real differences in the underlying populations (American for Black et al. and Portuguese and German for Soares et al.) or merely a difference in methodology cannot be determined from the data presented in the two chapters. The question could be addressed, however, by simply reclassifying both sets of transcripts, in each case using the alternate classificatory system and then analyzing the new classifications in terms of the validating data. It needs to be remembered, however, that the Soares study applied the same method to the mothers' AAIs, so these would also need to be reclassified. Moreover, that study was based on a hypothesis of continuity across generations. If the methods were compared, both hypotheses should be tested, including the dynamic-maturation hypothesis of continuity among the least endangered and discontinuity among the most endangered.

Although there are no group studies testing the hypotheses drawn from a dynamic-maturational approach to attachment theory, several case studies suggest the viability of the perspective. One of these details the conditions of physical abuse and parental pressure for performance that precedes a 4-year-old girl's organization of a compulsively compliant (A4) strategy with her mother and the effect of this strategy in reducing the danger of abuse to the child (Jacobsen & Miller, 1998). Another describes the process of individual change for an endangered child whose mother was extremely rejecting both physically and psychologically beginning from his birth (Hans & Bernstein, August 1995). Videotapes and discussions with Hans and Bernstein suggest that, in the absence of any closeness, warmth, or comforting contact and in the predictable threat of his mother's angry rejection for any trouble that he might cause, the boy organized as a "simple" Type A pattern in infancy, then reorganized to the more complex and self-protective compulsive compliant (A4) pattern in the preschool years. Ultimately, the boy's efforts to find expression for his need for affective engagement focused outside the family and in ways that could be considered both promiscuous (A5) and unacceptably maladaptive. At only 10 years of age, he was found fondling a younger girl and was accused of sexual abuse. There was no evidence that the boy intended harm or that he even understood the sexual aspects of the situation. To the contrary, desire for contact and comfort seems best to explain his behavior. This highlights the conflict between the self-protective function of strategies in the context for which they were organized and their consequences in other, less threatening contexts. This lack of applicability to differently organized contexts is true for all strategies, whether they are compulsive and obsessive strategies for danger that are applied in safe contexts or strategies for safety that are applied in dangerous contexts.

Chisholm describes this process for two children who were removed from a dangerous context, an orphanage in Romania, to the safer context of middle-class homes in Canada. In both cases, the children adapted their strategies to the new context. In one case, the process was an almost complete reorganization that permitted Type B functioning in the new context. The other case was more complex because the receiving home was physically safe but psychologically somewhat threatening. In this case, the child modified her behavior but retained many of the self-protective processes that she used in the orphanage. These processes continued to serve her in terms of immediate self-protection while, nevertheless, reducing her fit to the new environment and, in the context of the high expectations and limited flexibility of her adoptive parents, contributing to unsatisfying relationships.

The studies by Soares et al. and Crittenden et al. address the issue of transgenerational continuity. Both find evidence of such continuity, but both are limited by using assessment methods for the Adult Attachment Interview that constrain the range of possible patterns. In the Soares study, using the Grossmann method, the range was constrained to a secure/anxious distinction. This would obscure any changes between Type A and Type C as well as any subpattern changes within Types A or C. In the Crittenden study, using the Main and Goldwyn method, the range of adult patterns was constrained to the Ainsworth-based patterns, without the expansion of subclassifications now available using the dynamic-maturational method (Crittenden, 1998b, 1999). Given that this was a high-risk, maltreating sample, omission of the subclassifications tied to dangerous circumstances limits substantially the inferences that can be drawn from the findings regarding transgenerational continuity.

Life Changes, Including Unpredictable, Random Events

All researchers working in attachment acknowledge the influence of life events on the organization of attachment behavior. Most, however, think of this influence as operating within the set of patterns established by Ainsworth (with the possible addition of disorganization). Again, the perspective offered here is that the complexity of life changes and unforeseen random occurrences can lead not only to changes among Ainsworth patterns, but also to changes in the set of possibilities itself. Because several aspects of functioning may change at once, particularly in major threats, it becomes impossible to predict exactly how the system of child, parent, family, and context will reorganize and stabilize. Moreover, because many critical events are not related to, or caused by, preexisting aspects of the child or context, these events are unexpected and will affect development in ways that cannot be predicted from infant pattern of attachment. Although this uncertainty may make researchers uneasy, it creates great opportunity for humans to adapt to the ever-changing circumstances of life. It becomes possible that, even when imposed aspects of change are undesirable and self-threatening, the outcome can be greater integration, greater safety, and more satisfying relationships.

Populations with Greater Discontinuity

In spite of evidence of continuity of pattern of attachment, even across generations, there is also strong evidence of change in pattern of attachment in children across periods even as short as six months (e.g., Egeland & Farber, 1984; Sroufe, 1997; Sroufe, Carlson, Levy, & Egeland, in press; Urban et al., 1991; Vaughn et al., 1979). Understanding the reasons for these two apparently conflicting effects is important. The greatest evidence of life-span and transgenerational continuity comes from studies of middle-class, stable populations. That is, the circumstances of the individuals impose little change on them. In such cases, it is not possible to discern whether there is continuity because the individuals' mental processes resist change (i.e., are inflexible once initially organized in early childhood) or whether the circumstances around which the initial organization occurred are unchanged and well managed by the early strategy. That is, the continuity that is observed in stable and safe populations may be dependent on continuity of context rather than continuity of mental and behavioral functioning.

Populations facing unchanging, but complex, danger might show a different pattern. In these situations, strategies that are more complex than infant strategies might be needed. The hypothesis would be that, with development, individuals would change substrategy to a more contextually fine-tuned strategy. This issue is addressed in studies of children of depressed mothers (Teti & Gelfand, 1997a, 1997b), children at risk for behavior disorders (Fagot & Pears, 1996), and normative American adolescent girls (Black et al., chapter 16, this volume). In the first two of these studies, children facing threatening or dangerous circumstances more often showed changes in pattern of attachment at later assessment periods than children in stable and safe environments. In all three studies, endangered children more often used higher subscript strategies. These findings suggest that discontinuity within individuals reflects, at least some of the time, children's ability to use newly maturing potentials to construct more complex strategies that are adaptive, given the constraints of their developmental context.

Populations that experience instability and changing sorts of danger should show the most change. Many of the studies of risk populations focus on populations in which there are many and varied dangers, including dangers that affect one age period but not others. In such situations, there should be considerable flux in patterns of attachment, both from one assessment time to another and from one context or relationship to another. Of interest would be knowing whether the observed changes (i.e., the discontinuity) can be interpreted as reorganizing strategies to better fit changing conditions. If such evidence can be identified, it would be powerful in suggesting the flexibility of human functioning. Evidence of the alternative (that is, maintenance of a no longer adaptive strategy in the face of changing conditions) would be needed to determine that early organizations tended to be stable and fixed over time. It is probable that such an outcome will be found most often in cases of serious, life-threatening danger that occurs early in life and that it will be associated with later psychopathology.

CONCLUSION

It is proposed that a dynamic-maturational theory of attachment can better account for (1) developmental processes, (2) the wide range of variation seen in adult behavior, and (3) human adaptation under all types of geographic and social conditions than can theory that emphasizes life-span continuity within the Ainsworth patterns. Adaptability and flexibility are the hallmark characteristics of humans; change is the process by which we achieve them. This fits well with Bowlby's notion of developmental pathways that branch both at expected times in terms of maturational effects and at unexpected times as a result of accommodation to unpredictable events. Thus, the linear and almost predeterministic "trap" that some people think attachment theory imposes on development after infancy is not possible. Experience, either our own or that of our attachment figures, need not imprison us. To the contrary, maturation opens the door to continuing accommodation to an increasingly varied reality; events outside ourselves offer opportunities to use these maturing intellectual possibilities. The past is fixed, but its meaning is rewritten every time it is recalled. Maturation is the means, and mental integration is the process through which future functioning can be expanded to yield a nearly infinite range of human possibility.

CHAPTER NINETEEN

A Dynamic-Maturational Exploration of the Meaning of Security and Adaptation

Empirical, Cultural, and Theoretical Considerations

PATRICIA McKINSEY CRITTENDEN

The advantages of security of attachment have become a basic tenet of attachment theory. Nevertheless, when non-American and non-middle-class children are considered and when a disorganized or A/C classification is used, fewer than two-thirds of children are classified as *secure*. Furthermore, when attachment is assessed beyond infancy, fewer are secure. These observations motivate a reconsideration of the concept of security. In this closing chapter, some of the empirical, cultural, and theoretical meanings associated with the term *secure* are explored. In the first section, some puzzling data that challenge current notions of security are presented. In the second section, the issue is considered from the dynamic-maturational perspective on attachment theory; several speculative examples of how the model could be used to generate hypotheses about cultural variation are offered. In the final section, an alternative approach to conceptualizing self-protective strategies and adaptation is presented.

SOME PUZZLING FINDINGS

Of all the aspects of attachment that one could address, security seems, on the surface, to be the least problematic or controversial. Nevertheless, a close look at the accumulating data, varied classificatory methods, and expansions of attachment theory suggests quite the opposite. Defining and attributing meaning to security of attachment may underlay critical issues in the study of attachment and may determine how universal or culturally specific attachment theory will become. This section considers two aspects of defining security: the operationalization of the concept through assessments of attachment and its status as the normative and optimal form of attachment relationships.

Security and Classificatory Procedures

What Proportion of Humans Are Securely Attached? The various classificatory procedures that operationalize the concept of security differ in what is considered relevant to classification (the classificatory *method*) and in the array of possible classifications (the classificatory *system*). Although secure attachment is widely believed to be the normative pattern of attachment, accumulating data suggest greater complexity. For example, in their meta-analysis, van IJzendoorn and his colleagues have shown that using the original Ainsworth ABC classifications, 67% of 12-month-old American infants are classified as securely attached whereas, when the A/C or disorganized classifications are used, only 55% are deemed secure (van IJzendoorn & Kroonenberg, 1988; see Table 19.1). Is it the case that more elaborated classificatory methods and expanded models of the patterns yield reduced proportions of securely attached individuals?

It also appears from the data in Table 19.1 that preschool-aged children are substantially less secure than infants and, possibly, that adults may also be less secure. Are older people less often securely attached than infants?

The data in Table 19.2, drawn from the studies in this volume, suggest precisely these conclusions. When one considers the findings of high proportions of security (50% or higher) in Table 19.2, it becomes clear that all but two of these are characterized by (1) use of a nonelaborated classificatory method and nonexpanded classificatory system, (2) application of an infancy procedure to ages beyond 15–18 months, and/or (3) lack of videotaped evidence. The two exceptions are the Crittenden subsample of adequately reared children and the Rauh sample of normative children at 21 months classified with the ABCD method. Notably, these two have the lowest proportions of securely attached children within the "high secure" range. Moreover, the Crittenden subsample is unique in that not only were all "risk" children removed from this subgroup, but also every family was referred by a professional who, after working with the family in well-baby care, found the mother to be fully adequate. As to the Rauh sample, the same children were classified using the PAA as having only 17% Type B classifications. Which set of data is correct?

In this volume, Rauh, Ziegenhain, Müller, and Wijnroks (chapter 14) compared two classificatory methods applied to 12-month old German infants and three methods for 21-month-olds. At 12 months, using the Ainsworth ABC method, 59% of infants were securely attached whereas, using Main and Solomon's ABCD method, only 38% were considered secure. Based on Ainsworth's unidimensional maternal sensitivity scale applied during the first year of life, the Main and Solomon classifications were better validated. At 21 months, using the Ainsworth ABC method, 75% of toddlers were classified as securely attached. With Main and Solomon's ABCD method, 52% were found to be secure. Based on Crittenden's Preschool Assessment of Attachment, only 17% were securely attached. Which set of findings is correct, and does security increase or decrease from 12 to 21 months? When the Ainsworth scale of maternal sensitivity was used as a measure of validity for the 21-month

Table 19.1. Percentage of Subjects Classified as Securely Attached (Type B) in Studies Varying by Age, Context, and Classificatory System

Study	Age	ABC	ABCD	PAA[a]	C & M[b]	Ds/E/F[c]
Van IJzendoorn & Kroonenberg, 1988; Meta-analysis (USA)	12 mo	67%	55%			
Van IJzendoorn et al., 1992; Meta-analysis (clinical)	12 mo	(50%–66%)	(22%–51%)			
Crittenden & Claussen, 1996 (USA)	30 mo			32%	31%	
Fagot & Pears, 1996 (USA)	30 mo			35%		
Moore et al., 1994 (USA)	30 mo			39%		
Stevenson-Hinde & Shouldice, 1995 (UK), middle SES	54 mo				54%	
Turner, 1991 (UK), middle SES	2–6 yr				60%	
Speltz et al., 1990 (USA)	2–6 yr				73%	
(Clinical)	2–6 yr				(16%)	
Van IJzendoorn & Bakermans-Kranenberg, 1996; Meta-analysis (mixed nationalities)	Adult					58%
(Low SES)	Adult					(48%)
(Clinical)	Adult					(13%)
Fonagy et al., 1996 (UK), middle SES	Adult					61%
(Clinical)	Adult					22%

[a] Preschool Assessment of Attachment.
[b] Cassidy-Marvin Preschool System.
[c] Adult Attachment Interview.

Table 19.2. Distributions of Patterns of Attachment in Different Samples, at Different Ages, and in Different Cultures, Using Varied Classificatory Methods

Study, Sample, Age, Classificatory System	Type A	Type B	Type C	Other (A3–4); (C3–4)
Grossmann: German normative, 12 mo., ABC	50[a]	30	13	7-CC
Ahnert: German, 12 mo., ABC	42	45	10	X[b]
Ahnert: Russian, 12 mo., ABC	18	63	14	X
Teti: depressed, 12 mo., ABCD	17	20	23	40-D
Teti: nondepressed, 12 mo., ABCD	10	70	10	10-D
Teti: depressed, 21 mo., PAA	19 (50)	13	39 (50)	29-A/C, IO
Teti: nondepressed, 21 mo., PAA	26 (50)	44	22 (0)	9-A/C, IO
Moilanen: 18 mo., singleton, PAA	44 (25)[c]	22	22 (50)	6-IO
Moilanen: 18 mo., twins, PAA	40 (0)	40	17 (0)	2-IO
Lis: at adoption (18 mo.), written observation	20 (25)	0	80 (81)	X
Lis: at followup, 3 yr., written observation	7 (100)	93	0(0)	X
Crittenden: 12–30 mo., maltreated, A,B,C,A/C	31	28	8	33-A/C
Crittenden: 12–30 mo., adequate, A,B,C,A/C	27	60	0	13-A/C
Crittenden: 30–48 mo., maltreated, PAA	52 (77)	5	24 (30)	19-A/C, IO
Crittenden: 30–48 mo., adequate, PAA	21 (33)	58	21 (0)	0
Crittenden: maltreating mothers, AAI–M & G	36	7	57 (60)[d]	X
Crittenden: adequate mothers, AAI–M & G	28	41	31 (56)[d]	X
Rauh: 12 mo., ABC	25	59	9	X
Rauh: 12 mo., ABCD	16	38	7	39-D

(continued)

Table 19.2 *(continued)*

Study, Sample, Age, Classificatory System	Type A	Type B	Type C	Other (A3–4); (C3–4)
Rauh: 21 mo., ABC	11	75	8	X
Rauh, 21 mo., ABCD	3	52	3	39-D
Rauh: 21 mo., PAA	31 (52)	17	40(30)	9-A/C, IO
Bohlin: 4 yr., Cassidy-Marvin	17	62	21	X
Chisholm: 4.5 yrs., PAA	27 (42)	36 (38)[e]	14 (0)	20 A/C, IO
Lippe: 5–8 yrs., PAA	17 (17)	33	50 (17)	0
Lippe: 5–8 yrs., PAA	54 (42)	14	14 (50)	14 depr.
Black: 16 yr., AAI–(Dynamic-Maturation sys.)	31 (22)	34	17 (17)	17 (33)
Soares: 16–17 yr., AAI-(Grossmann system)	22 (A & C)	78	X	X
Soares: mothers, AAI-(Grossmann system)	30 (A & C)	70	X	X

[a] Entries consist of percentages of sample (or subsample).

[b] "X" indicates that this category was not used.

[c] Entries in parentheses consist of percentages of the cell proportion; thus, in this case, 25% of the Type A singletons were classified as A3 or A4.

[d] These entries refer to fearfully preoccupied classifications.

[e] This entry refers to "Secure Other."

classifications, there were no relations with the ABC classifications and equally strong relations for the ABCD and PAA classifications. When the two-dimensional CARE-Index assessment of maternal sensitivity (that differentiated maternal control from unresponsiveness) was applied to the same videotapes, there was no support for the ABC classifications at 21 months, mild support for the ABCD classifications in differentiating secure from anxious, and stronger support for the PAA in differentiating all three groups (Ziegenhain, Simo, & Rauh, August 1996). So how many 21-month-old infants were securely attached?

Some Problems with Reliability. The data in both Tables 19.1 and 19.2 suggest that age and classificatory method/system are issues to be resolved as we attempt to define security. They also confirm that high-risk status (i.e., exposure to danger) is associated with elevated rates of anxious attachment. The Strange Situations of 12-month-old infants from the former German Democratic Republic (GDR) and Soviet Russia in the Ahnert et al. study (chapter 4, this volume) highlight the issue of confusion of Type B with very anxious forms of attachment. The full set of Strange Situations was classified separately by Karin Grossmann and myself. Using the original ABC system, Grossmann found 42% secure. Using a method including both A/C and D classifications, I found 14% secure; overall, we had only 50% agreement, with the major disagreement being Type B versus very anxious attachment[1]. Conferencing the tapes did not resolve the disagreement. (Later it became clear that Grossmann and I agreed on the classification *if classification method and system were restricted to the original Ainsworth procedure;* we disagreed on whether these were appropriate restrictions.) The disagreement was both troubling to us and difficult to explain to the researchers. Ultimately, the Grossmann classifications were selected for analysis in Ahnert's study, and, with Ahnert's agreement, eight of the "disagreement" tapes were sent to five expert coders who were not told anything about the tapes.

We sought skilled coders who were internationally recognized, used varied classificatory methods and systems, and varied with regard to language and culture. Including Grossmann and myself, these tapes were classified by seven coders. Of these, four spoke German, with one from the former GDR; one (myself) was trained by Ainsworth, one by Main, three by Sroufe, and two by Crittenden. In terms of expertise, one was a clinician with a specialty in infancy, one an expert on disorganization, three had experience with child maltreatment, and two had experience with middle-class American and German infants and mothers.

---

[1] The same issue occurred in the early application of the Strange Situation to high-risk samples.

Originally, it had been intended that the results would be published in tabular form. This was not done because three of the coders were unable to assign classifications to the infants; they found the patterns of behavior to be too unusual to fit even the disorganized or A/C classifications. Three of the five coders found no evidence of security at all. The fourth coder identified three securely attached infants, and the fifth also found one of these to be secure. In the remaining cases, an assortment of disorganized and A/C combinations were most common, together with an occasional compulsive caregiving (A3) or feigned helpless (C4) classification.

Because there were no cases on which there was agreement on exact classification, but there was agreement regarding observed behavior, a descriptive approach was taken (Hinde, 1995). Among the coders' observations were that the mothers were unusually silent with little interaction, including a lack of soothing of upset infants and a lack of frontal positioning. Many mothers appeared sad and depressed, as compared to the strangers who appeared overbright and a bit intrusive in their willingness to approach and pick up the infants. Several of the infants were unusually passive and/or displayed unusual and unexpected shifts in behavior. Some infants seemed superficially cheerful but were vigilant of their mothers and were more easily calmed by the strangers than their mothers. More than one child was described as having autistic-like behavior (rocking, holding arms out at elbow level, blank stares, jerky movements, lying prone, huddling, reaching for the mother combined with looking away from her, screeching cries). Several of the infants who had been quite upset calmed themselves when their mothers returned.

Coder characteristics were considered in an attempt to understand the variation in classification. Training did not make a difference, as long as the coder recognized that some infants could be outside the system being applied. Being German did not affect the classifications, although the coder raised in the former GDR found the infants to be less disturbed than did other coders. Interestingly, the clinician was least concerned about "psychopathology," and the expert on disorganization found the tapes most unfamiliar. The coders with experience in child abuse and neglect felt that, although the tapes were very unusual and often disturbing, these infants did not resemble maltreated infants.

Using elaborated classificatory methods and/or expanded classificatory systems consistently reduced the proportion of Type B infants that was identified and increased the number of disorganized, A/C, A3, C4, and "unclassifiable" infants. Specifically, classificatory methods that (1) included the possibility of false positive behavior, (2) interpreted infant behavior in the light of preceding and concurrent maternal behavior, (3) compared behavior across all the episodes, and (4) considered behaviors not described by Ainsworth had the lowest proportions of Type B infants.

These findings are controversial but important. Because all of the coders were well trained and reliable, it becomes very important to understand why there was such great disagreement. (Similar issues have been reported by Kisilevsky and colleagues [1998] and Saarni [1998]). Furthermore, it is very significant that the disagreement was between Type B and "not-A-B-C-*or*-D," with most coders finding high levels of very anxious[2], even unrecognizable, attachment. Unfortunately, reliable validating data are not available because (1) the Ainsworth sensitivity measure was applied by coders who knew the dyads well and (2) the coders were not trained to reliability on a standardized set of videotapes and, therefore, may have used the sensitivity scale in culture-specific ways (see discussion in Chapter 7). Nevertheless, our ability to interpret the results of the Ahnert study hinges on the distinction between Type B and very anxious attachment, as does our understanding of security itself.

Cultural Variation and "Normalcy"

Cultural Variation in What Is Normal. Three classic studies suggest that there may be cultural variation in distributions of patterns of attachment: a North German sample had a high proportion of Type A infants (Grossmann et al., 1985), whereas Japanese (Miyake, Chen, & Campos, 1985) and Israeli (Oppenheim, Sagi, & Lamb, 1988; Sagi, Lamb, Lewkowicz, Shoham, Dvir, & Egtes, 1985) samples had high proportions of Type C infants. Although van IJzendoorn and Kroonenberg (1988) found greater within-culture than between-culture variation, it is IJzendoorn's conclusion that cultural differences in the distributions of pattern of attachment are not precluded by these findings (van IJzendoorn, 1990). Data from low income and risk samples consistently show substantial decreases in the proportion of children who are considered securely attached when contexts are less supportive and, especially, less safe (see Tables 19.1 and 19.2). In addition, if one looks beyond the attachment literature to the cross-cultural literature in general, it becomes apparent that cultures differ on a great many variables, but that the variables on which variation will be found depend on the specific cultures or subcultures being compared. Finding a way to summarize the diverse findings may require moving to a higher, meta-level of analysis. Both Sagi (1990) and van IJzendoorn (1990) have implied the need for a theory-based hypothesis regarding cultural differences. In keeping with the perspective offered in the

---

[2] As noted below, the terms applied to attachment patterns carry strong evaluative meanings. Consequently, where possible, alphanumeric identifiers have been used. Certainly, calling the "not-A-B-C-or-D" patterns "very anxious" imposes a negative evaluation on them. The lack of unbiased labels highlights an important issue in attachment research and helps to explain the intense feelings elicited by the coding of the Strange Situations in this study.

theory chapters in this volume, it is proposed that differences in the sorts of danger found in the compared cultures and the strategies that could be used to minimize the effects of these dangers constitute a basis for cultural differences in the use of self-protective strategies.

Understanding the Ahnert et al. Data from the GDR and Soviet Russia. This suggests a way to think about Ahnert's data. Presuming that the cases of disagreement regarding B versus very anxious are resolved in favor of a not-A-B-C-*or*-D classification (the majority finding for each of the eight cases), both the findings of the study itself (because the data used were biased toward Type B) and the interpretation of the findings change. If the Crittenden classifications of the entire sample had been used, the former GDR would have had many Type A and A/C infants, whereas the Russian sample would have had a bias toward Type C (i.e., B3 to C4). If this were more or less accurate, how could it be explained? Ahnert et al. provide the explanation in their introduction: the socialist culture sought to minimize the bond between mother and child and to foster the child's connection to the community. This is consistent with (1) the mothers' depressed appearance when they may have felt confusion between their natural proclivities and the cultural value that they should not comfort their infants who clearly wanted closeness and (2) the contrastingly bright, almost intrusive, behavior of the strangers who were licensed by the culture to approach and console the infants. In other words, the adults appeared to be acting in concert with the socialist values described by Ahnert et al. Both Bronfenbrenner (1970) for Soviet Russia and Leuzinger-Bohleber and Garlichs (1993) for the GDR report similar processes for older children using different measures. Such behavior can be expected to assist children to fit into the culture successfully, but it does so at some personal cost to the happiness and comfort of mothers and infants (cf. Hinde, 1991). Given a choice between long-term safety and immediate happiness, the mothers may have chosen safety for both themselves and their children. This seems adaptive and not psychopathological in the infants' developmental context (cf. Belsky, 1997b). However, as Grossmann points out, preparing an infant to fit well in one cultural context may reduce the fit to other contexts (Karin Grossmann with reference to infants from the United States, Japan, and Papua New Guinea, cited by Karen [1994, pp. 418–419]).

The Ahnert et al. study illustrates two issues that are central to theory: the problems of operationalizing attachment theory in coding procedures and, depending on what one considers valid observations relevant to classifying pattern of attachment, the issues of cultural influence on pattern of attachment (or, as I prefer to think of it, on mental and behavioral strategies for coping with danger). Ahnert's data are particularly fascinating because they were gathered before the political changes in the socialist countries. Because these changes have an impact on the types of danger experienced in the culture, these infants who began life in one cultural context but will develop in another provide a naturally occurring test of resilience. Which of these children will develop the adaptability to function well under both sets of cultural conditions? That people can manage this is abundantly clear. Some people who were very successful in the socialist culture have managed to adapt to the new conditions and be successful in them as well,[3] whereas others have become depressed at their losses, angry at failed expectations, or passively helpless as they await rescue from their misery. Learning what predicts how individuals will adapt is a crucial issue (cf. Jose et al., 1998). Follow-up of the Ahnert samples would be informative.

Psychopathology and Normative Distributions. What is psychopathological, and does it differ by culture? There is some evidence that rates of psychopathology may be relatively universal at about 15 to 20% of any given population (Dilling, Weyerer, & Castell, 1984; Hagnell, Öjesjö, Otterbeck, & Rorsman, 1994; Kessler, 1994; Roberts, Attkisson, & Rosenblatt, 1998; Rutter & Rutter, 1993; Schepank, 1987), whereas the diagnoses that are applied to the pathological individuals may be specific to cultures and even historical cohorts within cultures (Richters & Cicchetti, 1993). This could reflect different value judgments placed by both the culture and individuals on the various strategies for coping with danger (Bar-on et al., 1998). For example, comparison of two sets of AAI classifications drawn from the United Kingdom (Crittenden, April 1997) and Italy (Crittenden, 1999) suggests several (very preliminary) conclusions:

1. The distributions of the normative population differ, with the (middle-class) U.K. distribution having a Type A bias (specifically centering on B1-2/A1-2) and the Italian distribution having a Type C bias (B4/C1-2) and a second peak around A3-4.
2. The distributions of the population in treatment for psychopathology differ as almost an inverse of the normative distribution, that is, essentially never Type B and, for the British, Type C3-6, whereas, for the Italians, it is Types A4-5 and A4-5/C. This leads to the observation that what is considered psychopathological in British and Italian culture may not be the same and reflects what is considered normative and adaptive within each culture. It would be extremely interesting to know which attachment patterns were most closely associated with psychopathology in the former GDR and Soviet Russia. For example, would open and direct discussion of cultural/political discrepancies (a Type B-like

---

[3] Based on the perspective offered here, these resiliently adaptive individuals should fall along the integrated continuum from B3 to psychopathic AC. The actual proportion from different parts of this continuum might reflect the distribution in the pre-change distribution.

behavior) be a sufficiently dangerous strategy as to be considered psychopathological?

Meaning?

What do these findings mean? Is secure attachment a function of age, of context, of culture, and even of classificatory system? Are infants more securely attached than older children and adults? Do certain cultures display less secure attachment? Should we select classificatory systems by their ability to yield two-thirds of a middle-class, Western sample as securely attached? Does security vary, in predictable ways, across the life span? Do the ABC strategies differ in their adaptiveness, given contexts that differ in safety?

Although many of these questions cannot be answered empirically at this time, the data on different classificatory procedures are clear. Different classificatory methods and systems do yield different distributions. Moreover, whenever we look more closely at behavior and compare it across episodes and between mother and infant, we find fewer Type B children. Furthermore, whenever the array of possible classifications is expanded, there is a reduction of the number of children classified as securely attached. Finally, expanded classificatory systems consistently account for greater variance in validating variables than less differentiated systems. This indicates the importance of stating clearly the universe of classificatory options open to coders when reporting findings; failure to state this can lead to inaccurate comparisons and interpretations.

Furthermore, the data on risk are clear. Whenever children are at risk, that is, when they are exposed to danger, the proportion of securely attached children drops. The meaning of this is less clear. The hypothesis proposed here is that some anxiously attached children may be using the most adaptive strategy for reducing danger and increasing safety, given the constraints of their environment. If this is so, one must ask if the secure strategy of open and direct communication regarding feelings and intentions is always the best strategy. Possibly, use of all of the strategies, each in the appropriate context, is most adaptive. Unfortunately, in spite of the array of excellent assessments, no assessments of attachment fully assess the capacity to select and implement strategies that are adapted to specific and varied contexts. The notion of adaptability to varying contexts is addressed in the next section.

THEORETICAL ISSUES

Pattern of Attachment and Self-protective Strategies

Behind all of these issues lie more basic questions regarding the meaning and value of security of attachment. One of these questions concerns the ostensible superiority of security to all other strategies. Although there is considerable evidence that (in relatively safe contexts) Type B is the optimal strategy, the universality of this conclusion has been questioned (Sagi, 1990). Indeed, if security were as uniformly advantageous as it is reported to be, we must wonder why it is not "hard-wired" into our genetic heritage. That it is not implies that anxious attachment may have some protective value (Hinde & Stevenson-Hinde, 1990). This probably has to do with ecological variations in safety and the need of humans to respond flexibly to a wide variety of potential dangers. That is, it is hard to understand how safe environments and sensitive caregivers could have generated a selective advantage for those humans who displayed attachment behavior. To the contrary, only the relative ubiquity of danger and variation in parental protection could have resulted in the opportunity for attached children to fare better than children who were less attentive and responsive to changes in parental availability. Furthermore, because danger varies, the strategy that best identifies and protects children from danger may vary from individual to individual and context to context.

One problem in understanding security is the labels given to the ABC groups in infancy. These are both evaluative and inconsistent with regard to referent condition. "Secure" is clearly the most desirable label. It refers to an internal state that implies both feeling safe and the condition of actually being safe. Unsafe children are almost never found to be secure. "Avoidant" is the least desirable term. It refers to a behavior used by Type A infants but not by older Type A individuals. At later ages, all classificatory systems use other terms, for example, neutral, inhibited, or dismissing. "Ambivalent," on the other hand, is relatively undesirable and refers to an internal state that does not necessarily reflect actual differences in safety. This lack of synchrony in class of referent among the terms highlights a fundamental issue. Is security (1) a positive affective state, that is, happiness or comfort, (2) the condition of safety, (3) a particular set of behaviors, for example, signaling or approach on reunion, (4) the functional use of behavior to establish open and direct communication of thoughts and feelings, together with negotiation and compromise, or (5) a strategy for maximizing the probability of safety? Is it, in other words, a definable and stable state, a specific behavioral or functional strategy, or a systemic interaction of self with context such that the probability of safety is maximized? Is the Type B strategy the best strategy under all conditions?

On the answer to these questions will hinge our selection of classificatory procedures and thus the proportion of individuals identified as secure. I wish to propose that "strategy for maximizing the probability of safety, given variation in context" should be the defining characteristic of *adaptive* attachment. This leaves open the possibility that safety may be achieved in different ways under different circumstances. It also permits security, in both infancy and beyond infancy, a strategy of open and direct communication with attachment figures of needs and desires, together with negotiation of differences in these, that functions to protect the attached person, both physically and psychologically.

Because the term *secure* carries an inherent positive value (and anxious attachment an inherent negative value), the association of the word *secure* with Type B attachment may have misled us into making value judgments prematurely (Hinde, 1991; Sagi, 1990). On the other hand, the term *anxious* carries negative connotations, in spite of its self-protective function. Similarly, the terms associated with Types A and C carry only negative associations, even though the strategies have desirable features. For example, Type A functioning implies independence, predictability, and trustworthiness, whereas Type C individuals can be lively, persuasive, and loyal. That, of course, was Bowlby's point when he recommended to Ainsworth that she not label the groups until she knew the empirical meaning of the groupings. Although she followed Bowlby's advice with regard to her own data, others have applied the labels in preference to the letter codes. Nevertheless, it may still be premature to presume that we understand the value of strategies in all cultural contexts. It may be that the differences in the proportions of Type B children and adults that are reported in the literature are both real and also adaptive. To address this issue, we must consider the *function* of attachment behavior, that is, to promote safety. Because contexts vary, the "secure" pattern of open and direct communication of needs and desires may not always be protective. It is, however, generally comfortable, and it is this term that Ainsworth suggested when I was seeking a label for the B3 pattern for the Preschool Assessment of Attachment. I used the term, and, as with almost all of Ainsworth's suggestions, it not only fit the immediate circumstances, but it also opened the door to new and productive thought. Perhaps the Type B strategy is "comfortable" in both advantageous and dangerous ways, depending on the context in which it is applied.

Should the terminology be changed, and is it possible to select terms that are descriptive, nonpejorative, and suitable across the entire life span? Although I generally agree with Bowlby that the alphanumeric terminology might be best, it does seem that descriptive labels are useful. The dynamic-maturation model that I propose offers a simple rationale for selecting terms. The Type A strategy is organized around temporally ordered, "cognitive" information, whereas the Type C strategy is affectively organized. Type B is *balanced* with regard to these. From this perspective, it is easy to label Type C *affective*. Type A is more problematic: *cognitive? logical? temporal?* I prefer *cognitive* but recognize that this term does not carry its usual meaning and is not, therefore, immediately meaningful to everyone. In any case, it is important that the labels used carry both a descriptive and nonevaluative quality.

Finally, it is important to recognize that, when pattern of attachment is conceptualized using the dynamic-maturational approach, the patterns are not categorical. To the contrary, they are best described in terms of two dimensions: source of information (cognition and affect) and degree of integration. The pattern designations identify which transformations of information (e.g., falsified affect, distorted cognition) are used most frequently by individuals using specified patterns. Thus, the patterns can be organized around the extent to which they reflect Type A or Type C functioning.

Culture and Self-protective Strategies

Culture can be defined in many ways. From the perspective of attachment theory, the central issues are (1) sources of danger (both historic and current) and (2) the strategies for coping with danger. Although consideration of these issues can be accomplished somewhat from within a culture, comparisons among cultures can make clear assumptions that are built into cultures and, therefore, are largely invisible from within the culture (i.e., "It's a cinch fish didn't discover water," attributed to M. McLuhan). These assumptions become most evident when they are violated, as they are by maladaptive people within the culture and by people from other cultures. The perspective here is on variations in dangers experienced by different cultures and the effect that these may have on the way cultures organize.[4]

Several speculative examples are given: Finland, Sweden, Russia, Italy, and Egypt. Because there are not sufficient data to support the hypotheses, descriptive information is offered (Hinde, 1996, 1995). The interpretations are not meant as absolutes; instead, the intent is to demonstrate a way of thinking about culture that applies to groups of individuals including cultural groups,[5] the same concepts that are used to define individual self-protective attachment strategies. In the discussion that follows, cultures are described as being biased toward Type A or Type C *without regard to the proportion of Type B cases.* That is, if there is a difference in the proportion of Type A versus Type C and if that difference is also reflected in the subgroups within Type B, then the culture is described as being biased toward the more frequent pattern of these two. Differences in the extent of the bias are noted, when this is relevant, by the modal subclassification, ranging from B1-2 to A5-6 for Type A or from B4-5 to C7-8 for Type C (see Figure 18.3).

---

[4] For a similar perspective, see Bukowski & Sippola (1998), discussions of inhibition by Rubin (1998) and Chin, Hastings, Rubin, Chen, & Stewart (1998), and Hinde's finding regarding the effects of separation on rhesus monkeys (Hinde, 1991).

[5] The same process would work equally well for families (e.g., Byng-Hall, 1995).

Three Related Northern Cultures. Cultures develop over long periods of time and reflect not simply the current conditions, but also historical sources of danger, including geographic/climatic conditions (cf. Diamond, 1997). A comparison of Finland with its neighbors Sweden and Russia and with Italy may clarify my meaning. Historically, the danger in Finland has been the winter. Disease and starvation could be minimized if, during the short summer, one worked hard to prepare for winter. Thus, Finns (with a cultural bias toward Type A; see Moilanen et al., chapter 8, this volume) organized around a predictably dangerous future and inhibited activity based on immediate feelings in favor of safety later. Nevertheless, during the winter, the period of darkness was long, the food monotonous and meager, and the light and warmth faint. These conditions, particularly when feelings about them were inhibited and, therefore, also uncomforted, could lead to depression. On the other hand, expression of such feelings was futile and also dangerous. Family members experienced the same conditions, and expressing one's personal distress was a reminder to all of their own distress. Through affect contagion, uncontrolled expression of negative affect could endanger both one's self and one's family and lead, through the opposite (Type C) route, to depression. Silence, patience, and any "false" cheer that could be generated might be better. Thus, depression and its ultimate expression, suicide, were the dangers of both overinhibition of negative affect and unrestrained negative affect (see discussion in chapter 13, this volume).

In Adult Attachment Interviews, a bias toward inhibition of affect appeared as distanced and minimized discussions of the facts of childhood (which, in the past, often included much time alone and harsh, predictable punishment), told with little reference to the self and almost no expression of affect. In Strange Situations, Finnish infants were quiet and self-contained, as were their mothers. During departures and reunions, the infants concentrated on the toys and cried very little; there was very little physical contact. Instead, both mothers and infants were quiet and calm.

No wonder then that, along with being reliable and straightforward, Finns seem reserved, uncomfortable in exuberant social groups, and a bit melancholy even in the brilliance of long summer days. However, when Finns explain their culture to others, they focus on two historical events: the domination of Finland first by Sweden and later by Russia. Compared to many other countries, however, these two invasions had, in fact, relatively limited consequences. Finns were not sold into slavery, their sons were not murdered, their women were not raped and sent off in prostitution. Yet even now Finns retell these defeats with uneasy references to their powerful neighbors. In addition, only one generation ago as a result of World War II, many Finnish families were uprooted from Karelia (which became a part of Russia) and forced to relocate as refugees within current Finland. In addition, almost 90,000[6] Finnish children were sent to Sweden and other countries in part because, with the men at war, not enough food could be grown to feed the population. Often several such separations occurred, while among those children who remained in Finland, there was considerable malnutrition. One outcome is a still-continuing sadness among Finns. These events preoccupy their attention, whereas they do not dwell at length on the long winters.

Understanding this phenomenon requires thinking again about strategies and their function. Winter is the dominant and unrelenting danger, but it is one for which Finns are prepared. Winter and a strategy of inhibition of affect and organization around predictable outcomes are the ground Finns walk on. It is depression and invasion by powerful neighbors that are to be feared. These dangers are not so well addressed by the Type A strategy and are, therefore, more dangerous to Finns. It might well serve a culture biased toward Type A to remember the dangers of their own strategy carried too far, the limits of their strategy, and the treachery of their neighbors. Possibly the inscription carved in the stone fortress that defends Helsinki encapsulates this knowledge about danger and safety: *Seiso tässä omalla pohjallasi, äläkä luota vieraan apuun.* [Stand on your own ground and do not trust in the help of strangers.] Finns, however, do not inhibit affect completely. Culturally, it is channeled into the expressive arts, in which Finns excel. Personally, it is displayed, often with a poignant sincerity and warmth that is made more profound by comparison with Finnish reserve, when relationships are safe and self-protective strategies are not needed.

The neighbors themselves are of interest. Bohlin and her colleagues have noted the higher than expected proportion of Type C children in their Swedish sample (see Table 19.2). In a second sample of 25-month-old children classified using the PAA, this effect was even greater, as was a near absence of Type A children (Bohlin, personal communication, January 1999). Indeed, the bias in this subsample was toward B4/C1-2, with a significant number of C3-4 classifications. The very great preponderance probably reflects the interaction of (1) a cultural bias toward Type C with (2) near universal use of day care, and (3) a maturational effect that, at 24 months, coincides with the peak of the Type C effect of affective negotiation of hierarchy in relationships. This portrays a robust culture, unafraid of aggression and able to disarm it before it becomes dangerous. My own viewing of 25 Strange Situations of these Swedish mothers and their children is that the mothers were generally playful and nonrestrictive with children who sought attention with either threats or displays of incompetence and that these signals elicited responses only after repetition or intensification. Indeed, the majority of these Swedish children screamed quickly and loudly upon separation. In

[6] Live births in 1939 were 78,000 (*Statistical Yearbook of Finland,* 1992).

other words, Swedish culture may use the exaggerated display of affect strategically. Two points are of interest here. First, Sweden and Finland share the
geographic effects of winter, and yet the cultures appear to have selected different, indeed opposite, strategies. Why? Possibly, Sweden's more central location with regard to other European cultures is relevant to its greater focus on
interpersonal and hierarchical strategies. On the other hand, the different
genetic background of the cultures may be relevant (i.e., the genetic differences may reflect temperamental biases that affect selection of strategy). Or it
is possible that Sweden is undergoing a postwar change of strategy, from Type
A to Type C, reflecting the greater peace, prosperity, and safety of the end of
the twentieth century. (The epidemiological data on mental illness are consistent with this notion.) The issue, however, is not *why* different strategies were
selected, but rather accurate description of the variation and the function,
within each culture, of the strategies.

Finland's neighbor to the east is Russia. Not surprisingly, Russia is also a
culture biased toward Type C strategies and away from Type A. In this case,
however, my viewing of the Russian videotapes from the Ahnert sample suggests a different form of Type C, one that emphasizes passivity. The Russian
mothers in the Ahnert sample seemed more affectively in tune with (or sensitive to) their children, but also less responsive, than Bohlin's Swedish mothers. Put another way, the Russians seemed to commiserate with their children
but were less eager to take action as compared to the Swedes. They seemed to
submit to the burdens of life both without protest and also with sympathy for
their children. For a similar finding with regard to Russian adolescents, see
Jose et al. (1998). Although it may seem lacking in empirical support, my
viewing of Russian portraiture and family scenes in the State Tretyakov
Gallery was consistent with this perspective. The most outstanding feature was
the compelling and involving effect of the facial expressions and bodily poses
on the viewer; one was drawn affectively into the paintings. The expressions
themselves ranged from disarming to appealing to submissive and fearful,
except in the very small proportion of cases (about 10 to 15% of the whole) in
which the expression was of arrogance, power, and cruel cunning, that is, the
other half of the Type C strategy, in its extreme and ruthless form. Has
Russian culture organized around widespread use of a Type C2/4/6 strategy
of affective cohesion, shared and idealized values for the future, and the display of helpless submission that elicited protection (and sometimes domination) from the smaller proportion of powerful (and sometimes deceptively
wrathful) Type C3/5 leaders? If this hypothesis is entertained, then the recent
political changes in Russia seem to be more a change in appearance than a
cultural change in strategy.

Framed this way, Finland is located between two Type C cultures, one
robust and energetic and the other alternating between passively helpless and
powerful. While using a Type A strategy themselves, Finns shared with Swedes

a belief in being able to shape their own destiny and with Russians a melancholy over that which could not be controlled. In both cases, however, Finns felt the need to be alert to possible aggression and treachery.

Again, it is important to note that these are simplified hypotheses. Full description of self-protective strategies in any culture would require consideration of (1) subgroups with a culture and (2) the function in the culture of the nondominant strategies. That is, all cultures appear to have all patterns, with the differences being in the distribution of the patterns.

Two Mediterranean Cultures. Italy presents almost the opposite situation to Finland. Few people die of the cold in Italy, and the long summer makes it easy to set aside sufficient food for the winter. Earthquakes and volcanoes pose threats, but these are unpredictable and infrequent. Better to trust luck than to try to prepare. On the other hand, Italy's location and terrain make its land desirable, but historically travel between regions has been difficult. Not only have waves of outsiders sought to settle on the Italian peninsula, but also neighboring groups of people have sought to enlarge the share of land they controlled. Historically, for an Italian, the danger lay with other people, people who might want your land and who might be willing to deceive to get it. Differentiating friend from foe would be crucial under such circumstances. This could lead to a strategy of group cohesion, of mutual dependence on trusted others, and of customs, for example, food and language, that readily differentiated "us" from "them." Key elements of survival would become affective resonance within one's trusted group, threatening affect toward outsiders, use of false cognition to mislead others with regard to one's intentions, and expectation that others would use false affect and coercion. Of course, being forced to function so closely with others can be limiting and irritating. Stresses within one's group can create bitterness, coalitions, and changing balances of power. In such circumstances, the source of comfort and safety can also feel like restriction and control. Indeed, one could become quite ambivalent about trusted family relationships; the aphorism *"L'amore non é bello se non é litigarello"* [Love is not special if there is no struggle] captures some of these mixed feelings. The Type C strategy of alternating affective displays appears to typify many Italian adults (Crittenden, 1999).

But the distribution is not really that simple. Extreme Type C behavior seems almost to compel certain types of responses. The distribution of 146 Adult Attachment Interviews reported in Crittenden (1999) suggests a bimodal culture in which there is a considerable proportion of compulsive Type A patterns. This is supported by the histories reported in many AAIs. Type A3 speakers often report having had helpless, incompetent (Type C2/4) parents who needed rescue. Type A4 speakers often report having angry unpredictable (Type C3/5) parents who were watched vigilantly and obeyed promptly. Speakers classified as A5 often reported similar histories, combined with an ineffective strategy that, by adolescence, led to the speaker's choosing to withdraw from intimate human relationships. The reverse holds true for the histories reported by many of the Type C speakers: their parents were affectively distant and easily manipulated through the use of angry blame or incompetence. The process by which this occurs can be inferred from observing mothers and children in Strange Situations. At 12 months, many infants attempted to use avoidance during departures and reunion, but their mother rarely permitted it. Instead, they called goodbye at the door until the infant cried, and then they left. Similarly, on reunion, they called out until the avoiding infant reached and cried. Italian mothers appeared uncomfortable with infant avoidance. As preschoolers, many children either immediately satisfied maternal desires (a compulsive Type A pattern)[7] or struggled openly with the mother (Type C). Thus, Italy appears to be a complex culture in which balance is achieved through an alternation of strategies both across generations and within the culture. However, the dominant, that is, normative, strategy is Type C, generally in the B4-C1-2 range. In that context, it is individuals using one of the compulsive Type A strategies, that is, A3-5 or A3-5/C, who more often seek psychotherapy than individuals using a Type C strategy (Crittenden, 1999). This is consistent with the finding of higher rates of internalizing disorders among Italians than Americans (Tani & Schneider, 1997). To summarize, the normative Italian distribution suggests that the culture recognizes that linearity is not the most common causal relation among human events. Most are systemic; that is, there is a complicity of self even in unwanted outcomes. Aggressor and victim, right and wrong, blame and shame turn out to be conceptual dichotomies that are expressed far more complexly in real human lives.

The final example to consider is cultures typified by gender-based differences in the distributions of patterns of attachment. The findings of the Lippe and Crittenden study (chapter 6, this volume) suggest that Egypt is one such culture. In such cultures, girls and boys are raised quite differently and are expected to assume different, but complementary, roles as adults (Hofstede, 1984; Schneider, 1971). The function of the paired patterns probably varies from one such culture to another. In Egypt, the difference appears to be one of males assuming a dominance-based Type C strategy and bearing responsibility for both interpersonal obligations outside the family and overseeing, in a paternalistic and often authoritarian manner, the management of

---

[7] There is a similar finding regarding Italian children's social organization in which "leadership" was associated with well-behaved, polite, and socially correct children (a description that fits the compulsive Type A patterns well), whereas "sociability" was associated with well-liked, social, exuberant children who sought social contact (a description that is compatible with Type C patterns) (Casiglia, LoCoco, & Zappulla, 1998).

the family. Females appear more often to use a Type A strategy, possibly with an emphasis on compulsive compliance (A4), and bear responsibility for daily managing the home and children. On the surface, it appears that males are favored, and in many concrete ways they are; for example, they are given better food, more attention, and power. Girls seem relatively neglected and may even have a higher mortality rate as children (unlike Western Europe and North America where it is the boys who die in childhood more often). On the other hand, as women, females are idealized, treasured, and largely sequestered. Although our data do not provide such evidence, Lippe's experience with her Egyptian sample was that relations between the sexes are even more complex, with women acquiring a deceptive form of the Type C strategy as a means of wielding some power in relationships. Among the possible protective outcomes of this interplay of strategies is regulation of intracultural competition in a land of limited resources and space, establishment of boundaries for intrafamilial conflict and, therefore, protection of the children, and limits on population growth, again within the context of finite space and natural resources.

Culture, Strategy, and Individual Personality. An array of factors might account for cultural differences in coping strategies, that is, pattern of attachment. From this perspective, culture is construed as the means by which adults pass on to children the accumulated knowledge of the invariant aspects of the local danger and the best ways to protect themselves. Thus, cultures can be considered context-defined balances of risk and opportunity that are heavily weighted toward the accumulation of past experience.

Of course, I cannot assert that any of the specific interpretations are accurate. The superficial overviews of specific cultures that have been offered are precisely that: simplified and superficial hypotheses. Moreover, cultural strategies may both reflect each culture's specific environment and be affected by the context of neighboring cultures. In this way, they are like family systems whose constellation of strategies are reciprocally interactive. The point of this exercise is not to define culture, far less specific cultures, but rather to offer a new way to think productively about cultural differences, a way that can generate new respect for cultural variation as well as new perspectives for responding to this variation.

Does this imply that culture determines personality or even pattern of attachment? Absolutely not. But it is one source of influence in a hierarchy of systemic influences (Bronfenbrenner, 1979; Hinde, 1987; Vygotsky, 1987). The approach offered here focuses on one specified aspect of cultural influence (i.e., response to danger) that is consistent with the organization of dyadic attachment. But even this one aspect of culture has multiple effects depending on other levels of influence. Thus, some people behave in ways that are consistent with cultural mandates, whereas others defy them. Put another way, consistency in this aspect of culture influences *distributions* of self-protective strategies (a much narrower concept than personality), whereas individual experience in specific relationships is the process through which individuals organize their personal strategies.

In spite of the empirical limitations to the ideas presented here, there is an advantage to posing such hypotheses together with a clear statement of the theoretical rationale underlying them and a set of assessments that could test them. A theorist functions like a connect-the-dots artist, finding meaning in the empty space between bits of empirical evidence and eliminating the noisy bits that are not meaningful such that the whole appears clearly enough for the empiricist to test. It should be remembered, however, that empiricism cannot establish "truth." (It can rule out falsehood, but it cannot confirm the null hypothesis.) Consideration of danger and strategies for self-protection may provide a meaningful way to think about cultural differences in the distributions of attachment-defined strategies. The central point is that attachment figures must prepare their children to live successfully and safely in their context. When conditions are safe, the secure strategy is both the most adaptive and most satisfying; it leads to personal and interpersonal happiness. But in the context of danger, particularly unpredictable or deceptive danger, the secure, Type B strategy may be a dangerous strategy.

The Context of Human Evolution. We know little about the environment in which *Homo sapiens* evolved. But we can be sure that it was an environment with many and varying dangers. Evolution could be described as a process of progressive modification of genes, physiology, and behavior to increase safety under varied dangers. Attachment serves the function of promoting safety and must be presumed to have been selected in response to on-going dangerous conditions. It is hard to explain how attachment could have evolved under enduring safe conditions such as those characterized by highly sensitive mothers who provided a secure base for children's forays into a safe world. These things are desired but would not provide the impetus to complex genetic, neurological, and behavioral evolution. Only danger and the complexity of promoting survival and reproduction can provide the environmental pressure that would select for humans who display attachment behavior. Framed this way, it seems plausible that it is the *anxious* organizations that increased rates of survival under conditions of extreme danger, including danger from which parents could not protect children and from parents themselves. Thus, it may be anxious attachment that formed the basis for learning to transform sensory stimulation into meaningful information, for organizing complex strategies for self-protective interpersonal behavior, and for our evolved capacity for forming attachment relationships. (See Lesch et al., 1996, for evidence that genes associated with anxiety are dominant and present in the majority of humans.) Danger and anxious attachment drive the evolutionary process, whereas safety and security may reflect a comfortable resting state, a hiatus between periods of danger. (For an alternative perspective, see Belsky, 1997a.) This interpretation suggests the hidden danger of security as it is generally conceptualized. Too much comfort leads to complacency, which is the opening for danger – better a bit of wariness and doubt.

From this perspective, it is ironic to consider that we obsess over the anxiety disorders – disorders that are very uncomfortable but not fatal. They may be the protective price we pay for being so alert to danger and the essential need for self-protection. On the other hand, we do not even have a term for the "comfort disorders." These are so deadly that they do not survive in the gene pool!

The best adapted humans may be those who use many strategies and select them to increase maximally the probability of safety, *given current conditions* (Hinde, 1991). That is, a strategy is only as adaptive as it is appropriate for the context in which it is applied. I fear that we have naively assumed that the human context is naturally safe and transparent with regard to danger. Thus, the Type B strategy that is best suited to safe contexts has been treated as inherently superior to the other strategies. I wonder, however, what Ainsworth might have reported about the infant–mother relationship if her visit to Uganda had occurred during the terrorizing dictatorship of Idi Amin. I wonder if it isn't time to add complexity to attachment theory by recognizing that many developmental contexts are not now, and historically have not been, safe. It may, indeed, be more important to promote safety than to foster secure attachment as an end in itself. Furthermore, it may be time to recognize the achievement embodied in the non-B strategies that force children and adults to choose judiciously between needs and desires.

Maturation, Development, and Integration

The Process of Adaptation. Healthy human neonates are born with the potential to organize any (but not all) of the strategies. Flexibility of strategy, however, is not wholly possible in infancy. Instead, neonates respond to experience in innate and preconscious ways. When their environment does not readily meet their needs, they are uncomfortable and protest. With experience, however, they become able to predict and respond in an organized and adaptive manner to the unique contingencies of their family and cultural environment. In other words, the context largely determines which strategy infants will organize. With maturation and development, their responses become more complex and better adapted to unique features of their context. The process appears to be one of transforming a largely undifferentiated human infant with almost infinite potential into a specific boy or girl who reflects his or her contextual "address" in terms of both unique familial relationships and aspects of gender, ethnicity, nationality, and socioeconomic status.

Adolescence culminates in both maximum display of individual and group-membership identity factors (whether the group be peers or family) and the potential for self-reflective consciousness. It is consciousness and the intellectual ability to manage mental processes consciously, (i.e., metacognitively) that enables adults to realize their full human potential. That is, it is not until adulthood that the human mind is sufficiently mature that full integration is possible. At that time, however, adults from all contexts and using all strategies have the potential to become aware of their own strategy, a metacognitive function, and to consider its value under varied circumstances, that is, to use dispositional representations consciously as working models. Adults have the opportunity, in other words, to step outside of their developmental context and become fully human, thus both regaining the extraordinary potential of neonates and being able to use it to organize all of the strategies. In adulthood, this humanity is a conscious achievement maintained by active effort to understand and participate in the process of human communication about danger and safety in ways that maximize safety for everyone.

This does not imply conscious thought before action is taken. Achieving consciousness requires several hundred milliseconds; in this time, threat can become fatal danger. Furthermore, consciousness focuses thought, which necessarily narrows perception. This reduces vigilant scanning for signals of danger and thus increases risk in contexts in which danger is unpredictable or deceptive. Particularly for the anxious and very anxious strategies, preconscious implementation is critical for self-protection. That is, in certain situations, particularly those in which danger is close, deadly, and nearly imperceptible, reflection and problem solving are not protective but dangerous. Fast, precortical sensorimotor procedures and self-protective fight/flight/freeze responses to imaged information are more protective (Le Doux, Romanski, & Xagoraris, 1989). On the other hand, reflection is most useful when the danger is distant, either far in advance of the problem when new solutions can be practiced until they become procedural or after the threatening events have been survived (Crittenden, 1997b).

Adults of all attachment types have the possibility to discriminate contexts and to use all strategies in the appropriate context. Put this way, everyone must "earn" his or her adaptability. For the developmentally endangered, this means understanding the possibility of safety, discriminating its occurrence, and responding to it with open and direct communication and negotiation. For the developmentally safe, this means recognizing the possibility of danger, particularly pervasive and deceptive danger, being able to discriminate dangerous conditions from safe conditions, and responding to potential danger with self-protective strategies (i.e., the "anxious" strategies). Being unable to do this creates unnecessary risk. For example, recently in New York City, a

Danish woman left her baby outside in the baby carriage while she went into a restaurant for a meal, a common and safe practice in Denmark. A passerby thought the baby was abandoned and called the police. They put the baby in temporary care and filed charges of child neglect against the mother. The focus of the case became one of competing cultural norms. That confused the issue. The issue is what is safe and dangerous under the immediate conditions and, therefore, what strategy should be employed. Large cities are rarely safe, and the danger of New York City, in particular, is not a closely held secret. All of us, all the time and everywhere, must assess danger and organize our behavior to protect ourselves and our progeny. Fully integrated adults modify their behavior, not because it is culturally normative but because it is the safest thing to do.

Such mental flexibility creates the opportunity for maximum safety under the greatest range of conditions. It does not imply, however, that individuals use the Type B strategy or that they are happy. This suggests that adaptability is not security of attachment. Furthermore, it is not developmental history or an enduring state. Instead, adaptability may best be defined as a *process* in which not fully accurate dispositional representations are constantly reorganized into less inaccurate dispositional representations that permit flexible and adaptive use of all behavioral strategies without distorting the mental processing of information. That is, security refers to a specific strategy suitable to protective relationships in relatively safe contexts, whereas adaptability refers to a process of selecting strategies that promote survival under all kinds of conditions.

SECURITY AND ADAPTABILITY

In this chapter, I have proposed that variation and diversity in pattern of attachment are adaptive both to individuals and to cultures (cf. Marsella, 1998). This notion follows from an emphasis on the adaptiveness to our species of (1) a wide range of possible strategies, (2) a dynamic interplay among current circumstances, individuals' unique experience and attributes, and cultural/contextual factors, and (3) a long period of protected maturation in which to establish this adaptive flexibility. Thus, a central issue in attachment theory may be to distinguish between (1) mental processes, operating at various levels of consciousness, that promote implementation of self-protective strategies and (2) static models derived from incomplete or uninformed mental processes that implement past strategies even under changed conditions. The latter includes the misapplication both of self-protective strategies under safe conditions and of secure strategies under dangerous conditions, particularly deceptively dangerous conditions. Put another way, a distinction is made between (a) the observed organization of attachment behavior and (b) the mental process of perceiving and interpreting information to organize situation-specific, contextually adapted behavior. It is only when the underlying mental process is complete and informed by the full range of possible transformations of information that individuals can be deemed to be fully integrated. Behaviorally, this will appear as the flexible use of all necessary strategies as a function of contextual demands (cf. Hewlett, Lamb, Shannon, Leyendecker, & Schölmerich, 1998). Developmentally, this may not be possible prior to adulthood.

Put more explicitly, possibly a distinction should be made between adaptive functioning and secure, Type B attachment. Without doubt, secure attachment is associated with desirable outcomes, but whether this is directly attributable to a strategy of direct and open communication of intentions and desires and negotiation of differences in these is less clear. When danger is considered, it becomes clear that individuals using the Type B strategy rarely experience serious and deceptively dangerous conditions at the time that they are classified as Type B. Conversely, many people who face such danger use one or more of the Type A and C strategies for protection of themselves and their children. This is certainly adaptive in the immediate sense (Ainsworth, 1984). To be fully adaptive, however, I would propose that any individual demonstrate the ability to (1) use strategies that fit immediate circumstances such that they promote safety and comfort, (2) flexibly change strategy when circumstances change, (3) articulate consciously the motivations and processes for their behavior, and (4) articulate awareness of distorted, omitted, erroneous, and falsified information. The first two criteria require that a wide, even complete, array of anxious strategies be available in procedural and imaged memory from which they can be implemented without conscious consideration. For the full complement of deceptive strategies, this probably requires maturation that occurs in adolescence. The last two criteria, though not requiring elegant psychological formulations, do require a degree of self-reflective consciousness that permits intentional examination and manipulation of thought and behavior. This requires maturation that occurs during adulthood.

The focus on danger suggests that safety and comfort should not be assumed to be normative or stable. To the contrary, historical evidence indicates that developmental contexts are characterized by both danger and change. Those of us living in postindustrial, Western countries are fortunate enough to experience one of the most peaceful and safe periods in human experience. It is a period in which food is abundant, shelter available, and disease so rare that infant and child mortality are extremely low and most children do not lose their parents until well into the child's adulthood. Furthermore, in spite of crime and war, our cities and countries are safer for more people than ever before. Possibly it is these conditions and the research done on children living in these conditions that permit us to believe that safety and comfort are normative conditions and, therefore, that security is the normative and optimal pattern of attachment. A simple look at children raised outside this protected context suggests that most humans need other strategies for coping with danger and that flexibility in organizing and varying these strategies is very valuable.

Expanding the view of attachment relationships to include extradyadic influences (from family, community, and culture) permits children to benefit from many levels of knowledge, particularly those that are enduring and time-tested. It may also buffer the negative effect of having parents who, for whatever reason, are misguided. The nested effects of multiple, hierarchically different contexts promote variability, flexibility, and integration in individuals' mental and behavioral organization. Given that children survive until the maturational possibilities of adulthood can be realized, such a complex, interactive network of reciprocal influences fosters resilience even in the context of prior self-threatening experience.

What can we conclude? There are many ways to do it right. But in all cases "it" is the same: to protect self and progeny. The appropriate strategy depends on the context and the individual's maturation, but even then there are choices. Moreover, the choices that will work depend in part on the choices that others make, and these, in turn, are reciprocally dependent on one's own choices. Once made, however, choices change the context. In both families and cultures, the change usually results in a new context that maintains use of the selected strategy. In some cases, however, a pattern of instability is introduced and perpetuated. As for happiness and comfort, only B3 fully meets the requirement and it is secondary to safety. Any other strategy, however, that functions predictably and protectively and is understood among the participants, also leads to both equilibrium and considerable happiness and comfort. Moreover, these benefits are obtained without the risk of cheating that a naive use of the secure strategy elicits (Cosmides & Tooby, 1992).

I have sometimes heard that the dynamic-maturational perspective that I offer (which focuses on danger and emphasizes the adaptiveness of the Type A and Type C strategies) is too pessimistic, that it values security too little. It seems the opposite to me. The ability of humans to construct so many different strategies suited to so many different contexts has enabled us to survive and flourish under almost all possible conditions. Maturation, occurring slowly over two decades or more, increases the probability that a wide range of experiences will influence the development of both brain and mind. This is essential for flexibility. Given that change is the only certainty in life, too rapid closure on any mental or behavioral process, including the Type B strategy, would reduce humans' overall adaptability. Seen from this perspective, a dynamic-maturational approach to attachment theory makes it possible to value the full array of human functioning, without assigning pejorative meanings to the non-B patterns, and to feel optimism regarding the potential of any individual and culture to find a pathway to safety and comfort.

References

Abramson, L. Y., Seligman, M. E. P., & Teasdale, J. D. (1978). Learned helplessness in humans: Critique and reformulation. *Journal of Abnormal Psychology, 87,* 49–87.

Achenbach, T. M. (1991a). *Manual for the Child Behavior Checklist/4–18 and 1991 Profile.* Burlington: University of Vermont Department of Psychiatry.

Achenbach, T. M. (1991b). *Manual for the Teacher's Report Form and 1991 Profile.* Burlington: University of Vermont Department of Psychiatry.

Achenbach, T. M. (1991c). *Manual for the Youth Self Report Form and 1991 Profile.* Burlington: University of Vermont Department of Psychiatry.

Achenbach, T. M., Verhulst, F. C., Edelbrook, C., Baron, G. D., & Akkerhuis, G. W. (1987). Epidemiological comparison of American and Dutch children: II. Behavioral/emotional problems reported by teachers for ages 6 to 11. *Journal of the American Academy of Child and Adolescent Psychiatry, 26,* 326–332.

Ahnert, L., Krätzig, S., Meischner, T., & Schmidt, A. (1994). Sozialisationskonzepte für Kleinkinder: Wirkungen tradierter Erziehungsvorstellungen und staatssozialistischer Erziehungsdoktrinen im intra- und interkulturellen Ost-West-Vergleich [Socialization concepts for infants: The effects of traditional education concepts and state socialist education doctrines in an intra- and intercultural comparison]. In G. Trommsdorff (Ed.), *Psychologische Aspekte des sozio-politischen Wandels in Ostdeutschland* (pp. 94–110). Berlin, New York: Walter de Gruyter-Verlag.

Ahnert, L., Meischner, T., Schmidt, A., & Doskin, W. A. (1994). Krosskulturnoje isledowanie wsaimodeistwija s djetmi russkich i nemjetskich materej [Cross-cultural research on infant interaction in Russian and German samples]. *Voprosi psichologij, 5,* 20–30.

Ainsworth, M. D. S. (1962). Reversible and irreversible effects of maternal deprivation on intellectual development. In *Maternal deprivation* (pp. 42–62). New York: Child Welfare League of America.

Ainsworth, M. D. S. (1967). *Infancy in Uganda: Infant care and the growth of attachment.* Baltimore: Johns Hopkins University Press.

Ainsworth, M. D. S. (1973). The development of infant–mother attachment. In B. M. Caldwell & H. N. Riciutti (Eds.), *Review of child development research* (Vol. 3, pp. 1–94). Chicago: University of Chicago Press.

Ainsworth, M. D. S. (1979). Infant-mother attachment. *American Psychologist, 34,* 932–937.

Ainsworth, M. D. S. (1982). Attachment: Retrospect and prospect. In C. M. Parkes & J. Stevenson-Hinde (Eds.), *The place of attachment in human behavior.* New York: Basic Books.

Ainsworth, M. D. S. (1984). Attachment. In N. S. Endler & J. McV. Hunt (Eds.), *Personality and the Behavioral Disorders* (Vol. 1, 2nd ed.). New York: John Wiley.

Ainsworth, M. D. S. (1984, April). *Attachment, adaptation, and continuity.* Paper presented at the International Conference on Infant Studies, New York City.

Ainsworth, M. D. S. (1990). Epilogue: Some considerations relevant to theory and assessment regarding attachment beyond infancy. In M. Greenberg, D. Cicchetti, & E. M. Cummings (Eds.), *Attachment in the preschool years: Theory, research, and intervention* (pp. 463–488). Chicago: University of Chicago Press.

Ainsworth, M. D. S. (1993). Attachment as related to mother infant interaction. *Advances in Infancy Research, 8,* 1–50.

Ainsworth, M. D. S., Bell, S. M., & Stayton, D. J. (1971). Individual differences in Strange Situation behavior of one-year-olds. In H. R. Schaffer (Ed.), *The origin of human social relations.* London: Academic Press.

Ainsworth, M. D. S., Bell, S. M., & Stayton, D. J. (1974). Infant–mother attachment and social development: "Socialization" as a product of reciprocal responsiveness to signals. In P. M. Richards (Ed.), *The integration of a child into a social world* (pp. 99–135). Cambridge, England: Cambridge University Press.

Ainsworth, M. D. S., Blehar, M. C., Waters, E., & Wall, S. (1978). *Patterns of Attachment: A psychological study of the strange situation.* Hillsdale, NJ: Erlbaum Associates.

Ainsworth, M., & Eichberg, C. (1991). Effects on infant–mother attachment of mothers' unresolved loss of an attachment figure. In P. Marris, J. Stevenson-Hinde, & C. Parkes (Eds.), *Attachment across the life-cycle* (pp. 160–183). New York: Routledge.

Ainsworth, M. D. S., & Wittig, B. A. (1969). Attachment and exploratory behavior of one-year-olds in a strange situation. In B. M. Foss (Ed.), *Determinants of infant behavior* (Vol. 4, pp. 111–136). London: Methuen.

Alexander, T. G. (1986). *Mormonism in transition: A history of the Latter Day Saints, 1890–1930.* Urbana: University of Illinois Press.

Allen, J. P., Hauser, S. T., & Borman-Spurrell, E. (1996). Attachment theory as a framework for understanding sequelae of severe adolescent psychopathology: An 11-year follow-up study. *Journal of Consulting and Clinical Psychology, 64,* 254–263.

American Psychiatric Association (1987). *Diagnostic and statistical manual of mental disorders-III-revised.* Washington, DC: American Psychiatric Association.

Ames, E. W., & Carter, M. (1992). Development of Romanian orphanage children adopted to Canada [Abstract]. *Canadian Psychology, 33* (2), 503.

Andersson, B. E. (1989). Effects of public day-care: A longitudinal study. *Child Development, 60,* 857–866.

Arend, R., Grove, F. L., & Sroufe, L. A. (1979). Continuity of individual adaptation from infancy to kindergarten: a predictive study of ego resiliency and curiosity in preschoolers. *Child Development, 50,* 950–965.

Armsden, G. C., & Greenberg, M. T. (1987). The inventory of parent and peer attachment: Individual differences and their relationship to psychological well-being in adolescence. *Journal of Youth and Adolescence, 16,* 427–454.

Aro, H. M., Marttunen, M. J., & Lönnqvist, J. K. (1992). Trends in suicide mortality among young people in Finland. *Psychiatria Fennica, 23,* 29–39.

Attanasio, A., Rager, K., & Gupta, D. (1986). Ontogenity of cicardian rythmicity for melatonin, serotonin, and N-acetylserotonin in humans. *Journal of Pineal Research, 3,* 251–256.

Aubry, J. (1955). *La carence de soins maternels.* Paris: Centre Internationale de l'Enfance.

Bakarat, H. (1985). The Arab family and the challenge of social transformations. In E. Warnok Fernea (Ed.), *Women and the family in the Middle East: New voices of change.* Austin: University of Texas Press.

Bakwin, H., & Bakwin, R. M. M. (1972). *Clinical management of behavior disorders in children.* Philadelphia, London: Sanders Company.

Baran, B. (1985). Wyobrażenia o włagsnej przyszłosci dzieci wychowywanych poza rodziną. In M. Tyszkowa (Ed.), *Rozwój dziecka w rodzinie i poza rodziną* (pp. 205–225). Poznań: UAM.

Bar-On, D., Eland, J., Kleber, R. J., Krell, R., Moore, Y., Sagi, A. Soriano, E., Suedfeld, P., van der Velden, P. G., & van IJzendoorn, M. H. (1998). Multigenerational perspectives on coping with the Holocaust experience: An attachment perspective for understanding the developmental sequelae of trauma across generations. *International Journal of Behavioral Development, 22,* 315–338.

Bates, J. E., Maslin, C. A., & Frankel, K. A. (1985). Attachment security, mother–child interaction, and temperament as predictors of behavior-problem ratings at age three years. In I. Bretherton & E. Waters (Eds.), *Growing points of attachment theory and research. Monographs of the Society for Research on Child Development, 50*(1–2, Serial No. 209) (167–193).

Baumrind, D. (1970). Socialization and instrumental competence in young children. *Young Children, 26,* 104–119.

Bayley, N. (1969/1993). *Bayley scales of infant development.* New York: Psychological Corporation.

Beck, A. T. (1967). *Depression: Causes and treatment.* Philadelphia: University of Pennsylvania Press.

Beck, A. T., Steer, R. A., & Garbin, M. G. (1988). Psychometric properties of the Beck Depression Inventory: Twenty-five years of evaluation. *Clinical Psychology Review, 8,* 77–100.

Beck, A. T., Ward, C. H., Mendelson, M., Mock, J., & Erbaugh, J. (1961). An inventory for measuring depression. *Archives of General Psychiatry, 4,* 561–571.

Beeghly, M., & Cicchetti, D. (1996). Child maltreatment, attachment, and self-esteem: Emergence of an internal state lexicon in toddlers at high social risk. In M. E. Hertzig & E. A. Farber (Eds.), *Annual progress in child psychiatry and child development* (pp. 127–166). New York: Brunner/Mazel.

Behar, L., & Stringfield, S. (1974). A behavior rating scale for the preschool child. *Developmental Psychology, 10,* 601–610.

Belsky, J. (1988a). Infant day care and socioemotional development: The United States. *Journal of Child Psychology and Psychiatry, 29,* 397–406.

Belsky, J. (1988b). The "effects" of infant day care reconsidered. *Early Childhood Research Quarterly, 3,* 235–273.

Belsky, J. (1989). *Infant day care and attachment: Methodological, developmental and contextual considerations.* Paper presented at the 10th Biennial Meetings of ISSBD, Jyväskylä, Finland.

Belsky, J. (1995). Expanding the ecology of human development: An evolutionary perspective. In P. Moen & G. H. Elder (Eds.), *Examining lives in context: Perspectives on the human ecology of human development* (pp. 545–561). Washington, DC: American Psychological Association.

Belsky, J. (1997b). Variation in susceptibility to environmental influence: An evolutionary argument. *Psychological Inquiry, 8,* 182–186.

Belsky, J. (1997a). Attachment, mating, and parenting: An evolutionary interpretation. *Human Nature, 8,* 361–381.

Belsky, J., Fish, M., & Isabella, R. (1991). Continuity and discontinuity in infant negative and positive emotionality: Family antecedents and attachment consequences. *Developmental Psychology, 27,* 421–431.

Belsky, J., Hsieh, K., & Crnic, K. (1998). Infant positive and negative emotionality: One dimension or two? In M. E. Hertzig, & E. A. Farber (Eds.), *Annual progress in child psychiatry and child development* (pp. 29–44). Bristol, PA: Brunner/Mazel.

Belsky, J., & Isabella, R. (1988). Maternal, infant, and social-contextual determinants of attachment security. In J. Belsky & T. Nezworski (Eds.), *Clinical implications of attachment* (pp. 41–94). Hillsdale, NJ: Lawrence Erlbaum Associates.

Belsky, J., & Rovine, M. J. (1988). Nonmaternal care in the first year of life and security of infant–parent attachment. *Child Development, 59,* 157–167.

Belsky, J., Taylor, D., & Rovine, M. (1984). The Pennsylvania Infant and Family Development Project, III: The origins of individual differences in infant–mother attachment: Maternal and infant contributions. *Child Development, 55,* 718–728.

Belsky, J., & Youngblade, L. M. (1992). Parent–child antecedents of 5-year-olds' close friendships: A longitudinal analysis. *Developmental Psychology, 28,* 700–713.

Benes, F. M., Turtle, M., Khan, Y., & Farol, P. (1994). Myelination of a key relay zone in the hippocampal formation occurs in the human brain during childhood, adolescence, and adulthood. *Archives of General Psychiatry, 51,* 477–484.

Benn, R. K. (1986). Factors promoting secure attachment relationships between employed mothers and their sons. *Child Development, 57,* 1224–1231.

Benoit, D., & Parker, K. C. H. (1994). Stability and transmission of attachment across three generations. *Child Development, 65,* 1444–1456.

Berndt, T. J. (1982). The features and effects of friendship in early adolescence. *Child Development, 53,* 1447–1460.

Bernstein, V. J. (1988). Dramatic responses in a safe space: Helping parents to reach difficult babies. *Zero to Three,* 19–25.

Bernstein, V. J., & Hans, S. L. (1994). Predicting the developmental outcome of two-year-old children born exposed to methadone: The impact of social-environmental risk factors. *Journal of Clinical Child Psychology, 23,* 349–359.

Bernstein, V. J., Jeremy, R. J., & Marcus, J. (1986). Mother–infant interaction in multi-problem families: Finding those at risk. *Journal of the American Academy of Child Psychiatry, 25,* 631–640.

Bielicka, I., & Olechnowicz, H. (1967). A note on the rehabilitation of the family in the treatment of the orphan syndrome in infants. *Journal of Child Psychology, 8,* 139–142.

Bielicka, I., Stelmachowski, A., & Sztekiel, E. (1966). *O przysposobieniu (adopcji) dzieci.* Wasaw: Wydawnictwo Prawnicze.

Black, K. A., & McCartney, K. (1997). Adolescent females' security with parents predicts the quality of peer interactions. *Social Development, 6,* 91–110.

Blaney, P. H. (1986). Affect and memory: A review. *Psychological Bulletin, 99,* 229–246.

Block, J. H., Block, J., & Morrison, A. (1981). Parental agreement–disagreement on child-rearing orientations and gender-related personality correlates in children. *Child Development, 52,* 965–974.

Block, J. H., Jennings, P. H., Harvey, E., & Simpson, E. (1964). Interaction between allergic potential and psychopathology in childhood asthma. *Psychosomatic Medicine, 26*, 307–320.

Blos, P. (1962). *On adolescence: A psychoanalytic interpretation.* New York: Free Press.

Blos, P. (1979). *The adolescent passage: Developmental issues.* New York: International Universities Press.

Bluestein, D. L., Schultheiss, D. P., & Prezioso, M. S. (1993). *Attachment theory and career development: Current status and future directions.* Paper presented at the Annual Meeting of the American Psychological Association, Toronto.

Bohlin, G., Hagekull, B., Germer, M., Andersson, K., & Lindberg, L. (1989). Avoidant and resistant reunion behaviors as predicted by maternal interactive behavior and infant temperament. *Infant Behavior and Development, 12*, 105–117.

Bohman, M., & Sigvardsson, S. (1979). Long term effects of early institutional care: A prospective longitudinal study. *Journal of Child Psychology and Psychiatry and Allied Disciplines, 20*, 111–117.

Bornstein, M. H. (Ed.). (1989). *Maternal responsiveness: Characteristics and consequences.* San Francisco: Jossey-Bass.

Bowlby, J. (1951/1973). *Maternal care and mental health.* Geneva, Switzerland: World Health Organization.

Bowlby, J. (1969/1980). *Attachment and loss: Vol. 3. Loss.* New York: Basic Books.

Bowlby, J. (1973). *Attachment and loss: Vol. 2. Separation.* New York: Basic Books.

Bowlby, J. (1982). *Attachment and loss: Vol. 1. Attachment.* New York: Basic Books.

Bowlby, J. (1988). *A secure base.* New York: Basic Books.

Brazelton, T. B. (1961). Psychophysiologic reactions to the neonate: I. The value of the observation of the neonate. *Journal of Pediatrics, 58*, 508–512.

Brazelton, T. B., Koslowski, B. & Main, M. (1974). The origins of reciprocity: The early mother–infant interaction. In M. Lewis, & L. A. Rosenbloom (Eds.), *The effect of the infant on its caregiver* (pp. 49–76). New York: Wiley-Interscience.

Bretherton, I. (1985). Attachment theory: Retrospect and prospect. In I. Bretherton & E. Waters (Eds.), *Growing points of attachment theory and research. Monographs of the Society for Research on Child Development, 50* (1–2, Serial No. 209), 3–35.

Bretherton, I. (1987). New perspectives on attachment relations in infancy: Security, communication and internal working models. In J. D. Osofsky (Ed.), *Handbook of infant development* (pp. 1061–1100). New York: John Wiley.

Bretherton, I., Biringen, Z., Ridgeway, D., Maslin, C., & Sherman, M. (1989). Attachment: The parental perspective. *Infant Mental Health Journal, 10*, 203–221.

Bretherton, I., Ridgeway, D., & Cassidy, J. (1993). Assessing internal working models of attachment. In M. T. Greenberg, D. Cicchetti, & E. M. Cummings (Eds.), *Attachment in the preschool years* (pp. 273–308). Chicago: University of Chicago Press.

Bretherton, I., & Waters, E. (Eds.). (1985). Growing points in attachment theory and research. *Monographs of the Society for Research in Child Development, 50*, (Serial No. 209).

Bridger, S. (1987). *Women in the Soviet countryside.* Cambridge, England: Cambridge University Press.

Bridges, L. J., & Connell, J. P. (1991). Consistency and inconsistency in infant emotional and social interactive behavior across contexts and caregivers. *Infant Behavior and Development, 14*, 471–487.

Bronfenbrenner, U. (1970). *Two worlds of childhood: US and USSR.* New York: Russell Sage Foundation.

Bronfenbrenner, U. (1972). *Zwei Welten. Kinder in USA and UdSSR* [Two worlds of childhood. Children in the USA and the USSR]. Stuttgart: Deutsche Verlags-Anstalt.

Bronfenbrenner, U. (1979). *The ecology of human development: Experiments by nature and design.* Cambridge, MA: Harvard University Press.

Brugger von Nesslau, M. (1991). *Kindheit im zaristischen Rußland des 19. Jahrhunderts* [Childhood in Czarist Russia of the 19th century]. Dissertation: University of Zurich Press.

Bruner, J. S., & Bornstein, M. H. (1989). On interaction. In J. S. Bruner & M. H. Bornstein (Eds.), *Interaction in human development* (pp. 1–14). Hillsdale, NJ: Lawrence Erlbaum Associates.

Bryan, E. (1992). *Twins and higher multiple births.* London: Hodder & Stoughton.

Bukowski, W. M., & Sippola, L. K. (1998). Diversity and the social mind: Goals, constructs, culture, and development. *Developmental Psychology, 34,* 742–746.

Byng-Hall, J. (1995). *Rewriting family scripts, improvisation, and systems change.* New York: Guilford Press.

Caldwell, B. M., & Bradley, R. H. (1979). *Home observation for measurement of the environment.* Little Rock, AR: University of Arkansas.

Campbell, E. E. (1988). *Establishing Zion: The Mormon Church in the American West, 1847–1869.* Salt Lake City, UT: Signature Books.

Campbell, S. B., Cohn, J. F., Meyers, T. A., Ross, S., & Flanagan, C. (1993, March). Chronicity of maternal depression and mother-infant interaction. In D. Teti (Chair), *Depressed mothers and their children: Individual differences in mother-child outcome.* Symposium conducted at the meeting of the Society for Research in Child Development, New Orleans, LA.

CAPMAS/UNICEF (1989). *The situation of children in upper Egypt.* Prepared by Louise F. Allen. Cairo, Egypt: Nubar Printing House.

Carlson, E. A., Jacobvitz, D., & Sroufe, L. A. (1995). A developmental investigation of inattentiveness and hyperactivity. *Child Development, 66,* 37–54.

Carlson, V., Cicchetti, D., Barnett, D., & Braunwald, K. (1989). Disorganized/disoriented attachment relationships in maltreated infants. *Developmental Psychology, 25*(4), 525–531.

Casiglia, A. C., LoCoco, A., & Zappulla, C. (1998). Aspects of social reputation and peer relationships in Italian children: A cross-cultural perspective. *Developmental Psychology, 34,* 723–730.

Cassidy, J. (1988). Child–mother attachment and the self in six-year-olds. *Child Development, 59,* 121–134.

Cassidy, J. (1994). Emotion regulation: Influences of attachment relationships. In N. A. Fox (Ed.), *The development of emotion regulation: Biological and behavioral considerations. Monographs of the Society for Research in Child Development, 59* (2–3), 228–249.

Cassidy, J., & Berlin, L. J. (1994). The insecure/ambivalent pattern of attachment: Theory and research. *Child Development, 65,* 971–991.

Cassidy, J., Marvin, R. S., & The Working Group of the John D. and Catherine T. MacArthur Foundation on the Transition from Infancy to Early Childhood. (1991/1992). *Attachment organization in three- and four-year-olds: Coding guidelines.* Unpublished manuscript, University of Virginia at Charlottesville.

Chess, S., & Thomas, A. (1984). *Origins and evolution of behavior disorders: From infancy to early adult life.* Cambridge, MA: Harvard University Press.

Chin, X., Hastings, P. D., Rubin, K. H., Chen, H., & Stewart, S. L. (1998). Child-rearing attitudes and behavioral inhibition in Chinese and Canadian toddlers: A cross-cultural study. *Developmental Psychology, 68,* 571–591.

Chisholm, K. (1998). A three year follow-up of attachment and indiscriminate friendliness in children adopted from Romanian orphanages. *Child Development, 69* (4), 1090–1104.

Chisholm, K., & Carter, M. C. (1997). Attachment and indiscriminately friendly behavior. In E. W. Ames (Ed.), *The development of Romanian children adopted to Canada* (pp. 65–84). Ottawa: Human Resources Development Canada.

Chisholm, K., Carter, M. C., Ames, E. W., & Morison, S. J. (1995). Attachment security and indiscriminately friendly behavior in children adopted from Romanian orphanages. *Development and Psychopathology, 7,* 283–294.

Chisholm, K., & Savoie, L. (1992). Behavior and attachment problems of Romanian orphanage children adopted to Canada [Abstract]. *Canadian Psychology, 33*(2), 504.

Chung, Y. S., & Daghestani, A. N. (1989). Seasonal affective disorder. Shedding light on a dark subject. *Postgraduate Medicine, 86,* 309–314.

Cicchetti, D. (1993). Developmental psychopathology: Reactions, reflections, projections. *Developmental Review, 13,* 471–502.

Cicchetti, D., & Aber, J. L. (1986) Early precursors of later depression: An organizational perspective. In L. Lipsitt & C. Rovee-Collier (Eds.), *Advances in infancy research* (Vol. 1, pp. 87–137). Norwood, NJ: Ablex.

Cicchetti, D., & Barnett, D. (1991). Attachment organization in maltreated preschoolers. *Development and Psychopathology, 3,* 397–411.

Cicchetti, D., Cummings, E. M., Greenberg, M. T., & Marvin, R. S. (1990). An organizational perspective on attachment beyond infancy. In M. T. Greenberg, D. Cicchetti, & E. M. Cummings (Eds.), *Attachment in the preschool years: Theory, research, and intervention* (pp. 3–49). Chicago: University of Chicago Press.

Cicchetti, D., Rogosch, F. A., & Toth, S. L. (1998). Maternal depressive disorder and contextual risk: Contributions to development of attachment insecurity and behavior problems in toddlerhood. *Development and Psychopathology, 10,* 283–300.

Clarke-Stewart, A. K. (1989). Infant day-care: maligned or malignant? *American Psychologist, 44,* 266–273.

Cohen, J., & Cohen, P. (1983). *Applied multiple regression/correlation analysis for the behavioral sciences.* London: Erlbaum.

Cohn, D. A. (1990). Child–mother attachment of six-year-olds and social competence at school. *Child Development, 61,* 152–162.

Cohn, J. F., Campbell, S. B., Matias, R., & Hopkins, J. (1990). Face-to-face interactions of postpartum depressed and nondepressed mother-infant pairs at two months. *Developmental Psychology, 26,* 15–23.

Cohn, J. F., Campbell, S. B., & Ross, S. (1991). Infant response in the still-face paradigm at 6 months predicts avoidant and secure attachment at 12 months. *Development and Psychopathology, 3*(4), 367–376.

Cohn, J. F., Matias, R., Tronick, E. Z., Connell, D., & Lyons-Ruth, K. (1986). Face-to-face interactions of depressed mothers and their infants. In E. Z. Tronick & T. Field (Eds.), *Maternal depression and infant disturbance. New Directions for Child Development, 34* (pp. 31–44). San Francisco: Jossey-Bass.

Cole, P. M., Michel, M. K., & Teti, L. O. (1995). The development of emotion regulation and dysregulation: A clinical perspective. In N. A. Fos (Ed.), *The development of emotion regulation: Biological and behavioral considerations. Monographs of the Society for Research in Child Development, 59* (2–3), 73–100.

Cole-Detke, H., & Kobak, R. (1996). Attachment processes in eating disorder and depression. *Journal of Consulting and Clinical Psychology, 64,* 282–290.

Collins, N. L., & Read, S. J. (1990). Adult attachment, working models and relationship quality in dating couples. *Journal of Personality and Social Psychology, 58,* 644–663.

Connell, J. P. (1985). A new multidimensional measure of children's perceptions of control. *Child Development, 56,* 1018–1041.

Cosmides, L., & Tooby, J. (1992). Cognitive adaptations for social exchange. In J. Barkow, L. Cosmides, & J. Tooby, (Eds.) *The adapted mind* (pp. 163–228). New York: Oxford University Press.

Crandall, V. C., & Crandall, B. W. (1983). Maternal and childhood behaviors as antecedents of internal-external control perceptions in young adulthood. In H. M. Lefcourt (Ed.), *Research with the locus of control construct: Vol. 2. Developments and social problems* (pp. 53–103). New York: Academic Press.

Crittenden, P. M. (1981). Abusing, neglecting, problematic and adequate dyads: Differentiating by patterns of interaction. *Merril-Palmer Quarterly, 27,* 1–19.

Crittenden, P. M. (1985a). Maltreated infants: Vulnerability and resilience. *Journal of Child Psychology and Psychiatry, 26,* 85–96.

Crittenden, P. M. (1985b). Social networks, quality of child-rearing, and child development. *Child Development, 56,* 1299–1313.

Crittenden, P. M. (1987). Non-organic failure-to-thrive: Deprivation or distortion? *Infant Mental Health Journal, 8,* 51–64.

Crittenden, P. M. (1988a). Family and dyadic patterns of functioning in maltreating families. In K. Browne, C. Davies, & P. Stratton (Eds.), *Early prediction and prevention of child abuse* (pp. 161–189). Chichester: John Wiley.

Crittenden, P. M. (1988b). Relationship at risks. In J. Belsky & T. Nezworski (Eds.), *Clinical implications of attachment* (pp. 136–174). Hillsdale, NJ: Lawrence Erlbaum Associates.

Crittenden, P. M. (1988–1995). *The Preschool Assessment of Attachment, PAA.* Unpublished manual, Miami, FL.

Crittenden, P. M. (1990). Internal representational models of attachment relationships. *Infant Mental Health Journal, 11,* 259–277.

Crittenden, P. M. (1991, June 12–21). *Seminario di Studio e Training per l'uso del CARE-Index,* Modena, Italy.

Crittenden, P. M. (1992a). Quality of attachment in the preschool years. *Development and Psychopathology, 4,* 209–241.

Crittenden, P. M. (1992b). Treatment of anxious attachment in infancy and early childhood. *Development and Psychopathology, 4,* 575–602.

Crittenden, P. M. (1993a). Characteristics of neglectful parents: An information processing approach. *Criminal Justice and Behavior, 20,* 27–48.

Crittenden, P. M. (1993b). Comparison of two systems for assessing quality of attachment in the preschool years. In P. M. Crittenden (Chair), *Quality of attachment in the preschool years.* Symposium conducted at the Ninth Biennial Meeting of the International conference on Infant Studies, Paris.

Crittenden, P. M. (1994). Peering into the black box: An exploratory treatise on the development of self in young children. In D. Cicchetti & S. L. Toth (Eds.), *Rochester symposium on developmental psychopathology: Vol. 5. The self and its disorder* (pp. 79–148). Rochester, NY: University Press.

Crittenden, P. M. (1995a). Attachment and psychopathology. In S. Goldberg, R. Muir, & J. Kerr (Eds.), *Attachment theory: Social, developmental, and clinical perspectives* (pp. 367–406). Hillsdale, NJ: Analytic Press.

Crittenden, P. M. (Chair) (1995b, March). *Quality of attachment in the preschool years.* Symposium conducted at the Biennial Meeting of the Society for Research in Child Development, Indianapolis, IN.

Crittenden, P. M. (1996). Research on maltreating families: Implications for intervention. In J. Briere, L. Berliner, & T. Reid (Eds.), *APSAC Handbook on Child Maltreatment* (pp. 158–174). Thousand Oaks, CA: Sage Publications.

Crittenden, P. M. (1997a). Patterns of attachment and sexuality: Risk of dysfunction versus opportunity for creative integration. In L. Atkinson & K. J. Zuckerman (Eds.), *Attachment and psychopathology* (pp. 47–93). New York: Guilford Press.

Crittenden, P. M. (1997b). Toward an integrative theory of trauma: A dynamic-maturational approach. In D. Cicchetti & S. Toth (Eds.), *The Rochester Symposium on Developmental Psychopathology, Vol. 10. Risk, trauma, and mental processes* (pp. 34–84). Rochester, NY: University of Rochester Press.

Crittenden, P. M. (1997c). The effect of early relationship experiences on relationships in adulthood. In S. Duck (Ed.), *Handbook of personal relationships* (2nd ed., pp. 99–119). Chichester, England: John Wiley.

Crittenden, P. M. (1997d). Truth, error, omission, distortion, and deception: The application of attachment theory to the assessment and treatment of psychological disorder. In S. M. C. Dollinger & L. F. DiLalla (Eds.), *Assessment and intervention across the lifespan.* Hillsdale, NJ: Lawrence Erlbaum Associates.

Crittenden, P. M. (1998a). *CARE-Index Manual* (3rd revision). Unpublished manuscript, Miami, FL.

Crittenden, P. M. (1998b). Dangerous behavior and dangerous contexts: A thirty-five year perspective on research on the developmental effects of child physical abuse. In P. Trickett (Ed.), *Violence to children* (pp. 11–38). Washington, DC: American Psychological Association.

Crittenden, P. M. (1998c). *Patterns of attachment in adulthood: A dynamic-maturation approach to analyzing the Adult Attachment Interview.* Manuscript available from the author, Miami, FL.

Crittenden, P. M. (1999). Attaccamento in età adulta. *L'approccio dinamico-maturativo alla Adult Attachment Interview.* Edizione Italiana a cura di Graziella Fava Vizziello e Andrea Landini. Milano: Cortina.

Crittenden, P. M. (1999). Danger and development: The organization of self-protective strategies. In J. Vondra and D. Barnett, (Eds.) *Monographs of the Society for Research on Child Development* (pp. 145–171).

Crittenden, P. M., & Claussen, A. H. (1996). *Quality of attachment in young children and risk for psychopathology.* Tampere, Finland: World Association of Infant Mental Health.

Crittenden, P. M., Partridge, M. F., & Claussen, A. H. (1991). Family patterns of relationship in normative and dysfunctional families. *Development and Psychopathology, 3,* 491–512.

Crittenden, P., Vorria, P., Kakitsis, P., Denegri, Z., Papalgoura, Z., Claussen, A. H., & Poleomarkaki, E. (1992, September). *Comparison of mother–child relationship of Greek children raised in institutional care with those raised at home.* Paper presented at the 5th European Conference on Developmental Psychology, Seville, Spain.

Crockenberg, S. B. (1981). Infant irritability, mother responsiveness and social support influences on the security of infant-mother attachment. *Child Development, 52,* 857–865.

Cronbach, L. J., & Meehl, P. E. (1955). Construct validity in psychological tests. *Psychological Bulletin, 52,* 281–302.

Cummings, E. M., & Davies, P. T. (1994). Maternal depression and child development. *Journal of Child Psychology and Psychiatry, 35,* 73–112.

Cummings, E. M., & Davies, P. T. (1996). Emotional security as a regulatory process in normal development and the development of psychopathology. *Development and Psychopathology, 7,* 123–139.

Daehler, M., & Greco, C. (1985). Memory in very young children. In M. Pressley & C. Brainerd (Eds.), *Cognitive learning and memory in children* (pp. 49–79). New York: Springer.

Damasio, A. R. (1994). *Descartes' error: Emotion, reason, and the human brain.* New York: Avon Books.

Darling, N., & Steinberg, L. (1993). Parenting style as context: An integrative model. *Psychological Bulletin, 63,* 1266–1281.

Davies, P. T., & Cummings, E. M. (1994). Marital conflict and child adjustment: An emotional security hypothesis. *Psychological Bulletin, 116,* 387–411.

Dawson, G., Klinger, L. G., Panagiotides, Spieker, S., & Frey, K. (1992). Infants of mothers with depressive symptoms: Electroencephalographic and behavioral findings related to attachment status. *Development and Psychopathology, 4,* 67–80.

Dekovic, M., Gerris, J. R. M., & Janssens, J. M. A. M. (1989, July). *Parental cognitions, parent–child interaction and social-cognitive development of the child.* Paper presented at the Tenth Biennial Meetings of the International Society for the Study of Behavioral Development, Jyvaskyla, Finland.

DeMulder, E. K., & Radke-Yarrow, M. (1991). Attachment with affectively ill and well mothers: Concurrent behavioral correlates. *Development and Psychopathology, 3,* 227–242.

Denham, S. A., Renwick, S. M., & Holt, R. W. (1991). Working and playing together: Prediction of preschool social emotional competence from mother–child interaction. *Child Development, 62,* 242–249.

Devereux, G. (1968). *From anxiety to method in the behavioral sciences.* The Hague: Mouton.

De Wolff, M. S., & van IJzendoorn, M. H. (1997). Sensitivity and attachment: A meta-analysis on parental antecedents of infant attachment. *Child Development, 68,* 571–591.

Diamond, J. (1997). *Guns, germs, and steel: The fates of human societies.* New York: W. W. Norton.

Diekstra, R. F. W. (1993). The epidemiology of suicide and parasuicide. *Acta Psychiatria Scandinavica,* Suppl. *371,* 9–20.

Dilling, W., Weyerer, S., & Castell, R. (1984). *Psychische Erkrankungen in der Bevölkerung.* [Psychological Illness in the population]. Stuttgart, Germany: Enke.

Dontas, C., Maratos, O., Fafoutis, M. & Karangelis, A. (1985). Early social development in institutionally reared Greek infants: Attachment and peer interaction. In I. Bretherton & E. Waters (Eds.), *Growing points of attachment theory and research. Monographs of the Society for Research on Child Development, 50*(1–2, Serial No. 209) (pp. 136–146).

Downey, G., & Coyne, J. C. (1990). Children of depressed parents: An integrative review. *Psychological Bulletin, 108,* 50–76.

Dozier, M., & Kobak, R. (1992). Psychophysiology in adolescent attachment interviews: Converging evidence for deactivating strategies. *Child Development, 6,* 1473–1480.

Dubrovina, I. V., & Puzskaia, A. G. (Eds.) (1990). *Psikhicheskoe razvitie vospitannikov detskogo doma* [Psychic development of the caretaking persons in the infant's home]. Moscow: Pedagogika.

Dunn, J. (1984). *Sisters and brothers.* London: Fontana.

Easterbrooks, M. A. (1989). Quality of attachment to mother and to father: Effects of perinatal risk status. *Child Development, 60,* 825–830.

Egeland, B., Breitenbucher, M., & Rosenberg, D. (1980). Prospective study of the significance of life stress in the etiology of child abuse. *Journal of Consulting and Clinical Psychology, 48,* 195–205.

Egeland, B., & Farber, E. A. (1984). Infant–mother attachment: Factors related to its development and changes over time. *Child Development, 55,* 753–771.

Egeland, B., & Sroufe, L. A. (1981a). Attachment and early maltreatment. *Child Development, 52,* 44–52.

Egeland, B., & Sroufe, A. (1981b). Developmental sequellae of maltreatment in infancy. In R. Rizley & D. Cicchetti (Eds.), *New directions for child development: Developmental perspectives on child maltreatment* (Vol. 11, pp. 77–92). San Francisco: Jossey-Bass.

Ekholm, B., & Hedin, A. (1987). Studies of day care center climate and its effects on children's social and emotional behavior. *Early Child Development and Care, 27,* 43–57.

Elicker, J., Englund, M., & Sroufe, L. A. (1992). Predicting peer competence and peer relationships in childhood from early parent–child relationships. In R. D. Parke & G. W. Ladd (Eds.), *Family–peer relationships: Modes of linkage.* Hillsdale, NJ: Lawrence Erlbaum Associates.

El Safty, M. (1979). Parental attitudes toward the socialization of children in the Egyptian Muslim middle class families. *International Journal of Sociology of the Family, 9,* 177–195.

Emde, R. N., & Sorce, J. F. (1983). The rewards of infancy: Emotional availability and maternal referencing. In J. D. Call, E. Galenson, & R. L. Tyson (Eds.), *Frontiers of infant psychiatry* (pp. 17–30). New York: Basic Books.

Engels, F. (1966). Der Ursprung der Familie, des Privateigentums und des Staates [The origin of the family, of private property and of the state]. In K. Marx & F. Engels (Eds.), *Ausgewählte Schriften in zwei Bänden* (Vol. 2, pp. 155–282). Berlin: Dietz-Verlag.

Epstein, S. (1979). The stability of behavior: I. On predicting most of the people much of the time. *Journal of Personality and Social Psychology, 37,* 1097–1126.

Epstein, S. (1980). The stability of behavior: II. Implications for psychological research. *American Psychologist, 35,* 790–806.

Erikson, E. H. (1950). *Childhood and society.* New York: W. W. Norton.

Erikson, E. H. (1968). *Identity: Youth and crisis.* New York: W. W. Norton.

Erickson, M. F., Sroufe, L. A., & Egeland, B. (1985). The relationship between quality of attachment and behavior problems in preschool in a high-risk sample. In I. Bretherton & E. Waters (Eds.), *Growing points of attachment theory and research. Monographs of the Society for Research on Child Development, 50*(1–2, Serial No. 209) (pp. 147–166).

Fagot, B. I., & Kavanaugh, K. (1990). The prediction of antisocial behavior from avoidant attachment classifications. *Child Development, 61,* 864–873.

Fagot, B. I., & Kavanagh, K. (1993). Parenting during the second year: Effects of children's age, sex, and attachment classification. *Child Development, 64,* 258–271.

Fagot, B. I., & Pears, K. (1996). Changes in attachment during the third year: Consequences and predictions. *Development and Psychopathology, 8,* 325–344.

Farrell-Erickson, M., & Egeland, B. (1994). *Throwing a spotlight on the developmental outcomes for children: Findings of a seventeen-year follow-up study.* Paper presented at the Children in the shadows: The fate of children in neglecting families, University of Minnesota.

Fava Vizziello, G. (1990, 1991). *Training per l'uso del WMCI.* Dipartimento di Psicologia dello Sviluppo e della Socializzazione, Università degli Studi di Padova, Italia.

Fava Vizziello, G., Palacio-Espasa, F., & Cassibba, R. (1992). Modalités de reorganisation des enfants de 9 à 30 mois, suite à la séparation des parants à la crèche, *Neuropsychiatrie de l'Enfant et Adolescent, 40,* 431–448.

Feuerstein, R. (1980). *Instrumental enrichment: An intervention program for cognitive modifiability.* Baltimore, MD: University Park Press.

Field, T. M. (1984). Early interactions between infants and their postpartum depressed mothers. *Infant Behavior and Development, 7,* 517–522.

Field, T. M. (1986). Models for reactive and chronic depression in infancy. In E. Z. Tronick & T. M. Field (Eds.), *Maternal depression and infant disturbance* (pp. 47–60). San Francisco: Jossey-Bass.

Field, T. M. (1987). Interaction and attachment in normal and atypical infants. *Journal of Consulting and Clinical Psychology, 55,* 853–859.

Fischer, J. L. (1981). Transitions in relationship style from adolescence to young adulthood. *Journal of Youth and Adolescence, 10,* 11–23.

Fleiss, J. L. (1981). *Statistical methods for rates and proportions.* New York: John Wiley & Sons.

Fleiss, J. L. (1986). *The design and analysis of clinical experiments.* New York: John Wiley & Sons.

Fonagy, P. (1991). Maternal representations of attachment during pregnancy predict the organization of infant–mother attachment at one year of age. *Child Development, 62*(5), 891–905.

Fonagy, P., Steele, H., & Steele, M. (1991). Maternal representations of attachment during pregnancy predict the organization of infant–mother attachment in one year of age. *Child Development, 62,* 891–905.

Fox, N. (1977). Attachment of kibbutz infants to mother and metapelet. *Child Development, 48,* 1228–1239.

Fox, N. A., & Davidson, R. J. (1987). Electroencephalogram asymmetry in response to the approach of a stranger and maternal separation in 10-month-old infants. *Developmental Psychology, 23,* 233–240.

Fox, N. A., Kimmerly, N. L., & Schafer, W. D. (1991). Attachment to mother/attachment to father: A meta-analysis. *Child Development, 62,* 210–225.

Frankel, K., Maslin-Cole, C., & Harmon, R. J. (1991, April). *Depressed mothers of preschoolers: What they say is not what they do.* Paper presented at the biennial conference of the Society for Research in Child Development, Seattle, WA.

Freitag, M. K., Belsky, J., Grossmann, K., & Grossmann, K. E. (1996). Continuity in parent–child relationships from infancy to middle childhood and relations with friendship competence. *Child Development, 67*(4), 1437–1454.

Fremmer-Bombik, E., Rudolph, J., Veit, B., Schwarz, G., & Schwarzmeier, I. (1989). *The Regensburg method of analyzing the Adult Attachment Interview.* Unpublished manual, Lehrstuhl für Psychologie IV, Universität Regensburg.

Gaensbauer, T. J., Harmon, R. J., Cytryn, L., & McKnew, D. H. (1984). Social and affective development in infants with a manic-depressive parent. *American Journal of Psychiatry, 141,* 223–229.

Geertz, C. (1989). *Works and lives: The anthropologist as author.* Stanford, CA: Stanford University Press.

Geertz, C. (1995). *After the fact: Two countries, four decades, one anthropologist.* Cambridge, MA: Harvard University Press.

Gelfand, D. M., & Teti, D. M. (1990). The effects of maternal depression on children. *Clinical Psychology Review, 10,* 329–353.

Gelfand, D. M., Teti, D. M., Seiner, S. A., & Jameson, P. B. (1996). Helping mothers fight depression: Evaluation of a home-based intervention program for depressed mothers and their infants. *Journal of Clinical Child Psychology, 25*(4), 406–422.

Gelinier-Ortiques, M. C., & Roudinesco, J. (1955). Maternal deprivation, psychogenic deafness and pseudo-retardation. In G. Caplan (Ed.), *Emotional problems of early childhood* (pp. 231–251). New York: Basic Books.

George, C., Kaplan, N., & Main, M. (1985). *An adult attachment interview.* Unpublished manuscript, University of California at Berkeley, Department of Psychology.

Gergen, K., Gulerce, A., Lock, A., & Misra, G. (1996). Psychological science in cultural context. *American Psychologist, 51,* 496–503.

Gewirtz, J. L. (1965). The course of infant smiling in four child-rearing environments in Israel. In B. M. Foss (Ed.), *Determinants of infant behavior* (Vol. 3., pp. 205–248). London: Methuen.

Goldberg, S., Perrotta, M., Minde, K., & Corter, C. (1986). Maternal behavior and attachment in low-birth-weight twins and singletons. *Child Development, 57*(1), 34–46.

Goldfarb, W. (1945a). Psychological privation in infancy and subsequent adjustment. *American Journal of Orthopsychiatry, 14,* 247–255.

Goldfarb, W. (1945b). Effects of psychological deprivation in infancy and subsequent stimulation. *American Journal of Psychiatry, 102,* 18–33.

Goldsmith, H. H., & Alansky, J. A. (1987). Maternal and infant temperamental predictors of attachment: A meta-analytic review. *Journal of Consulting and Clinical Psychology, 55*(6), 805–816.

Goldsmith, H. H., Bradshaw, D. L., & Rieser-Danner, L. A. (1986). Temperament as a potential developmental influence on attachment. In J. Lerner & R. Lerner (Eds.), *New directions for child development: Temperament and social interaction during infancy and childhood* (Vol. 31). San Francisco: Jossey-Bass.

Goldsmith, H. H., & Campos, J. J. (1990). The structure of temperamental fear and pleasure in infants: A psychometric perspective. *Child Development, 61,* 1944–1964.

Gottlieb, R., & Wiley, P. (1984). *America's Saints.* New York: G. P. Putnam's Sons.

Greenberg, M., Siegel, J., & Leitch, C. (1983). The nature and importance of attachment relationships to parents and peers during adolescence. *Journal of Youth and Adolescence, 12*(5), 373–386.

Groop, L. C., & Tuomi, T. (1997). Non-insulin-dependent diabetes mellitus – a collision between thrifty genes and an affluent society. *Annals of Medicine, 29,* 37–53.

Grossmann, K. E. (1977). Skalen zur Erfassung mütterlichen Verhaltens von Mary D. S. Ainsworth [Mary Ainsworth's maternal behavior scales]. In K. E. Grossmann (Ed.), *Entwicklung der Lernfähigkeit in der sozialen Umwelt* [Development of learning ability in the social environment] (pp. 96–105). Munich, Germany: Kindler Verlag.

Grossmann, K., Fremmer-Bombik, E., Friedl, A., Grossmann, K. E., Spangler, G., & Suess, G. (1989). Die Ontogenese emotionaler Integrität und Koherenz [The ontogeny of emotional integrity and coherency]. In E. Roth (Ed.), *Denken und Fühlen: Aspekte Kognitiv-emotionaler Wechselwirkung,* (pp. 36–55). Berlin: Springer-Verlag.

Grossmann, K., Fremmer-Bombik, E., Rudolph, J., & Grossmann, K. E. (1988). Maternal attachment representations as related to child–mother attachment patterns and maternal sensitivity and acceptance of her infant. In R. A. Hinde & J. Stevenson-Hinde (Eds.), *Relations within families* (pp. 241–260). Oxford: Oxford University Press.

Grossmann, K. E., & Grossmann, K. (1981). Parent–infant attachment relationship in Bielefeld: A research note. In K. Immelmann, G. W. Barlow, L. Petrinovich, & M. Main (Eds.), *Behavioral development: The Bielefeld interdisciplinary project.* London: Cambridge University Press (English). Berlin: Parey Verlag (German).

Grossmann, K. E., & Grossmann, K. (1990). The wider concept of attachment in cross-cultural research. *Human Development, 33,* 31–47.

Grossmann, K. E., & Grossmann, K. (1991). Attachment quality as an organizer of emotional and behavioral responses in a longitudinal perspective. In C. M. Parkes, J. Stevenson-Hinde, & P. Marris (Eds.), *Attachment across the life cycle* (pp. 93–114). London: Tavistock/Routledge.

Grossmann, K. E., & Grossmann, K. (1994). Bindungstheoretische Grundlagen psychologisch sicherer und und unsicherer Entwicklung [Basic aspects of attachment theory for secure and insecure development]. *GWG Zeitschrift der Gesellschaft für wissenschaftliche Gesprächspsychotherapie, 96,* 26–41.

Grossmann, K. E., & Grossmann, K. (in preparation). Emotional organization and concentration on reality in a life course perspective.

Grossmann, K. E., Grossmann, K., Huber, F., & Wartner, U. (1981). German children's behavior towards their mothers at 12 months and their fathers at 18 months in Ainsworth's Strange Situation. *International Journal of Behavioral Development, 4,* 157–181.

Grossmann, K., Grossmann, K. E., Spangler, G., Suess, G., & Unzner, L. (1985). Maternal sensitivity and newborns' orientation responses as related to quality of attachment in northern Germany. In I. Bretherton & E. Waters (Eds.), *Growing points of attachment theory and research* (pp. 233–278). *Monographs of the Society for Research on Child Development, 50*(1–2, Serial No. 209) (pp. 233–256).

Grossmann, K. E., Scheurer-Englisch, H., & Stephan, C. (1989, July). *Attachment research: Lasting effects and domains of validity.* Paper presented at the Tenth Biennial Meetings of ISSBD, Jyväskylä, Finland.

Grotevant, H., & Cooper, C. (1985). Patterns of interaction in family relationships and the development of identity and role-taking skill in adolescence. *Child Development, 56,* 415–428.

Gunnarsson, L. O. (1978). Children in day-care and family care in Sweden: A follow-up. *Research Bulletin, No 21, Department of Education.* Göteborg: University of Göteborg.

Hagekull, B., & Bohlin, G. (1992). Prevalence of problematic behaviors in four-year-olds. *Scandinavian Journal of Psychology, 33,* 359–369.

Hagekull, B., & Bohlin, G. (1994). Behavioral problems and competencies in four-year-olds: Dimensions and relationships. *International Journal of Behavioral Development, 17,* 311–327.

Hagekull, B., & Bohlin, G. (1995). Day care quality, family and child characteristics and socioemotional development. *Early Childhood Research Quarterly, 10,* 505–526.

Hagnell, O., Öjesjö, L., Otterbeck, L., & Rorsman, B. (1994). Prevalence of mental disorders, personality traits and mental complaints in the Lundby Study. *Scandanavia Journal of Social Medicine,* Supplementum 50, 1–17.

Hans, S. L. (1989). Developmental consequences of prenatal exposure to methadone. In D. E. Hutchings (Ed.), *Prenatal abuse of licit and illicit drugs. Annals of the New York Academy of Sciences, 562,* 195–207.

Hans, S. L., & Bernstein, V. J. (1995, August). *Parent–child interaction of dyads in which the children were exposed to methadone in utero: Infancy through adolescence.* Paper presented at the Annual Meeting of the American Psychological Association, New York.

Harlow, H. F. (1978). Uczuciowość. In R. Zazzo (Ed.), *Przywiązanie* (pp. 68–83). Warsaw: PWN.

Harrington, D. M., Block, J. H., & Block, J. (1978). Intolerance of ambiguity in preschool children: Psychometric considerations, behavioral manifestations, and parental correlates. *Developmental Psychology, 14,* 242–256.

Hårsman, I. (1984). *The emotional and social adjustment of infants to day-care centers.* Paper presented at the International Conference on Infant Studies, New York.

Harter, S. (1982). The perceived competence scale for children. *Child Development, 53,* 87–97.

Harter, S. (1988). *Self-Perception Profile for Adolescents.* Denver: University of Denver.

Hartman, E. J., & Haavind, H. (1981). Mothers as teachers and their children as learners. In W. P. R. Robinson (Ed.), *Communication in development, European Monographs in Social Psychology* (Vol. 24, pp. 129–158). London: Academic Press.

Hartman, L., Roger, M., Lemaire, B. J., Massias, J. F., & Chaussain, J. L. (1982). Plasma and urinary melatonin in male infants during the first 12 months of life. *Clinica Chimica Acta, 121,* 37–42.

Hatem, M. (1987). Toward the study of the psychodynamics of mothering and gender in Egyptian families. *International Journal of Middle East Studies, 19,* 287–306.

Hawley, D. J., & Wolfe, F. (1994). Effect of light and season on pain and depression in subjects with rheumatic disorders. *Pain, 59,* 227–234.

Head, T., & Williams T. M. (1995, March). *Children's and their parents' conceptualizations of attachment.* Paper presented in the symposium Quality of Attachment in the Preschool Years. Society for Research in Child Development, Indianapolis, IN.

Herjanic, B., & Reich, W. (1982). Development of a structured psychiatric interview for children: Agreement between child and parent on individual symptoms. *Journal of Abnormal Child Psychology, 10,* 307–324.

Hertsgaard, L., Gunnar, M., Erickson, M. F., & Nachmias, M. (1995). Adrenocortical response to the Strange Situation in infants with disorganized/disoriented attachment relationships. *Child Development, 66,* 1100–1106.

Hesse, E. (1996). Discourse, memory, and the Adult Attachment Interview: A note with emphasis on the emerging cannot classify category. *Infant Mental Health Journal, 17,* 4–11.

Hewlett, B. S., Lamb, M. E., Shannon, D., Leyendecker, B., & Schoelmerich, A. (1998). Culture and early infancy among central African foragers and farmers. *Developmental Psychology, 34,* 653–661.

Hill, J., & Holmbeck, G. (1986). Attachment and autonomy during adolescence. *Annals of Child Development, 3,* 145–189.

Hille, B. (1985). *Familie und Sozialisation in der DDR* [Family and socialization in the GDR]. Opladen: Leske & Budrich Verlag.

Hinde, R. A. (1987). *Individuals, relationships & culture: Links between ethology and the social sciences.* Cambridge, England: Cambridge University Press.

Hinde, R. A. (1991). Relationships, attachment, and culture: A tribute to John Bowlby. *Infant Mental Health Journal, 12,* 154–163.

Hinde, R. A. (1992). Developmental psychology in the context of the other behavioral sciences. *Developmental Psychology, 28,* 1018–1029.

Hinde, R. A. (1995). A suggested structure for a science of relationships. *Personal Relationships, 2,* 1–15.

Hinde, R. A. (1996). Describing relationships. In A. E. Auhagen & M. von Salisch (Eds.), *The diversity of human relationships* (pp. 7–35). New York: Cambridge University Press.

Hinde, R. A., & Stevenson-Hinde, J. (1990). Attachment: Biological, cultural, and individual desiderata. *Human Development, 33,* 62–72.

Hinshaw, S. P., Lahey, B. B., & Hart, E. L. (1993). Issues of taxonomy and comorbidity in the development of conduct disorder. *Development and Psychopathology, 5*(1–2), 31–49.

Hoem, B., & Hoem, J. M. (1987). *The Swedish family: Aspects of contemporary developments* (Stockholm Research Reports in Demography, No 43). Stockholm: University of Stockholm.

Hofstede, G. (1984). Hofstede's cultural dimensions: An independent validation using Rokeach's value survey. *Journal of Cross-cultural Psychology, 15,* 417–433.

Hoodfar, H. (1995). Child care and child health in low-income neighborhoods of Cairo. In E. Warnok Fernea (Ed.), *Childhood in the Muslim Middle East.* Austin: University of Texas Press.

Hunter, F., & Youniss, J. (1982). Changes in functions of three relations during adolescence. *Developmental Psychology, 18,* 806–811.

Hwang, C. P., & Broberg, A. G. (1992). The historical and social context of child care in Sweden. In M. E. Lamb, K. J. Sternberg, C. P. Hwang, & A. G. Broberg (Eds.), *Child care in context.* Hillsdale, NJ: Lawrence Erlbaum Associates.

Isabella, R. A. (1993). Origins of attachment: Maternal interactive behavior across the first year. *Child Development, 64,* 605–621.

Isabella, R. A., Belsky, J., & von Eye, A. (1989). Origins of infant–mother attachment: An examination of interactional synchrony during the infant's first year. *Developmental Psychology, 25*(1), 12–21.

Izard, C. E., Haynes, M., Chisholm, G., & Baak, K. (1991). Emotional determinants of infant–mother attachment. *Child Development, 62,* 906–917.

Jacobsen, T., & Hofmann, V. (1997). Children's attachment representations: Longitudinal relations to school behavior and academic competency in middle childhood and adolescence. *Developmental Psychology, 33*(4), 703–710.

Jacobsen, T., & Miller, L. J. (1998). Compulsive compliance in a young maltreated child. *Journal of the American Academy of Child and Adolescent Psychiatry, 37*(5), 462–463.

Jacobsen, T., Ziegenhain, U., Müller, B., Rottmann, U., Hofmann, V., & Edelstein, W. (1992). *Predicting stability of mother–child attachment in day-care children from infancy to age six.* Unpublished poster, presented at the 5th World Congress of the World Association of Infant Psychiatry and Allied Disciplines, Chicago.

Jacobson, S. W., & Frye, K. F. (1991). Effect of maternal social support on attachment: Experimental evidence. *Child Development, 62,* 572–582.

Jacobvitz, D., & Sroufe, L. A. (1987). The early caregiver–child relationship and attention-deficit disorder with hyperactivity in kindergarten: A prospective study. *Child Development, 58,* 1488–1495.

Jarvis, P. A., & Creasey, G. L. (1991). Parental stress, coping, and attachment in families with an 18-month-old infant. *Infant Behavior and Development, 14,* 383–395.

Jeremy, R. J., & Hans, S. L. (1985). Behavior of neonates exposed in utero to methadone as assessed on the Brazelton scale. *Infant Behavior and Development, 8,* 323–336.

Jose, P. E., D'Anna, C. A., Cafasso, L. L., Bryant, F. B., Chiker, V., Gein, N., & Zhezmer, N. (1998). Stress and coping among Russian and American early adolescents. *Developmental Psychology, 34,* 757–769.

Julien, D., Markman, H. J., Lindahl, K., Johnson, H. M., & Van Widenfelt, B. (1987). *Interactional Dimensions Coding System.* Denver: University of Denver.

Jurga, M. (1985). Doświadczenie społeczne i rozwój osobowości wychowanek domów dziecka. In M. Tyszkowa (Ed.), *Rozwój dziecka w rodzinie i poza rodziną* (pp. 153–202). Poznań: UAM.

Kagitcibasi, C., & Berry, C. W. (1989). Cross-cultural psychology: Current research and trends. In M. R. Rosensweig & W. P. Lynman (Eds.), *Annual Reviews of Psychology, 40,* 493–531.

Karen, R. (1994). *Becoming attached: Unfolding the mystery of the infant–mother bond and its impact on later life.* New York: Warner.

Katkovsky, W., Crandall, V. C., & Good, S. (1967). Parental antecedents of children's beliefs in internal-external control of reinforcement in intellectual achievement situations. *Child Development, 28,* 765–776.

Kauffman, R., & Kauffman, R. W. (1994). *The Latter Day Saints: A study of the Mormons in the light of economic conditions.* Urbana: University of Illinois Press.

Kauppila, A., Kivel, E., Pakarinen, A., & Vakkuri, O. (1987). Inverse seasonal relationship between melatonin and ovarian activity in humans in a region with a strong seasonal contrast in luminosity. *Journal of Clinical Endocrinology and Metabolism, 65,* 823–828.

Keller, H., Völker, S., & Zach, U. (1997). Attachment in cultural context. *ISSBD Newsletter, 1*(31), 1–3.

Keller, M., Beardslee, W., Dorer, D., Lavori, P., Samuelson, H., & Klerman, G. (1986). Impact of severity and chronicity of parental affective illness on adaptive functioning and psychopathology in children. *Archives of General Psychiatry, 43,* 930–937.

Kelly, G. A. (1955). *The psychology of personal constructs.* New York: W. W. Norton.

Kessler, R. C. (1994). The National Comorbidity Survey of the United States. *International Review of Psychiatry, 6*(4), 365–376.

Kirkpatrick, L. A., & Davis, K. E. (1994). Attachment style, gender, and relationship stability: A longitudinal analysis. *Journal of Personality and Social Psychology, 66,* 502–512.

Kirkpatrick, L. A., & Hazan, C. (1994). Attachment styles and close relationships: A four-year prospective study. *Personal Relationships, 1,* 123–142.

Kisilevsky, B. S., Hains, S. M. J., Lee, K., Muir, D. W., Xu, F., Fu, G., Zhao, Z. Y., & Yang, R. L. (1998). The still-face effect in Chinese and Canadian 3- to 6-month-old infants. *Developmental Psychology, 34,* 629–639.

Klein, P. S. (1992). Cognitive and emotional interplay in early development: Mediation role of parents. *Advances in cognition and educational practice, 1A,* 169–194.

Klein, P. S., & Feuerstein, R. (1985). Environmental variables and cognitive development. In S. Harel & N. J. Anastasiow (Eds.), *The at-risk infant: Psycho/socio/medical aspects.* Baltimore, MD: Paul H. Publishing.

Klinge, M. (1994). *A brief history of Finland.* Helsinki, Finland: Otava.

Klominek, W. (1981). *Rozwój dzieci adoptowanych w nowym środowisku rodzinnym w 10–15 lat po przysposobieniu* (pp. 1–11). Warsaw: TPD ZG.

Kobak, R., & Cole, H. (1994). Attachment and meta-monitoring: Implications for adolescent autonomy and psychopathology. In D. Cicchetti & S. L. Toth (Eds.), *Rochester symposium on developmental psychopathology: Vol. 5. Disorder and dysfunctions of the self* (pp. 267–297). Rochester, NY: University of Rochester Press.

Kobak, R. R., Cole, H. E., Ferenz-Gillies, R. & Fleming, W. S. (1993). Attachment and emotion regulation during mother–teen problem solving: A control theory analysis. *Child Development, 64,* 231–245.

Kobak, R. R., & Sceery, A. (1988). Attachment in late adolescence: Working models, affect regulation, and representations of self and others. *Child Development, 59,* 135–146.

Kobak, R., Sudler, N., & Gamble, W. (1991). Attachment and depressive symptoms during adolescence: A developmental pathway analysis. *Development and Psychopathology, 3,* 461–474.

Kostovic, I., Judas, M., Petanjek, Z., & Simic, G. (1995). Ontogenesis of goal-directed behavior: Anatomo-functional considerations. *International Journal of Psychophysiology, 19,* 85–102.

Lamb, M. E. (1987). Predictive implications of individual differences in attachment. *Journal of Consulting and Clinical Psychology, 55*(6), 817–824.

Lamb, M. E., Hwang, C. P., Bookstein, F. L., Broberg, A., Hult, G., & Frodi, M. (1988). Determinants of social competence in Swedish preeschoolers. *Developmental Psychology, 24,* 58–70.

Lamb, M. E., & Sternberg, K. J. (1989). *Tagesbetreuung* [Daycare]. In H. Keller (Ed.), *Handbuch der Kleinkindforschung* (pp. 587–608). Berlin: Springer.

Lamb, M. E., & Sternberg, K. J. (1990). Do we really know how daycare affects children? *Journal of Applied Developmental Psychology, 11,* 351–379.

Lamb, M. E., Thompson, R. A., Gardner, W. P., Charnov, E. L., & Estes, D. (1984). Security of infantile attachment as assessed in the "strange situation": Its study and biological interpretation. *The behavioral and brain sciences, 7,* 127–171.

Lamb, M. E. Thompson, R. A., Gardner, W., & Charnov, E. L. (1985). *Infant–mother attachment: The origins and developmental significance of individual differences in Strange Situation behavior.* Hillsdale, NJ: Lawrence Erlbaum Associates.

Lamb, M. E., Sternberg, K. J., Hwang, C. P., & Broberg, A. G. (Eds.). (1992). *Child care in context. Cross-cultural perspectives.* Hillsdale, NJ: Lawrence Erlbaum Associates.

Lapsley, D. K, Rice, K. G., & FitzGerald, D. P. (1990). Adolescent adaptation hypothesis. *Journal of Counseling and Development, 68*(5), 561–565.

Lazzarini, A., & Rissone, A. (1982). L'inserimento all'asilo nido: un'esperienza di separazione e un'occasione di cambiamento. *Giornale di Neuropsichiatria dell' Età Evolutiva, II, 4,* 373–385.

Lederberg, A. R., & Mobley, C. E. (1990). The effect of hearing impairment on the quality of attachment and mother–toddler interaction. *Child Development, 61,* 1596–1604.

Le Doux, J. E., Romanski, L., & Xagoraris, A. (1989). Indelibility of subcortical emotional memories. *Journal of cognitive neuroscience,* 1, 238–243.

Lefcourt, H. M. (1982). The social antecedents of locus of control. In H. M. Lefcourt (Ed.), *Locus of control: Current trends in theory and research* (pp. 131–147). Hillsdale, NJ: Lawrence Erlbaum Associates.

Lesch, J. E. (1996). Immunology dichotomized. *Science,* 273, 75–76.

Lesch, K.-P., Benegel, D., Heils, A., Sabol, S., Greenberg, B., Petri, S., Benjamin, J., Müller, C., Hamer, D., & Murphy, D. (1996). Association of anxiety-related traits with a polymorphism in the serotonin transporter gene regulatory region. *Science,* 274, 1527–1530.

Leuzinger-Bohleber, M., & Garlichs, A. (1993). *Früherziehung West-Ost. Zukunftserwartungen, Autonomieentwicklung und Beziehungsfähigkeit von Kindern und Jugendlichen.* [Early education West-Ost: Expectations for the future, development of autonomy, and ability to bond in children and youths] Weinheim/München: Juventa-Verlag.

Levine, L., Tuber, S., Slade, A., & Ward, M. (1991). Mothers' mental representations and their relationship to mother–infant attachment. *Bulletin of the Menninger Clinic,* 55(4), 454–469.

LeVine, R. A. (1977). Child rearing as cultural adaptation. In P. H. Leidermann, S. R. Tulkin, & A. Rosenfeld (Eds.), *Culture and infancy* (pp. 15–27). New York: Academic Press.

Lewis, M., & Feiring, C. (1989). Infant, mother, and mother–infant behavior and subsequent attachment. *Child Development,* 60, 831–837.

Lewis, M., Feiring, C., McGuffog, C., & Jaskir, J. (1984). Predicting psychopathology in six-year-olds from early social relations. *Child Development,* 55, 123–136.

Lieberman, A. F., & Pawl, J. H. (1988). Clinical applications of attachment theory. In J. Belsky & T. Nezworski (Eds.), *Clinical implications of attachment* (pp. 327–347). Hillsdale, NJ: Lawrence Erlbaum Associates.

Lippe, A. L. von der (in press). The impact of maternal schooling and occupation on child-rearing attitudes and behaviors in low-income neighborhoods in Cairo, Egypt. *International Journal of Behavior Development.*

Lippe, A. L. von der, & Hartman, E. (1996). *Mothers as mediators of meaning in the development of cognitive competence in Egyptian children.* Resources of Education (RIE), ERIC Document Reproduction Services (EDRS), Clearinghouse on Elementary and Early Childhood Education, Urbana-Champaign: University of Illinois.

Lis, S. (1978). Znaczenie opieki matki zastąpczej dla psychoruchowego rozwoju dziecka wychowywanego poza rodziną. *Zeszyty Naukowe Instytutu Psychologii Uniwersytetu Warszawskiego,* 10, 3–55.

Lis, S. (1992). *Socjalizacja dziecka w środowisku pozarodzinnym.* Warsaw: PWN.

Lissina, M. I. (1985). *Child-adult-peers. Patterns of communication.* Moscow: Progress Publishers.

Lofland, J., & Lofland, L. H. (1984). *Analyzing social settings: A guide to qualitative observation and analysis.* Belmont, CA: Wadsworth Publishing Co.

Lütkenhaus, P., Bullock, M. & Geppert, U. (1987). Toddler's action: Knowledge, control, and the self. In F. Halisch & J. Kuhl (Eds.), *Motivation, intention and volition* (pp. 145–162). Berlin: Springer.

Lynch, M., & Cicchetti, D. (1997). The role of self-organization in the promotion of resilience in maltreated children. *Development and Psychopathology,* 9, 797–815.

Lynch, M., & Cicchetti, D. (1998). An ecological-transactional analysis of children and contexts: The longitudinal interplay among child maltreatment, community violence, and children's symptomology. *Development and Psychopathology, 10,* 235–257.

Lyons-Ruth, K., Connell, D. B., Grunebaum, H., & Botein, S. (1990). Infants at social risk: Maternal depression and family support services as mediators of infant development and security of attachment. *Child Development, 61,* 85–98.

Lyons-Ruth, K., Easterbrooks, M. A., & Cibelli, C. D. (1997). Infant attachment strategies, infant mental lag, and maternal depressive symptoms: Predictors of internalizing and externalizing problems at age 7. *Developmental Psychology, 33*(4), 681–692.

Lyons-Ruth, K., Repacholi, B., McLeod, S., & Silva, E. (1991). Disorganized attachment behavior in infancy: Short-term stability, maternal and infant correlates, and risk-related subtypes. *Development and Psychopathology, 3,* 377–396.

Maccoby, E. E. (1992). The role of parents in the socialization of children: An historical overview. *Developmental Psychology, 28,* 1006–1017.

Maccoby, E., & Jacklin, C. N. (1987). Gender segregation in childhood. *Advances in Child Development and Behavior, 20,* 239–287.

Maccoby, E. E., & Martin, J. A. (1983). Socialization in the context of the family: Parent–child interaction. In P. H. Mussen (Series Ed.) & E. M. Hetherington (Vol. Ed.), *Handbook of child psychology: Vol. 4. Socialization, personality, and social development* (4th ed., pp. 1–101). New York: John Wiley.

MacDonald, K. B. (Ed.). (1988). *Sociobiological perspectives on human development.* New York: Springer-Verlag.

MacDonald, K. B. (1992). Warmth as a developmental construct: An evolutionary analysis. *Child Development, 63,* 753–773.

Main, M. (1981). Avoidance in the service of attachment: A working paper. In K. Immelmann, G. W. Barlow, L. Petrinovich, & M. Main (Eds.), *Behavioral development: The Bielefeld Interdisciplinary Project.* Cambridge: Cambridge University Press.

Main, M. (1991). Metacognitive knowledge, metacognitive monitoring, and singular (coherent) vs. multiple (incoherent) model of attachment: Findings and directions for future research. In C. M. Parkes & J. Stevenson-Hinde (Eds.), *Attachment across the lifecycle* (pp. 127–159). New York: Routledge.

Main, M., & Cassidy, J. (1988). Categories of response to reunion with the parent at age 6: Predictable from infant attachment classification and stable over a 1-month period. *Developmental Psychology, 24,* 415–426.

Main, M., & Goldwyn, R. (in press). Adult attachment classification systems. In M. Main (Ed.), *A typology of human attachment organization: Assessed in discourse, drawing, and interviews.* Cambridge: Cambridge University Press.

Main, M., & Hesse, E. (1990). Parents' unresolved traumatic experiences are related to infant disorganized attachment status: Is frightened and/or frightening parental behavior the linking mechanism? In M. T. Greenberg, D. Cicchetti, & E. M. Cumming (Eds.), *Attachment in the preschool years. Theory, research, and intervention* (pp. 161–182). Chicago: University of Chicago Press.

Main, M., Kaplan, N., & Cassidy, J. (1985). Security in infancy, childhood, and adulthood: A move to the level of representation. In I. Bretherton & E. Waters (Eds.), *Growing points of attachment theory and research* (pp. 66–104). *Monographs of the Society for Research on Child Development, 50* (1–2, Serial No. 209) (pp. 66–104).

Main, M., & Solomon, J. (1986). Discovery of a new, insecure-disorganized/disoriented attachment pattern. In T. B. Brazelton & M. Yogman (Eds.), *Affective development in infancy* (pp. 95–124). Norwood, NJ: Ablex.

Main, M., & Solomon, J. (1990). Procedures for identifying infants as disorganized-disoriented during the Ainsworth Strange Situation. In M. Greenberg, D. Cicchetti, & E. M. Cummings (Eds.), *Attachment in the preschool years: Theory, research, and intervention* (pp. 121–160). Chicago: University of Chicago Press.

Main, M., Tomasini, L., & Tolan, W. (1979). Differences among mothers of infants judged to differ in security. *Developmental Psychology, 15,* 472–473.

Mainemer, H., & Gilman, L. C. (1992). The experiences of Canadian parents adopting children from Romanian orphanages [Abstract]. *Canadian Psychology, 33*(2), 503.

Mainemer, H., Gilman, L. C., & Ebbern, H. (1997). Parenting stress. In E. W. Ames (Eds.), *The development of Romanian children adopted to Canada* (pp. 85–95). Ottawa: Human Resources Development Canada.

Makarenko, A. S. (1983). *Ein Buch für Eltern* [A book for parents]. Berlin: Verlag Volk and Wissen.

Malatesta, C. Z., Culver, C., Tesman, J. R., & Shephard, B. (1989). The development of emotion expression during the first two years of life. *Monographs of the Society for Research in Child Development, 54* (1–2, Serial. No. 219) (pp. 125–136).

Mangelsdorf, S., Gunnar, M., Kestenbaum, R., Lang, S., & Andreas, D. (1990). Infant proneness-to-distress temperament, maternal personality, and mother-infant attachment: Associations and goodness of fit. *Child-Development, 61*(3), 820–831.

Marris, P. (1991). The social construction of uncertainty. In P. Marris, J. Stevenson-Hinde, & C. Parkes (Eds.), *Attachment across the life-cycle* (pp. 77–90). New York: Routledge.

Marsella, A. J. (1998). Toward a "global-community psychology": Meeting the needs of a changing world. *American Psychologist, 53,* 1282–1291.

Marvin, R. S., & Mossler, D. (1976). A methodological paradigm for the description and analysis of non-verbal expressions: coy expression. *Representative Research in Social Psychology, 7,* 133–139.

Marvin, R. S., & Stewart, R. B. (1990). A family systems framework for the study of attachment. In M. T. Greenberg, D. Cicchetti, & E. M. Cummings (Eds.), *Attachment in the preschool years: Theory, research, and intervention* (pp. 51–86). Chicago: University of Chicago Press.

Marx, K. (1981). *Das Kapital, Vol 1.* Berlin/Germany: Dietz Verlag.

Masitova, G. H. (1977). *Razvitie differencial'nyh bzaimootnosenij s okruzajuscimi vzroslymi u mladencev* [Interindividual development of interaction patterns between caretaking adults and children]. Unpublished dissertation, Moscow University, Moscow.

Masitova, G. H. (1979). *Vzaimootnosenija s okruzajuscimi vzroslymi kak faktor razvitija licnosti rebjonka na pervom godu zizni* [Interaction with caretaking adults as a factor for individual personal development in the first year of life]. *Voprosy psihologii licnosti,* 62–74.

Matas, L., Arend, L., & Sroufe, L. A. (1978). Continuity of adaptation in the second year: The relationship between the quality of attachment and later competent functioning. *Child Development, 49,* 547–556.

Matejček, Z. (1962). Sledováni duševního vývoje ústavních detí detskou psychiatrickou slouzbou stredoceskeho kraje. *Ceskoslovenska Pediatrie, 17,* 621–627.

Matejček, Z. (1964). Psychologické sledováni detí v domovech ze zvýšenou péči. *Ceskoslovenska Pediatrie, 19,* 21–25.

Matejček, Z. (1967). Vývoj osobnosti ústavních detí. *Psychológia a Patopsychológia Dietata, 3,* 17–31.

Mazumdar, P. M. H. (1995). *Species and specificity: An interpretation of the history of immunology.* New York: Cambridge University Press.

McMullan, S., & Fisher, L. (1992). Developmental progress of Romanian orphanage children in Canada [Abstract]. *Canadian Psychology, 33*(2), 504.

Messerjakova, S. J. (1979). *Psihologiceskij analiz "kompleksa ozivlenija" u mladencev* [Psychological analysis of the "activity complex" in children]. Unpublished dissertation, Moscow University, Moscow.

Minde, K., Corter, C., Goldberg, S., & Jeffers, D. (1990). Maternal preference between premature twins up to age four. *Journal of the American Academy of Child and Adolescent Psychiatry, 29,* 367–374.

Mitchell, S. K., Bee, H. L., Hammond, M. A., & Barnard, K. E. (1985). Prediction of school and behavior problems in children followed from birth to age eight. In W. K. Frankenburg, R. N. Emde, & J. W. Sullivan (Eds.), *Early identification of children at risk.* New York: Plenum Press.

Miyake, K., Chen, S., & Campos, J. J. (1985). Infant temperament, mother's mode of interaction, and attachment in Japan: An interim report. *Monographs of the Society for Research in Child Development, 50,* 276–297.

Moilanen, I. (1979). *To be born as a twin – risks and sequelae.* Thesis, Acta Universitatis Ouluensis (Series D Medica No 50).

Moilanen, I. (1987). Inter-twin relationships and mental health. *Nordisk Psykiatrisk Tidskrift, 41,* 279–284.

Montoli Perani, R. A. (1985). Un bambino va all'asilo nido; un'esperienza di lavoro clinico nel territorio. *Giornale di Neuropsichiatria dell'Età Evolutiva, 5,* 327–332.

Murray, L. (1992). The impact of postnatal depression on infant development. *Journal of Child Psychology and Psychiatry, 33,* 543–561.

Nagayama, H., Sasaki, M., Ichii, S., Hanada, K., Okawa, M., Ohta, T., Asano, Y., Sugita, Y., Yamazaki, J., & Koshaka, M. (1991). Atypical depressive symptoms possibly predict responsiveness to phototherapy in seasonal affective disorder. *Journal of Affective Disorders, 23,* 185–189.

Naslund, B., Persson-Blennow, I., McNeil, T. F., Kaij, L., & Malmquist-Larsson, A. (1984). Deviations on exploration, attachment, and fear of strangers in high-risk and control infants at one year of age. *American Journal of Orthopsychiatry, 54,* 569–577.

Newberger, C. M., & Cook, S. J. (1983). Parental awareness and child abuse: A cognitive-developmental analysis of urban and rural samples. *American Journal of Orthopsychiatry, 53,* 512–524.

NICHD Early Child Care Research. (1997). The effects of infant child care on infant–mother attachment security: Results of the NICHD study of early child care. *Child Development, 68*(5), 860–879.

Ogawa, J. R., Sroufe, L. A., Weinfield, N. S., Carlson, E. A., & Egeland, B. (1997). Development and the fragmented self: Longitudinal study of dissociative symptomatology in a nonclinical sample. *Development and Psychopathology, 9*(4), 855–879.

Olechnowicz, H. (1957). Choroba szpitalna (hospitalizm) u małego dziecka wychowywanego poza rodziną. *Pediatria Polska, 7,* 837–849.

Oppenheim, D., Sagi, A., & Lamb, M. E. (1988). Infant–adult attachments on the kibbutz and their relation to socioemotional development 4 years later. *Developmental Psychology, 24,* 427–433.

Osofsky, J. D., & Connors, K. (1979). Mother–infant interaction: An integrative view of a complex system. In J. D. Osofsky (Ed.), *Handbook of Infant Development* (pp. 519–548). New York: John Wiley.

Ostner, I. (1990). Integration durch Segregation. Weibliche Identität im Wandel [Integration through segregation. Changing female identities]. *Studium Generale.* Heidelberg: Heidelberger Verlagsanstalt.

Partonen, T. (1994). Effects of morning light treatment on subjective sleepiness and mood in winter depression. *Journal of Affective Disorders, 30,* 47–56.

Patterson, G. R. (1982). *A social learning approach to family intervention: Vol. 3. Coercive family process.* Eugene, OR: Castalia.

Pedersen, D. R., & Moran, G. (1995). A categorical description of infant–mother relationships in the home and its relation to Q-sort measures of mother–infant interaction. In E. Waters, B. E. Vaughn, G. Posada, & K. Kondo-Ikemura (Eds.), Caregiving, cultural, and cognitive perspectives on secure-base behavior and working models. New growing points of attachment theory and research *Monographs of the Society for Research in Child Development, 60* (2–3, Serial No. 244). (pp. 111–132).

Pilgrim, V. E. (1993). *Muttersöhne* [Mammas' boys]. Hamburg/Germany: Rowohlt Verlag.

Provence, S., & Lipton, R. C. (1962). *Infants in institutions.* New York: International Universities Press.

Przetacznikowa, M. (1967). Odrebności w rozwoju psychicznym dzieci do lat trzech wychowywanych w żłobkach i w rodzinach. *Materiały do Nauczania Psychologii,* serial II, 2, 719–733.

Pujol, J., Vendrell, P., Junque, C., Marti-Vilalta, J. L., et al. (1993). When does human brain development end? Evidence of corpus callosum growth up to adulthood. *Annals of Neurology, 34,* 71–75.

Quintana, S., & Kerr, J. (1993). Relational needs in late adolescent separation-individuation. *Journal of Counseling and Development, 71,* 349–354.

Radke-Yarrow, M., Cummings, E. M., Kuczynski, L., & Chapman, M. (1985). Patterns of attachment in two- and three-year-olds in normal families and families with parental depression. *Child Development, 56,* 884–893.

Raja, S. N., McGee, R., & Stanton, W. R. (1992). Perceived attachments to parents and peers and psychological well-being in adolescence. *Journal of Youth and Adolescence, 21,* 471–485.

Rauh, H. (1990). Die Rolle der Mutter in der Sozialisation des kleinen Kindes [The role of the mother in the socialization of infants]. In R. Schmitz-Scherzer, A. Kruse, & E. Olbrich (Eds.), *Altern – Ein lebenslanger Prozess der sozialen Interaktion.* Festschrift zum 60. Geburtstag von Frau Professor Ursula Maria Lehr (pp. 411–423). Darmstadt, Germany: Steinkopff.

Rauh, H., Dillmann, S., Müller, B., & Ziegenhain, U. (1995). Anfänge der Persönlichkeitsentwicklung in der frühen Kindheit [Origins of personality development in infancy]. In A. Kruse & R. Schmitz-Scherzer (Eds.), *Psychologie der Lebensalter* (pp. 107–122). Darmstadt, Germany: Steinkopff.

Rauh, H., Rottmann, U., & Ziegenhain, U. (1987, 1990). Anpassung von Kleinkindern an neue Settings im ersten Lebensjahr [Adaptation of infants to novel settings in the first year of life]. *"Frühkindliche Anpassung"* to the German Science Foundation (Ra 373/5-1 bis 5-3). Unpublished research proposal, Free University of Berlin, Institute for Psychology.

Raven, J. C., Court, J. H., & Raven, J. (1992). *Standard Progressive Matrices.* London: Oxford University Press.

Recommended Dietary Allowance 10th Edition (1989). Washington, DC: National Academy of Sciences.

Reimer, M. S., Overton, W. F., Steidl, J. H., Rosenstein, D. S., & Horowitz, H. (1996). Familial responsiveness and behavioral control: Influences on adolescent psychopathology, attachment, and cognition. *Journal of Research on Adolescence, 6,* 87–112.

Reyes, M. B., Routh, D. K., Jean-Gilles, M. M., Sanfilippo, M. D., et al. (1991). Ethnic differences in parenting children in fearful situations. *Journal of Pediatric Psychology, 16,* 717–726.

Rice, K. G. (1990). Attachment in adolescence: A narrative and meta-analytic review. *Journal of Youth and Adolescence, 19,* 511–538.

Richman, A. L., Miller, P. M., & LeVine, R. A. (1992). Cultural and educational variations in maternal responsiveness. *Developmental Psychology, 28*(4), 614–621.

Richters, J. E., & Cicchetti, D. (1993). Developmental considerations in the investigation of conduct disorder. *Development and Psychopathology, 5,* 331–344.

Ritvo, S., & Solnit, A. (1958). Influences of early mother–child interactions on identification process. *Psychoanalytic Study of the Child, 13,* 64–86.

Roberts, R. E., Attkisson, C. C., & Rosenblatt, A. (1998). Prevalence of psychopathology among children and adolescents. *American Journal of Psychiatry, 155,* 715–725.

Robin, M., & Casati, I. (1994). Are twins different from singletons during early childhood? *Early Development and Parenting, 3,* 211–221.

Robin, M., Josse, D., & Tourrette, C. (1988). Mother–twin interaction during early childhood. *Acta Geneticae Medicae Gemellologiae, 37,* 151–159.

Robin, M., Kheroua, H., & Casati, I. (1992). Effects of early mother–twin relationships from birth to age 3, on twin bonding. *Acta Geneticae Medicae Gemellologiae, 41,* 143–148.

Rocznik demograficzny. (1976). Wasaw: Zarzad Wydawnictw Statystycznych i Drukarni.

Rocznik statystyczny Ministerstwa Zdrowia i Opieki Spolecznej 1976. (1976). Warsaw: MZiOS.

Rodning, C., Beckwith, L., & Howard, J. (1991). Quality of attachment and home environments in children prenatally exposed to PCP and cocaine. *Development and Psychopathology, 3,* 351–366.

Roggman, L. A., Langlois, J. H., & Hubbs-Tait, L. (1987). Mothers, infants, and toys: Social play correlates of attachment. *Infant Behavior and Development, 10,* 233–237.

Roggman, L. A., Langlois, J. H., Hubbs-Tait, L. & Rieser-Danner, L. (1994). Infant daycare, attachment, and the "file-drawer problem." *Child Development, 65,* 1429–1443.

Rogoff, B. Mistry, J. Göncü, A., & Mosier, C. (1991). Cultural variation in the role relations of toddlers and their families. In M. H. Bornstein (Ed.), *Cultural approaches to parenting* (pp. 173–183). Hillsdale, NJ: Lawrence Erlbaum Associates.

Rogosch, F. A., Cicchetti, D., & Aber, J. L. (1995). The role of child maltreatment in early deviations in cognitive and affective processing abilities and later peer relationship problems. *Development and Psychopathology, 7,* 591–609.

Rosen, K. S., & Rothbaum, F. (1993). Quality of parental caregiving and security of attachment. *Developmental Psychology, 29,* 358–367.

Rosenstein, D. S., & Horowitz, H. A. (1996). Adolescent attachment and psychopathology. *Journal of Consulting and Clinical Psychology, 64,* 244–253.

Ross, S., & Jennings, K. (1992, May). *Mother–infant interaction and infant attachment security in clinically depressed mothers.* Paper presented at the eighth International Conference on Infant Studies, Miami, FL.

Rothbart, M. K., & Ahadi, S. A. (1994). Temperament and the development of personality. *Journal of Abnormal Psychology, 103*(1), 55–66.

Rottmann, U., & Ziegenhain, U. (1988). *Bindungsbeziehung und außerfamiliale Tagesbetreuung im frühen Kleinkindalter. Die Eingewöhnung einjähriger Kinder in die*

Krippe [Attachment relations and daycare experience in infancy: The familiarization of one-year-olds with daycare]. Unpublished dissertation, Free University of Berlin, Institute for Psychology, Berlin.

Rubin, K. H. (1998). Social and emotional development from a cultural perspective. *Developmental Psychology, 34,* 611–615.

Rutter, M. (1981). *Maternal deprivation reassessed.* New York: Penguin Books.

Rutter, M., & Maughan, B. (1997). Psychosocial adversities in childhood and adult psychopathology. *Journal of Personality Disorders, 11*(1), 4–18.

Rutter, M., & Rutter, M. (1993). *Developing minds: Challenge and continuity across the lifespan.* New York: Basic Books.

Saarni, C. (1998). Issues of cultural meaningfulness in emotional development. *Developmental Psychology, 34,* 647–652.

Sagi, A. (1990). Attachment theory and research from a cross-cultural perspective. *Human Development, 33,* 10–22.

Sagi, A., Donnel, F., Harel, Y., Joels, T., & Tuvia, M. (1989, July). *Multiple caregiving quality of care, and infant–metapelet attachment on Israeli Kibbutzim.* Paper presented at the Tenth Biennial Meetings of ISSBD, Jyväskylä, Finland.

Sagi, A., Lamb, K., Lewkowicz, K. S., Shoham, R., Dvir, R., & Estes, D. (1985). Security of infant–mother-father, and -metapelet attachments among kibbutz-reared Israeli children. In I. Bretherton & E. Waters (Eds.), *Growing points of attachment theory and research Monographs of the Society for Research on Child Development, 50*(1–2, Serial No. 209). (pp. 257–275).

Sakin, J., & Teti, D. M. (1995). *Maternal and child correlates of attachment quality among toddlers.* Unpublished manuscript, University of Maryland, Baltimore County, MD.

Sameroff, A. J. (1994). Models of development and developmental risk. In C. H. Zeanah (Ed.), *Handbook of infant mental health* (pp. 3–13). New York: Guilford Press.

Sameroff, A., & Chandler, M. (1975). Reproductive risk and the continuum of caretaking casualty. In F. Horowitz, M. Hetherington, S. Scarr-Salapatek, & G. Siegel (Eds.), *Review of child development research* (Vol. 4, pp. 187–244). Chicago: University of Chicago Press.

Sameroff, A. J., Seifer, R., & Zax, M. (1982). Early development of children at risk for emotional disorder. *Monographs of the Society for Research in Child Development, 47*(7, Serial No. 199) (pp. 82–90).

Scarr, S., & Eisenberg, M. (1993). Child care research: Issues, perspectives, and results. In L. W. Porter & M. R. Rosenzweig (Eds.), *Annual Review of Psychology* (Vol. 44, pp. 613–644). Palo Alto, CA: Annual Reviews.

Scarr, S., & McCartney, K. (1983). How people make their own environments: A theory of genotype-environment effects. *Child Development, 54,* 424–435.

Scarr, S., Phillips, D., & McCartney, K. (1990). Facts, fantasies and the future of child care in the United States. *Psychological Science, 1,* 26–35.

Schacter, D. L., & Tulving, E. (1994). What are the memory systems of 1994? In D. L. Schacter & E. Tulving (Eds.), *Memory systems 1994* (pp. 1–38). Cambridge, MA: Bradford.

Schaffer, H. R. (1966). Activity level as a constitutional determinant of infantile reaction to deprivation. *Child Development, 37,* 595–602.

Schepank, H. (Ed.) (1987). *Epidemiology of psychogenic disorders – the Mannheim study. Results of a field survey.* Berlin, Germany: Springer.

Schmidt-Kolmer, E., & Schmidt, H. H. (1962). Über Frauenarbeit und Familie [On woman labor and family]. *Einheit, 12,* 89–99.

Schneider, J. (1971). On vigilance and virgins: Honor, shame, and access to resources in Mediterranean societies. *Ethology, 10,* 1–23.

Schneider-Rosen, K. (1993). The developmental reorganization of attachment relationships: Guidelines for classification beyond infancy. In M. T. Greenberg, D. Cicchetti, & E. M. Cummings (Eds.), *Attachment in the preschool years: Theory, research, and intervention* (pp. 185–220). Chicago: University of Chicago Press.

Schneider-Rosen, K., Braunwald, K. G., Carlson, V., & Cicchetti, D. (1985). Current perspectives in attachment theory: Illustrations from the study of maltreated infants. In I. Bretherton & E. Waters (Eds.), *Growing points of attachment theory and research* (pp. 194–210). *Monographs of the Society for Research on Child Development, 50*(1–2, Serial No. 209) (pp. 194–210).

Schneider-Rosen, K., & Cicchetti, D. (1984). The relationship between affect and cognition in maltreated infants: Quality of attachment and the development of visual self-recognition. *Child Development, 55,* 648–658.

Schore, A. N. (1994). *Affect regulation and the origin of self: The neurobiology of emotional development.* Hillsdale, NJ: Lawrance Erlbaum Associates.

Seefeldt, L. (1997). *Models of parenting in maltreating and non-maltreating mothers.* Dissertation presented to the faculty of the School of Nursing at the University of Wisconsin at Milwaukee, Milwaukee, WI.

Segall, M. H., Lonner, W. J., & Berry, J. W. (1998). Cross-cultural psychology as a scholarly discipline: On the flowering of culture in behavioral research. *American Psychologist, 53,* 1101–1110.

Seifer, R., Sameroff, A. J., Dickstein, S., Keitner, G., Miller, I., Rasmussen, S., & Hayden, L. C. (1996). Parental psychopathology, multiple contextual risks, and one-year outcomes in children. *Journal of Clinical Child Psychology, 25*(4), 423–435.

Seifer, R., & Schiller, M. (1995). The role of parenting sensitivity, infant temperament, and dyadic interaction in attachment theory and assessment. In E. Waters, B. E. Vaughn, G. Posada & K. Kondo-Ikemura (Eds.), *Caregiving, cultural, and cognitive perspectives on secure-base behavior and working models. New growing points of attachment theory and research. Monographs of the Society for Research in Child Development, 60* (2–3, Serial No. 244) (pp. 146–174).

Seligman, M. E. P. (1975). *Helplessness: On depression, development, and death.* San Francisco, CA: W. H. Freeman and Co, Publishers.

Sharabany, R., Gershoni, R., & Hofman, J. E. (1981). Girlfriend, boyfriend: Age and sex differences in intimate friendship. *Developmental Psychology, 17,* 800–808.

Shaver, P. R. (1989). *Links between adults' early attachment relationships and affiliative and work patterns at maturity.* Paper presented at the 10th Biennial Meetings of ISSBD, Jyväskylä, Finland.

Shaw, D., Keenan, K., & Vondra, J. (1994). Developmental precursors of externalizing behavior: Ages 1 to 3. *Developmental Psychology, 30,* 355–364.

Shepherd, G., & Shepherd, G. (1984). *A kingdom transformed: Themes in the Development of Mormonism.* Salt Lake City: University of Utah Press.

Sieder, R. (1987). *Sozialgeschichte der Familie* [A social history of the family]. Frankfurt am Main: Suhrkamp Verlag.

Sigman, M., & Wachs, T. D. (1991). Structure, continuity, and nutritional correlates of caregiver behavior pattern in Kenya and Egypt. In M. H. Bornstein (Ed.), *Cultural approaches to parenting.* Hillsdale, NJ: Lawrence Erlbaum Associates.

Smith, P. B., & Pederson, D. R. (1988). Maternal sensitivity and patterns of infant–mother attachment. *Child Development, 59,* 1097–1101.

Soares, I. (1992). *Representação da vinculação na idade adulta e na adolescência. Estudo intergeracional: mãe-filho(a)* [Attachment representation in adolescence and adulthood. An intergenerational study: mother–son/daughter]. Unpublished doctoral dissertation, Faculty of Psychology and Education, University of Porto.

Sorokina, A. I. (1987). *Razvitie emotsii v obshchenii so vzroslymi u detei pervogo goda zhizni* [The development of emotions in interaction with adults during the first year of life]. Unpublished dissertation, Moscow University, Moscow.

Spangler, G., & Grossmann, K. E. (1993). Biobehavioral organization in securely and insecurely attached infants. *Child Development, 64,* 1439–1450.

Speltz, M. L., Greenberg, M. T., & Deklyen, M. (1990). Attachment in preschoolers with disruptive behavior: A comparison of clinic referred and non-problem children. *Development and Psychopathology, 2,* 31–46.

Spieker, S. J., & Booth, C. L. (1988). Maternal antecedents of attachment quality. In J. Belsky & T. Nezworski (Eds.), *Clinical implications of attachment* (pp. 95–135). Hillsdale, NJ: Lawrence Erlbaum Associates.

Spitz, R. A. (1945). Hospitalism. An inquiry into the genesis of psychiatric conditions in early childhood. *Psychoanalytic Study of the Child, 1,* 53–74.

Spitz, R. A. (1958). *La première anneé de la vie de l'enfant.* Paris: PUF.

Spitz, R. A., & Wolf, K. M. (1946). Anaclitic depression: An inquiry into the genesis of psychiatric conditions in early childhood. *Psychoanalytic Study of the Child, 2,* 313–342.

SPSS Inc. (1983). *SPSSX. A complete guide to SPSSX language and operations.* New York: McGraw-Hill.

Sroufe, L. A. (1983). Infant–caregiver attachment and patterns of adaptation in preschool: Roots of maladaptation and competence. In M. Perlmutter (Ed.), *Minnesota Symposium in Child Psychology* (Vol. 16, pp. 41–81). Hillsdale, NJ: Lawrence Erlbaum Associates.

Sroufe, L. A. (1985). Attachment classifications from the perspective of infant–caregiver relationships and infant temperament. *Child Development, 56,* 1–14.

Sroufe, L. A. (1990). An organizational perspective on the self. In D. Cicchetti & M. Beeghly (Eds.), *The self in transition: Infancy to childhood* (pp. 281–307). Chicago: University of Chicago Press.

Sroufe, L. A. (1997). Psychopathology as an outcome of development. *Development and Psychopathology, 9*(2), 251–268.

Sroufe, L. A., Carlson, E. A., Levy, A. K., & Egeland, B. (1999). Implications of attachment theory for developmental psychpathology. *Development and Psychopathology, 11*(1), 1–13.

Sroufe, L. A., & Jacobvitz, D. (1989). Diverging pathways, developmental transformations, multiple ethologies and the problem of continuity in development. *Human Development, 32,* 196–203.

Sroufe, L. A., & Waters, E. (1977). Attachment as an organizational construct. *Child Development, 48,* 1184–1199.

Sroufe, A., & Waters, E. (1997). On the universality of the link between responsive care and secure base behavior. *ISSBD Newsletter, 1*(31), 3–5.

Stalker, C., & Davies, F. (1995). Attachment organization and adaptation in sexually abused women. *Canadian Journal of Psychiatry, 40,* 3–10.

Statistical Yearbook of Finland. (1992). *Valtion painatuskeskus: Statistics Finland* (Vol. 87, new series). Helsinki, Finland.

Stern, D. N. (1989). The representation of relational patterns: Developmental Considerations. In A. J. Sameroff & R. N. Emde (Eds.), *Relationship disturbances in early childhood* (pp. 52–69). New York: Basic Books.

Stern, D. N. (1992, January). *Basi dell'intervento clinico nei primi anni di vita,* Venice: Italy: Seminario di Studio.

Stern, D. N. (1995). *The motherhood constellation: A unified view of parent–infant psychotherapy.* New York: Basic Books.

Stern-Brushweiler, N., & Stern, D. N. (1988, September). *Conceptualization of different approaches to the maternal representation of her infant in various mother-infant therapies.* Paper presented at the 3rd Biennial Conference of the International Association for Infant Mental Health, Providence, RI.

Stevens, J. P. (1980). Power of the multivariate analysis of variance tests. *Psychological Bulletin, 88,* 728–737.

Stevenson-Hinde, J. (1991). Temperament and attachment: An eclectic approach. In P. Bateson (Ed.), *The development and integration of behavior* (pp. 315–329). Cambridge: Cambridge University Press.

Stevenson-Hinde, J., & Shouldice, A. (1990). Fear and attachment in 2.5 year olds. *British Journal of Developmental Psychology, 8,* 319–333.

Stevenson-Hinde, J., & Shouldice, A. (1995). Maternal interactions and self-reports related to attachment classification at 4.5 years. *Child Development, 66,* 583–596.

Suess, G. J. Grossmann, K. E., & Sroufe, L. A. (1992). Effects of infant attachment to mother and father on quality of adaptation in preschool: From dyadic to individual organization of self. *International Journal of Behavioral Development, 15,* 43–65.

Susman-Stillman, A., Kalkoske, M., Egeland, B., & Waldman, I. (1996). Infant temperament and maternal sensitivity as predictors of attachment security. *Infant Behavior and Development, 19,* 33–47.

Szajnberg, N. M., Skrinjaric, J., Moore, A. (1989). Affect attunement, attachment, temperament and zygosity: A twin study. *Journal of the American Academy of Child and Adolescent Psychiatry, 28,* 249–253.

Takahashi, K. (1990). Are the key assumptions of the "Strange Situation" procedure universal? A view from Japanese research. *Human Development, 33,* 23–30.

Tal, C., & Klein, P. S. (1996). *Mediation of behavior and attachment in mother–infant interaction.* Ramat Gan, Israel: Bar Ilan University.

Tani, F., & Schneider, B. H. (1997). Self-reported symptomology of socially rejected and neglected Italian elementary-school children. *Child Study Journal, 27,* 301–317.

Teti, D. M., & Gelfand, D. M. (1997a). Maternal cognitions as mediators of child outcomes in the context of postpartum depression. In L. Murray & P. J. Cooper (Eds.), *Postpartum depression and child development* (pp. 136–164). New York: Guilford Press.

Teti, D. M., & Gelfand, D. M. (1997b). The Preschool Assessment of Attachment: Construct validity in a sample of depressed and nondepressed families. *Development and Psychopathology, 9*(3): 517–536.

Teti, D. M., Gelfand, D. M., Messinger, D. S., & Isabella, R. (1995). Maternal depression and the quality of early attachment: An examination of infants, preschoolers, and their mothers. *Developmental Psychology, 31,* 364–376.

Teti, D. M., & Nakagawa, M. (1990). Assessing attachment in infancy: The Strange Situation and alternate systems. In E. D. Gibbs & D. M. Teti (Eds.), *Interdisciplinary assessment of infants: A guide for early intervention professionals.* (pp. 191–214). Baltimore, MD: Paul H. Brookes.

Thompson, R. (1993). Socioemotional development: Enduring issues and new challenges. *Developmental Review, 13,* 372–405.

Thompson, R. A., Lamb, M. E., & Estes, D. (1982). Stability of infant–mother attachment and its relationship to changing life circumstances in an unselected middle-class sample. *Child Development, 53,* 144–148.

Tizard, B. (1977). *Adoption: A second chance.* London: Open Books.

Tizard, B., & Hodges, J. (1978). The effect of early institutional rearing on the development of eight year old children. *Journal of Child Psychology and Psychiatry, 19,* 99–118.

Tizard, B., & Rees, J. (1974). Comparison of the effects of adoption, restoration to the natural mother, and continued institutionalization on the cognitive development of 4-year-old children. *Child Development, 45,* 92–99.

Tizard, B., & Rees, J. (1975). The effect of early institutional rearing on the behavior problems and affectional relationships of 4-year-old children. *Journal of Child Psychology and Psychiatry, 16,* 61–74.

Tizard, J., & Tizard, B. (1974). The institution as an environment for development. In M. P. M. Richards (Ed.), *The integration of a child into a social world* (pp. 137–152). London: Cambridge University Press.

Trivers, R. (1985). *Social evolution.* Menlo Park, CA: Benjamin Cummings.

Tronick, E. Z., & Gianino, A. F. (1986). The transmission of maternal disturbance to the infant. In E. Z. Tronick & T. Field (Eds.), *Maternal depression and infant disturbance* (pp. 5–12). San Francisco: Jossey-Bass.

Tulving, E. (1979). Memory research: What kind of progress? In G. Nilsson (Ed.), *Perspectives on memory research: Essays in honor of Uppsala University's 500th anniversary* (pp. 19–34). Hillsdale, NJ: Lawrence Erlbaum Associates.

Tulving, E. (1985). How many memory systems are there? *American Psychologist, 40,* 385–398.

Turner, P. (1991). Relations between attachment, gender, and behavior with peers in preschool. *Child Development, 62,* 1475–1488.

UNDP (1996). *Human Development Report 1996. Principal coordinators: M. ul Haq & R. Jolly.* New York/Oxford: Oxford University Press.

Urban, J., Carlson, E., Egeland, B., & Sroufe, A. (1991). Patterns of individual adaptations across childhood. *Development and Psychopathology, 3,* 445–460.

Vandell, D. L., Owen, M. T., Wilson, K. S., & Henderson, V. K. (1988). Social development in infant twins: Peer and mother–child relationships. *Child Development, 59*(1), 168–177.

van den Boom, D. (1994). The influence of temperament and mothering on attachment and exploration: An experimental manipulation of sensitive responsiveness among lower-class mothers with irritable infants. *Child Development, 65,* 1457–1477.

van den Boom, D. (1995). Do first-year intervention effects endure? Follow-up during toddlerhood of a sample of Dutch irritable infants. *Child Development, 65,* 1798–1816.

van IJzendoorn, M. H. (Ed.) (1990). Special topic: Cross-cultural validity of attachment theory. *Human Development, 33*(1), 3–9.

van IJzendoorn, M. H., & Bakermans-Kranenburg, M. J. (1996). Attachment representations in mothers, fathers, adolescents, and clinical groups: A meta-analytic search for normative data. *Journal of Consulting and Clinical Psychology, 64,* 8–21.

van IJzendoorn, M. H., Goldberg, S., Kroonenberg, P. M., & Frenkel, O. J. (1992). The relative effects of maternal and child problems on the quality of attachment: A meta-analysis of attachment in clinical samples. *Child Development, 63,* 840–858.

van IJzendoorn, M., Kranenburg, M., Zwart-Woudstra, H, van Busschbach, A., & Lambermon, M. W. E. (1991). Parental attachment and children's social-emotional development: Some findings on the validity of the Adult Attachment Interview in the Netherlands. *International Journal of Behavioral Development, 14*(4), 375–394.

van IJzendoorn, M. H., & Kroonenberg, P. M. (1988). Cross-cultural patterns of attachment: A meta-analysis of the Strange Situation. *Child Development, 59,* 147–156.

van IJzendoorn, M. H., Sagi, A., & Lambermon, M. W. E. (1992). The multiple caretaker paradox: Some data from Holland and Israel. In R. C. Pianta (Eds.), *Beyond the parent: The role of other adults in children's lives* (New directions in child development, Vol. 57). San Francisco: Jossey-Bass.

Vatutina, N. (1983). *Rebjenok postupaet v detskij sad* [The entry of the child into the nursery school]. Moscow/Russia: Prosvescenie.

Vaughn, B. E., Deane, K. E., & Waters, E. (1985). The impact of out-of-home care on child–mother attachment quality. Another look at some enduring questions. In I. Bretherton & E. Waters (Eds.), *Growing points of attachment theory and research. Monographs of the Society for Research and Child Development, 50* (1–2, Serial No. 209), (pp. 110–135).

Vaughn, B. E., Egeland, B., Sroufe, A., & Waters, E. (1979). Individual differences in infant–mother attachment at twelve and eighteen months: Stability and change in families under stress. *Child Development, 50,* 971–975.

Vaughn, B. E., Stevenson-Hinde, J., Waters, E., Kotsaftis, A., Lefever, G. B., Shouldice, A., Trudel, M., & Belsky, J. (1992). Attachment security and temperament in infancy and early childhood: Some conceptual clarifications. *Developmental Psychology, 28*(3), 463–473.

Vaughn, B. E., Taraldson, B. Crichton, L., & Egeland, B. (1980). Relationships between neonatal behavioral organization and infant behavior during the first year of life. *Infant Behavior and Development, 3,* 47–66.

Vereijken, C. M. J. L., Riksen-Walraven, J. M., & Kondo-Ikemura, K. (1997). Maternal sensitivity and infant attachment security in Japan: A longitudinal study. *International Journal of Behavioral Development, 21*(1), 35–49.

Vondra, J. I., Shaw, D. S., & Kevenides, M. C. (1995). Predicting infant attachment classification from multiple, contemporaneous measures of maternal care. *Infant Behavior and Development, 18,* 415–426.

Vondra, J. I., Shaw, D. S., Swearingen, L., Cohen, M., & Owens, E. B. (in press). Attachment stability and emotional and behavioral regulation from infancy to preschool age. *Development and Psychopathology.*

von Eye, A., & Brandtstädter, J. (1988). Evaluating developmental hypothesis using statement calculus and nonparametrc statistics. In P. B. Baltes, D. L. Featherman, & R. M. Lerner (Eds.), *Life-span development and behavior,* 8 (pp. 61–97). Hillsdale, NJ: Lawrence Erlbaum Associates.

Vygotskij, L. S. (1982/1983). *Sobranie socinenij.* (Selected Papers, Vols. 1–3). Moscow/Russia: Pedagogika.

Vygotsky, L. S. (1987). *The collected works of L. S. Vygotsky.* R. W. Rieber & A. S. Carlton (Eds.) and N. Minick (Trans.). New York: Plenum Press.

Ward, M. J., & Carlson, E. A. (1995). Associations among adult attachment representations, maternal sensitivity, and infant–mother attachment in a sample of adolescent mothers. *Child Development, 66,* 69–79.

Warren, S. L., Huston, L., Egeland, B., & Sroufe, L. A. (1997). Child and adolescent anxiety disorders and early attachment. *Journal of the American Academy of Child and Adolescent Psychiatry, 36*(5), 637–644.

Wartner, U., Grossmann, K., Fremmer-Bombik, E., & Suess, G. (1994). Attachment patterns at age six in South Germany: Predictability from infancy and implications for preschool behavior. *Child Development, 65*(4), 1014–1027.

Waters, E., Merrick, S., Treboux, D., Crowell, J., & Albersheim, L. (in press). Attachment security in infancy and early adulthood: A 20-year longitudinal study. *Child Development.*

Weber-Kellermann, I. (1987). *Die Deutsche Familie: Versuch einer Sozialgeschichte* [The German family. An attempt of a social history]. Frankfurt am Main: S. Fischer Verlag.

Wechsler, D. (1974). *Manual for the Wechsler Intelligence Scale for Children – Revised.* New York: Psychological Corporation.

Weinfield, N. S., Sroufe, A., & Egeland, B. (in press). Attachment from infancy to early adulthood in a high-risk sample: Continuity, discontinuity and their correlates. *Child Development.*

Weiss, R. S. (1982). Attachment in adult life. In C. M. Parkes & J. Stevenson-Hinde (Eds.), *The place of attachment in human behavior.* New York: Basic Books.

White, B. L., & Watts, J. C. (1973). *Experience and environment: Major influences on the development of the young child: Vol. 1.* Englewood Cliffs, NJ: Prentice-Hall.

Wikan, U. (1982). Life among the poor in Cairo. London, England: Tavistock Publications.

Wolfe, D. A. (1985). Child-abusive parents: An empirical review and analysis. *Psychological Bulletin, 97,* 462–482.

Wolkind, S. N. (1974). Sex differences in the aetiology of antisocial disorders in children in long-term residential care. *British Journal of Psychiatry, 125,* 125–130.

Yarrow, L. J. (1961). Maternal deprivation: Toward an empirical conceptual re-evaluation. *Psychological Bulletin, 58,* 459–490.

Yarrow, L. J. (1964). Separation from parents during early childhood. In M. L. Hoffman & L. W. Hoffman (Eds.), *Review of Child Development Research* (pp. 89–136). New York: Russell Sage Foundation.

Yokoyama, Y., Shimizu, T., & Hayakawa, K. (1995). Maternal partial attachment for one of a pair of twins and the influence of childrearing environments. *Nippon Koshu Eisei Zasshi, 42,* 104–112.

Zeanah, C. H. (1990; 1991). *Seminario di studio per la codifica della Strange Situation.* Dipartimento di Psicologia dello Sviluppo e della Socializzazione, Università degli Studi di Padova, Italia.

Zeanah, C. H., & Barton, M. L. (1989). Introduction: Internal representations and parent–infant relationships. *Infant Mental Health Journal, 10*(3), 135–141.

Zeanah, C. H., Keener, M. A., & Anders, T. F. (1986). Adolescent mothers' prenatal fantasies and working models of their infants. *Psychiatry, 49,* 193–203.

Ziegenhain, U., Klopfer, U., Dreisörner, R., & Rauh, H. (1992). *MUSKA. Skalen zur Bewertung des emotionalen und kommunikativen Ausdrucks der Bezugsperson in der Interaktion mit dem Kinde* [Scales for assessing and evaluating the emotional and communicative expression of the caretaker in the interaction with the infant]. Unpublished manuscript, Free University of Berlin, Institute for Psychology, Berlin.

Ziegenhain, U., Müller, B., & Rauh, H. (1996). Frühe Bindungserfahrungen und Verhaltensauffälligkeiten bei Kleinkindern in einer sozialen und kognitiven

Anforderungssituation [The influence of attachment quality and intensity of attachment insecurity on cognitive performances and emotional states of 20-month-old infants in a test situation]. *Praxis der Kinderpsychologie und Kinderpsychiatrie, 45*(3–4), 95–102.

Ziegenhain, U., Rauh, H., & Müller, B. (1996). Emotionale Anpassung von Kleinkindern an die Krippenbetreuung [Infants' emotional adaptation to day care]. In L. Ahnert (Ed.), *Tagesbetreuung für Kinder unter 3 – Theorien und Tatsachen.* Göttingen: Hogrefe.

Ziegenhain, U., Simo, S. & Rauh, H. (1996). Quality of attachment and continuity or discontinuity in maternal sensitivity over the infant's first two years. Poster presented at the XIVth Biennial ISSBD Meetings, Quebec City, Canada, August 12–16, 1996.

Zimmerman, P. (in preparation). *Kontinuität von Bindungsbeziehungen* [Continuity of attachment relationships]. Doctoral dissertation, Universität Regensburg, Regensburg, Germany.

Zoll, D. A., Lyons-Ruth, K., & Connell, D. (1984, August). *Infants at psychiatric risk: Maternal behavior, depression, and family history.* Paper presented at the 92nd Annual Convention of the American Psychological Association, Toronto.

Index

Note: Page numbers followed by *f* indicate figures; page numbers followed by *t* indicate tables.